MyWritingLab™ Online Course (access code r...)

MyWritingLab is an online homework, tutorial, and assessment p... ...p... ...des engaging experiences for today's instructors and students.

Writing Help for Varying Skill Levels

For students who enter the course at widely varying skill levels, MyWritingLab provides unique, targeted remediation through personalized and adaptive instruction. Starting with a pre-assessment known as the Path Builder, MyWritingLab diagnoses students' strengths and weaknesses on prerequisite writing skills. The results of the pre-assessment inform each student's Learning Path, a personalized pathway for students to work on requisite skills through multimodal activities. In doing so, students feel supported and ready to succeed in class.

Respond to Student Writing with Targeted Feedback and Remediation

MyWritingLab unites instructor comments and feedback with targeted remediation via rich multimedia activities, allowing students to learn from and through their own writing.

- When giving feedback on student writing, instructors can add links to activities that address issues and strategies needed for review. Instructors may link to multimedia resources in Pearson Writer, which include curated content from Purdue OWL.
- In the Writing Assignments, students can use instructor-created peer review rubrics to evaluate and comment on other students' writing.
- Paper review by specialized tutors through Tutor Services is available, as is plagiarism detection through TurnItIn.

Learning Tools for Student Engagement

Learning Catalytics

Generate class discussion, guide lectures, and promote peer-to-peer learning with real-time analytics. MyLab and Mastering with eText now provides Learning Catalytics—an interactive student response tool that uses students' smartphones, tablets, or laptops to engage them in more sophisticated tasks and thinking.

MediaShare

MediaShare allows students to post multimodal assignments easily—whether they are audio, video, or visual compositions—for peer review and instructor feedback. In both face-to-face and online course settings, MediaShare saves instructors valuable time and enriches the student learning experience by enabling contextual feedback to be provided quickly and easily.

Direct Access to MyLab

Users can link from any Learning Management System (LMS) to Pearson's MyWritingLab. Access MyLab assignments, rosters, and resources, and synchronize MyLab grades with the LMS gradebook. New direct, single sign-on provides access to all the personalized learning MyLab resources that make studying more efficient and effective.

Proven Results

No matter how MyWritingLab is used, instructors have access to powerful gradebook reports. These reports provide visual analytics that give insight to course performance at the student, section, or even program level.

Visit www.mywritinglab.com for more information.

THE CURIOUS WRITER

Concise Fifth Edition

Bruce Ballenger

Boise State University

New!
2016
MLA
Updates

PEARSON

Boston   Columbus   Indianapolis   New York   San Francisco   Amsterdam
Cape Town   Dubai   London   Madrid   Milan   Munich   Paris   Montréal   Toronto   Delhi
Mexico City   São Paulo   Sydney   HongKong   Seoul   Singapore   Taipei   Tokyo

Vice President and Editor in Chief: Joseph Opiela
Program Manager: Eric Jorgensen
Product Marketing Manager: Ali Arnold
Field Marketing Manager: Joyce Nilsen
Media Producer: Marisa Massaro
Content Producer: Laura Olsen
Media Editor: Tracy Cunningham
Project Manager: Rebecca Gilpin

Text Design, Project Coordination, and
  Electronic Page Makeup: Integra
Design Lead: Barbara Atkinson
Cover Designer: Jenny Willingham
Cover Illustrations: Infiniti
Senior Manufacturing Buyer: Roy L. Pickering, Jr.
Printer/Binder: LSC Communications/Crawfordsville
Cover Printer: Lehigh-Phoenix Color/Hagerstown

Acknowledgments of third-party content appear on pages CR-1–CR-3, which constitute an extension of this copyright page.

PEARSON, ALWAYS LEARNING, and MYWRITINGLAB are exclusive trademarks owned by Pearson Education, Inc. or its affiliates in the United States and/or other countries.

Unless otherwise indicated herein, any third-party trademarks that may appear in this work are the property of their respective owners and any references to third-party trademarks, logos, or other trade dress are for demonstrative or descriptive purposes only. Such references are not intended to imply any sponsorship, endorsement, authorization, or promotion of Pearson's products by the owners of such marks, or any relationship between the owner and Pearson Education, Inc., or its affiliates, authors, licensees, or distributors.

Library of Congress Cataloging-in-Publication Data
Names: Ballenger, Bruce P., author.
Title: The curious writer/Bruce Ballenger.
Description: Concise edition. | Hoboken : Pearson Higher Education, [2017] |
   Includes index.
Identifiers: LCCN 2015041633 | ISBN 978-0-13-412070-6 | ISBN 0-13-412070-1
Subjects: LCSH: English language—Rhetori—Handbooks, manuals, etc. |
Interdisciplinary approach in education—Handbooks, manuals, etc. |
Academic writing—Handbooks, manuals, etc.
Classification: LCC PE1408 .B37 2017 | DDC 808/.042—dc23
LC record available at http://lccn.loc.gov/2015041633

1   17

Student Edition ISBN 13: 978-0-13-467939-6
Student Edition ISBN 10:   0-13-467939-3

A la Carte Edition ISBN 13: 978-0-13-470306-0
A la Carte Edition ISBN 10:   0-13-470306-5

PEARSON
www.pearsonhighered.com

Contents

Chapter 10 Re-Genre: Repurposing Your Writing for Multimedia Genres 346

Preface

I have a friend, a painter, who teaches art at my university, and his introductory courses teach the subskills of painting, things like how to use a brush, mix paints, and understand color theory. Common sense suggests that such fundamentals are the starting place for any creative activity, including writing. But college writers walk into our classes with a lifetime of language use. They already know a lot about making meaning with words, more than they think they know. Yet there is much to teach, and perhaps the most powerful thing we can teach them is that writing isn't just for getting down what you know but for discovering what you think. I've learned to never underestimate the power of this discovery process, and that's why discovery is the beating heart of this book.

What's New in This Edition?

The fifth edition of *The Curious Writer* is substantially revised and includes a groundbreaking new chapter on "re-genre." As always, I have also made revisions throughout with the overall aim of making the book more teachable and more reflective of the world in which today's students live. Here's what you will find:

- **A completely new chapter on repurposing ("re-genre-ing") writing (Ch. 10)** encourages students to transform academic writing into contemporary genres such as blogs, audio and video podcasts, infographics, and more. In creating these transformations, students gain a deeper rhetorical knowledge of genre conventions, strengths, and limitations.
- **A thoroughly reorganized and revised chapter on argument (Ch. 6)** now offers clearer, more comprehensive guidance on what an argument is and how to write one—knowledge and skills that are at the center of almost all good writing.
- **A significantly revised chapter on critical analysis (Ch. 7)** widens its focus beyond literature to include images, objects, ads, and more—any "texts" in our lives that may have ambiguous meanings.
- **A significantly revised section on research** includes updated information about data searches, a new section on online interviews and surveys, and expanded coverage of plagiarism and synthesizing sources.
- **New readings and illustrations throughout** offer fresh perspectives on current topics to engage students more effectively.

Inquiry in the Writing Classroom

Writing instructors often vaguely refer to the importance of "critical thinking"; it is, we say, something that good writing encourages. *The Curious Writer* suggests that we might focus more explicitly on *inquiry*. Most of us already teach inquiry, although we may not all realize it. For example, our writing classes invite students to be active participants in making knowledge in the classroom through peer review. When we ask students to fastwrite or brainstorm, we encourage them to suspend judgment and openly explore their feelings or ideas. And when we urge students to see a draft as a first look at a topic, and revision as a means of discovering what they may not have noticed before, we teach a process that makes discovery its purpose. Indeed, most composition classrooms create a "culture of inquirers."

　　We can do this more effectively if we take five key actions:

1. **Create an atmosphere of mutual inquiry.** Students are used to seeing their teachers as experts who know everything. But in an inquiry-based classroom, instructors are learners too. They ask questions not because they already know the answers but because there might be answers they haven't considered.

2. **Emphasize questions before answers.** The idea that student writers should begin with an inflexible thesis or a firm position on a topic before engaging in the process of writing is anathema to inquiry-based learning. Questions, not preconceived answers, lead to new discoveries.

3. **Encourage a willingness to suspend judgment.** To suspend judgment demands that we trust that the process will lead us to new insights. This requires both faith in the process and the time to engage in it. The composition course, with its emphasis on process, is uniquely suited to nurture such faith.

4. **Introduce a strategy of inquiry.** Announcing that we're teaching an inquiry-based class is not enough. We have to introduce students to the strategy of inquiry we'll be using. In the sciences, the experimental method provides a foundation for investigations. What guidance will we give our students in the composition course?

5. **Present inquiry in a rhetorical context.** An essay, a research project, an experiment, any kind of investigation is always pursued with particular purposes and audiences in mind. In an inquiry-based class, the situation in which the inquiry project is taking place is always considered.

The Curious Writer is built on all of these elements. It features a strategy of inquiry that is genuinely multidisciplinary, borrowing from the sciences, the social sciences, and the humanities. Each project presented in Chapters 3 through 7, for example, leads students toward subjects that offer the most potential for learning. Rather than write about what they already know, students are encouraged to choose topics that they want to learn more about. In addition, the discussion questions that follow the student and professional essays do more than simply test students' comprehension or reduce the reading to a single theme. In many cases, these questions are open ended and can lead students in many directions. And throughout, I have tried to maintain a voice and persona that suggests I am working along with the students as a writer and a thinker—which is exactly the experience of mutual inquiry that I try to create in my classes. Finally, *The Curious Writer* is organized around a strategy of inquiry that is present in every assignment and nearly every exercise. I revisit the model "The Spirit of Inquiry," which is introduced in Chapters 1 and 2, in every subsequent chapter. This inquiry strategy is the thematic core of the book.

The Inquiry Strategy of *The Curious Writer*

A strategy of inquiry is simply a process of discovery. The model I use in this book borrows partly from science through its insistence on continually looking closely at the "data" (sensory details, facts, evidence, textual passages, and so on) and using that data to shape or test the writer's ideas about a subject. But the heart of the model is the alternating movement between two modes of thinking—creative and critical—in a dialectical process. One way of describing this movement is as a shifting back and forth between suspending judgment and making judgments (see Figure A).

This inquiry strategy works with both reading and writing, but in Chapter 2, "Reading as Inquiry," I offer four categories of questions—those that explore, explain, evaluate, and reflect—that I think will help guide students in reading most texts more strategically. These types of questions will be most evident in the follow-up questions to the many readings throughout *The Curious Writer*.

Finally, a strategy of inquiry is useful only if it makes sense to students; I've tried very hard, particularly in the first section of the book, to make the model comprehensible.

How This Book Is Organized

Because the inquiry-based approach is central to *The Curious Writer*, it's crucial for students to work through Chapter 1, "Writing as Inquiry," and Chapter 2, "Reading as Inquiry." Chapters 3 through 7 focus on "inquiry projects." The range of assignments in these chapters should satisfy the needs of most composition instructors. If your university is lucky enough to have a two-semester sequence, *The Curious Writer* includes assignments suitable for both courses, including personal, argument, and research essays.

The book's focus on genres of writing also makes it appealing for advanced composition courses. For example, assignments such as the personal essay and the review help students see how to apply what they've learned to distinct rhetorical situations and help them to understand how those situations shape the genres.

In recent years, I've become interested in reading strategies, a topic that I never mentioned as a novice teacher. There just didn't seem to be enough time.

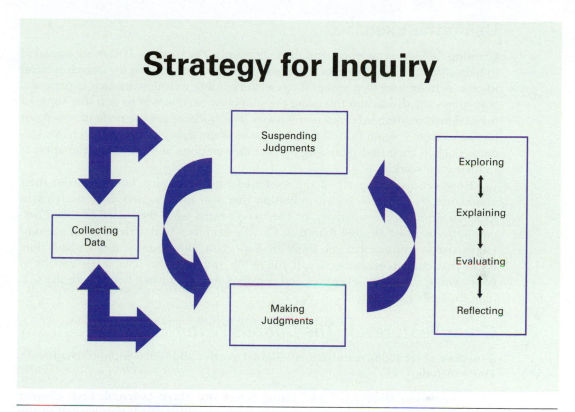

Figure A   In nearly every assignment in *The Curious Writer,* students will use this strategy of inquiry.

But skillful reading is always an important part of teaching writing, and so I've found new ways in *The Curious Writer* to link the reading and writing processes, beginning in Chapter 2, "Reading as Inquiry." I've also expanded the discussion to reading images. This emphasis on visual rhetoric echoes the latest developments in composition in response to the growth of the Web and the growing visual literacy of our students.

Finally, the approach of *The Curious Writer* grows in part from my own scholarship on research writing, particularly the criticism that research is too often isolated in the writing course in a "research paper" assignment. This book makes research a part of every assignment, from the personal essay to the proposal, emphasizing that it is a useful source of information, not a separate genre.

This is the third textbook I've written with the "curious" moniker. Because all are inquiry-based, the word is a natural choice. And although I'm very interested in encouraging my students to be curious researchers, readers, and writers, I also hope to remind my colleagues who use the books that we should be curious, too. We should model for our students our own passion for inquiring into the world.

Using the Exercises

Learning follows experience, and the exercises in *The Curious Writer* are intended to help students make sense of the ideas in the text. I often plan the exercises as an in-class activity, and then assign the relevant reading to follow up that experience. Sometimes the discussion following these in-class exercises is so rich that some of the assigned reading becomes unnecessary. The students get the main idea without having to hear it again from the author. More often, though, the reading helps students deepen their understanding of what they've done and how they can apply it to their own work.

However, assigning all of the exercises isn't necessary. Don't mistake their abundance in the book as an indication that you must march your students in lockstep through every activity, or they won't learn what they need to. *The Curious Writer* is more flexible than that. Use the exercises and activities that seem to emphasize key points that you think are important. Skip those you don't have time for or that don't seem necessary. If you're like me, you also have a few rabbits of your own in your hat—exercises and activities that may work better with the text than the ones I suggest.

Other Features of *The Curious Writer*

A number of recurring features are designed to offer additional support to students. These include:

- **Learning Objectives and Using What You Have Learned.** Each chapter begins by establishing learning objectives, which are then revisited at the end of each chapter to reinforce the chapter's content. Notes throughout the chapter highlight where the objectives come into play.
- **Features of the Form.** These charts in Chapters 3 through 7 summarize the particular features and conventions of the genre being explored.
- **Inquiring into the Details.** These boxed features dig deeper into specific, relevant topics.
- **Prose+.** This feature reflects the increasing importance of visual literacy by offering images for analysis.

Resources for Instructors and Students

The following resources are available to qualified adopters of Pearson English textbooks.

The Instructor's Resource Manual

ISBN 0-13-412158-9/978-0-13-412158-1
This manual, written by my colleague Michelle Payne, includes sample syllabi as well as a helpful introduction that offers general teaching strategies and ideas for

teaching writing as a form of inquiry. It also provides a detailed overview of each chapter and its goals, ideas for discussion starters, handouts and overheads, and a large number of additional writing activities that teachers can use in their classrooms to supplement the textbook.

PowerPoint Presentation

A downloadable set of PowerPoint slides can be used by instructors who want to accompany chapter readings and discussions with presentable visuals. These slides, also designed by Michelle Payne, illustrate each learning objective and key idea in the text in visual form. Each slide includes instructors' notes.

MyWritingLab

MyWritingLab is an online practice, tutorial, and assessment program that provides engaging experiences for teaching and learning.

MyWritingLab includes most of the writing assignments from your accompanying textbook. Now, students can complete and submit assignments, and teachers can then track and respond to submissions easily—right in MyWritingLab—making the response process easier for the instructor and more engaging for the student.

In the Writing Assignments, students can use instructor-created peer review rubrics to evaluate and comment on other students' writing. When giving feedback on student writing, instructors can add links to activities that address issues and strategies needed for review. Instructors may link to multimedia resources in Pearson Writer, which include curated content from Purdue OWL. Paper review by specialized tutors through SmartThinking is available, as is plagiarism detection through TurnItIn.

MyWritingLab unites instructor comments and feedback with targeted remediation via rich multimedia activities, allowing students to learn from and through their own writing.

Writing Help for Varying Skill Levels

For students who enter the course at widely varying skill levels, MyWritingLab provides unique, targeted remediation through personalized and adaptive instruction. Starting with a pre-assessment known as the Path Builder, MyWritingLab diagnoses students' strengths and weaknesses on prerequisite writing skills. The results of the pre-assessment inform each student's Learning Path, a personalized pathway for students to work on requisite skills through multimodal activities. In doing so, students feel supported and ready to succeed in class.

Learning Tools for Student Engagement

Learning Catalytics. Generate class discussion, guide lectures, and promote peer-to-peer learning with real-time analytics. MyLab and Mastering with eText now provides Learning Catalytics—an interactive student response tool that uses students' smartphones, tablets, or laptops to engage them in more sophisticated tasks and thinking.

MediaShare. MediaShare allows students to post multimodal assignments easily—whether they are audio, video, or visual compositions—for peer review and instructor feedback. In both face-to-face and online course settings, MediaShare saves instructors valuable time and enriches the student learning experience by enabling contextual feedback to be provided quickly and easily.

Direct Access to MyLab. Users can link from any Learning Management System (LMS) to Pearson's MyWritingLab. Access MyLab assignments, rosters, and resources, and synchronize MyLab grades with the LMS gradebook. New direct, single sign-on provides access to all the personalized learning MyLab resources that make studying more efficient and effective.

Visit www.mywritinglab.com for more information

REVEL for *The Curious Writer,* 5/e by Bruce Ballenger

REVEL is designed for the way today's composition students read, think, and learn. In English, reading is never the endgame. Instead—whether in a textbook, an exemplar essay, or a source—it begins a conversation that plays out in writing. REVEL complements the written word with a variety of writing opportunities, brief assessments, model documents, and rich annotation tools to deepen students' understanding of their reading. By providing regular opportunities to write and new ways to interact with their reading, REVEL engages students and sets them up to be more successful readers and writers—in and out of class.

Video and Rich Multimedia Content. Videos, audio recordings, animations, and multimedia instruction encourage students to engage with the text in a more meaningful way.

Interactive Readings and Exercises. Students explore reading assignments through interactive texts. Robust annotation tools allow students to take notes, and low-stakes assessments and writing exercises enable students to engage meaningfully with the text outside of the classroom.

Integrated Writing Assignments. Minimal-stakes, low-stakes, and high-stakes writing tasks allow students multiple opportunities to interact with the ideas presented in the reading assignments, ensuring that they come to class better prepared.

Pearson eText

An interactive online version of *The Curious Writer* is available as an eText, which brings together the many resources of the MyLabs with the instructional content of this successful book to create an enhanced learning experience for students.

Acknowledgments

Making this book has been a team effort. From the first edition of *The Curious Writer*, I've been lucky to have an extraordinarily gifted group of Pearson people working with me, including Joe Opiela, who first encouraged me to write this book, and a remarkable team of development editors and production staff. In particular, I'd like to thank Ginny Blanford, whose editorial insight helped me enormously to rethink my work here, from tightening sentences to restructuring entire chapters. Her firm but always friendly guidance kept the project on track and kept me from panic. Dr. Michelle Payne, a colleague at Boise State and a longtime friend, has been involved in the development of this book since the beginning, reviewing chapters, writing instructor's manuals, and developing teaching materials. Michelle's help with the argument chapter in this edition was instrumental. And finally, for the last few editions, I've enlisted the help of my daughter, Becca. I'm endlessly proud of her, which is as it should be.

My students are also key collaborators, though they often don't know it. For their assistance in the fifth edition, I'd like to thank Hailie Johnson-Waskow, Andrea Oyarzabal, Bernice Olivas, Seth Marlin, Amy Garrett, Amanda Stewart, Kersti Harter, Micaela Fisher and many others whose work may not appear here but who taught the teacher how to teach writing.

Reviewers of books like these can be crucial to their development. For the first four editions, I relied on feedback from the following folks:

Susan Achziger, Community College of Aurora; Jeffrey T. Andelora, Mesa Community College; Ken Autrey, Francis Marion University; Ellen Barker, Nicholls State University; Sandra Barnhill, South Plains College; Angela Cardinale Bartlett, Chaffey College; Melissa Batai, Triton College; Patrick Bizzaro, East Carolina University; Jennifer Black, McLennan Community College; Sara M. Blake, El Camino College; Pamela S. Bledsoe, Surry Community College; James C. Bower, Walla Walla Community College; Libby Bradford Roeger, Shawnee Community College; Mark Browning, Johnson County Community College; Shanti Bruce, Nova Southeastern University; Jo Ann Buck, Guilford Technical Community College; Carol Burnell, Clackamas Community College; Susan Butterworth, Salem State College; Sharon Buzzard, Quincy College; Maria A. Clayton, Middle Tennessee State University; Dr. Keith Coplin, Colby Community College; Donna Craine, Front Range Community College; Rachelle Darabi, Indiana University/Purdue University–Fort Wayne; Jason DePolo, North Carolina A&T State University; Brock Dethier, Utah State University; Rosemarie Dombrowski, Arizona State University (DPC); Virginia B. Earnest, Holmes Community College–Ridgeland; Terry Engebretsen, Idaho State University; John Christopher Ervin, University of South Dakota; Kevin Ferns, Woodland Community College; Greg Giberson, Salisbury University; Daniel Gonzalez, University of New Orleans; Gwendolyn N. Hale, Savannah State University; Michael Hammond, University of San Francisco; Shari Hammond, Southwest Virginia Community College; Vicki M. Hester, St. Mary's University; Nels P. Highberg, University of Hartford; Charlotte Hogg, Texas Christian University; Anneliese Homan, State Fair Community

College; Shelly Horvath, University of Indianapolis; Dawn Hubbell-Staeble, Bowling Green State University; Chad Jorgensen, Metropolitan Community College; Lilia Joy, Henderson Community College; David C. Judkins, University of Houston; William Klein, University of Missouri–St. Louis; Robert Lamm, Arkansas State University; Mary C. Leahy, College of DuPage; Lynn Lewis, University of Oklahoma; Steve Luebke, University of Wisconsin–River Falls; Michael Lueker, Our Lady of the Lake University; Rosemary Mack, Baton Rouge Community College; Kara M. Manning, The University of Southern Mississippi; James C. McDonald, University of Louisiana–Lafeyette; Rhonda McDonnell, Arizona State University; Jacqueline L. McGrath, College of DuPage; Amanda McGuire Rzicznek, Bowling Green State University; James J. McKeown, Jr., McLennan Community College; Eileen Medeiros, Johnson & Wales University; Bryan Moore, Arkansas State University; John D. Moore, Eastern Illinois University; Margaret P. Morgan, University of North Carolina–Charlotte; Dr. Peter E. Morgan, University of West Georgia; Tom Moriarty, Salisbury University; Brigid Murphy, Pima Community College; Jason E. Murray, University of South Dakota; Robin L. Murray, Eastern Illinois University; Amy Ratto Parks, University of Montana; Dorothy J. Patterson, Oakwood College; Susan Pesznecker, Clackamas Community College; Betty Porter, Indiana Wesleyan University; Steven R. Price, Mississippi College; Lynn Raymond, UNC Charlotte; Mark Reynolds, Jefferson Davis Community College; David H. Roberts, Samford University; Elaine J. Roberts, Judson College; Kristie Rowe, Wright State University; Kathleen J. Ryan, University of Montana; Teryl Sands, Arizona State University; Robert A. Schwegler, University of Rhode Island; Heath Scott, Thomas Nelson Community College; Bonita Selting, University of Central Arkansas; Mark A. Smith, Lock Haven University of Pennsylvania; Vicki Stieha, Northern Kentucky University; Elizabeth A. Stolarek, Ferris State University; Marian Thomas, Boise State University; Ruthe Thompson, Southwest Minnesota State University; Lisa Tyler, Sinclair Community College; Marjorie Van Cleef, Housatonic Community College; Worth H. Weller, Indiana University Purdue University–Fort Wayne; Ann R. Wolven, Lincoln Trail College; Richard T. Young, Blackburn College; and BJ Zamora, Cleveland Community College.

And for this fifth edition, reviewers include Susan Achziger, Community College of Aurora; Sarah Allen, University of Northern Colorado; Scott D. Banville, Nicholls State University; Lynn Chrenka, Ferris State University; Brianne M. DiBacco, University of Southern Indiana; Seán Henne, West Shore Community College; Rosemary Mack, Baton Rouge Community College; Amanda McGuire Rzicznek, Bowling Green State University; James J. McKeown, Jr., McLennan Community College; Eileen Medeiros, Johnson & Wales University; Steve Moore, Arizona Western College; Siskanna Naynaha, Lane Community College; and Ashley Bissette Sumerel, University of North Carolina at Wilmington.

Finally, I want to thank my daughters, Rebecca and Julia, who allow themselves to be characters in all of my books. They are both actors, and like good theater people, they are more than willing to play their parts in these texts, no matter what roles I assign. I'm especially grateful to Karen, my wife, who has endured multiple editions of these books and their hold on my attention, which has often come at her expense. She's the beacon I follow through this blizzard of words, always guiding me home.

BRUCE BALLENGER

1

Writing as Inquiry

Learning Objectives

In this chapter, you'll learn to

1.1 Reflect on and revise your beliefs about yourself as a writer.

1.2 Understand what kinds of questions will sustain inquiry into any subject.

1.3 Practice a method of writing and thinking that will help you generate ideas.

1.4 Apply rhetorical knowledge to make choices in specific writing situations.

Yesterday in class, Tina wrote an essay about whether adultery is forgivable. She isn't married but has good friends who are, a couple she said everyone thought had the "perfect" marriage. The woman's husband, apparently, had an affair. Tina, who is in a pretty tight relationship with her boyfriend, has strong feelings about cheating on a partner. It ticks her off. "If it happened to me," she wrote, "I would have dumped him." Tina's essay could easily have become a rant about infidelity—a blunt, perhaps shrill argument about adultery's immorality or the depravity of two-timing men. It wasn't. Instead, she wondered about the relationship between friendship and love in marriage. She wondered about what kind of communication between spouses might short-circuit cheating. She wondered how attitudes towards sex differ between men and women. Many of these questions were explored by Michel de Montaigne, a sixteenth-century writer we were studying in that class, and Tina began to wrap his thinking around hers as she struggled to make sense of how she felt about what happened to her friends.

Tina was engaged in an act of inquiry.

Her motive was to *find out* what she thought rather than prove what she already knew. And writing was the way Tina chose to think it through.

Many of us admit that we really don't like to write, particularly when forced to do it. Or we clearly prefer certain kinds of writing and dislike others: "I just like to write funny stories," or "I like writing for myself and not for other people," or "I hate writing research papers." I can understand this, because for years I felt much the same way. I saw virtually no similarities between a note to a friend and the paper I wrote for my philosophy class in college. Words had power in one context but seemed flimsy and vacant in another. One kind of writing was fairly easy; the other was like sweating blood. How could my experiences as a writer be so fundamentally different? In other words, what's the secret of writing well in a range of writing contexts *and* enjoying it more in all contexts? Here's what I had to learn:

1. You don't have to know what you think before you're ready to write. Writing can be a way of *discovering* what you think.

2. A key to writing well is understanding the *process* of doing it.

They're not particularly novel ideas, but both were a revelation to me when I finally figured them out late in my career as a student, and they changed for good the way I wrote. These two insights—that writing is a means of discovery and that reflecting on how we write can help us write—are guiding principles of this book. I won't guarantee that after they read *The Curious Writer*, haters of writing will come to love it or that lovers of writing won't find writing to be hard work. But I hope that by the end of the book, you'll experience the pleasure of discovery in different writing situations, and that you'll understand your writing process well enough to adapt it to the demands of whatever situation you encounter.

Motives for Writing

Why write? To start, I'd propose two motives, one obvious and the other less so:

1. To share ideas or information—*to communicate.*

2. To think—*to discover.*

These two motives for writing—to *communicate* with others and to *discover* what the writer thinks and feels—are equally important. And both may ultimately relate to what I call our *spirit of inquiry*, which is born of our deeper sense of wonder and curiosity or even confusion and doubt, our desire to touch other people, our urge to solve problems. The spirit of inquiry is a kind of perspective toward the world that invites questions, accepts uncertainty, and makes each of us feel some responsibility for what we say. This inquiring spirit should be familiar to you. It's the feeling you had when you discovered that the sun and a simple magnifying glass could be used to burn a hole in an oak leaf. It's wondering what a teacher meant when he said that World War II was a "good" war and Vietnam was a "bad" war. It's the questions that haunted you yesterday as you listened to a good friend describe her struggles with anorexia. The inquiring spirit even drives your quest to find a smartphone, an effort that inspires you to read about the technology and visit the *Consumer Reports* website at consumerreports.org. Inquiry was Tina's motive when she decided to turn her academic essay on adultery away from a shrill argument based on what she already believed into a more thoughtful exploration of why people cheat.

Beliefs About Writing and Writing Development

Most of us have been taught about writing since the first grade. We usually enter college with beliefs not only about what makes a good paper and what "rules" of writing to follow, but also about how we can develop as writers. As I mentioned earlier, I've learned a lot about writing since my first years in college, and a big part of that learning involved unraveling some of my prior beliefs about writing. In fact, I'd say that my development as a writer initially had more to do with *unlearning* some of what I already knew than it did with discovering new ways to write. But you have to make your beliefs explicit if you're going to make decisions about which are helpful and which aren't. So take a moment to find out what your beliefs are and to think about whether they actually make sense.

1.1
Reflect on and revise your beliefs about yourself as a writer.

Exercise 1.1

This I Believe (and This I Don't)

STEP ONE: From the following list, identify the one belief about writing that you agree with most strongly and the one that you're convinced isn't true.

1. Writing proficiency begins with learning the basics and then building on them, working from words to sentences to paragraphs to compositions.

2. The best way to develop as a writer is to imitate the writing of the people you want to write like.

3. People are born writers like people are born good at math. Either you can do it or you can't.

4. The best way to develop as a writer is to develop good reading skills.

5. Practice is the key to a writer's development. The more a writer writes, the more he or she will improve.

6. Developing writers need to learn the modes of writing (argument, exposition, description, narration) and the genres (essays, research papers, position papers, and so on).

7. Developing writers should start with simple writing tasks, such as telling stories, and move to harder writing tasks, such as writing a research paper.

8. The most important thing that influences a writer's growth is believing that he or she can improve.

9. The key to becoming a better writer is finding your voice.

STEP TWO: Look over the following journal prompts (for more on journals, see the "Inquiring into the Details: Journals" box). Then spend five minutes writing in your journal about *why* you agree with the one belief and disagree with the other. This is an open-ended "fastwrite." You should write fast and without stopping, letting your thoughts flow in whatever direction they go. In your fastwrite, you can respond to any or all of the prompts to whatever extent you want.

Rules for Fastwriting

1. There are no rules.
2. Don't try to write badly, but give yourself permission to do so.
3. To the extent you can, think through writing rather than before it.
4. Keep your pen moving.
5. If you run out of things to say, write about how weird it is to run out of things to say until new thoughts arrive.
6. Silence your internal critic to suspend judgment.
7. Don't censor yourself.

Journal Prompts

- *What* do you mean, exactly, when you say you agree or disagree with the belief? Can you explain more fully why you think the belief is true or false?

- *When* did you start agreeing or disagreeing with the belief? Can you remember a particular moment or experience as a student learning to write that this agreement or disagreement connects to?

- *Who* was most influential in convincing you of the truth or falsity of the belief?

One Student's Response

Bernice's Journal

EXERCISE 1.1
STEP TWO

I used to be a firm believer in the idea of born writers—it was a genetic thing. People were gifted with the gold pen genes, or they weren't. Writing as a process involved a muse, inspiration, and luck. Things uncontrollable by the writer. Then I started writing, mostly for my 101 class, and I started to feel powerful when I put words on paper. In control. The idea of my voice, my words, just being on the page and other people reading it and maybe liking it was a rush. I was always the girl who specialized in the art of being unnoticed, unseen, blending in. My Comp 101 prof. liked my writing and pushed me really hard to work on my basics, to think about my process, to prewrite and revise. I started to see a clear distinction between how to write and what to write. How is all mixed up with the process, with discipline, with practice and perseverance.... The how isn't something you are born with; it's something you develop, something you practice, a skill you hone.... Becoming a good writer takes learning how to write, figuring out a process that works for you, and then letting your voice be heard on the page.

Inquiring into the Details

Journals

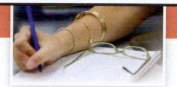

Here are five things that make a journal especially useful for writers:

- *Feel comfortable writing badly.* Whether print or digital, the journal must be a place where you're able to largely ignore your internal critic.

- *Use it throughout the writing process.* Journals can be indispensable for invention whenever you need more information, not just at the beginning. They can also be a place where you talk to yourself about how to solve a writing problem.

- *Write both specifically and abstractly.* Sometimes you'll be trying to be as concrete as possible, generating details, collecting facts, exploring particular experiences. Other times, use the journal to think in more-abstract language, thinking through ideas, reflecting on process, analyzing claims.

- *Don't make any rules about your journal.* These rules usually begin with a thought like "I'll only write in my journal when...." Write in your journal whenever you find it useful, and in any way that you find useful, especially if it keeps you writing.

- *Experiment.* Your journal will be different from my journal, which will be different from the journal of the woman sitting next to you in class. The only way to make a journal genuinely useful is to keep trying ways to make it useful.

Unlearning Unhelpful Beliefs

You won't be surprised when I say that I have a lot of theories about writing development; after all, I'm supposedly the expert. But we are *all* writing theorists, with beliefs that grow out of our successes and failures as people who write. Because you don't think much about them, these beliefs often shape your response to writing instruction without your even knowing it. For example, I've had a number of students who believe that people are born writers. This belief, of course, would make any kind of writing class a waste of time, because writing ability would be a matter of genetics.

A much more common belief is that learning to write is a process of building on basics, beginning with words and then working up to sentences, paragraphs, and perhaps whole compositions. This belief was very common when I was taught writing. I remember slogging my way through Warriner's *English Grammar and Composition* in the seventh and eighth grades, dutifully working through chapter after chapter.

Today, along with a lot of experts on writing instruction, I don't think that this foundational approach to writing development is very effective. While I can still diagram a sentence, for example, that's never a skill I call on when I'm composing.

Unlearning involves rejecting common sense if it conflicts with what actually works.

And yet building on the basics seems like common sense, doesn't it? This brings up an important point: Unlearning involves rejecting common sense *if* it conflicts with what actually works. Throughout this book, I hope you'll constantly test your beliefs about writing against the experiences you're having with it. Pay attention to what seems to work for you and what doesn't. Mostly, I'd like you at least initially to play what one writing instructor calls the *believing game*. Ask yourself, *What will I gain as a writer if I try believing this is true?* For example, even if you've believed for much of your life that you should never write anything in school that doesn't follow an outline, you might discover that abandoning this "rule" sometimes helps you to use writing to *discover* what you think.

The Beliefs of This Book

Allatonceness. One of the metaphors I very much like about writing development is offered by writing theorist Ann E. Berthoff. She said learning to write is like learning to ride a bike. You don't start by practicing handlebar skills, move on to pedaling practice, and then finally learn balancing techniques. You get on the bike and fall off, get up, and try again, doing all of those separate things at once. At some point, you don't fall and you pedal off down the street. Berthoff said writing is a process that involves allatonceness (all-at-once-ness), and it's simply not helpful to try to practice the subskills separately. This book shares the belief in the allatonceness of writing development.

Believing You Can Learn to Write Well. Various other beliefs about writing development—the importance of critical thinking, the connection between reading and writing, the power of voice and fluency, and the need to listen to voices other than your own—also help to guide this book. One belief, though, undergirds them all: *The most important thing that influences a writer's growth is believing that he or she can learn to write well*. Faith in your ability to become a better writer is key. From it grows the motivation to learn how to write well.

Faith isn't easy to come by. I didn't have it as a writer through most of my school career, because I assumed that being placed in the English class for underachievers meant that writing was simply another thing, like track and math, that I was mediocre at. For a long time, I was a captive to this attitude. But then, in college I wrote a paper I cared about; writing started to matter, because I discovered something I really wanted to say and say well. This was the beginning of my belief in myself—and of my becoming a better writer. Belief requires motivation, and one powerful motivator is to approach a writing assignment as an opportunity to learn something—that is, to approach it with what I have called the spirit of inquiry.

Habits of Mind

When I first started teaching writing, I noticed a strange thing in my classes. What students learned about writing through the early assignments in the class didn't seem to transfer to later assignments, particularly research papers. What was I doing wrong? I wondered. Among other things, what I'd failed to make clear to my students was that certain "habits of mind" (or *dispositions*, as one writer terms them) could be consistently useful to them, in writing papers in my course and in any course involving academic inquiry—habits related to seeing writing as a process of discovery. We'll look at several closely related habits here; later in this chapter, you'll see how they play a role in the writing process.

Starting with Questions, Not Answers

A lot of people think that writing is about recording what you already know, which accounts for those who choose familiar topics to write on when given the choice. "I think I'll write about _____," the thinking goes, "because I know that topic really well and already have an idea what I can say." Writers who write about what they know usually start with answers rather than questions. In some writing situations this makes a lot of sense, because you're being asked specifically to prove that you know something. I'm thinking of an essay exam, for instance.

1.2
Understand what kinds of questions will sustain inquiry into any subject.

But more often, writing in a university is about inquiry, not reporting information. It's about discovery. It's about finding the questions that ultimately lead to interesting answers.

Making the Familiar Strange. Starting with questions rather than answers changes everything. *It means finding new ways to see what you've seen before.* Take this for example:

What is it? An iPhone, of course. Not much more to say, right? But imagine that your purpose isn't to simply provide the quickest answer possible to the simple factual question *What is it?* Consider instead starting with questions that might inspire you to think about the iPhone in ways you haven't before; for example,

- *What does it mean* that iPhone owners spend twice as much time playing games as other smartphone users?

- *What should be done* about the environmental impacts of iPhone production in China?

Both these questions lead you to potentially new information and new ways of seeing that familiar phone in your pocket. They promise that you'll discover something you didn't know before.

Questions open up the inquiry process, while quick answers close it down. When you discover what you think, you don't cook up a thesis before you start—you discover the thesis as you explore. But to work, the inquiry process demands something of us that most of us aren't used to: suspending judgment.

Suspending Judgment

We jerk our knee when physicians tap the patellar tendon. If everything is working, we do it reflexively. We're often just as reflexive in our responses to the world:

- "What do you think of American politicians?"

  "They're all corrupt."

- "Is it possible to reconcile economic growth with the preservation of natural resources?"

  "No."

- "Isn't this an interesting stone?"

  "It's just a rock."

We make these judgments out of habit. But this habit is in fact a way of seeing, based on this premise: Some things are really pretty simple, more or less black-and-white, good or bad, boring or interesting. Academic inquiry works from another, very different premise: The world is really a wonderfully complex place, and *if we look closely and long enough*, and ask the right questions, we are likely to be surprised at what we see. A condition of inquiry is that you *don't* rush to judgment; you tolerate uncertainty while you explore your subject. Academic inquiry requires that you see your preconceptions as hypotheses that can be tested, not established truths. It is, in short, associated with a habit of *suspending* judgment.

> *It's okay to write badly. Resist the tendency to judge too soon and too harshly.*

Being Willing to Write Badly

In a writing course such as this one, the challenge of suspending judgment begins with how you approach your own writing. What's one of the most common problems I see in student writers? Poor grammar? Lack of organization? A missing thesis? Nope. *It's the tendency to judge too soon and too harshly.* A great majority of my students—including really smart, capable writers—have powerful internal critics, or, as the novelist Gail Godwin once called them, "Watchers at the Gates." This is the voice you may hear when you're starting to write a paper, the one that has you crossing out that first sentence or that first paragraph over and over until you "get it perfect."

The only way to overcome this problem is to suspend judgment. In doing so, you essentially tell your Watcher this: *It's okay to write badly.* Godwin once suggested that writers confront their internal critics by writing them a letter.

> Dear Watcher,
>
> Ever since the eighth grade, when I had Mrs. O'Neal for English, I've been seeing red. This is the color of every correction and every comment ("awk") you've made in the margins on my school writing. Now, years later, I just imagine you, ready to pick away at my prose every time I sit down to write. This time will be different....

It might help to write your internal critic a letter like this. Rein in that self-critical part of yourself, and you'll find that writing can be a tool for *invention*—a way to generate material—and that you can *think through writing* rather than waiting around for the thoughts to come. You need your internal critic. But you need it to work with you, not against you. Later in this chapter, I'll show you how to accomplish this.

Searching for Surprise

Starting with questions, making the familiar strange, suspending judgment, and writing badly—all are related to searching for surprise. In fact, one of the key

1.3
Practice a method of writing and thinking that will help you generate ideas.

benefits of writing badly is *surprise*. This was a revelation for me. I was convinced that you never pick up the pen unless you know what you want to say. Once I realized I could write badly and use writing not to *record* what I already knew, but to *discover* what I thought, this way of writing promised a feast of surprises that made me hunger to put words on the page. If you're skeptical that your own writing can surprise you, try the following exercise.

Conditions That Make "Bad" Writing Possible

1. Willingness to suspend judgment
2. Ability to write fast enough to outrun your internal critic
3. Belief that confusion, uncertainty, and ambiguity help thought rather than hinder it
4. Interest in writing about "risky" subjects, or those about which you don't know what you want to say until you say it

Exercise 1.2

A Roomful of Details

STEP ONE: Spend ten minutes brainstorming a list of details based on the following prompt. Write down whatever comes into your mind, no matter how silly. Be specific and don't censor yourself.

Try to remember a room you spent a lot of time in as a child. It may be your bedroom in the back of your house or apartment, or the kitchen where your grandmother made thick, red pasta sauce or latkes. Put yourself back in that room. Now look around you. What do you see? What do you hear? What do you smell?

Brainstorming

- Anything goes.
- Don't censor yourself.
- Write everything down.
- Be playful but stay focused.

STEP TWO: Examine your list. If things went well, you will have a fairly long list of details. As you review the list, identify the one detail that surprises you the most, a detail that seems somehow to carry an unexpected charge. This might be something that seems connected to a feeling or a story. You might be drawn to a detail that confuses you a little. Whatever its particular appeal, circle it.

STEP THREE: Use the circled detail as a prompt for a seven-minute fastwrite. Begin by focusing on the detail: What does it make you think of? And then what? And then? Alternatively, begin by simply describing the detail more fully: What does it look like? Where did it come from? What stories are attached to it? How does it make you feel? Avoid writing in generalities. Write about specifics—that is, particular times, places, moments, and people. Write fast, and chase after the words to see where they want to go. Give yourself permission to write badly.

You may experience at least three kinds of surprise after completing a fast-writing exercise such as the one above:

1. Surprise about *how much* writing you did in such a short time

2. Surprise about discovering a topic you didn't expect to find

3. Surprise about discovering a *new way of understanding or seeing a familiar topic*

One Student's Response

Bernice's Journal

EXERCISE 1.2
STEP THREE

DETAIL: STAINLESS STEEL COUNTERS

When I was five or six my father and I made cookies for the first time. I don't remember what prompted him to bake cookies, he liked to cook but he didn't read very well so he didn't like to use cook books. I remember sitting on the cold stainless steel, the big red and white cook book splayed over my lap. I was reading it out loud to my dad. The kitchen was warm but everything gleamed; it was industrial and functional. It was the only room in our house that still looked like it belonged to the "Old Pioneer School." My dad and uncles had renovated every other room into bedrooms, playrooms, family rooms. The place was huge but cozy, it was home. I remember reading off ingredients until I got to the sugar. It called for 3/4 cup and I didn't understand the fraction. I thought it meant three or four cups. We poured so much sugar into the bowl. The cookies were terrible. Hard and glassy, too sweet and brittle. It wasn't until years later that I understood that my dad didn't understand the measurement either. He was persistent though. We pulled down every cook book in the house until we found one that described the measuring cups and what they meant. We started all over and our

> second batch was perfect. My dad is one of the smartest people I know, inventive, imaginative but he only has a rudimentary education. He can read and write enough to get by, he's gifted with numbers, but I can't help looking back and wondering what he could have been, what he could have done for the world if just one person had taken him by the hand and showed him what he showed me. If just one person had told him not to give up, to keep trying, that in the end it will be worth all the work, I wonder who he could have been if one person had seen his curiosity and imagination and fostered it instead of seeing his muscles and capable hands and putting him to work. If just one person had told him that his mind was the greatest tool he possessed. If just one person baked cookies with him.

The kind of surprises you encounter doing this sort of writing may not always be profound. They may not even provide you with obvious essay topics. With any luck, though, by hunting for surprises in your own work, you will begin to experience the pleasure of writing *to learn*. That's no small thing, particularly if you've always believed that writers should have it all figured out before they pick up the pen.

Writing Situations and Rhetorical Choices

1.4

Apply rhetorical knowledge to make choices in specific writing situations.

The following isn't good writing, is it?

> im happy to be back w/u guys it was a too long of a weekend- dancing friday then? u hailey and i runnin tomorrow- sounds fun 2 me

Actually, the answer is, of course, that it depends.

Writing occurs in a writing situation, and different writing situations are associated with different types of writing and forms of communication—different genres and media. Think of how many writing situations we encounter these days and how many types of writing we do. For example, besides writing part of this textbook chapter, I wrote e-mails to an editor and a student, freewrote in my journal, drafted some text for a web page, sent a text to my daughter, and posted a comment on Facebook.

In each case, the writing situation demanded something different from me. In each, however, I had to make appropriate *rhetorical* choices—choices related to the following four considerations:

- **Purpose for writing:** What is the text trying to do?
- **Audience:** For whom is it intended?
- **Subject:** What is it about?
- **Genre/Medium:** What type of writing—what form of communication—would work best in view of my purpose, audience, and subject? What are its strengths and limitations, and what are its conventions?

That is, to write effectively, I had to think about why I was writing, to whom I was writing, what I was writing about, and what type of text I was writing. The effectiveness of my writing depended on my making appropriate choices in light of these considerations. And the rhetorical choices that we make in a writing situation are wide ranging; they include not only big choices (What's the best genre for accomplishing my purpose with this audience?), but also many smaller choices (Is it okay to say "ur" instead of "you're"?).

Now let's go back to the text message, written by my daughter to a friend.

Rhetorical Consideration	The Text Message
Purpose	Expressive and informational purposes: to reinforce intimacy; to plan
Audience	A close friend, with considerable shared knowledge
Subject	Personal details related to knowledge of a shared experience
Genre/Medium	Text message; limited to 160 characters, with a shorthand shared by users

Based on this analysis, my daughter's text message is clearly good writing after all. It uses the conventions of the genre/medium to fulfill its purpose—reinforce intimacy and make a Friday-night plan—for the audience the writer had in mind. My daughter used her *rhetorical knowledge* to make choices that resulted in an effective piece of writing. Of course, she would think it is weird to call her understanding of how to write a text message "rhetorical knowledge." But that's exactly what it is. She just doesn't think about it that way.

But what happens when you *do* think about it?

1. You become more skillful at composing in writing situations with which you are familiar.

2. You can learn to master unfamiliar writing situations much more quickly.

You have more rhetorical knowledge than you think. After all, you've been writing and speaking all your life. But when you start becoming aware of this knowledge, it becomes more powerful, and you become a better writer. Throughout *The Curious Writer*, I'll encourage you to think rhetorically.

In the next years of college, you'll be encountering unfamiliar writing situations, so learning to reflect on how each involves *rhetorical choices* will make you a much better communicator. (By the way, we also use this rhetorical knowledge to analyze how well someone else communicates, which is the focus of Chapter 2.) Learning to write well, then, isn't simply learning how to craft transitions, organize information, and follow grammatical "rules"—it's also learning to recognize that each writing situation asks you for something different. For example, in college writing situations, the basic rhetorical considerations, as in Figure 1.1, "Thinking rhetorically," may be expanded with questions such as these:

- What is the purpose of the assignment? To interpret or analyze? Synthesize or summarize? Argue or explore?

- What is the subject, and what does that imply about my approach? Are there certain ways of writing about topics in history, psychology, or literature that differ from writing about topics in biology, social science, or business?

- Am I writing for an expert audience or a general audience? For my instructor or my peers?

- What is the form or genre for this assignment, and what are its conventions? What kind of evidence should I use? How is it organized?

You won't always have control over all of these choices. In college, you'll get writing assignments that may supply you with a purpose: "Write an essay that compares the energy efficiency of solar panels with that of a conventional coal power plant." Sometimes the form isn't up to you: "Write a five-page argument paper." But even when you have such constraints, you still have a lot of rhetorical choices to make—things like: "Should I use the first person? What evidence do I need, and where should it come from?"

Each genre and medium imposes its own conditions on the writer. For example, my daughter's text message can't be more than 160 characters, and that

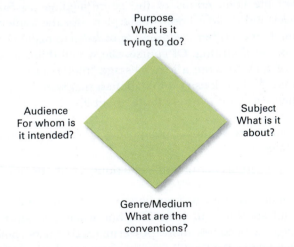

Purpose
What is it
trying to do?

Audience
For whom is
it intended?

Subject
What is it
about?

Genre/Medium
What are the
conventions?

Figure 1.1   Thinking rhetorically. Rhetorical choices involve four considerations: purpose, subject, audience, and genre/medium. Each consideration is associated with questions. For genre/medium, these include conditions and conventions regarding what you can say and especially how you say it. While all considerations have always been important in rhetorical thinking, genre and medium are especially critical to consider now that you may have alternatives to writing traditional term papers, including PowerPoints, podcasts, video, visuals, and a host of other multimodal approaches.

limitation inspired, among other things, a shorthand for composing that uses characters sparingly. Considering genre and medium is especially important now that the forms of communication have expanded radically, even in academia. You may write not just a term paper. You might do a PowerPoint, make a poster, build a web page, collaborate on a wiki, or produce a podcast.

Thinking about rhetorical contexts increases the chance that you'll make good choices when you solve problems as a writer, particularly in revision. Much like riding Berthoff's bike, in composing, writers usually think about purpose, audience, subject, and genre/medium all at once, drawing on their experience with similar writing situations.

A First Reflection on Your Writing Process

There is a process for doing almost anything—fixing a broken washing machine, learning how to play tennis, studying for the SAT, and, of course, writing. Why, then, do some English teachers seem to make such a big deal out of reflecting on your writing process? Here's why:

- First, the process of writing, like any process that we do frequently, is not something that we think about.

- As a consequence, when we write, we tend to focus just on *what* and not on *how*, just on the product and not on the process. And then, when problems arise, we don't see many options for solving them—we get stuck and we get frustrated.

- If, however, we start to pay attention to how we write in a variety of situations, two things happen: We become aware of our old habits that don't always help and may actually hinder our success with writing. Second—and this is most important—we begin to understand that there are actually *choices* we can make when problems arise, and we become aware of what some of those choices are.

- In short, *the more we understand the writing process, the more control we get over it.* Getting control of the process means the product gets better.[1]

A Case Study

Here's an example of what I mean. Chauntain summarized her process this way: "Do one and be done." She always wrote her essays at the last minute and only wrote a single draft. She approached nearly every writing assignment the same way: Start with a thesis, and then develop five topic sentences that support the thesis, with three supporting details under each. This structure was a container

---

[1]There is considerable research in learning theory that confirms these conclusions; in particular, so-called metacognitive thinking—the awareness of how you do things—increases the transfer of relevant knowledge from one situation to another. In other words, what you learn about how to do something in one situation gets more easily activated in another situation.

into which she poured all her prose. Chauntain deliberated over every sentence, trying to make each one perfect, and as a result, she spent considerable time staring off into space searching for the right word or phrase. It was agony. The papers were almost always dull—she thought so too—and just as often she struggled to reach the required page length. Chauntain had no idea of any other way to write a school essay. As a matter of fact, she thought it was really the *only* way. So when she got an assignment in her economics class to write an essay in which she was to use economic principles to analyze a question that arose from a personal observation, Chauntain was bewildered. How should she start? Could she rely on her old standby structure—thesis, topic sentences, supporting details? She felt stuck.

Because she failed to see that she had choices related to both process and this particular writing situation, she also had no clue what those choices were. That's why we study process. It helps us solve problems such as these. And it must begin with a self-study of your own habits as a writer, identifying not just how you tend to do things, but the patterns of problems that might arise when you do them.

Thinking About Your Process

You will reflect on your writing and reading processes again and again throughout this book, so that by the end you may be able to tell the story of your processes and how you are changing them to produce better writing more efficiently. Now is a good time to begin telling yourself that story.

What do you remember about your own journey as a writer both inside and outside of school? One of my earliest, most pleasant memories of writing is listening to the sound of the clacking of my father's old Royal typewriter in the room down the hall as I was going to sleep. I imagine him there now, in the small study that we called the "blue room," enveloped in a cloud of pipe smoke. It is likely that he was writing advertising copy back then, or perhaps a script for a commercial in which my mother, an actress, would appear. I loved the idea of writing then. The steady hammering of typewriter keys sounded effortless yet at the same time solid, significant. This all changed, I think, in the eighth grade when it seemed that writing was much more about following rules than tapping along to a lively dance of words.

Spend some time telling your own story about how your relationship to writing evolved.

When you get a writing assignment, your habit may be to compose carefully. This assignment, in contrast, is all about invention—about generating ideas.

Exercise 1.3

Literacy Narrative Collage

In your journal, create a collage of moments, memories, and reflections related to your experience with writing. *For each prompt, write fast for about four minutes. Keep your pen or fingers on the keyboard moving, and give yourself permission to write badly.* After you've responded to one prompt, skip a line and move on to the next one. Set aside about twenty minutes for this generating activity.

1. What is your earliest memory of writing? Tell the story.

2. We usually divide our experiences as writers into private writing and school writing, or writing we do by choice and writing we are required to do for a grade. Let's focus on school writing. Tell the story of a teacher, a class, an essay, an exam, or a moment that you consider a *turning point* in your understanding of yourself as a writer or your understanding of school writing.

3. Writing is part of the fabric of everyday life in the United States, and this is truer than ever with Internet communication. Describe the roles that writing plays in a typical day for you. How have these daily roles of writing changed in your lifetime so far?

4. What is the most successful (or least successful) thing you've ever written in or out of school? Tell the story.

Congratulations. You've made a mess. But I hope this collage of your experiences as a writer is an interesting mess, one that brought some little surprises. As you look at these four fragments of fastwriting, you might begin to sense a pattern. Is there a certain idea about yourself as a writer that seems to emerge in these various contexts? It's more likely that one, or perhaps two, of the prompts really took off for you, presenting trails you'd like to continue following. Or maybe nothing happened. For now, set your journal aside. You may return to this material if your instructor invites you to draft a longer narrative about your writing experiences, or you might find a place for some of this writing in your portfolio.

Now that you've spent some time telling a story of your background as a writer, use the following survey to pin down some of your habits and experiences related to school writing. The questions in the survey can help you develop a profile of your writing process and help you identify problems you might want to address by altering your process.

Exercise 1.4

What Is Your Process?

STEP ONE: Complete the Self-Evaluation Survey.

Self-Evaluation Survey

1. When you're given a school writing assignment, do you wait until the last minute to finish it?

    Always———Often———Sometimes———Rarely———Never

2. How often have you had the experience of learning something you didn't expect through writing about it?

    Very often————Fairly often————Sometimes————Rarely————Never

3. Do you generally plan out what you're going to write before you write it?

    Always————Often————Sometimes————Rarely————Never

4. *Prewriting* describes activities that some writers engage in before they begin a first draft. Prewriting might include such invention activities as freewriting or fastwriting, making lists, brainstorming or mapping, collecting information, browsing the web, talking to someone about the essay topic, reading up on it, or jotting down ideas in a notebook or journal. How much prewriting do you tend to do for the following types of assignments? Circle the appropriate answer.

    ■ A personal narrative:

    A great deal————Some————Very little————None————Haven't
    written one

    ■ A critical essay about a short story, novel, or poem:

    A great deal————Some————Very little————None————Haven't
    written one

    ■ A research paper:

    A great deal————Some————Very little————None————Haven't
    written one

    ■ An essay exam:

    A great deal————Some————Very little————None————Haven't
    written one

5. At what point(s) in writing an academic paper do you often find yourself getting stuck? Check all that apply.
    ❑ Getting started
    ❑ In the middle
    ❑ Finishing
    ❑ I never/rarely get stuck (go on to question 9)
    ❑ Other: _____

6. If you usually have problems getting started on a paper, which of the following do you often find hardest to do? Check all that apply. (If you don't have trouble getting started, go on to question 7.)
    ❑ Deciding on a topic
    ❑ Writing an introduction
    ❑ Finding the time to begin
    ❑ Figuring out exactly what I'm supposed to do for the assignment
    ❑ Finding a purpose or focus for the paper

❏ Finding the right tone

❏ Other: _____

7. If you usually get stuck in the middle of a paper, which of the following cause(s) the most problems? Check all that apply. (If writing the middle of a paper isn't a problem for you, go on to question 8.)

❏ Keeping focused on the topic

❏ Finding enough information to meet page-length requirements

❏ Following my plan for how I want to write the paper

❏ Bringing in other research or points of view

❏ Organizing all my information

❏ Trying to avoid plagiarism

❏ Worrying about whether the paper meets the requirements of the assignment

❏ Worrying that the paper just isn't any good

❏ Messing with citations

❏ Other: _____

8. If you have difficulty finishing a paper, which of the following difficulties is/are typical for you? Check all that apply. (If finishing isn't a problem for you, go on to question 9.)

❏ Composing a last paragraph or conclusion

❏ Worrying that the paper doesn't meet the requirements of the assignment

❏ Worrying that the paper just isn't any good

❏ Trying to keep focused on the main idea or thesis

❏ Trying to avoid repeating myself

❏ Realizing I don't have enough information

❏ Dealing with the bibliography or citations

❏ Other: _____

9. Rank the following list of approaches to revision so that it reflects the strategies you use *most often to least often* when rewriting academic papers. Rank the items 1–6, with the strategy you use most often as a 1 and the strategy you use least often as a 6.

_____ I just tidy things up—editing sentences, checking spelling, looking for grammatical errors, fixing formatting, and performing other proofreading activities.

_____ I look for ways to reorganize existing information in the draft to make it more effective.

_____ I try to fill holes by adding more information.

_____ I do more research.

_____ I change the focus or even the main idea, rewriting sections, adding or removing information, and changing the order of things.

_____ I rarely do any revision.

10. Finally, do you tend to impose a lot of conditions on when, where, or how you think you write most effectively? (For example, do you need a certain pen, do you always have to write on a computer, do you need to be in certain kinds of places, must it be quiet or noisy, do you write best under pressure?) Or can you write under a range of circumstances, with few or no conditions? Circle one.

     Lots of conditions———Some———A few———No conditions

If you impose conditions on when, where, or how you write, list some of those conditions here:

1.

2.

3.

STEP TWO: In small groups, discuss the results of the survey. Begin by picking someone to tally the answers to each question. Post these on the board, a large sheet of paper, or a spreadsheet, so they can then be added up for the class. Analyze the results for your group. In particular, discuss the following questions:

- Are there patterns in the responses? Do most group members seem to answer certain questions in similar or different ways? Are there interesting contradictions?
- Based on these results, what "typical" habits or challenges do writers in your class seem to share?
- What struck you most?

Problem Solving in Your Writing Process

If you took the survey, you probably uncovered some problems with your writing process. The great news for those of us who struggle with certain aspects of writing—and who doesn't?—is that you can do something about it. As you identify the obstacles to doing better work, you can change the way you approach writing tasks. For instance, consider some of the more common problems students struggle with and some ideas about how _The Curious Writer_ can help you with them.

Writing Problem	Possible Cause	A Solution
Consistently writes short. Often can't meet page requirements for assignments.	Writer works from scarcity. Begins the draft with too little information on the topic.	Focus on invention. Generate more material *before* you begin the draft, through research, fastwriting, etc. (see "Inquiring into the Details: Invention Strategies" in this chapter).
Dislikes revision, especially if it involves more than "tidying" things up.	Writer spends a great deal of time writing the first draft and trying to make it "perfect." Gets over-committed to the initial approach to the topic.	Write a fast draft and then do deeper revision. Attack the draft physically (see Revision Strategy 11.18 in Chapter 11).
Writer's block.	Internal critic is too harsh too early in the writing process. Often involves anxiety about audience.	Find a place where you can write badly without it feeling like a performance. A journal or notebook often works (see "Inquiring into the Details: Journals" in this chapter).
Dislikes open-ended assignments. Would rather be told what to write about.	Writer may be unused to valuing own thinking. Little experience with assignments in which writer must discover own purpose.	Use your own curiosity and questions to drive the process. Craft questions that are useful guides for exploration and promise discovery and learning (see "Starting with Questions, Not Answers" in this chapter).
Struggles with focus. Able to write a lot but can't seem to stay on topic.	Writer doesn't exploit key opportunities to look at writing critically, to evaluate and judge what she has generated.	Effectively combine invention with evaluation, generating with judging, by using a process that makes room for both as you write (see "The Nature of the Writing Process" below).

The Nature of the Writing Process

Earlier you saw Chauntain's writing process. Here was my writing process when I was in school:

1. Get the assignment. Find out when it is due and how long it is supposed to be.
2. Wait until the night before it is due and get started.
3. Stare off into space.
4. Eat ice cream.

5. Write a sketchy outline.

6. Write a sentence; then cross it out.

7. Stare off into space.

8. Write another sentence, and then squeeze out a few more.

9. Think about Lori Jo Flink, and then stare off into space.

10. Write a paragraph. Feel relief and disgust.

Suspending judgment feels freer, exploratory.... Making judgments shifts the writer into an analytical mode.

I would get the work done eventually, but the process was agonizing and the product mediocre. What did I conclude from this back then? That I wasn't good at writing, which was no big surprise because I pretty much hated it. Something happened to me to change that view, of course, because you hold my book in your hands. I came to understand the problems in my writing process: I viewed writing as a straight march forward from beginning to end, one where I had to wait for something to come into my head and then try to get it down. At all costs, I avoided things like new ideas or other ways of seeing a topic—anything that might get in the way of the drive to the conclusion. If I thought about anything, it was trying to find the "perfect" way of saying things or worrying about whether I was faithfully following a certain structure. I rarely learned anything from my writing. I certainly never expected I should.

The Writing Process as Recursive and Flexible

But this straight march isn't the way experienced writers work at all. The writing process isn't a linear trajectory, but a looping, recursive process—one that encourages *thinking*, not simply recording the thoughts that you already have. Writing doesn't involve a series of steps that you must follow in every situation; on the contrary:

- The writing process is *recursive*, a much messier zigzag between collecting information and focusing on it, exploring things and thinking about them, writing and rewriting, reviewing and rearranging, and so on. For example, invention strategies are useful at many points in the writing process.

- The process is *flexible* and always influenced by the writing situation. For instance, experienced writers have a keen sense of audience, and they use this to cue their choices about a change in tone or whether an example might help clarify a point. These are exactly the kinds of adjustments you make in social situations all the time.

A System for Using Writing to Think

What do I mean when I say the writing process encourages thinking? Usually, when we imagine someone who is "deep in thought," we see him staring off into space with a furrowed brow, chin nested in one hand. He is not writing. He may be

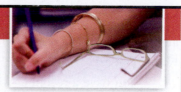

Inquiring into the Details

Invention Strategies

Invention is a term from rhetoric that means the act of generating ideas. While we typically think of *rhetoric* as something vaguely dishonest and often associated with politics, it's actually a several-thousand-year-old body of knowledge about speaking and writing well. Invention is a key element in rhetoric. It can occur at any time during the writing process, not just at the beginning in the "prewriting" stage. Some useful invention strategies include:

■ *Fastwriting:* The emphasis is on speed, not correctness. Don't compose, don't think about what you want to say before you say it. Instead, let the writing lead, helping you discover what you think.

■ *Listing:* Fast lists can help you generate lots of information quickly. They are often in code, with words and phrases that have meaning only for you. Let your lists grow in waves—think of two or three items and then pause until the next few items rush in.

■ *Clustering:* This nonlinear method of generating information, also called *mapping*, relies on *webs* and often free association of ideas or information. Begin with a core word, phrase, or concept at the center of a page, and build branches off it. Follow each branch until it dies out, return to the core, and build another. (For an example, see p. 78.)

■ *Questioning:* Questions are to ideas what knives are to onions. They help you cut through to the less obvious insights and perspectives, revealing layers of possible meanings, interpretations, and ways of understanding. Asking questions complicates things but rewards you with new discoveries.

■ *Conversing:* Conversing is fastwriting with the mouth. When we talk, especially to someone we trust, we work out what we think and feel about things. We listen to what we say, but we also invite a response, which leads us to new insights.

■ *Researching:* This is a kind of conversation, too. We listen and respond to other voices that have said something, or will say something if asked, about topics that interest us. Reading and interviewing are not simply things you do when you write a research paper, but activities you use whenever you have questions you can't answer on your own.

■ *Observing:* When we look closely at anything, we see what we didn't notice at first. Careful observation of people, objects, experiments, images, and so on generates specific information that leads to informed judgments.

thinking about what he's *going* to write, but in the meantime the cursor is parked on the computer screen or the pen rests on the desk. Thinking like this is good—I do it all the time. But imagine if you also make thought external by following your thinking on paper or screen and not just in your head. Here is some of what happens:

- You have a record of what you've thought that you can return to again and again.

- As you *see* what you've just said, you discover something else to say.

- Because the process of thinking through writing is slower than thinking in your head, you think differently.
- Because externalizing thought takes mental effort, you are more immersed in thought, creating what one theorist called a state of "flow."

As I've already mentioned, thinking through writing is most productive when you suspend judgment, reining in your internal critic. You may actually do some pretty good thinking with some pretty bad writing.

Using writing as a way of thinking is even more powerful if there is a *system* for doing it that reliably produces insight. One method, which we could call a *dialectical system*, exploits two different kinds of thinking—one creative and the other critical, one wide open and the other more closed. So far in this chapter, we've focused on the creative side, the generating activities I've called "writing badly" that restrain your internal critic. But you need that critical side. You need it to make sense of things, to evaluate what's significant and what's not, to help you figure out what you might be trying to say. If you use both kinds of thinking, "dialectically" moving back and forth from one to the other, then you're using a method that is at the heart of the process you'll use throughout *The Curious Writer*.[2] Try the next exercise to see how this might work for you.

Exercise 1.5

Two Kinds of Thinking

Let's return to the subject you began writing about in Exercise 1.3—your experiences as a writer—but focus on something that was probably part of your response to the third prompt in that exercise: your experience with writing technology.

Using Creative Thinking

STEP ONE: What are your earliest memories of using a computer for writing? In your journal or on the computer, begin by telling the story and then let the writing lead from there. Keep your pen or the cursor moving, and allow yourself to write badly.

---

[2] For Greek philosophers such as Plato, dialectic was a way of arriving at truth through back-and-forth conversation between two people who were open to changing their minds. Similarly, the process of writing and thinking I propose here is a back and forth between two parts of yourself—each receptive to the other—in an effort to discover your own "truths," ideas, and insights.

STEP TWO: Brainstorm a list of words or phrases that you associate with the word *literate* or *literacy*.

Reread what you just wrote in steps 1 and 2, underlining things that surprise you or that seem significant or interesting to you. Skip a line and move on to step 3.

Using Critical Thinking

STEP THREE: Choose one of the following sentence frames as a starting point. Complete the sentence and then develop it as a paragraph. This time, compose each sentence while thinking about what you want to say before you say it and trying to say it as well as you can.

> *What I understand now about my experiences with writing on computers that I didn't understand when I started out is _____.*
>
> *When they think about writing with computers, most people think _____, but my experience was _____.*
>
> *The most important thing I had to discover before I considered myself "computer literate" was _____.*

Reflecting

If you're like most people, then the parts of this exercise where you creatively generated material felt different than the part where you judged as you wrote. But *how* were they different? How would you distinguish between the experiences of generating and judging? Talk about this or write about it in your journal.

A Writing Process That Harnesses Two Currents of Thought

The two parts of Exercise 1.5 involving creative and critical thinking were designed to show you the difference between the two and also to simulate the shift between them, the shift from suspending judgments to making judgments—something I referred to as "dialectical" thinking. In the first two steps, you spent some time fastwriting without much critical interference, trying to generate some information from your own experience. In the third step, which began with "seed" sentences that forced you into a more reflective, analytical mode, you were encouraged to look for patterns of meaning in what you generated.

   As you probably noticed, these two distinct ways of thinking each have advantages for the writer:

- *Suspending judgment* feels freer, is exploratory, and may spark emotion.
- *Making judgments* shifts the writer into an analytical mode, one that might lower the temperature, allowing writers to see their initial explorations with less feeling and more understanding.

Thus, creative thinking creates the conditions for discovery—new insights or ways of seeing—while critical thinking helps writers refine their discoveries and focus on the most significant of them.

The Sea and the Mountain. Here's another way to conceptualize creative and critical thinking (see Figure 1.2):

- When you write creatively, you plunge into the sea of information. You don't swim in one direction, but eagerly explore in all directions, including the depths.

- When you write critically, you emerge from the water to find a vantage point—a mountain—from which to see where you've swum. From the mountain (which occasionally erupts and belches forth two words: "So What?"), you are able to see patterns that aren't visible from the water. You are able to make judgments about what you encountered there: What's significant? What isn't? Why?

The key is not to stay on the mountain. Instead, you take the patterns you saw and the judgments you made and plunge back into the sea, this time with a stronger

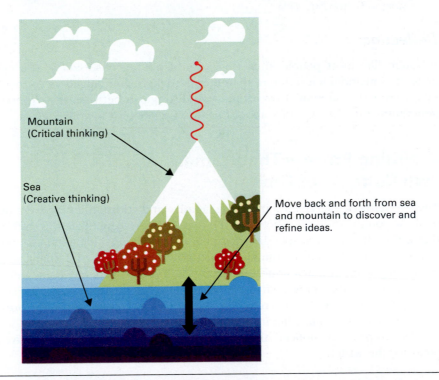

Figure 1.2   Generating insight using critical and creative thinking. Thinking to inquire is like the movement back and forth from the sea of information to the mountain of reflection. In one you explore, and on the other you evaluate. Insight develops when you continually move back and forth; as you refine your ideas, when in the sea, you swim in ever smaller circles with a stronger sense of purpose.

sense of purpose. You're clearer about what you want to know and where you need to swim to find it. This back and forth between mountain and sea continues until you've discovered what you want to say. In fact, you made just this sort of movement in Exercise 1.2 and then in Exercise 1.5 when you moved from generating to judging. It is a process of induction and deduction, working upwards from specifics to infer ideas, and then taking those ideas and testing them against specifics.

Figure 1.3 lists yet other ways in which you can visualize the movement between creative and critical thinking. In narrative writing, for instance, creative thinking helps you generate information about *what happened*, while critical thinking may lead you to insights about *what happens*. Likewise, in research writing, investigators often move back and forth between their *observations of* things and their *ideas about* them.

As you work through the book, you'll find it easier to shift between contrasting modes of thought—from collecting to focusing, from generating to judging, from showing to telling, from exploring to reflecting, from believing to doubting, from playing to evaluating. In short, you'll become better able to balance creative and critical thinking. You'll know when it's useful to open up the process of thinking to explore and when it's necessary to work at making sense of what you've discovered.

Answering the *So What?* Question. An important function on the critical thinking side is to make sure you can answer the one question you must answer when writing for an audience:

So what?

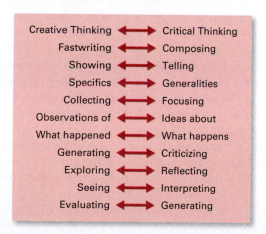

Creative Thinking	Critical Thinking
Fastwriting	Composing
Showing	Telling
Specifics	Generalities
Collecting	Focusing
Observations of	Ideas about
What happened	What happens
Generating	Criticizing
Exploring	Reflecting
Seeing	Interpreting
Evaluating	Generating

Figure 1.3   Alternating currents of thought. When writers alternate between creative and critical thinking, they move back and forth between two opposing modes of thought—the creative and the critical. One seems playful and the other judgmental; one feels open ended and the other more closed. Activities such as fastwriting and brainstorming promote one mode of thought, and careful composing and reflection promote the other.

So what? can be a pretty harsh question, and I find that some students tend to ask it too soon in the writing process, before they've fully explored their topic. A danger is that this can lead to frustration. You may, for example, have found yourself high and dry if you've tried to reflect on possible meanings of a moment you've written about for only eight minutes. Another danger is that the writer is tempted to seize on the first convenient idea or thesis that comes along. This abruptly ends the process of inquiry before the writer has had a chance to explore.

When you can't come up with an answer to the *So what?* question, the solution is usually to generate more information.

A Writing Process Driven by Questions

The inquiry approach is grounded in the idea that the writing process depends, more than anything else, on finding good questions to address.

I recently visited teachers in Laredo, Texas, and I told them that with a good question, even the most boring topic can become interesting. I would prove it, I said, and picked up a lemon that was sitting on a table and asked everyone, in turn, to ask a question about the lemon or about lemons. Twenty minutes later, we had generated sixty questions. In the process, we began to wonder how the scent of lemons came to be associated with cleanliness, why lemons appeared so often in wartime British literature, why the lime and not the lemon is celebrated in local Hispanic culture. We wondered a lot of interesting things that we never expected to wonder about, because a lemon is ordinary. Questions can make the familiar world we inhabit yield to wonder.

The point is this: *There are no boring topics—just wrong questions.*

But what are *good* inquiry questions? Obviously, for a question to be good, you have to be interested in it. Furthermore, others must also have a stake in the answer, because you'll be sharing what you learn.

Usually, when we investigate something we don't know much about, we start by asking informational questions. Say you're interested in the Disney Corporation's sustainability projects. You first need to know what those are. You might search online and read about Disney's commitment to recycling or to energy efficiency. This is basic background information—facts about what has already been said about a topic. But in college writing, you're usually not writing a report or a summary of what's known about a topic. Just explaining what Disney is doing to reduce emissions isn't enough. You have to *do* something with that information. This involves that critical mind that we talked about earlier, one that asks you to make judgments.

Different types of questions lead to different kinds of judgments. And it's landing on the appropriate type of question for your project that will launch you into meaningful inquiry. These question types include the following:

- *Value questions:* Is it good or bad? Useful or useless?

- *Relationship questions:* Are they similar or dissimilar? Is there a cause and effect? What's the connection?

- *Policy questions:* What should be done?
- *Interpretation questions:* What might it mean?
- *Hypothesis questions:* What is the best explanation?
- *Claim questions:* Are the assertions valid? What is most persuasive?

You can apply these kinds of questions to nearly any topic, depending on what interests you about it. For example, in Figure 1.4 I tried to imagine how someone exploring Disney's sustainability programs might use each of these question types. With a little factual background, it isn't hard to start framing possible inquiry questions that can really steer your project in different—and possibly interesting—directions.

A good question not only lights your way into a subject, but may also illuminate what form you could use to share your discoveries. Certain kinds of writing—reviews, critical essays, personal essays, and so on—are often associated with certain types of questions, as you can see in Figure 1.4. In Part 2 of *The Curious Writer*, which features a range of inquiry projects from the personal essay to the research essay, you'll see how certain questions naturally guide you towards certain kinds of writing.

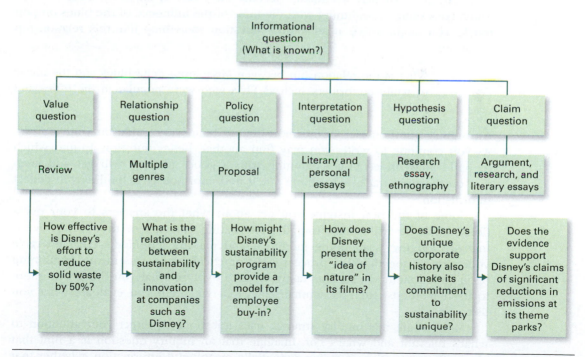

Figure 1.4 Categories of inquiry questions. The inquiry process often begins with informational questions: What is already known about this? As writers learn more about their topics, they refine their questions so that they are more likely to lead to analysis or argument rather than mere report. Some of these questions are associated with certain kinds of writing that are covered in this book.

A Strategy for Inquiry: Questioning, Generating, and Judging

If you combine the power of good questions with the back-and-forth process of writing creatively and critically, you have a strategy of inquiry that you can use for every assignment in this book. The key is to alternately generate—topics, ideas, questions—and judge. Typically, you begin exploring a subject, sometimes generating some initial thoughts through fastwriting, listing, or other invention methods. But like landscape shots in photography, subjects cover a huge amount of ground. You need to narrow your subject and eventually arrive at a yet narrower topic, or some *part* of the landscape to look at more closely. As an example, take popular music. That's a huge subject. But as you write and read about it a little, you may begin to see that you're most interested in the blues, and especially in its influence on American popular music. This last might seem promising as a general topic.

With a tentative topic in hand, you then need to search for a few inquiry questions about your topic that both interest you and will sustain your project. These are the questions that will help you focus your topic, that will guide your research, and that may eventually become the heart of an essay draft on your topic. For example, beginning with the topic of the influence of the blues on pop music, you might arrive at an inquiry question something like this relationship question:

> What is the relationship between Mississippi delta blues and the music of white performers such as Elvis who were popular in the fifties and sixties?

An inquiry question may be no more than a temporary guide on your journey. As you continue to write, you may find another, better question around which to build your project. But beginning with a good question will get and keep you on the right track—something you'll find enormously helpful as you collect information.

Some of the best insights you get about what the answers to your questions might be will come from the alternating currents of thought—generating and judging, suspending judgment and making judgments—that energize your writing and thinking processes. In practical terms, this means combining open-ended methods, such as fastwriting, to explore what you think with more focused methods, such as summarizing, that will help you evaluate what you discover.

Most of all, this inquiry strategy uses questions to direct your attention to what's relevant and what's not. Imagine that an inquiry question is a flint that gives off sparks when it strikes potentially meaningful information, whether that information comes from personal experiences or research. These sparks are the things that will light your way to discoveries about your topic. In Part 2 of this book, you'll be led through this process in the last part of each chapter, as you *open up* your thinking about topics (generate), *narrow down* those topics through focused questioning (judge), *try out* various approaches (generate), *think about* criteria (judge)—and finally, develop, draft, and revise your writing.

The inquiry strategy I'm proposing should work with nearly any topic. Let's try one in Exercise 1.6.

Exercise 1.6

A Mini Inquiry Project: Cell Phone Culture

The alternating currents of thought—generating and judging, exploring and evaluating, opening up and focusing, mountain and sea—can be put to work in any situation where you want to figure out what you think. Writing is a key part of the system. In this exercise, I'll guide you to think one way and then another. Later, you may find you do this on your own without thinking about it. But for now, let me guide you.

More than 90 percent of us now have cell phones, and according to one study, about a third of people aged eighteen to twenty-nine say that they "couldn't live without" them. Cell phones make us feel safer, and of course they're an enormous convenience. But they've also introduced new annoyances into modern life, like the "halfalogue," the distracting experience of being subjected to one half of a stranger's conversation with someone on their cell phone. It's a technology that is fundamentally changing our culture—our sense of community and connection, our identities, the way we spend our time. But how? Try exploring that question for yourself, to see if you can discover what *you* find interesting about the topic.

Invention: Generating

STEP ONE: Let's first take a dip in the sea of information. Recent research on "cell phone addiction" suggests that, as with Internet addiction, "overuse" of the technology can result in anxiety, depression, irritability, and antisocial behavior. This research also suggests that college students are particularly vulnerable to cell phone addiction. One survey to determine whether someone is cell phone addicted asks some of the following questions:

- Do you feel preoccupied about possible calls or messages on your mobile phone, and do you think about it when your cell is off?
- How often do you anticipate your next use of the cell phone?
- How often do you become angry and/or start to shout if someone interrupts you when you're talking on a cell phone?
- Do you use a cell to escape from your problems?

Start by exploring your reaction to this list in a fastwrite in your journal, print or digital. Write for at least three minutes, but write longer if you can. What do you make of the whole idea of "cell phone addiction"? What does this make you think about? And then what? And then?

Judging

STEP TWO: Reread your fastwrite, underlining anything that you find interesting, surprising, or possibly significant. Pay particular attention to anything that might have surprised you. Then thoughtfully finish the following sentence.

One interesting question that this raises for me is: _____?

Generating

STEP THREE: Focus on the question you came up with in step 2. Return to the sea and write about specific *observations, stories, people, situations, or scenes* that come to mind when you consider the question you posed. Don't hesitate to explore other questions as they arise as well. Let the writing lead. Write fast for *at least* another three minutes without stopping.

Judging

STEP FOUR: Review what you just wrote, thoughtfully complete the following sentence, and then follow that first sentence for as long as you can compose here, thinking about what you're going to say before you say it, rather than fastwriting.

So far, one thing I seem to be saying is that we. . . .

Finding a Question

STEP FIVE: You haven't generated much writing on cell phone culture yet, but if you've written for ten minutes or so, you should have enough information to take a stab at writing a tentative inquiry question. Using the question categories in Figure 1.4, try to draft a question about cell phones, cell phone culture, cell phone addiction, or any other topic suggested by your writing. Remember, the question should be one of the following:

- A value question: Is it any good?
- A policy question: What should be done?
- A hypothesis question: What is the best explanation?
- A relationship question: What is the relationship between _____ and _____?
- An interpretation question: What might it mean?
- A claim question: What does the evidence seem to support?

Reflecting on the Process

STEP SIX: In your journal, or on an online discussion board, answer the following questions about what you've just drafted.

1. What, if anything, do I understand now that I didn't before?
2. What most surprised me?
3. What's the most important thing I take from this?

Reflective Inquiry About Your Writing

I should be a really good guitar player. I've played since I was eleven. I'm okay. But among my other problems was a lousy sense of rhythm—at least until recently, when I began playing with my friend Richard, who can play skillfully in all the ways I can't. How did I solve the rhythm problem by playing with Richard? What exactly did I learn to do that helped me adjust my strum so I could provide passably good backup to Richard's leads?

To get better at a process, we need to ask questions about it. And to answer these questions, we have to have three things:

1. Some knowledge of how the process is done or how it might be done
2. The language to define the problem
3. Some ideas about possible solutions

Since the beginning of this chapter, I've argued that taking the time to reflect on your knowledge and think about writing, and paying attention to how you use this knowledge and thinking as you write, is well worth the effort. It will speed up your learning, help you to adapt more easily to a range of writing situations, and make writing less frustrating when things go wrong. Experts call this "reflective inquiry," and they observe that experienced professionals in many fields often do this kind of thinking. In a way, reflective inquiry is thinking *about* thinking. It isn't easy. But it is also one of the most important ways in which we *transfer* what we know from one situation to another. Reflective thinking is key to making the most of your learning in this writing course.

You've tried your hand at reflective inquiry in several exercises so far, including the previous one on "cell phone culture." Let's get a little more practice with it before we move on.

Exercise 1.7

Scenes of Writing

Think about the writing and thinking you've done about yourself as a writer in this chapter. Review your notes from all of the exercises you tried that asked you to reflect on that (Exercise 1.1, your beliefs about writing; Exercise 1.3, your literacy collage; and Exercise 1.4, the survey on your writing process). Now imagine the kind of writer *you would like to be.*

Scene 1

A month ago, you got a writing assignment in your philosophy course: a twelve-page paper that explores some aspect of Plato's dialogues. It's the night before the paper is due. Describe the scene. What are you doing? Where? What's happening? What are you thinking? If you can, make use of the various types of writing that can convey scene: setting, action, description, narration, dialogue.

Scene 2

Rewrite scene 1. This time, script it as you *wish* it would look.

Finally, imagine that each scene is the opening of a film. What would they be titled?

Reflective Inquiry

Think about the terms we've used in this chapter to talk about the writing process—terms such as these:

- *Prewriting*
- *Revision*
- *Focusing*
- *Critical and creative thinking*
- *Invention*
- *Reflection*
- *Exploration*
- *Inquiry questions*
- *Habits of mind*
- *Suspending judgment*
- *Genre*
- *Alternating currents of thought*
- *Writing situation*
- *Rhetorical choices*

Draft a 200- to 250-word essay or discussion-board post about your own writing process—past, present, or future—that uses as much of the terminology of the writing process as you find relevant and useful to your essay or post.

Using What You Have Learned

Remember the learning goals at the beginning of the chapter?

1. **Reflect on and revise your beliefs about yourself as a writer.** In this chapter, you started to tell yourself the story of yourself as a writer. Like any good story, you tell it for a reason: What does it tell you about the kind of writer you think you've been? Is that the writer who will work for you now as you deal with a wider range of writing situations in college and out of college? The great thing is that if your beliefs about yourself are holding you back, you can change them. And you will as you work your way through this book. Reflect continuously on what you do as a writer that works for you (and on what you do that doesn't). This isn't just an academic exercise; it is knowledge that you can put to work to help solve your writing problems.

2. **Understand what kinds of questions will sustain inquiry into any subject.** Academic inquiry is driven by questions that will keep you thinking. But what kinds of questions will sustain your investigation of a subject over time? In this chapter, you learned how you can start with an informational question—What is known about a topic?—and refine that into a question that will help you discover what you want to say. You'll see later how these questions often lead to certain kinds of writing. The ability to understand what kinds of questions will guide your writing and thinking is something that you can draw on in nearly every college class.

3. **Practice a method of writing and thinking that will help you generate ideas.** Throughout *The Curious Writer*, you'll use the technique you were introduced to here: using your creative mind to explore and generate material, and using your critical mind to narrow down and evaluate what you've generated. As you get more practice with this method, you'll find that you may not even think about it but instead shift naturally from withholding judgment to making judgments. If this works for you, you'll find that it's a powerful way to use writing to discover what you think in nearly any writing situation.

4. **Apply rhetorical knowledge to make choices in specific writing situations.** In this book, *rhetoric* is never a bad word. You learned here that the term doesn't describe someone who blows smoke in an attempt to deceive, but rather represents a way of thinking about how to communicate effectively. Rhetoric is a system for analyzing writing situations by looking at purpose, audience, and genre, so that you can see more clearly what your choices are when you're composing any kind of text. You already have considerable rhetorical understanding. Anyone with any skill in social situations does. But as you become more conscious of rhetorical analysis, you'll discover how fundamental it is to speaking and writing well.

2

Reading as Inquiry

Learning Objectives

In this chapter, you'll learn to

2.1 Apply reading purposes relevant to reading in college.

2.2 Examine your existing beliefs about reading and how they might be obstacles to reading effectively.

2.3 Recognize reading situations and the choices about approaches to reading that they imply.

2.4 Understand the special demands of reading to write, and practice doing it.

2.5 Understand some conventions of academic writing and recognize them in texts.

You've been reading all of your life. Why read a chapter on the subject, especially in a book about writing? Well, I'm going to argue that reading in college is different from much of the reading you've done in school up until now. To start with, the *kinds* of reading, or *genres*, you'll encounter will range widely from poems to journal articles with dense academic prose. You'll also be reading subjects about which you may have very little prior knowledge. It's hard to overstate what a difference lacking knowledge about a subject makes in your ability to understand what you read and use what you read in your writing. When readers know a lot about a subject, they have mental categories and hierarchies for that subject—slots into which the new information they read is organized—which makes it easier for them to retrieve and use the information later in their writing. In contrast, when readers don't know much about the subject of their reading—and that's often the case in undergraduate inquiry-based projects—they don't know what to make of what they're reading. We can picture their mental process as a scrambled struggle to simply understand the text. Going on to actually *use* the information in their writing will be an entirely different, and much bigger, problem. You've probably experienced these situations, and they don't feel good. You're bored or frustrated with what you're reading. You can't focus. All you want to do is watch *Keeping Up with the Kardashians* on TV, and you actually hate that program.

An obvious solution to this problem is to develop some knowledge about a topic so you can read with more understanding. But there are other strategies, too, that can help you read—and use—difficult texts in unfamiliar genres, and I'll introduce you to them in this chapter. They include the following:

- *Be clear about your goals in reading a text.*

- *Use questions to drive the process.* In reading to inquire there are four types of questions that can direct your attention as you read: exploring, explaining, evaluating, and reflecting questions.

- *See a text in its rhetorical context.* In other words, you can work more effectively with any kind of reading if you can see the kind of work its author *intended* it to do.

- *Understand that reading is a process.* The more you reflect on how you do it, including in different situations, the more control you gain over the process.

- *Write as you read.* You can apply creative and critical thinking to generating insights about texts, too, through tools such as a double-entry journal (described further on in this chapter).

- *Understand the features of academic discourse.* Knowing what to look out for will help you understand what you're reading.

Purposes for Academic Reading

Why read? We pick up a book for pleasure, read a news website for information, and so on. But I'd like to be more specific. What are the purposes for reading in college? First imagine some typical contexts for academic reading. You might, for example,

- Read a textbook to acquire knowledge about a subject. You may be required to demonstrate what you've learned on a test or in a paper.

- Read a textbook (such as this one) that is a guide to a process. You use it to help you *do* something—write, perform an experiment, design a website.

2.1
Apply reading purposes relevant to reading in college.

- Read a journal article or short story closely, to analyze the arguments of the article or interpret the meaning of the story.
- Read material you have found online, to see how you might use the information in your own writing or to prepare a presentation.

Reading with the spirit of inquiry turns books, essays, and articles into one side of a dialogue that you're having with an author.

Each of these reading situations involves multiple purposes, and in each case one or two purposes are especially important. Although reading is a cognitively complex thing, I'd propose that the purposes of academic reading boil down to four—to *explore, explain, evaluate,* and *reflect.*

Imagine that each purpose involves asking a text different kinds of questions. We don't typically start reading with questions in mind. I know when I was an undergraduate, the question I usually had when I was reading a textbook (aside from "When will I be done so I can go play the guitar?") was "Will this be on the test?" On my really deep thinking days, I might read an assigned article in, say, my environmental studies class and wonder, "Do I agree or disagree with this?" These are reasonable questions. But they aren't very good guides for reading well. The research on reading says that the best readers have conscious goals when they read. These goals can be expressed as questions. Here, then, are some general questions that can express the different purposes. Notice that you can ask these questions about both the text and parts of the text.

Purpose	Some Examples of Readers' Questions
Explore	What could I learn from this? What does this make me think?
Explain	What do I understand this to be saying?
Evaluate	Is this persuasive? How do I interpret this?
Reflect	How is this put together? What do I notice about how I'm thinking about this?

Each of these questions will lead you to read the same text in a different way. In using the purposes and questions, keep in mind that we often have more than one main purpose for reading a text. For example, when we read a biology textbook to learn about cell structure for a test in two weeks, we will read it to explore *and* explain. When we have to analyze a website as a source for an academic paper, we have to make a judgment about whether it has persuasive content (evaluate) *and* think about how it's designed to be persuasive (reflect).

But to demonstrate how each of these purposes might change the way you read a text, we'll try to apply each of them separately in the following exercise.

Exercise 2.1

Using the Four Purposes for Academic Reading

Every year, the *Chronicle of Higher Education* publishes data about last year's college undergraduates. Here's a table (Figure 2.1) from that report that describes students' employment levels outside of school. Read the table using the four purposes for reading—exploring, explaining, evaluating, and reflecting—one at a time.

Explore

STEP ONE: First just figure out what you make of this information. Data tell stories. What are some of the stories the data in this table seem to be telling? Make a list of these in your journal. Some inferences are probably obvious. For example, part-time students clearly work more than full-time students. No surprise there. Work towards teasing out some of the less obvious implications, especially those that you find surprising. When you're done, look at your list of inferences. What questions do they raise? For example, private college students who are full-time clearly work less than full-time students enrolled in public schools. And yet, if they attend part-time, students enrolled at private colleges work *far more than* part-time students at public institutions. Why? What might explain this?

Percentage of college students age 16 to 24 who were employed, by hours worked per week, October 2009				
	Full-time students		**Part-time students**	
	Worked 20 or more hours	**Worked less than 20 hours**	**Worked 20 or more hours**	**Worked less than 20 hours**
All undergraduates	23%	16%	62%	11%
Female	25%	18%	64%	12%
Male	21%	13%	59%	10%
Hispanic	27%	10%	60%	12%
White	24%	19%	63%	13%
Black	20%	9%	64%	n/a
Asian	12%*	9%	n/a	n/a
By type of institution attended:				
Public 2-year	28%	16%	59%	11%
Public 4-year	24%	15%	63%	13%
Private 4-year	13%	20%	80%	n/a
* Large margin of error				
Note: The designation "n/a" means no figures were provided because statistical standards were not met. For that reason, no figures were provided for American Indians or Pacific Islanders.				
Source: Census Bureau				

Figure 2.1   Employment patterns for college undergraduates

Explain

STEP TWO: Turn your list from step 1 into a fat paragraph that summarizes what you think are the story lines in this table. What are the things it seems to be saying?

Evaluate

STEP THREE: Based on your reading of the data in the table, make a one-sentence assertion about what you think is *the most significant finding*. Write this down in your journal.

Reflect

STEP FOUR: Statistical tables are inevitably selective on what data they include. They also group information into categories that make the data easier to understand but may obscure important results. In this table, students' employment was categorized into students who work more than twenty hours and students who work less than twenty hours. Does this seem sensible to you? Make a case for or against using that distinction.

In class, or on the online discussion board, talk about your experience with reading for each of these four purposes.

- Which step of the exercise was hardest for you?
- With which of these purposes do you typically read texts in school? Which are new to you?
- How did each reading purpose change the focus of your reading?

We always have a purpose for reading something, but we rarely think much about it. In this section, I've tried to convince you that you'll read much more skillfully and efficiently—particularly in college—when you do consider *why* you're reading something. The advantages of this awareness are huge: You'll know what to look for in a text that's relevant to the task. You'll know what questions to ask yourself to evaluate what you're reading. And you'll know what you might use from a text in your own writing. There's another thing that will help, too. Reading, like writing, is something you've done much of your life, and you've developed habits and beliefs that govern how you approach reading. These can help you or they can hurt you. But you can't determine that until you know what they are.

2.2

Examine your existing beliefs about reading and how they might be obstacles to reading effectively.

Beliefs About Reading

You have theories about reading much like you have theories about writing—including beliefs about what makes a "good" reader and about yourself as a reader. They're not beliefs you're aware of, probably, but they profoundly affect how you read everything you read. Through an exercise that gets you thinking a little about your own literacy history, let's start to tease some of these beliefs out into the open so you can get a look at them.

Exercise 2.2

A Reader's Memoir

Generating

STEP ONE: There is considerable evidence that attitudes about reading are heavily influenced by how reading is viewed at home. Were there books around when you were growing up? Did your parents encourage you to read? Did they read? Fastwrite for five minutes about your memories of reading as a child in your home. Describe what you remember, and try to be as specific as possible.

Judging

STEP TWO: Speculate about the beliefs these early experiences with reading might have encouraged. In your journal, compose an answer to this inquiry question: *What is the relationship between my early reading experiences at home and my current beliefs about reading?*

Generating

STEP THREE: Now think about your reading experiences in school up until now. Fastwrite for five minutes, telling stories about your experiences with particular books or teachers, especially those that might have influenced the way you think of reading and of yourself as a reader.

Judging

STEP FOUR: As before, try to summarize how these experiences in school might have influenced how you view yourself as a reader now. Answer this question: *What is the relationship between my experiences reading in school and my current beliefs about reading and myself as a reader?*

One Common Belief That Is an Obstacle

I hope that Exercise 2.2 revealed some of the beliefs that shape how you feel about reading. When I wrote about my memories of reading at home, I realized that I had been lucky to grow up in a family that celebrated reading but that I had preferred to "read" television instead of a book. I can see now how this made me a reluctant reader who lacked confidence in his reading ability. When I wrote about my memories of academic reading, I immediately remembered—with revulsion—tanking on the reading portion of the SAT, and I realized that for years I'd thought the only purpose of reading in school is to say back what it said in a test or a paper.

My belief about school reading is a common one, and for good reason. Most reading instruction seems to focus on comprehension—you know, the SAT- or ACT-inspired kind of situation in which you are asked to read something and then

Only by understanding how we read in certain situations can we acquire more control over what we get out of the reading experience.

explain what it means. This often becomes an exercise in recall and vocabulary, an analytical challenge in only the most general way. Essentially, you train yourself to distinguish between specifics and generalities and to loosely follow the author's reasoning. In English classes, sometimes we are asked to perform a similar exercise with stories or poems—what is the theme, or what does it mean?

Instruction and assignments such as these encourage students to see reading as an archaeological expedition where they must dig for hidden meaning. The "right" answers to the questions are in the text, like a buried bone; you just have to find them. The trouble with this approach is the belief that it tends to foster, which is that *all meaning resides in the text and the reader's job is merely to find it*. This belief limits the reader's interaction with the text. If meaning is fixed within the text, embedded like a bone in antediluvian mud, then all the reader has to do is dig. Digging isn't a bad thing, but reading can be so much more than laboring at the shovel and sifting through dirt.

Reading Situations and Rhetorical Choices

2.3
Recognize reading situations and the choices about approaches to reading that they imply.

This chapter began with a list of typical reading situations you might encounter as an undergraduate. You read a textbook to acquire information for a test. You mine an article for material to put in a paper or analyze a short story to interpret its theme, and so on. In each of these situations, you're going to make choices about *how* you read that text. Usually, these choices are governed by habit. This is the way you *always* read a textbook or a short story.

I'm going to try to convince you to make these choices differently. First, they should be conscious choices. For example, earlier we talked about purpose-directed reading. To read by asking questions based on your purpose is to make conscious choices.

Recall from Chapter 1 that to write effectively in a writing situation, you need to make appropriate rhetorical choices and that one of the considerations these are based on is your writing purpose. Similarly, in a reading situation, to read effectively you make choices based in part on your reading purpose.

When you're reading for a writing assignment, your purpose for reading basically has already been determined. For example, you might get an assignment like this in an English class:

- *Closely read and **explicate** the poem by Mary Oliver.*

Or perhaps you get an assignment like this in a marketing class:

- *Find and read company websites for mission statements and **explain** how companies distinguish between goals and objectives.*

In each of these situations, what you need to do is to start by *reading the assignment rhetorically*, to make sure you understand your purpose for reading. The main clue is usually the verb: *explicate, explain, argue, summarize, interpret, analyze*, and so on. These verbs tell you what you are supposed to do with what you read.

Frequently, however, you will have much less direction than this on what to do with your reading. Sometimes reading is just a part of a larger project, presentation, or paper, and *you* have to figure out what to do with every text you encounter. In these cases, you will need to figure out your purpose along with three other considerations that affect the choices you make about how to read something. These considerations, which I'll call *frames for reading*, are similar to those that come into play in rhetorical choices for writing.

Four Frames for Reading

- **Your purpose:** Why are you reading this text? (To explore, explain, evaluate, and/or reflect?)

- **Your knowledge of the genre/medium:** What do you know about this kind of text, and what do you therefore expect? What is it trying to do, and for whom was it likely written?

- **Your knowledge of the subject:** What do you already know about the subject of the reading? What biases might you have about it?

- **Self-perception:** How good do you think you are at reading a text in this genre and on this subject?

These considerations inevitably affect our reading. For example, a few years ago, when I was a novice at the shorthand of text messaging, I was painfully aware that I lacked genre knowledge. What do those abbreviations mean? When one of my daughters sent me a message, my first concern was decoding some of it. As I gained familiarity with the form, the problem of genre knowledge faded and I could focus more immediately on *why* they were telling me what they were telling me. They were asking for money? They wanted me to back off on the boyfriend? Experienced readers are aware of these frames and deliberately look at a text through them in order to make their reading more efficient.

Reading Scenarios

Consider a couple of scenarios involving academic reading and how an experienced writer might apply the four frames for reading.

Scenario #1. You're assigned two chapters in your college physics textbook for an exam. You don't know physics, much less college physics. Based on your feelings about reading textbooks and your inexperience with the subject, you're not feeling good about the time you'll spend reading for the assignment.

Faced with this situation, an experienced reader might apply the four frames as follows:

1. *Purpose.* I'm reading this to be able to explain what I know on an exam. I'd better pay attention to key concepts and terms when I read it and make sure

I can explain them to myself. I think I'll write a summary in my notebook of the key ideas—and a running list of terms and definitions—as I read. This is gonna slow me up but in the end will be worth it.

2. *Genre/medium knowledge.* I know that textbooks for intro courses are intended for readers with low subject knowledge, but even so, it might be a struggle for me to understand and remember terms. Textbooks usually have clues about what's important—I'll pay particular attention to terms that are emphasized by length of treatment and visual cues such as italics and headings.

3. *Subject knowledge.* I don't know much about physics, so I can't skip around when I read this. I'll need to work through the text from the beginning and not move on to a new section until I think I understand the current one.

4. *Self-perception.* I stink at science and don't much like reading textbooks. Because I know I'm going to get frustrated, I'll allow some extra time to get through this—maybe reading over a few days rather than in one sitting.

Scenario #2. You're writing a research essay for your composition class on the impact of climate change in Australia, a place that one observer noted is a kind of "miner's canary" on the issue—in other words, likely to be among the first to experience problems and provide a warning sign for what is to come in the rest of the world. The question you're asking is whether chronic water shortages in the Outback are really climate related. Along with other material, you've found a great article in *Rolling Stone Magazine* that seems really on topic.

Here's how an experienced reader might approach reading the article:

1. *Purpose.* No one is telling me why I should read this article. I've got to figure that out. The *Rolling Stone* piece might be the most strongly stated thing I've read so far that argues that climate change is responsible for Australia's environmental problems. I'm going to read it to find some of those passages. Maybe I can use them in my paper. I'm also going to pay particular attention to the evidence provided on water shortages.

2. *Genre/medium knowledge.* This is *Rolling Stone*, not an academic article. It won't provide the quality of evidence that a journal article would. I also know that because of the magazine's youthful audience and its focus on popular music, *Rolling Stone* might be prone to overstating things a bit for dramatic effect. I'm going to read a little more critically.

3. *Subject knowledge.* I know a fair amount about the climate-change issue, and because I feel really strongly about it, I'm going to try to read this article critically, as a doubter more than a believer (see "Inquiring into the Details: Reading Perspectives"). What is the writer ignoring? Does he address counterarguments?

4. *Self-perception.* This article should be easy for me to read and understand.

Inquiring into the Details

Reading Perspectives

One of the best ways to read strategically is to consciously *shift* our perspective while we read. Like changing lenses on a camera or changing the angle, distance, or time of day to photograph something, this shift in reading perspective illuminates different aspects of a text. Here are some of the perspectives you might take:

- **Believing:** What the author says is probably true. Which ideas can I relate to? What information should I use? What seems especially sound about the argument?

- **Doubting:** What are the text's weaknesses? What ideas don't jibe with my own experience? What are the gaps in the information or the argument? What isn't believable about this?

- **Updating:** What does this add to what I already know about the subject?

- **Hunting and gathering:** What can I collect from the text that I might be able to use?

- **Interpreting:** What might be the meaning of this?

- **Pleasure seeking:** I just want to enjoy the text and be entertained by it.

- **Connecting:** How does this information relate to my own experiences? What is its relationship to other things I've read? Does it verify, extend, or contradict what other authors have said?

- **Reflecting:** How was this written? What makes it particularly effective or ineffective?

- **Resisting:** This doesn't interest me. Why do I have to read it? Isn't *Survivor* on television right now?

Exercise 2.3

Reading a Life

Here's a scenario for you to consider, one that involves reading a different kind of text—a photograph. I'd like you to apply the four frames for reading to this photograph, much the way I applied them in the previous two scenarios.

First, some background. One of the many ways we all make inferences about other people is by paying attention to the details of their lives. What things do they value? What is their behavior in significant social situations? What groups do they belong to? While we may do this informally all the time, academics and writers do it, too—for example, when they study members of social or cultural groups or when they plan to write a profile of someone. One academic version of this is called *ethnography*. It relies on very close observations of people in the places that

their groups typically inhabit. Photographs can be an important source of data for such inquiries.

The photograph above, "Ruth's Vanity (on the day she died)," potentially tells us a lot about who Ruth Smith was, through the things on her vanity and on the dresser that is visible in the mirror above the vanity. I'd like you to think about how to read this photograph by applying the four frames for reading: purpose, genre/medium knowledge, subject knowledge, and self-perception. Explain, as I did in the previous scenarios, how each frame might influence *how* you read this photograph: Number each frame, and then write a brief paragraph explaining how the frame influences how you read the photograph to make inferences about Mrs. Smith. Your instructor may ask you to do this in your journal, submit it as a short response, or post it to the online discussion board.

Reading situations, like writing situations, can really differ, and each asks something different from you. There is no one "right" way to read well, or to write well, in most situations. Instead, there are choices. These choices are rhetorical; in every reading situation, you need to think about your purpose in reading the text, about the text itself—its subject, its genre/medium, and the author's likely purpose and audience—and about your self-perception in relation to the text's subject and genre/medium. You need to think about what these frames together imply about how you *might* approach the text. It's not a science. There's no formula to follow. Mostly, you simply want to be a *flexible* reader and writer, one who can read a situation well enough to make decisions about how to approach it. This becomes possible when you pay attention to your process.

A Process for Reading to Write

The process of reading to write is going to be different from, say, that of reading for pleasure. For example, lately I'm reading books about rafting the Colorado River. My motives are both learning and pleasure, but I really don't plan on writing anything about rafting, so I'm not as active a reader as I am when I'm reading something for, say, an essay I'm writing or a book I'm researching. I spend considerably less time taking notes, marking passages, mining the bibliography, and doing other things like that. I'm less worried about *what I can do* with what I'm reading.

Not long ago, I was working on an essay in which I was exploring why certain landscapes—usually the ones we know best from our childhoods—often get under our skins even if we no longer live in those places. My reading for this project led me to all kinds of sources—articles in anthropology, history, and literary works. This reading was enjoyable, but it was also work. In the back of my mind, I was always asking, *Does this relate to the questions I'm interested in?* It was a reading process that was much more directed by my purposes—by my desire to use what I was reading in my own writing.

2.4

Understand the special demands of reading to write, and practice doing it.

Questions for the Process of Reading to Write

So far we've explored the various ways we might approach academic reading situations in general. We've explored questions like these: What are typical situations? How might reading frames such as purpose or genre knowledge influence what we do? Now let's look specifically at processes for those reading situations—typical in college—in which you have to write about what you read, especially when this involves inquiry into a topic.

What Do I Want to Know? Inquiry is driven by questions, not answers. What do you want to know? In Chapter 1 (see "A Writing Process Driven by Questions" on pp. 28–29), I explained that inquiry into most topics about which you know little often begins with informational questions: What is known about the impact

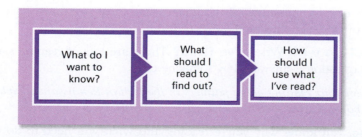

Figure 2.2   Reading to write is one of the most goal-oriented types of reading. First, you are guided by your research question: What do you want to know? If you know this, you know what to look for and how to use it in your own work.

of climate change in the Australian Outback? Why are reality shows so popular? In the beginning of an inquiry project, this larger goal—to develop some background knowledge—provides some guidance for how you should read, but the reins will be pretty loose. You're likely to wander around a lot. That's okay as a start, but the reading and writing processes need the discipline of good questions that will keep you focused.

Consider some writing I did about theories of dog training. This writing actually originated with the behavior of our golden retriever: Ada was being bad—jumping on people, barking, and generally being a pest. Ada's behavior inspired some research on websites, in books, and even in academic articles. At first, I just wanted to know what the schools of thought were on getting Ada in line—a question of fact. Before long, I knew enough to come up with much better questions, more specific and more directive, which changed not only what I was reading, but also how I read it. From the question "What are theories of dog training?" I ended up asking, "What is the relationship between the use of shock collars and dog aggression and submission?"

Obviously, the second question is a much better guide to what to read and what to ignore. That one step of focusing the reading process on a narrower question, taken at an appropriate point, can then make a huge difference in the efficiency of the process.

What Should I Read to Find Out? Should I buy a new iPhone? Who cares? Well, I care. But because this is a question in which only I have a stake, I'm likely to read all kinds of things to help me answer the question. I won't be picky. But suppose my question were less personal and more academic, or less concerned with just me and instead addressed to a larger audience—for example, "Do people's emotional attachments to their iPhones have any of the qualities of clinical addiction?" With this question, I'll be a lot more picky about what I read. I'll look in the usual places—some quality websites—but I'll also check out some books on addictive behavior and search scholarly articles, probably in psychology, to see if anyone has studied users' emotional bonds to their cell phones.

In other words, *what* you read (the kinds of texts you focus on) is determined not just by the question you're asking but the context in which you're asking it—the rhetorical choices related to your writing: Who are you writing for and why? What kinds of information will that audience find most persuasive? Are there certain kinds of evidence they would expect you to offer?

What Do I Do with What I've Read? There are lots of reading situations in which this question is answered by someone else:

> *Based on your reading about painters in the Italian Renaissance, explain in 250 words how an artist such as Caravaggio chose his subject matter.*

In this case, you know why you're reading and what you need to do with what you've read—explain a particular point. But in many reading situations, especially those that are inquiry based, you'll have considerable freedom to determine not only your own purposes for your reading, but also, more specifically, how you might use some of it in your paper or presentation. For example, are you reading a book chapter to find an explanation for a particular idea? Are you analyzing a statistical table to find evidence that supports a point you're trying to make?

In either type of reading situation, to actually do something with what you've read, you first have to know what you think about what you've read. How can you possibly make a decision about whether to quote an author or summarize someone's ideas or select this fact or another if you don't know what *you* make of what the text is saying? If you don't know much about the Italian Renaissance, let alone Caravaggio, then at the very least you'll need to try to *understand* as much as you can from your reading about both.

We've already talked about how reading isn't a monologue. "Blah, blah, blah," says a text, and you mindlessly write, "The text says, 'Blah, blah, blah.'" That's a monologue, not a conversation. You're not talking with—or back to—what you're reading; you're parroting what you've read. In the next section, I'll propose a method for encouraging conversations with what you read that will help you to discover what you think.

Having a Dialogue with What You Read

A typical process for reading to write:

1. Google some keywords on a topic.
2. Go to the first link that seems promising and click on it.
3. If the site seems relevant, read it once quickly online. Bookmark or print.
4. Go read something else and repeat the process.
5. Hope that you'll remember what you've read when you have to write on the topic.

Another standard version of the process:

1. Get a reading assignment.
2. Read it once, maybe twice. Highlight a few things.
3. Compose something quickly about what you've read for the assignment, looking for slots to insert what you highlighted.

These are passive readings. While they're fine for some reading tasks, they don't work well when you have to write or talk about what you read in a paper or for a presentation.

Imagine an alternative scenario: An assigned reading, a book, or an article is open in front of you, but so is your notebook. Your pen is poised to mark up the text—underlining, making marginal notes, adding question marks next to confusing passages and checkmarks next to those you think are important. When you're finished with your first reading, you go back and focus on what you marked. On the left-hand page of your notebook, you write down quoted passages that seem important; you jot down some facts that struck you. You might add a summary of a key idea or paraphrase the author's assertions. Then, on the right-hand page of your notebook, you fastwrite for five minutes, thinking about what you just read, looking at the notes you collected on the opposing page to spur you along.

What I'm proposing, quite simply, is that you write while you read. But I'm also suggesting a method for doing this writing that some call a "double-entry note-book" or "dialogue journal." If you're using a notebook, you use the left-hand page to collect important ideas, facts, quotations, or arguments from what you've read, and then you use the right-hand page to think about them through writing. You

Inquiring into the Details

Reading the Visual

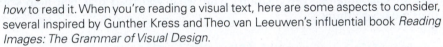

As you know by now, it helps enormously when reading a new text to have some knowledge of *how* to read it. When you're reading a visual text, here are some aspects to consider, several inspired by Gunther Kress and Theo van Leeuwen's influential book *Reading Images: The Grammar of Visual Design*.

- *Framing:* As in writing, what the photographer, advertiser, painter, or designer chooses to include in an image and what she chooses to leave out profoundly affect the story, idea, or feeling that an image communicates. Framing might also establish a viewer's distance from the action. An up-close-and-personal image suggests intimacy, while a long shot has the opposite effect.

- *Angle:* A front-on view of a subject creates a different effect than looking up, or down, at it.

- *Relationships:* One of the most important of these is the relationship between you and the image itself. Is the subject of an image looking directly at the viewer or look-ing away? In the first case, the subject seems to make some kind of demand, and in the second, the subject perhaps makes an invitation to simply be an onlooker.

- *Color:* Designers know that color affects mood. Not surprisingly, for example, red is a color that communicates feelings of passion and energy. White suggests "purity" and innocence. Yellow is sunny and joyous. For further analysis on color and emotion in visuals, search the web on the subject.

- *Arrangement:* In writing, we give certain information emphasis by where we place it in a sentence, in a paragraph, or in the composition as a whole. Visual information also uses the physical arrangement of objects for emphasis, making some things larger or smaller, in the foreground or background, to one side or the other. Kress and van Leeuwen, for example, suggest we perceive the left side of an image as information that is a "given," things that viewers readily accept, while the right side is perceived as "new," information that viewers aren't familiar with. Thus, the right side becomes a key feature for communicating a message.

- *Light:* What is most illuminated and what is in shadows—and everything in between—also influences what is emphasized and what is not. But because light is something we strongly associate with time and place, it also has an emotional impact.

can use this method with any kind of text, including visual texts. See how the double-entry journal technique works for you to analyze an image. (You can find some ideas about analyzing images in "Inquiring into the Details: Reading the Visual.")

Exercise 2.4

Double-Entry Journaling with a Visual Text

Advertisements make arguments. They are carefully designed to combine text and images to persuade a particular audience to *do* something: buy a product, join an organization, vote for a referendum, make a donation. You know this, of course. But most of us are generally unaware of the methods of visual arguments. We don't think much about how they use visual language to direct our gaze and touch our emotions (see "Inquiring into the Details: Reading the Visual" for more on how visual texts are designed to persuade). To read an advertisement with these things in mind involves *rhetorical analysis*. Up until now, we've looked at analyzing the rhetorical situations we find ourselves in as readers. Now we'll turn our attention to analyzing texts. What is the intended audience of an ad? What are the appeals designed specifically for that audience? How does the ad use emotion? How was it composed to emphasize certain ideas or feelings?

In Chapter 6, on writing arguments, we'll look at this kind of rhetorical analysis more closely, but for now, select an advertisement from a magazine, or focus on a screen ad on your computer. Try to find one with lots going on visually. Take a close look. Then practice using the double-entry journal technique to analyze the ad's visual argument.

STEP ONE: Here are the questions for reading your ad:

- What specifically are the appeals in the advertisement, and to whom are they directed?

- What specific evidence in the ad would you point to as examples of those appeals?

- Do you think they are persuasive for the intended audience? Why or why not?

Following the instructions below, use two blank opposing pages in your journal to explore these questions.

STEP TWO: On the left-hand page, collect some information from the ad. Make a list of everything you look at in the ad, *in the order you look at it*. What do you see first? Then what? Then what? Be as specific as you can. When you've got a satisfactory list, circle those items that you think are particularly effective.

STEP THREE: On the right-hand page, explore your thinking about what you've collected. Begin a fastwrite by explaining to yourself what you notice about the *order* of the details you noticed in the ad. How did the ad direct your gaze?

Then explore the items you circled on the other side of the page. Why were they effective. For whom? What kind of audience response might they get? How would these visual arguments convince a person to buy what is advertised?

STEP FOUR: Go back to the questions in step 1. How would you answer them?

STEP FIVE: Reflect in writing, in class, or on your class's online discussion board about your experience using the double-entry journal to analyze your ad.

- What worked? What didn't?
- How might you apply the double-entry journal to other reading situations?
- What did the method encourage you to do in the exercise that you don't usually do when you read?

Techniques for Keeping a Double-Entry Journal. You're going to discover ways to make a reading journal work best for you. But if the journal is going to help you have *conversations* with what you read, there are some essential elements.

1. **Focus on what the author or text actually says.** That's the beauty of the left-facing page of a double-entry journal. Because it contains passages, facts, ideas, and claims from your reading, you're working with what the text said, not with what you vaguely remember that it said.

2. **Try to suspend judgment.** When we feel strongly about what we're reading, it's human nature to decide right away whether we agree or disagree with an author or come to a quick conclusion about what a text says and what it means. But you can use writing—and especially the open-ended, exploratory process of fastwriting—to really think things through before you come to conclusions.

3. **Use questions.** Sometimes, as in Exercise 2.4, the questions are provided to direct your reading. More often, you read to discover the questions that interest you about a topic. These will fuel bursts of writing that lead you towards having something to say about what you read.

4. **Read to write and write to read.** This is fundamental. No matter what technique you use to include what you read in your writing, you should always write *as you read* and, if possible, immediately after.

The double-entry journal method I'm proposing here typically involves a notebook and a pen, but if you prefer to work on a tablet or laptop, you can accomplish much the same thing with a two-column Word or Pages document. If you use a notebook, imagine that the spiral binding that divides opposing pages is a kind of table. On the left sits a text and an author; on the right sits you. You're having a conversation across that imaginary table. What do you talk about?

First, you have to try to understand what a text is saying. That's what the left-hand page is for—to try to collect information and ideas from what you're reading that you think are central to understanding the reading. On the right-hand page of your journal, you respond to, think and ask questions about, and explore what you've collected on the opposite page.

Exercise 2.5

Reading Creatively, Reading Critically

Now that you've seen how the double-entry journal can help you analyze an image, let's try it with a more familiar kind of text. I published the essay "The Importance of Writing Badly" some years ago, but I think it still expresses several of the main ideas behind this book. I'd like you to read the piece critically, though, using the double-entry journal method I just described.

As before, you'll use opposing pages of your journal.

STEP ONE: Read the essay once through, marking it up. (Make a copy if you don't want to write in your book.) Read it a second time and, on the left-hand page of your notebook, carefully *copy* lines or passages from the essay that

- Connected with your own experience and observations
- Raised questions for you
- Puzzled you
- Seemed to be key points
- Evoked disagreement or agreement or made you think differently
- Were surprising or unexpected

The Importance of Writing Badly
Bruce Ballenger

I was grading papers in the waiting room of my doctor's office the other day, and he said, "It must be pretty eye-opening reading that stuff. Can you believe those students had four years of high school and still can't write?"   1

I've heard that before. I hear it almost every time I tell a stranger that I teach writing at a university.   2

I also hear it from colleagues brandishing red pens who hover over their students' papers like Huey helicopters waiting to flush the enemy from the tall grass, waiting for a comma splice or a vague pronoun reference or a misspelled word to break cover.   3

And I heard it this morning from the commentator on my public radio station who publishes snickering books about how students abuse the sacred language.   4

I have another problem: getting my students to write badly.   5

6   Most of us have lurking in our past some high priest of good grammar whose angry scribbling occupied the margins of our papers. Mine was Mrs. O'Neill, an eighth-grade teacher with a good heart but no patience for the bad sentence. Her favorite comment on my writing was "awk," which now sounds to me like the grunt of a large bird, but back then meant "awkward." She didn't think much of my sentences.

7   I find some people who reminisce fondly about their own Mrs. O'Neill, usually an English teacher who terrorized them into worshipping the error-free sentence. In some cases that terror paid off when it was finally transformed into an appreciation for the music a well-made sentence can make.

8   But it didn't work that way with me. I was driven into silence, losing faith that I could ever pick up the pen without breaking the rules or drawing another "awk" from a doubting reader. For years I wrote only when forced to, and when I did it was never good enough.

9   Many of my students come to me similarly voiceless, dreading the first writing assignment because they mistakenly believe that how they say it matters more than discovering what they have to say.

10   The night before the essay is due they pace their rooms like expectant fathers, waiting to deliver the perfect beginning. They wait and they wait and they wait. It's no wonder the waiting often turns to hating what they have written when they finally get it down. Many pledge to steer clear of English classes, or any class that demands much writing.

11   My doctor would say my students' failure to make words march down the page with military precision is another example of a failed education system. The criticism sometimes takes on political overtones. On my campus, for example, the right-wing student newspaper demanded that an entire semester of Freshman English be devoted to teaching students the rules of punctuation.

12   There is, I think, a hint of elitism among those who are so quick to decry the sorry state of the sentence in the hands of student writers. A colleague of mine, an Ivy League graduate, is among the self-appointed grammar police, complaining often about the dumb mistakes his students make in their papers. I don't remember him ever talking about what his students are trying to say in those papers. I have a feeling he's really not that interested.

13   Concise, clear writing matters, of course, and I have a responsibility to demand it from students. But first I am far more interested in encouraging thinking than error-free sentences. That's where bad writing comes in.

14   When I give my students permission to write badly, to suspend their compulsive need to find the "perfect way of saying it," often something miraculous happens: Words that used to trickle forth come gushing to the page. The students quickly find their voices again, and even more important, they are surprised by what they have to say. They can worry later about fixing awkward sentences. First, they need to make a mess.

15   It's harder to write badly than you might think. Haunted by their Mrs. O'Neill, some students can't overlook the sloppiness of their sentences or their lack of

eloquence, and quickly stall out and stop writing. When the writing stops, so does the thinking.

The greatest reward in allowing students to write badly is that they learn that language can lead them to meaning, that words can be a means for finding out what they didn't know they knew. It usually happens when the words rush to the page, however awkwardly.   16

I don't mean to excuse bad grammar. But I cringe at conservative educational reformers who believe writing instruction should return to primarily teaching how to punctuate a sentence and use *Roget's Thesaurus*. If policing student papers for mistakes means alienating young writers from the language we expect them to master, then the exercise is self-defeating.   17

It is more important to allow students to first experience how language can be a vehicle for discovering how they see the world. And what matters in this journey—at least initially—is not what kind of car you're driving, but where you end up.   18

Page #	Notes from Reading	Exploratory Response
	■ Direct quotations ■ Summaries of key ideas ■ Paraphrases of assertions, claims ■ Facts, specific observations, data ■ Premises and reasons ■ Interesting examples or case studies	■ Focused fastwrite on material in left-hand column or page. ■ What's relevant to the question? ■ What questions does it raise? ■ What do I think and feel about this? ■ How does it change the way I think about the subject? ■ What surprised me? ■ What's the most important thing I take away from the reading? ■ How does it connect to what I've heard, seen, or read before?

Figure 2.3   An approach to keeping a double-entry journal. Note that you should keep track of page numbers (if any) in the reading from which you collected information and put them in the left-hand column or page. Particularly when doing research, you should begin by jotting down key bibliographic information about each source.

STEP TWO: Now use the right-hand page of your notebook to think further about what you wrote down on the left-hand page. Use the questions in Figure 2.3 as prompts for a focused fastwrite. Write for five or six minutes without stopping.

STEP THREE: Reread what you've written. Again, on the right-hand page of your notebook, write your half of the following imaginary dialogue with someone who is asking you about the idea of "bad writing."

> Q: I don't understand how bad writing can help anyone write better. Can you explain it to me?
>
> A:
>
> Q: Okay, but is it an idea that makes sense to you?
>
> A:
>
> Q: What exactly (i.e., quotation) does Ballenger say that makes you feel that way?
>
> A:

STEP FOUR: Finish the exercise by reflecting in your journal for five minutes on what, if anything, you noticed about using the double-entry journal to have a "conversation" with a text. In particular:

- How did it change the way you usually read an article such as this one?
- How might you adapt it for other situations in which you have to read to write?
- What worked well? What didn't?
- Do you think the method encouraged you to think more deeply about what you read?

Alternatives to the Double-entry Journal. Though the double-entry journal nicely structures your thinking about what you read between collecting and evaluating, generating and judging, it's hardly the only method for writing as you read. Here are some other approaches you can try:

1. **Three-Act Notes.** This is a simple but effective way of thinking about what you just read. Immediately after you finish the text, set it aside and fastwrite for as long as you can, exploring your response. Act 1: In your notebook or in Word, begin with this seed sentence: *The thing that strikes me most about this is …* and follow it from there, writing as fast as you can. Act 2: Return to the reading. Review your underlinings and reread what you thought were interesting passages, tables, or data. Jot down a bulleted list of key concepts, facts, statistics, or claims that you harvest from this review. Act 3: End with another fastwrite—*second thoughts*—in which you focus on one or more of the bulleted items. Explore what you find significant, interesting, or relevant.

2. **After-words.** At a minimum, spend a few minutes immediately after you finish reading something by beginning with a summary: *What I understand this to be saying is….* Get this down first, and then fastwrite your thoughts about the argument, key concept, or significant findings you highlighted in your summary. How does it change the way you think about the topic? How does it connect with other things you've read? What do you find surprising?

Wrestling with Academic Discourse: Reading from the Outside In

The one thing that most influences your ability to understand and use what you read is prior knowledge. If you're reading about an unfamiliar topic—say, the biology of the Palouse worm, a creepy, disturbingly large creature that lives deep underground in northern Idaho—then you will have to work harder than if you read about a familiar topic. In college, unfortunately, much of what you read will be about subjects that are new to you. This means, quite simply, that you may struggle. You'll get frustrated. In your worst moments, you might want to throw an assigned reading out the window. I did that once.

But here's the good news: The more you learn about a topic, the more competent you'll feel. And it isn't just topic knowledge that will make you feel this way. It's also learning to understand the *discourse* of a particular discipline. You learn how to read, for instance, the discourse of biologists who write about worms, or the discourse social workers use to write to each other about poverty. There are all kinds of *discourse communities*, or groups of people who share certain ways of thinking, asking questions, and communicating—not just scholarly ones. Electricians share certain ways of communicating with each other. So do surfers.

It might seem that reading specialized discourses such as these is just about deciphering jargon. It's actually about much more than that. Academic discourse, for example, includes not just the language insiders use, but also

- The kinds of questions participants typically ask that guide research in the field
- Preferred methods for answering questions
- The kinds of evidence a discourse community considers persuasive
- Conventions for reporting discoveries

Even a couple of sentences on the same topic—the appeal and the effects of watching reality television—can yield some hints about how discourses differ.

EXAMPLE 1

There has been a considerable interest in how real reality television shows are as well as how such programming creates and reinforces gender and racial stereotypes (Cavender and Bond-Maupin 1993; Eschhotz et al. 2002; Estep and Macdonald 1983; Oliver 1994; Prosise and Johnson 2004).[1]

---

[1]Monk-Turner, Elizabeth, et al. "Are Reality TV Crime Shows Continuing to Perpetuate Crime Myths?" *The Internet Journal of Criminology*, 2007, www.internetjournalofcriminology.com/Monk-Turner%20et%20al%20-%20Reality%20TV%20Crime%20Shows.pdf.

> ## EXAMPLE 2
>
> **Reality TV: An Insider's Guide to TV's Hottest Market[2]**
>
> For all of Reality's faults, I still liken critics who blanketly bash it while favoring sit-coms and dramas to wine snobs who can't just enjoy an orange soda now and then.

The first example is from an academic journal and the second from a popular book. It isn't hard to draw some contrasts between them. Imagine that you are asked, based on just these two sentences, to infer a list of "rules" (or conventions) for academic writing. What would they be? For example, what would you say about the kinds of evidence that seem necessary in academic writing and the preferred methods of answering questions? What would you infer about the conventions for reporting discoveries?

What you're doing here with just a couple sentences is the kind of rhetorical analysis that will help you understand how to read—and later, how to write—in discourses that may not be familiar to you. Let's look at academic discourses specifically to see what features they might share.

Features of Academic Discourse

2.5

Understand some conventions of academic writing and recognize them in texts.

There isn't a single academic discourse. There are *discourses*. Academic discourse varies from discipline to discipline. Why? Though all academic disciplines—from those in the humanities to those in the natural sciences—are dedicated to creating new knowledge, they each look at different aspects of the world. Some, say, look at language. Others observe natural phenomena. A few, like math, work with often highly abstract concepts or ideas. Because the materials for discovery differ, the methods of discovery do, too. These differences naturally lead to unique ways of describing things and reporting them. Before long, you have different discourse communities.

Despite all these differences, it is possible to make some observations about academic discourse that apply across discourse communities. As you become more experienced reading texts in various fields, you will begin to recognize some of these basic patterns, and this will help immensely with your academic reading.

1. **Billboards.** Academic writers announce, usually somewhere near the beginning of an article, what they are going to do.
2. **Reviews.** Like the first example about reality shows, academic texts often include a review of what others have already said on a topic. This is also near the beginning.

---

[2]Devolld, Troy. *Reality TV: An Insider's Guide to TV's Hottest Market*. Michael Weise Productions, p. 22.

3. **Hedges.** Contrary to the popular assumption that academic texts usually deal in certainty, much academic writing qualifies assertions. They signal caution by using words such as *appear to be, tend*, or *suggest*.

4. **Signposts.** Most academic subjects are complicated neighborhoods, and scholarly writing offers plenty of explicit direction about deviations in an argument (e.g., *however*), presentation of reasons (e.g., *because*), and evidence (e.g., *for example*).

5. **Questions.** Academic writing is about inquiry and discovery, and these arise from questions to explore or problems to solve. Identifying the question or the problem that an academic article proposes to address is key to understanding what it's about; knowing the question driving the research also makes the path authors took to a study's conclusions much more obvious.

These five conventions are some handholds that you can seize as you wrestle your way through much academic discourse. Figure 2.4 may also help you understand how scholarly articles typically organize their content.

I distinctly remember the first time I had to read articles in biology, my undergraduate major. I was lost. I felt stupid. And I vowed to avoid scholarly books and articles if at all possible. In the Internet age, this kind of avoidance can seem even more possible. But the truth is that, even if it's more possible, it's not a good idea. Popular writing on the web can help you to develop a working knowledge of your topic—and this will help you begin to understand the scholarship—but it is the academic sources that will always lead you to the deepest, richest understandings of the things that interest you. Now is the time to learn how to break

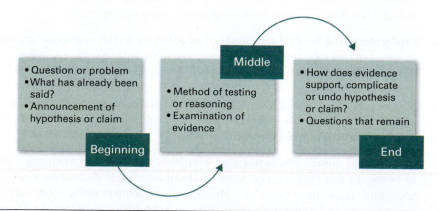

Figure 2.4 How academic articles are organized. Scholarly articles have a beginning, middle, and end, like stories do. Beginnings "billboard" the research question and review the literature. In the middle, writers tell what happened in their own investigation of the question, and in the end, they analyze the significance of what they've found.

through the initial reaction to academic prose—"This is so boring!"—and enter the messy, exciting marketplace where knowledge is made. That, after all, is the business of the university, and, as a curious writer and reader, you're invited to become a part of it.

Using What You Have Learned

Reflect on the learning goals introduced at the beginning of the chapter.

1. **Examine your existing beliefs about reading and how they might be obstacles to reading effectively.** As you become a more experienced reader in college, your beliefs about your own competence should *evolve* along with your understanding of how different kinds of texts work. In the days ahead, think about this. Are you thinking about reading any differently than when you began the course ?

2. **Apply reading purposes relevant to reading in college.** Your purpose for much of the reading you do will be decided by you. You're researching a paper or a presentation, for instance, and you collect all kinds of texts. How do you want to *use* them? To explore, explain, evaluate, or reflect? What "frames" will you use to make that decision?

3. **Recognize reading situations and the choices about approaches to reading that they imply.** Just as there is no "right" way to write in all situations, there is no "right" way to read whenever you have a reading assignment. Hopefully, you will see that each situation implies certain choices. Think about what they are and you'll read much more strategically.

4. **Understand the special demands of reading to write, and practice doing it.** The best way to jumpstart your engagement with a text is *to write* while you read and after. Always have a pen in your hand. We think in dialogue with a text. It is from this conversation that we collaborate with a text to discover our own ideas about something. Throughout *The Curious Writer*, I'll encourage you to keep up this dialogue, using some form of the double-entry journal and through questions.

5. **Understand some conventions of academic writing and recognize them in texts.** In this chapter, you learned about *academic discourse,* a weighty-sounding term that describes the range of conventions that scholarly communities use to ask questions, choose methods, and report on discoveries. Whatever major you end up in, you'll be required to learn some of the conventions of academic discourse in your field. Don't let anyone tell you that academic discourse is just one thing—it varies from scholarly community to scholarly community—but we have explored general features of much academic writing, features such as how many scholarly articles are organized.

3

Writing a Personal Essay

Learning Objectives

In this chapter, you'll learn to

3.1 Use personal experiences and observations to drive inquiry.

3.2 Apply the exploratory thinking of personal essays to academic writing.

3.3 Identify the characteristics of personal essays in different forms.

3.4 Use invention strategies to discover and develop a personal essay topic.

3.5 Apply revision strategies that are effective for shaping narratives.

Writing About Experience and Observations

Most us were taught and still believe that we need to know what we are going to write about before we actually pick up the pen or sit in front of the computer. My student Lynn was typical.

"I think I'll write about my experience organizing the street fair," she told me the other day. "That would be a good topic for a personal essay, right?"

"Do you think so?" I said.

"Well, yes, because I already know a lot about it. I'll have a lot to write about."

"Okay, but is there anything about this experience that you want to understand better?" I said. "Anything about it that makes you curious?"

"Curious? It was just a street fair," she said.

"Sure, but is there something about what happened that makes you want to look at the experience again? Is there a chance that you might learn something about yourself, or about street fairs, or about the community, or about people, or…?"

Lynn was probably sorry she asked. What I should have said was much more to the point: The best personal essay topics are those that raise questions you may not know the answers to. They are head-scratching topics, experiences that you look back at and say to yourself, "What was *that* about?" They are likely not experiences you have already figured out, or that you choose simply because you know them well. The best topics ask to be written about because they make you wonder *Why did I do that? What does that mean? Why did that happen? How did I really feel? What do I really think?*

Like all other forms of inquiry, the personal essay is driven by questions, but more than any other form, it is a vehicle for writers to work through their thinking and feeling on a subject, directly in front of their readers. The drama of the personal essay is watching a writer *coming to know.*

The personal essay is a vehicle for writers to work through their thinking and feeling on a subject, directly in front of their readers.

As a form, the *personal* essay places the writer at center stage. This doesn't mean that once she's there, her responsibility is to pour out her secrets, share her pain, or confess her sins. Some essays do have these confessional qualities, but more often they do not. Yet a personal essayist, no matter the subject of the essay, is still *exposed*. There is no hiding behind the pronoun *one*, as in "one might think" or "one often feels," no lurking in the shadows of the passive voice: "An argument will be made that.…" The personal essay is first-person territory.

In this sense, the personal essay is much like a photographic self-portrait. Like a picture, a good personal essay tells the truth, or it tells *a* truth about the writer/subject, and it often captures the writer at a particular moment in time. This explains why the experience of taking a self-portrait, or of confronting an old picture of oneself taken by someone else, can create the same feeling of exposure that writing a personal essay often creates.

But it does more. When we gaze at ourselves in a photograph, we often see it as yanked from a larger story about ourselves, a story that threads its way through our lives and gives us ideas about who we were and who we are. This is what the personal essay demands of us: We must somehow present ourselves truthfully and measure our past against our present. In other words, when we hold a photograph of ourselves, we know more than the person we see there knew, and as writers of the personal essay, we must share that knowledge and understanding with readers.

Though the personal essay may be an exploration of a past experience, it needn't always be about memories. A personal essay can instead focus on some aspect of writers' present lives, just as long as it raises questions that interest them. Just last week, for example, my students spent two days at the local zoo, taking notes on what they saw there, and from this came personal essays about feeling caged, the hunger for eye contact with wild things, and the irony of a bald eagle, our national symbol, missing its right wing.

Motives for Writing a Personal Essay

Essai was a term coined by the sixteenth-century French nobleman Michel de Montaigne, a man who endured plague epidemics, the bloody civil war between French Catholics and Protestants, and his own bouts of ill health. His tumultuous and uncertain times, when old social orders and intellectual traditions were under assault, proved to be ideal ferment for the essay. The French verb *essayer* means "to attempt" or "to try," and the essay became an opportunity for Montaigne to work out his thoughts about war, the education of children, the evils of doctors, and the importance of pleasure. The personal essay tradition inspired by Montaigne is probably unlike what you are familiar with from high school. The high school essay is often formulaic—a five-paragraph theme or thesis-example paper—while the personal essay is an open-ended form that allows for uncertainty and inconclusiveness. It is more about *the process of coming to know* than presenting *what* you know. The personal essay attempts *to find out* rather than *to prove.*

It is an ideal form of inquiry if your purpose is exploratory and if you're particularly interested in working out the possible relationships between your subject and yourself. Because the personal essay is openly subjective, the writer can't hide. The intruding *I* confronts the writer with the same questions over and over again: *Why does this matter to me? What do I make of it? How does this change the way I think of myself and the way I see the world?* Because of this, one of the principal dangers of the personal essay is that it can become narcissistic; it can go on and on about what the writer thinks and feels, and the reader can be left with that nagging question—*So what?* The personal essayist must always find some way to hitch the particulars of his or her experience to something larger—an idea, a theme, or even a feeling that readers might share.

On the other hand, one of the prime rhetorical advantages of the personal essay is its subjectivity. Because it is written with openness and honesty, the essay can be a very intimate form, inviting the reader to share in the writer's often concealed world. The *ethos* of personal essayists, or their credibility, revolves around the sense that they are ordinary people writing about ordinary things. In the personal essay, we often get to see the face sweating under the mask.

3.1
Use personal experiences and observations to drive inquiry.

The Personal Essay and Academic Writing

In some ways, the personal essay might seem like a dramatic departure from the kind of academic writing you may have done in other classes. Explicitly subjective and sometimes tentative in its conclusions, the personal essay is a relatively open form that is not predictably structured like much academic writing. Additionally,

3.2
Apply the exploratory thinking of personal essays to academic writing.

the tone of the personal essay is conversational, even intimate, rather than imper-sonal and removed. So, if your sociology or economics professor will never ask for a personal essay, why bother to write one in your writing class?

It's a fair question. While the pleasures of personal essay writing can be rea-son alone to write these essays, there are also other important reasons related to your academic work. Writing a personal essay will encourage you to:

- **Emphasize invention.** More than any other writing assignment, the per-sonal essay encourages writers to suspend judgment. Since essayists' motives are to find out what they didn't know they knew, the form makes exploration the main engine of inquiry. This places emphasis on invention—techniques like fastwriting or research that *generate* information and ideas—a process you can use (and will throughout *The Curious Writer*) in any assignment.

- **Practice dialectical thinking.** The personal essay is *inductive* like scien-tific thinking; it looks closely at the data of experience and attempts to infer from that information theories about the way things are, and then returns to the experience with new understanding.

- **Expose the drama of coming to know.** The essay emphasizes the *process* of learning about yourself and your subject, exposing your reasoning and the ways you use knowledge to get at the truth of things. Reflecting on these components can tell you a lot about how you think.

- **Establish your role as narrator.** We tend to think of narrators as a literary device, or something that is only relevant when writing in the first person. But you narrate all of your writing, from the least formal personal responses to the most formal academic essays. You are always the guiding hand, lead-ing readers through the material. Writing personal essays makes that role visible, of course, and it's a powerful experience for those who aren't used to feeling present in their writing. This presence is something you can carry into all the writing you do, even when you don't use first person.

Inquiring into the Details

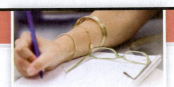

The Power of Narrative Thinking

In a classic study of the culture of the Kpelle tribe in Liberia, anthropologists presented tribal mem-bers with twenty items—garden and kitchen tools, fruits and vegetables, clothing, etc.—and asked them to organize the items in a way that made "sense." What the Kpelle did surprised the anthropologists. In-stead of putting the items in conceptual categories—garden tools in one category, food in another—the Kpelle put them in functional ones. The potato and knife were paired because "you take the knife and cut the potato."

In the West, we are mostly trained as school writers to use the kind of categorical, conceptual thinking that leads us quite naturally to write that way, too. When we write thesis-driven essays, for example, we organize the writing hierarchically, starting with a main idea and subordinating everything that comes after it. One theorist called this "paradigmatic" thinking. Personal essays call on a different kind of thinking, the kind that the Kpelle tribesmen used, and a key part of this thinking is looking for relationships—particularly causal ones—between things that are seen in a particular context. It's the kind of thinking that is behind storytelling. We want to make sense of an experience by finding reasons that might help explain it, and we do this not by trying to organize information into conceptual categories but by examining the particulars of the experience.

What's powerful about this kind of narrative thinking is that instead of stripping away context so that it's easier to manage abstract ideas, narrative thinking makes the evidence found in particular times and places central to understanding. While academia seems to emphasize paradigmatic thinking, narrative thinking is a part of some disciplines like anthropology, teacher education, and nursing, all communities of practice that are vitally interested in trying to interpret what happens to particular groups of people in specific contexts. The personal essay is an instrument to engage in this kind of narrative thought.

Features of the Form

Feature	Conventions of the Personal Essay
Inquiry questions	What does it mean to me? What do I understand about this now that I didn't then?
Motives	Self-discovery is often the motive behind writing a personal essay—the essay is in first person, and the essayist is center stage.
Subject matter	Essayists often write about quite ordinary things; they find drama in everyday life, past or present. Personal essays can be about taking a walk, breaking up on Facebook, the housefly on your beer glass. In some ways, the real subject of a personal essay is the writer herself and how she makes sense of her world.
Structure	Essays often tell stories, but, unlike some fiction, they both show *and* tell, using both narrative and exposition, sometimes alternating between the two. When about the past, there are two narrators in the essay—the "then-narrator" and the "now-narrator." One describes what happened and the other describes what the narrator makes *now* of what happened. The thesis may come near the end rather than at the beginning. And the essay isn't necessarily chronological.

3.3

Identify the characteristics of personal essays in different forms.

(continued)

Feature	Conventions of the Personal Essay
Sources of information	Like any essay, the personal essay might use all four sources of information—memory, observation, reading, and interview. But it is likely to lean most heavily on memory and observation.
Language	Personal essays work in two registers—the more general language of reflection and the very specific details of experience and observation. This specific language is often sensory: What did it look like exactly? What did you hear? How did it feel?

Prose+

Josh Neufeld's "A Matter of Perspective" is a kind of personal essay. The theme—the idea that we all have moments in our lives when we feel "very, very small"—speaks not only to Josh's experience, but to our own. A graphic essay such as this one exploits image and text in combination, amplifying the power of each.

READINGS

▶ ## Personal Essay 1

Try this exercise: Think about things, ordinary objects, that you have held onto all these years because you simply can't throw them away. They *mean* something to you. They are reminders of another time, or a turning point in your life, or a particular moment of joy, or sadness, or perhaps fear. Consider a few of mine: a green plaster Buddha, handmade; a glow-in-the-dark crucifix; an old pair of 7 × 50 Nikon binoculars; a 1969 Martin D 28 guitar; a brown-handled flathead screwdriver with a touch of red nail polish on the handle; a homemade lamp made from a wooden wallpaper roller; a red dog collar. While they are meaningless to you, to me each of these objects carries a charge; they remind me of a story, a moment, a feeling. The personal essay makes space for writers to explore the meanings of such ordinary things.

Taking Things Seriously: 75 Objects with Unexpected Meanings, the book from which the following short essay was taken, is a gallery of objects—a bottle of dirt, a Velveeta Cheese box, a bear lamp, a pair of shells, and more—that are displayed along with the meditations on their significance by the writers who have carefully kept the objects as reminders on a shelf, in a closet, by their beside. Laura Zazulak's short essay focuses on a doll that she snatched from a neighbor's trash can. Just telling a story about what happened is not enough in a personal essay. The essay must have something to say to someone else. As you read Zazulak's brief piece, consider what that something might be.

Every Morning for Five Years

Laura Zazulak

1   Every morning for five years, I was not so welcomingly greeted by my middle-aged, developmentally disabled neighbor across the street. Scotty never smiled and seemed to hate everyone. He never left the perimeter of his mother's lawn and apparently didn't know how to do anything but rake, shovel, take out the trash, and yell in a high-pitched voice. I'd pull out of my driveway and see him there, wearing a neon orange hunting cap, raking absolutely nothing at the same spot that he'd raked the day before. I'd think to myself, "Don't make eye contact!" But I always did. He'd stare at me and neither of us would blink.

2   Near the end of my fifth year on the street, Scotty stopped coming out of his house. At first, I was thankful. But as time passed, I began to worry. Then one Saturday morning in the middle of January I noticed that his window was wide open. Later that day, a police car showed up. Maybe Scotty and his mother got into one of their

screaming matches again? Then a funeral-home van pulled up and they brought out Scotty's body. Although it came as a surprise to me to discover that he knew how miserable his life was, he had killed himself.

The next day Scotty's uncle came over and began furiously carting things off to the dump. He left behind a garbage can in the driveway piled with all of Scotty's earthly possessions. I noticed two little pink feet sticking up into the air.   3

After dark, I crept across the street to the garbage can, armed with a travel-sized bottle of hand sanitizer. I looked left, then right. I dashed forward, tugged at the feet, and then ran as fast as I could back into my own backyard with my prize. Only then did I look at what I'd rescued. I would like you to meet Mabel.   4

Inquiring into the Essay

Throughout *The Curious Writer*, I'll invite you to respond to readings using questions related to the four motives for reading discussed in Chapter 2. The following questions, therefore, encourage you to explore (*What do I think about this?*), explain (*What do I understand that this is saying?*), evaluate (*What's my judgment about this?*), and reflect to discover (*How does this work?* or *How am I thinking about it?*) and shape what you think about the reading. In Chapter 2, I encouraged you to write while you read and after. Try that now using the double-entry journal technique introduced in Chapter 2 (see pp. 52–53). As soon as you finish your first reading of "Every Morning for Five Years," open up your journal and on the right-hand page, fastwrite your response to the explore and explain questions above. Write for at least three minutes. Then go back to Zazulak's essay and on the left-hand page, jot down sentences or passages from it that you think are important to your understanding of it. Build your responses to the questions that follow from these first thoughts about what you just read.

1. **Explore.** All of the essays in the book *Taking Things Seriously*, including Zazulak's, have this to say: It is remarkable how much meaning we can invest in the ordinary when we take the time to notice it. This is an idea you can explore on your own. Brainstorm a list of objects that might have "unexpected significance" to you. Choose one and fastwrite about it for four minutes. Then skip a line, choose another, and write for another four minutes. If this is interesting to you, repeat this process over a few days and create a collage of brief stories that four or five objects inspired. Are there any themes that seem to run through all of them? Do they speak to each other in any way?

2. **Explain.** Explain how the photograph and the essay work together to create meanings that might not be apparent if we had either one without the other.

3. **Evaluate.** Personal essays like "Every Morning for Five Years" *imply* their meaning rather than state it explicitly. In that way, an essay like this one is more like a short story. Make an argument for your own understanding of the meaning of Zazulak's essay, and use passages from the piece to support your claim.

4. **Reflect.** One of the features of the personal essay is two narrators: the "now-narrator" and the "then-narrator." One looks back on an experience from the present, applying knowledge that the "then-narrator" did not have. From this comes fresh insight. But these two narrators aren't always obvious. Can you see them in this essay?

▶ Personal Essay 2

One of the ways that personal essays differ from the thesis-proof structure of much school writing is that they are *end-weighted*—the full meaning of the essay emerges later in the work. The conventional academic essay is *front-weighted*, with the thesis often parked in the first paragraph or two. You can see that end-weighted structure in Ginny Blanford's lovely personal essay about an adopted daughter, a survivalist dog, and a moment when the recognition of loss led towards the light. This is how personal essays work—the writer wonders about something she's experienced and uses the writing to arrive at some new understanding, an understanding that wasn't apparent when the experience happened. It is a process that begins with questions, not answers, and often starts with a gut feeling that there is some meaning there, just out of reach. We write personal essays to find that meaning.

The Dog That Made Us a Family
By Ginny Blanford

We inherited my daughter Liana when she was not quite 5. She had been adopted from China by my closest friend of 30 years, Linda, a single 51-year-old woman, tiny and fragile-looking but full of steel. Linda had a history of various illnesses, and my husband later told me that when she walked happily off the plane on Christmas Day in 1994, with her round, worried-looking Chinese baby wrapped in bright red and clutching a teddy bear, he had a premonition that we would eventually raise this child. Three years later, my best friend died—complications from Crohn's disease—and Liana came home with us. I was 55, a fulltime textbook editor with two almost-grown daughters. My husband, an English professor, was 48. I was looking forward to a few years of empty nesting and then some grandchildren. Starting over with a feisty kindergartner was, to be candid, not in my plans.   1

Shortly after she came to us, Liana began asking for a dog. She had been passed from family to family during her mother's six-month illness, indulged by people who wanted to make her happy. She was not used to hearing the word "no." I love dogs—I had grown up with a beautiful collie named Sunbeam—but I already had one unexpected new responsibility and I didn't want another. Initially our apartment was our excuse: too little space. But four years later we moved to a house, and we could no longer resist Liana's pleas. So off we went to an animal shelter.   2

Molly was a regal chow mix, chestnut red with a feathery tail that wagged all the time. She was gentle but energetic. As long as Liana and my husband, John, promised to do the walking, I decided I could handle having a dog. So we brought Molly home. Twenty-four hours later I opened the front door, and a red streak pushed by me—Molly, bolting out the door, through a neighbor's yard, into a nearby woods. Liana ran after her, screaming, and John headed out, too, into the dark, drizzling rain, frequently catching sight of the dog and then losing the trail.   3

Liana came back into the house, sat on her new dog's bed and cried. In her four years with us, she had hardly ever cried. And she had hardly ever mentioned her adoptive mother, my best friend. I almost resented that she seemed to have moved past grief without a second thought. But now she sobbed. She howled. Her thick black hair stuck to her cheeks, wet with tears. She wrapped her arms around herself, then around me, squeezing hard. She cried for three hours—until well after John returned. "She's gone," Liana moaned. "My dog is gone. My mother is dead. I loved my dog. Why did my mother die?"   4

She hadn't moved past grief, it turned out. She had just buried it, deep beyond reach, until now.   5

For John, finding Liana's dog became a mission. Luckily, we had taken some cell-phone photos of Molly during her few hours with us, and we sent them out to all the   6

(continued)

(*continued*)

shelters in the area. After three weeks I gave up. But then we got a call. A woman had spotted a dog matching Molly's picture 15 miles away, in the woods near her home—across two highways, two rivers and I-95. As John often points out, Molly could have easily made it back to the shelter she'd left if she'd only had an E-ZPass.

7   Despite repeated sightings, Molly somehow stayed out of reach. For two more months our dog lived in the woods. The wonderful woman who'd noticed Molly left scraps on her back porch and enlisted the neighborhood kids to report sightings. The food would be gone every morning, but the red dog eluded them all. Finally John hired a team of animal facilitators—they used to be called dogcatchers—and they set out a cage. For another week Molly ignored it until they changed the bait, at John's suggestion, from tuna to steak. Then she walked in, and she came home.

8   For five years now, Molly has slept with Liana every night. When Liana is away, her dog paces. Molly's tail still wags, but she is 7 now, a little slower and much less rambunctious. Liana, a tiny beauty of 15 with fashionably black nails and a loyal circle of ebullient friends, has moved on to "Twilight" and the Jonas Brothers. She still loves dogs, but she'd prefer the Paris Hilton model—a yappy little dog that she can dress up and put on like a pair of rhinestone earrings. Sometimes it seems as though Liana hardly remembers when her dog ran away and she hollered for her dead mother. But John and I remember, because that was the moment that Liana and our lost friend and our lost dog all came together, and we became a family.

Inquiring into the Essay

In the last chapter I argued that writing about what you read right after you read it is the best way to both understand and analyze the text. Use these questions for some writing in your journal about "The Dog That Made Us a Family."

1. **Explore.** The last time that I cried deeply—the chest-rattling, breath-choking kind of crying—was when my dog Stella died suddenly and unexpectedly from post-surgical complications. I sensed then, as Blanford does in this essay, that those tears were not just about a dog. Fastwrite about your own experience of losing a pet, or losing something or someone dear to you, exploring the event and your reaction. Ask yourself, too, whether your feelings of loss might have been amplified by other things going on in your life at the time. What were those other things?

2. **Explain.** The narrative begins with an adopted child, and then continues with the adoption of a dog, who runs away soon after. The child, who lost her first mother, grieves for both lost dog and lost mother. The narrator's husband, after much effort, finds the dog, who is reunited with the child and her family. This is the situation. But what is the *story*? What is this narrative really about?

3. **Evaluate.** Because the motive behind personal essays is to find out, rather than to prove, we don't often see them as making an argument. But if you were to read "The Dog That Made Us a Family" as an essay trying to make a claim about how families work, or what the best ways to deal with loss might be, or whatever else, what would that claim be?

4. **Reflect.** While there's no formula for structuring a personal essay, one thing you often see is the movement between the "now-narrator" (the writer looking back from the present) and the "then-narrator" (the writer who is telling what happened). See if you can identify the movement between these two narrators in the essay. Where do you see it?

THE WRITING PROCESS

Inquiry Project   Writing a Personal Essay

Inquiry questions: What does it mean to me? What do I understand about this now that I didn't understand then?

Here are some approaches to writing a personal essay as an inquiry project—a traditional essay and some multimodal methods. Your instructor will give you further guidance on the details of the assignment.

Write a personal essay on a topic that you find confusing or that raises interesting questions for you. Topics need not be personal, but they should arise from your own experiences and observations. The essay should offer a central insight about what you've come to understand about yourself and/or the topic. In other words, you will "essay" into a part of your life, past or present, exploring the significance of some memories, experiences, or observations. Your motive is personal discovery—reaching that new insight.

Your essay should do all the following (see also the Features of the Form box earlier in this chapter on pp. 65–66 for typical features of the personal essay):

- Do more than tell a story. There must be a *purpose* behind telling the story that speaks in some way to someone else. It should, ultimately, answer the *So what?* question.
- Include some reflection to explain or speculate about what you understand *now* about something that you didn't understand *then*. Your essay should have both a then-narrator and a now-narrator, one narrator who remembers what happened and one narrator who views what happened with the understanding you have now.
- Be richly detailed. Seize opportunities to *show* what you mean rather than simply explain it.

Prose+

There are all sorts of possibilities for creating a personal essay that go beyond the usual written text by exploiting images, sound, and even video. You might consider experimenting with the online version of the personal essay genre: the blog.

Study the genre first by reading some online blogs, and then model yours after your favorites. You can publish your essay on the web using Blogger, Wordpress, or other blogging software.

Finally, consider writing a personal essay modeled after "Every Morning for Five Years" (pp. 68–69). Begin with a digital photograph of an object that is meaningful to you, and then explore its significance.

Writing Beyond the Classroom

Essaying "This I Believe"

The essay genre, which has been around for about five hundred years, is a vibrant and increasingly common form of writing on the radio and for online audio. Why? One reason might be that the intimacy of the essay—the sense of a writer speaking directly to a reader without the masks we often wear when we write—seems particularly the voice of writing embodied in speech. Certainly, the ease with which we can "publish" essays as podcasts accounts for the explosion of online essayists.

This I Believe, a program heard on public radio (thisibelieve.org), is typical of radio programs that actively seek to broadcast student essays (which are subsequently published as podcasts). The program was begun in the 1950s by famed journalist Edward R. Murrow, who invited radio listeners and public figures to submit very brief (350- to 500-word) essays that stated some core belief that guided their "daily lives." As revived by the nonprofit organization This I Believe, the program is enormously popular and features work from people in all walks of life, including college students who may have written a "This I Believe" essay in their writing courses.

The program's website offers this advice to essayists:

1. Find a way to succinctly and clearly state your belief.
2. If possible, anchor it to stories.
3. Write in your own voice.
4. "Be positive," and avoid lecturing the listener.

What Are You Going to Write About?

With the personal essay, nearly anything goes. Essayists write about everything from their struggles with eating disorders, adjusting to life after military service, or dealing with the loss of a sibling to what we typically consider utterly commonplace things: a walk, negotiating the use of an armrest with a fellow airplane passenger, a fondness for weird hats. Whatever you write about, what matters most is that you've chosen the topic because you aren't quite sure what you want to think about it. Write about what confuses you, what puzzles you, or what raises itchy questions.

The process for discovering a topic (see Figure 3.1) begins simply with what I call opening up, or generating lots of material. Open the warehouse of memory

3.4

Use invention strategies to discover and develop a personal essay topic.

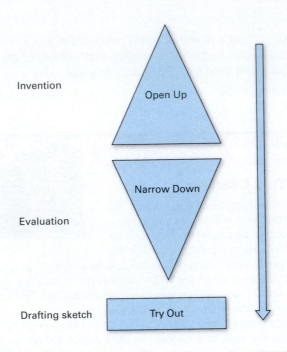

Figure 3.1   To discover a personal essay topic, we'll follow a pattern that will be repeated in every assignment chapter. It emphasizes "invention", or spending some time first simply exploring possibilities through writing, brainstorming, and visualizing. From there, you'll narrow down the material, focusing on the most promising material for a first draft, or "sketch".

and walk around, or open your eyes and look around you *now*. Just collect some things, without judging their value for this project.

Opening Up

Even if you've already got an idea for a personal essay topic, spend some time exploring the possibilities before you make a commitment. It doesn't really take much time, and there's a decent chance you'll discover a great topic for your essay that you never would have thought of otherwise.

The journal prompts that follow will get you going. What you're after is to stumble on an interesting topic. Actually, it's more like stumbling through the *door* to an interesting topic—a door that gives you a look at what you might fruitfully explore with more-focused writing. Try several prompts, looking for a topic that might, after some writing, raise questions such as these:

- *Am I uncertain about what this might mean?*
- *Is this topic more complicated than it seemed at first?*
- *Might I understand these events differently now than I did then?*

Listing Prompts. Lists can be rich sources of topic ideas. Let them grow freely, and when you're ready, use a list item as the focus of another list or an episode of fastwriting. The following prompts should get you started thinking about both your experiences and your observations.

1. Make a list of experiences or places that you can't forget. Reach into all parts and times of your life.

2. Make a list of "turning points," moments in your life in which you sensed that things changed for you in some fundamental way.

3. Make quick lists from the following prompts: toys from childhood, regrets, firsts (kisses, disappointments, losses of innocence, memories, relationships, etc.).

Fastwriting Prompts. Early on, fastwriting can help you settle on a narrower topic, *if* you allow yourself to write "badly." Then use a more-focused fastwrite, trying to generate information and ideas within the loose boundaries of your chosen topic.

1. Choose an item from a list you've created to use as a prompt. Just start fastwriting about the item; perhaps start with a story, a scene, a situation, a description. Follow the writing to see where it leads.

2. Most of us quietly harbor dreams—we hope to be a professional dancer, a good parent, an activist, a marketing executive, an Olympic luger, or a novelist. Begin a fastwrite in which you explore your dreams. When the writing stalls, ask yourself questions: *Where did this dream come from? Do I still believe in it? In what moments did it seem within reach? In what moments did it fade?* Plunge into those moments.

3. What was the most confusing time in your life? Choose a moment or scene that stands out in your memory of that time, and, writing in the present tense, describe what you see, hear, and do. After five minutes, skip a line and choose another moment. Then another. Make a collage.

4. Begin with this prompt: "You know that feeling when...." For example, you know that feeling when you wake up after something terrible happened the day before, and for a minute you forget, and the world feels fresh and new but then it hits you that, no, the world is not right? Come up with your own "you know that feeling" statement, and then tell yourself the story.

Visual Prompts. Images trigger ideas, and so can more-visual ways of thinking. Let's try both. Boxes, lines, arrows, charts, and even sketches can help us see more of the landscape of a subject, especially connections between fragments of information that aren't as obvious in prose. The clustering or mapping method is useful to many writers early in the writing process as they try to discover a topic. Figure 3.2 shows my cluster from the first prompt listed here.

1. What objects would you most regret losing in a house fire? Choose a most-treasured object as the core for a cluster. Build a web of associations from it, returning to the object in the core whenever a strand dies out.

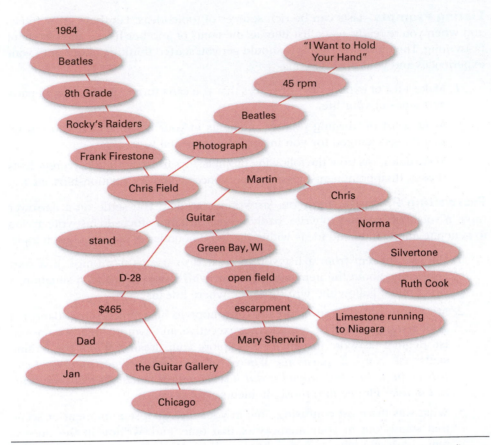

Figure 3.2   A cluster built around the one object I would most regret losing in a house fire: my Martin guitar

2. Find a photograph from your past, perhaps like the one from mine that opens this chapter. Fastwrite about what you see in the picture, what you don't see, and a story that it inspires.

3. Draw a long line on a piece of paper in your journal. This is your life. Divide the line into segments that seem to describe what feels like distinct times in your life. These don't have to correspond to familiar age categories such as adolescence or childhood; they could correspond to periods in your life that you associate with a place, a relationship, a dilemma, a job, a personal challenge, and so on. In any case, make the segments chronological. Examine your timeline, and, as a fastwrite prompt, put two of these periods in your life together. Explore what they had in common, particularly how the earlier period might have shaped the later one.

4. Get on Google Earth. Find the town or city where you were born or lived as a young child. Zoom in on your neighborhood. Fastwrite about what this makes you remember. Alternatively, find the house you live in now. Using the "street view" feature, "walk" down the street, stopping at the homes of interesting neighbors that you know or have observed. With the image on the screen, fastwrite in your journal, telling yourself stories about the people in your neighborhood.

Research Prompts. Things we hear, see, or read can be powerful prompts for personal essays. It's tempting to believe that personal essays are always about the past, but just as often essayists are firmly rooted in the present, commenting and pondering on the confusions of contemporary life. In that sense, personal essayists are researchers, always on the lookout for material. Train your eye with one or more of the following prompts.

1. Put this at the top of a journal page: "Things People Do." Now go outside and find a place to observe people. Write down a list of everything you see people doing. Choose one action you find interesting and fastwrite about it. Is it weird? Why?

2. Look up the definition of "infatuation." Write it down at the top of a journal page, and then write for five minutes about your experience and observations of infatuations with people, things, places, ideas.

Narrowing Down

Okay, you've generated some "bad" writing about your experiences and observations. Can any of it be shaped into a personal essay? Are there any clues about a topic you could develop with more-focused fastwriting? These are particularly tough questions when writing a personal essay, because most of us are inclined to think that the only one who could possibly care about what happened to us or what we observe is ourselves (or maybe Mom).

Don't make the mistake of judging the material too soon or too harshly. Personal essayists write successfully about any topic—often including quite ordinary things—so don't give up on a promising topic this early in the game. But first, how do you decide what's promising?

What's Promising Material and What Isn't? The signs of a promising personal essay topic include the following:

- **Abundance.** What subject generated the most writing? Do you sense that there is much more to write about?
- **Surprise.** Did you see or say something you didn't expect about a topic?
- **Confusion.** What subject raises questions you're not sure you can answer easily?

In the personal essay, this last item—confusion and uncertainty—may yield the most-fertile topics. All of the questions listed at the beginning of the "Opening Up" section are related in some way to a feeling that some experience or observation—even if it's familiar to you—has yet to yield all of its possible meanings.

Questions About Purpose and Audience. Who cares about my middling career as a high school cross-country runner? Who cares that I grew to love that gritty neighborhood in Hartford? Who cares that I find high school reunions weird? When we write about ourselves, we can't help but wonder why anyone, other than ourselves, *would* care. Maybe they won't. But if you discover something about your life that helps you to understand it better—even in a small way—you will begin to find an audience. After all, we are interested in understanding our own, often ordinary lives, and perhaps we can learn something from you.

To find an audience for a personal essay, you have to discover something to say about your experiences and observations that speaks to others—a larger theme that comments on what your story might mean. People don't read personal essays for "morals" about life, but for insights that arise from the recognition that what happened to you might be a category of experience you share with others. An essay about the death of your father could offer insights about how we adapt to loss. An essay about going to the zoo might say something about how zoos trigger our desire for connection to animals. Can you see that in both of these examples, there is a shift from "I" to "we," and from "me" to "us"? This shift signals the necessary change from your observations of something to your ideas about it, from your memory of what happened to your insight about what happens, from the sea of experience to the mountain of reflection. This is the change that readers of personal essays are looking for.

Trying Out

A few years ago, shortly after attending my fortieth high school reunion, I began working on a personal essay about my experiences attending these affairs. As I generated "bad writing" on the subject of high school reunions, I kept returning to the same question: If I find these reunions generally weird and unsatisfying, why do I keep going? Using this inquiry question, I tried out my topic with the focused fastwrite that follows:

> *Last fall, I went to my 40th high school reunion...I had been to the 10th and the 20th, both of which required travel, once from the East coast and once from the West. I have no idea why I went to the effort...I didn't like high school...and I don't have many friends left in the Chicago suburb where I grew up. Why does anyone go to a high school reunion? I wonder if I've gone because...like it or not...high school is part of the narrative of our growing up that is at once mysterious and utterly familiar. I can remember everything...my failure to make the swim team that my brother was a star on...breaking the mercury barometer in physics class with my*

elbow while cleaning chalk erasers at the window…the sexual thrill of sitting on a bench next to Suzie Durment at a football game and feeling her thigh press close to mine. And yet I can't explain so much of high school…It just doesn't make sense. Why would I run cross country for four years and absolutely hate every minute of it?…How could I so thoroughly mishandle the kindness and affection of Jan Dawe, my first serious girlfriend?…And why all those years did I still pine for Lori Jo Flink, a girl from the 7th grade?…I guess that's one reason I go to my high school re-union…To enjoy the melancholy of seeing Lori Jo again and to relish the bittersweet taste of rejection.…She always comes…Yet when I did see her this time it wasn't the same. We had a very brief conversation… "I looked you up on the Internet," she said, and was promptly swept to the dance floor by Larry Piacenza…She looked me up on the Internet…This should have given me a thrill but it didn't…Why not?…These days I've been stripping the siding off so many old narratives about myself, stories that I've mistaken for walls that bear weight…Perhaps I tossed Lori Jo on that pile of discarded lumber…along with the desire to attend another high school reunion. As I'm counting the gifts of middle age, I gladly add this one.

What I hope you notice in my focused writing on reunions is how I keep using questions to tease out meaning, starting with a question I'd never really asked myself before: Why do I go to high school reunions? Why would anyone? These inquiry questions pulled me out of the sea of experience and onto the mountain of reflection (highlighted passages), where I begin to see a possible answer: I go to reunions to revive old stories about myself that may no longer matter. In the personal essay, judging involves *reflection*. What do we make of what happened then that we didn't quite see until now? What might our observations of the world around us now *say* about that past world and, maybe more important, about ourselves?

Questions for Reflection. In Chapter 1, I talked about thinking with writing as a movement back and forth between the creative and critical minds. In a way, personal essays and other narrative genres make this movement of the mind visible. For example, in Ginny Blanford's essay on p. 71, "The Dog That Made Us a Family," if you look closely you'll see the subtle movement from telling the story to reflecting on its meaning, culminating with this line: *She hadn't moved past grief, it turned out. She had just buried it, deep beyond reach, until now.* This is the "now-narrator," the writer who has the benefit of time and experience since something happened, attempting to make sense of it as she looks back. The "then-narrator" is in charge of telling what happened; the "now-narrator" takes a stab at saying *what happens*, what it might mean.

Now that you've tried out your topic, put yourself in the now-narrator's perspective, answering questions such as these:

- What do you understand now about this topic that you didn't fully understand when you began writing about it? Start some writing with this phrase: "As I look back on this now, I realize that…."

- What seems to be the most important thing you're trying to say so far?
- How has your thinking changed about your topic? Finish this seed sentence as many times as you can in your notebook: *Once I thought* _____, *and now I think* _____.

Writing the Sketch

Throughout *The Curious Writer*, I'll encourage you to write what I call "sketches." As the name implies, this is a first look at something roughly drawn. It is a pretty rough draft of your piece, perhaps no more than about 300–400 words, with a tentative title. Though it may be sketchy, your sketch should be reader-based prose. You want someone else to understand what it's about. Don't assume others know what you know. When you need to, explain things.

A sketch is a good starting point for a personal essay in any mode. If you're working on a radio essay, for example, the sketch will be much the same as one that you write for a conventional essay. It's simply a very early script.

Choose your most promising material, and tell the story. If it's drawn from memory, incorporate both what happened then and what you make of it now. If it's built on observations, make sure they are detailed, anchored to particular times and places, and in some way significant.

You may or may not answer the "So what?" question in your sketch, though you should try. Don't muscle the material too much to conform to what you already think; let the writing help you figure out what you think.

To summarize, then, in a sketch try to do the following:

- Have a tentative title.
- Keep it relatively short.
- Write it fast.
- Don't muscle it to conform to a preconceived idea.
- Write to be read, with an audience in mind.
- Make it specific instead of general.

▶ Student Sketch

Amanda Stewart's sketch, "Earning a Sense of Place," faintly bears the outlines of what might be a great personal essay. When they succeed, sketches are suggestive; it is what they're not quite saying that yields promise. On the surface, "Earning a Sense of Place" could seem simply a piece about Amanda's passion for skiing. So what? And yet, there are lines here that point to larger ideas and unanswered questions. For example, Amanda writes that the "mental reel" of her swishing down a mountain on skis is "the image that sustains me when things are hard, and when I want to stop doing what is right and start doing what is easy." Why is it that such a mental image can be sustaining in hard times? How well does this mental image work? The end of the sketch is even more suggestive. This really might be a piece about trying to find a "sense of place" that doesn't rely on such images; in a sense, the sketch seems to be trying to say that joy on the mountain isn't enough.

The pleasure of writing and reading a sketch is in looking for what it might teach you, learning what you didn't know you knew.

I've highlighted portions of the text to illustrate a revision exercise that follows Amanda's essay.

Earning a Sense of Place

Amanda Stewart

The strings to my earflaps stream behind me, mixing with my hair as a rooster-tail flowing behind my neck. Little ice crystals cling to the bottom of my braid and sparkle in the sunlight. The pompom on top of my hat bobs up and down as I arc out, turning cleanly across the snow. I suck in the air, biting with cold as it hits my hot lungs, and breathe deep as I push down the run. 1

This is what I see when I picture who I want to be. It's the image that sustains me when things are hard, and when I want to stop doing what is right and start doing what is easy. I have made so many terrible decisions in the past that I know how far astray they lead me; I don't want that. I want the girl in the mental reel in her quilted magenta jacket and huge smile. She's what I grasp at when I need help getting through the day. 2

She's an amalgam of moments from the past mixed with my hopes for the future. I love to ski, and have since my parents strapped little plastic skis onto my galoshes when I was a year and a half old. From that day I flopped around our snow-covered yard, I've been in love with skiing. It's the only time I feel truly comfortable. Day to day I often feel so awkward. I wonder if my hair is right, or if my clothes fit. Last night, my roommate had a boy over, and as he sat on the couch talking to me, all I felt was discomfort and awkwardness. I didn't know what to say, felt judged, felt out of place. I never feel that way on skis. Even floundering in heavy, deep snow, or after a fall that has packed my goggles with snow and ripped the mittens off my hands I know exactly what to do. I'm a snow mermaid, only comfortable in my medium. I often wish I could trade in my walking legs for something like a tail that is more truly me. 3

My dad's coffee cup at home says, "I only work so I can ski," and for him, it's true. Sometimes I feel like I only push through my daily life so I can get to the next mountain and zip up my pants and go. I don't want to live like that though: it's too much time looking forward to something, and not enough looking at what I'm living in. I need to appreciate my life as it is, snowy cold or sunny warm. That sense of place I have on skis can probably be earned here on the flat expanses of campus just as easily as I got it pushing myself down the bunny slopes so long ago. I just have to earn it. 4

Moving from Sketch to Draft

Here's the journey with the assignment you've taken so far:

1. You've generated some "bad writing," openly exploring possibilities for personal essay topics while suspending judgment.

2. You landed on a tentative topic.

3. You tried out this topic through more writing, some of it still "bad."

4. Your critical mind took over as you began to judge what you have so far. What questions does this material raise for you? What might it *mean*? With judgment comes a growing concern for audience. Why would they care about this?

5. You tried out the topic in a sketch. It's written with an audience in mind.

At the heart of the process I'm describing is a movement from "writer-based" to "reader-based" prose. This movement occurs with any type of writing, but it's particularly tricky with the personal essay. When you're writing about yourself, there is always this: *Who cares?*

The movement from sketch to draft must address this question. But how?

Evaluating Your Own Sketch. One way to assess whether your sketch might be meaningful to someone other than you is to look for the balance between narrative and reflection, or the then-narrator and the now-narrator. Try this:

- Take two highlighters, each a different color.

- Go through your sketch from beginning to end, using one color to highlight text that's storytelling, what happened or what you saw (the then-narrator), and then use the other color to highlight text that is explanatory, more-general commentary about what happened or what you saw (the now-narrator). What's the pattern of color?

There are several possibilities here:

1. **One color dominates.** Your sketch is mostly narrative or mostly summary, all then-narrator or all now-narrator. A personal essay that is mostly narrative usually fails to address the "So what?" question. It seems to tell a story without a purpose. On the other hand, a personal essay that is all explanation fails to engage readers in the writer's *experiences*. It's all telling and no showing. Personal essays must both show *and* tell.

2. **One color dominates except at the end.** Typically, there is all narrative until the very end, when the writer briefly reflects, much like the formula for a fable, with its moral at the end. This can seem predictable to readers. But you can work with it in revision by taking the reflection at the end and using it to reconceive the essay *from the very beginning*. Can you take the ending and use its insight to organize your thinking in a revision?

3. **The colors alternate.** Sometimes this is the most interesting type of personal essay, because the two narrators are in genuine collaboration, trying to figure out what happened and what it *means*.

In my markup of Amanda's sketch (p. 83), you can see how there is some shifting in the pattern of color. But exposition dominates. Her revision might need more story, more *showing* readers what happened that has made her think the things she now thinks.

If our personal experiences and observations are to mean anything to someone else, then they must, at the very least, both show and tell. They should, through details, descriptions, and scenes, invite an audience into the sea of our experiences. But they must also be clear about the *reason* behind the invitation—about what we have come to understand and want our audience to understand. In revising your sketch, focus on these two concerns above all.

Reflecting on What You Learned. In Chapter 1, I introduced the dialectical method of thinking through writing that moves back and forth between creative thinking and critical thinking, generating and judging. Highlighting the two narrators in your sketch is a way to actually see yourself thinking that way *in your own writing*—or not, depending on the patterns of color you see. Make a journal entry about this. In your sketch, which of the two narrators is more active, and why do you think that's so? In a revision of this sketch, how might you address any imbalance between the two? Where could the now-narrator tell more, or where could the then-narrator show more?

Developing

In the last section, you focused on using a sketch to identify the *purposes* of telling someone else about your memories, experiences, or observations. For example, in the sample sketch, Amanda seems to be telling us about her love for skiing because that love suggests a longing that most of us feel: to transfer the confidence we feel in one part of our lives to every other part. The key to developing your draft is to arrive at a fuller understanding of what your purpose is in telling your own stories *and then to rebuild your essay around that insight from the beginning*.

In other words, as you begin your revision, focus on exploring the answer to these questions:

- What might this essay be saying, not only about me, but more generally about people who find themselves in similar situations? Sometimes the best way to get at this insight is through a pronoun shift: Instead of "What does my story tell *me*?", consider "What might it be trying to tell *us*—people who might have experienced something similar?" In other words, shift from "I" to "we." What do *we* seem to do or say in the situations you're writing about?

- What questions does the essay raise that might be interesting, not only to me, but also to others who do not know me?

Fastwrite in your journal about these questions for as long as you can. One word of caution, though, and I can't stress it enough: YOU DO NOT NEED TO BE PROFOUND. Most of us aren't philosophers or really deep thinkers. We are ordinary people who are just trying to make sense of our lives and work towards those little insights that make us understand things a little better.

As you get a grip on the purpose behind your essay, you can focus your efforts on developing those parts of the narrative that are relevant. What scenes, anecdotes, details, observations, facts, stories, and so on might focus your attention—and later your readers' attention—on what you're trying to say about the topic?

To do so, try some of the following strategies:

- *Explode a moment.* Choose a scene or moment in the story or stories you're telling that seems particularly important to the meaning of the essay. Reenter that moment and fastwrite for a full seven minutes, using all your senses and as much detail as you can muster.

- *Rewrite the lead.* Think about where you might begin that would best dramatize the question, dilemma, problem, or idea that you're exploring. Find a scene, description, fact, profile, or event that points the beginning of the essay towards your purpose in telling the story.

- *Research.* Yes, research can be a great source of information for narrative essays, too. Say you're writing about your observations of pacing animals in the zoo. Is there scholarship on boredom in captive animals? (I can answer that—yep.)

- *Generate.* Cluster the idea or question you're exploring to discover other personal stories or details that might expand the ways you're looking at things. Brainstorm lists of details to flesh out scenes. Fastwrite about the question driving your essay, telling yourself the story of what you initially thought and what you think now about the question. Build those insights into the draft.

Drafting

As you begin drafting, consider the pieces that come together to make a strong personal essay:

1. *Question.* While personal essays might lead to a thesis, they always begin with a question—something that the writer is trying to understand by exploring certain experiences and observations. When you draft you have a tentative idea of what this question is.

2. *Lead.* Find a way to begin your essay that dramatizes that question or highlights the dilemma you're exploring. This gives your essay a sense of purpose from the start.

3. *Now- and Then-Narrator.* Most personal essays move back and forth throughout between what happened (then-narrator) and what the writer is starting to understand about its meaning (now-narrator).

4. *End-Weight.* Unlike conventional thesis-proof essays, personal essays are end-weighted. They accumulate meaning throughout, often culminating in the major point of insight. This insight is neither profound nor extremely general, but some understanding that you've worked hard to come to as you consider the question that arises from certain experiences you've had.

Methods of Development. Narrative is an especially useful method of development for personal essays. How might you use it to develop your subject?

Narrative Narrative can work in a personal essay in at least three ways. You can use it to:

1. Tell an extended story of what happened.
2. Tell one or more anecdotes, or brief stories, that somehow address the question behind your interest in the topic.
3. Tell the story of your thinking as you've come to understand something you didn't understand before.

Often, a single essay uses narrative in all three types of ways.

Consider beginning your draft with the anecdote or the part of the story you want to tell that best frames the question, dilemma, or idea that is the focus of your essay (see "Inquiring into the Details: More Than One Way to Tell a Story"). If you're writing about the needless destruction of a childhood haunt by developers, then consider opening with the way the place looked *after* the bulldozers were done with it—description related to the end of your narrative.

Time in writing is nothing like real time. You can ignore chronology, if doing so serves your purpose. You can write pages about something that happened in seven minutes or cover twenty years in a paragraph. The key is to tell your story or stories in ways that emphasize what's important.

Using Evidence. How do you make your essay convincing, and even moving, to an audience? It's all in the details. Like most stories, the personal essay thrives on particularity: What exactly did it look like? What exactly did she say? What exactly did it sound and smell like at that moment? Evidence that gives a personal essay authority consists of details that make a reader believe the writer can be trusted to observe keenly and to remember accurately. Both the professional essays in this chapter are rich in detail. There is the neighbor with the "neon orange hunting cap" who rakes the same spot every day in Laura Zazulak's "Every Morning for Five Years," and the description of the teenage Liana "with fashionably black nails and a loyal circle of ebullient friends" in Ginny Blanford's "The Dog That Made Us a Family." This focus on the particular—what it exactly looked like, smelled like, felt like, sounded like—makes an essay come alive for both writer and reader.

As you draft your essay, remember the subtle power of details. Tell, but always show, too.

Workshopping

At this stage in writing the personal essay—the first full draft—what you may need most are responses that address the issues you've worked on most in your sketch: Does the draft clearly answer the "So what?" question (purpose)? Is it clear what one main thing the essay is trying to say (meaning)? All other revision concerns are subordinate to these questions. Why? Because without a clear purpose and clear sense, it's impossible to make any judgments about content.

Annie Dillard, a writer of many nonfiction books and essays, once said that she believed that the biggest challenge in writing comes down to this basic question: *What to put in and what to leave out.* In a personal essay such as the one you're working on, you might conclude that the answer to the question is equally basic (simple): You tell the "whole" story. Yet the truth is that you never do, even in telling a story to friends. We shape and shade a story depending on our motive for telling it. The same is true in prose. Your purpose and what you are trying to say are the two things that determine what belongs in a story and what doesn't. So this is where you should begin.

Questions for Readers. The following box, which focuses on these two key concerns, can help you to guide your peers' response to your first draft.

Questions for Peer Reviewers	
1. Purpose	What would you say this essay is about? Do you have a clear sense of *why* I'm writing about this topic?
2. Meaning	Most essays need to say one fricking thing (S.O.F.T.). What would you say is the point of this draft? What is the main thing I seem to be saying about this topic?

Reflecting on the Workshop. After the workshop session, do a follow-up entry in your notebook that explores these questions:

- What main impression did you take away from the conversation about your draft?
- What do you think worked in the draft?
- What do you think needs work?
- What was/were your favorite sentence or passages in the draft? Why?

Revising

3.5

Apply revision strategies that are effective for shaping narratives.

Revision is a continual process—not a last step. You've been revising—"reseeing" your subject—from the first messy fastwriting in your journal. But the things that get your attention vary depending on where you are in the writing process. With your draft in hand, revision becomes your focus through what I'll call "shaping and tightening your draft."

Shaping. Shaping focuses on larger concerns first: purpose and meaning—the very largest concerns, which you've looked at if you workshopped your draft—and the next-to-largest concerns of information and organization. It starts with knowing what your essay is about—your inquiry question and maybe your theme—and then revising to make every element of the draft focused on that question or idea.

What to Cut and What to Add   A key to revising a personal essay, then, is this: *Given my essay's purpose and meaning, what should I cut and what should I add?*

- What information—scenes, descriptions, observations, explanations—is no longer relevant to the purpose and meaning?

- What information is missing that should be added to help readers understand and, in a small way, experience, so that they will appreciate my point?

The Question of Time   Revising a narrative essay also involves the question of time. Consider this in two ways:

1. Where will the information to develop your story come from—from the past or from the present? The then-narrator is master of the past: What happened? And then what? The now-narrator is charged with commenting from the present: What do I make of what happened from where I sit now? Personal essays that tell stories need information from both past and present.

2. How does time organize the information in the draft? Do you tell your story chronologically? Is that the best way to structure the essay? What might happen, for example, if you begin in the middle of the story, or even at the end? Will that better dramatize the question or dilemma that you're exploring?

Research   I'm not talking about extensive research, but about quick searches for background information, relevant facts, and maybe even something on what other writers or experts have said. Here's an example. I was writing an essay in which I recalled a total solar eclipse that happened in August 1964. Did it really? A quick web search confirmed it, but I also got information about exactly how long it lasted, and this information helped strengthen the scene I was writing. Say you're writing an essay about iPhone infatuation. Why not look up a definition of "infatuation" and then do some quick research on how students use their iPhones in a typical day?

Other Questions for Revision   Make sure you address the following questions as you revise:

- Does the draft begin in a way that gives your readers a sense of where the essay is going? Is your purpose clear? (This is especially important for podcast essays.)

- Is there too much explaining? Narrative essays are usually built on the backbone of story—anecdote, scene, and description. This is how we help the audience appreciate, in some small way, the experiences that have inspired the insights we want to share. Personal essays *do* need to tell, but they must also *show*.

- By the end of your essay, will the reader appreciate the significance of the story you're telling? Have you said what you need to say about how, though it's your own experience, the meaning you discover might apply to others as well?

Polishing. When you are satisfied with the shape of your draft, focus on paragraphs, sentences, and words. Are your paragraphs coherent? How do you manage transitions? Are your sentences fluent and concise? Are there any errors in spelling or syntax?

Before you finish your draft, work through the following checklist:

✓ Every paragraph is about one thing.
✓ The transitions between paragraphs aren't abrupt.
✓ The length of sentences varies in each paragraph.
✓ Each sentence is concise. There are no unnecessary words or phrases.
✓ You've checked grammar, particularly for verb agreement, run-on sentences, unclear pronouns, and misused words (*there/their, where/were,* and so on).
✓ You've run your spellchecker and proofed your paper for misspelled words.

▶ Student Essay

Military veterans often bring their rich, complicated experiences into my writing classes, and because what they've seen and done often raises questions they can't easily answer, they learn to love the personal essay. Seth Marlin served in Iraq. In the essay "Smoke of Empire," he recalls that during his first night in the country, there was a stench he didn't recognize. It turns out this stench was the smell of things—often perfectly good things—burning. The refuse of war. This memory inspires a meditation on war, waste, and empire.

The piece was written for the radio, and Seth produced an audio essay using Audacity software that blended his vocal reading of "Smoke of Empire" with music that gave the essay even more power. As you read Seth's essay, keep in mind that he wrote it with the idea that his audience would hear it a single time. Consider as you read it how that changed his approach to the writing. You can also listen to the essay at bruceballenger.com.

Smoke of Empire

Seth Marlin

1   When I was in Iraq, we used to have this rotating detail. Call it "*Hajji*-watch." Bring in local guys, pay them ten bucks to move sandbags, haul trash. Post a couple soldiers with rifles in case anyone gets froggy. Locals try to sell you stuff, turn them down. They ask for soap, shampoo, toothpaste, say you don't have any. That's the order they drill into you: *Do Not Buy, Sell, or Give Items to Local Nationals.*

2   Locals were poor. Dirt poor. Steal the gloves out of your pocket if they thought they'd get some use. Who could blame them? One guy I saw stole a bedroll once; another, maybe fifteen,

jacked a soccer-ball, said it was for his little brother. Our squad-leader said it was contraband, said the ball would be waiting for him when he came back next week, soon as he got a memorandum from the base-commander.

That kid never got his ball, you kidding me? Lot of poor guys with families; that line stretched two miles up the road back into town. He'd have been lucky to get in at all. I doubt he ever got that ball back; most likely, it just went to the burn-pit.   3

* * *

Fun fact: Wars generate waste. The Department of Defense estimates that its wars each generate ten pounds of garbage per service member per day. At over 150,000 service members deployed, that's a lot of trash. Unfortunately, the locals tend not to cotton to your leaving messes all over their soil; thus, in the name of diplomacy, the invaders have to clean up after themselves. On places like Joint Base Balad, all that refuse goes to one place: the burn-pit.   4

Picture a base, fifteen miles across, set in a swath of palm-dotted farmland. Now picture on part of that a landscape of hills, valleys, and craters—all of it garbage, all bigger than a dozen football fields. Now picture that on fire. Through the haze, you might see the figures who manage all that incoming drek—orange-turbaned Sikhs wearing blue jumpsuits, some of them wearing goggles and surgical masks if they're lucky. These pits are typically run by private contractors; OSHA guidelines mean little to nothing here. Your tax dollars at work.   5

My first night in Iraq, I remember looking west from my trailer and being surprised to see a sunset of blazing orange. It was at least two hours after dusk, and the stars were out, at least a couple anyway. Then I realized that *that wasn't sunlight I was seeing*—that it was *flames*. Those weren't clouds I was seeing, but rather smoke. I didn't know what all that was yet, only that it took up half the northern sky. But oh, I learned. The first thing I learned about was the smell, like burning oak-leaves mixed with scorched plastic and warping aluminum. Wood, fabric, paper, metal—if it burned, they burnt it. If not, they threw something on it until it did. On a clear day it threw smoke a half-mile high; on the cold days during the rainy season, October through March, the flames got tamped down by the constant downpour. Made the world smell like a half-smoked cigarette, all wet soot and chemicals. Made you gag passing through it on your way to the motor pool. During the summer months the ashes blew into the town just north of us, a little two-rut burg called Yethrib. Turned the air gray, sent hot embers raining down on the farmers' fields. Sitting in a tower on a weeklong rotation of guard-duty, I remember watching one day as some hundred-odd acres of sunflower, sorghum, and lentils went up in flames. An entire season's crops destroyed, in a part of the country where the median income was two dollars a day.   6

* * *

I remember convoying home from bridge-sites late at night; I used to peer over the steering-wheel and look for the banded floodlights, the blood-red haze of smoke. Waste never sleeps. On a bulletin-board in my platoon's Ops office, I remember they'd posted a memo signed by two Air-Force lieutenants-colonel. The memo cited the effects of long-term   7

(continued)

(continued)

exposure to the smoke, expressed outrage at the lack of incinerators, ordered the memo posted in every company headquarters, every permanent file of every soldier in service on that base. I'm sure that memo's still in my record somewhere; then again, the VA does have a tendency to lose things.

8   I saw a lot of strange, scary, moving things during my time deployed. Sunrises over the Tigris, Sumerian ruins, farmers praying in their fields at dawn. But the image that sticks with me is the burn-pit. Why? Maybe because the sight of all that waste, made tangible, left some mark on me, like tracking mud on floors as a guest, uninvited. War is consumption, I've realized. Conspicuous consumption. It's embarrassing, really: this is the democracy we bring to a foreign nation, consumption and waste. Look at all we've got. Fast-food, electronics, medicine. You can't have any, and we're going to burn it all right in front of you.

9   You know, the last night I was writing this I pulled up Google Earth, pinned down where I was posted. Our old motor-pool was taken down, bulldozed over; our old living-areas and trailers had been carted away. Even the burn-pit was silent, but it still sits there, like a grease-stain you can see from the air. Big sign in English: "NO DUMPING," it says, while behind it sits a mountain of blackened, twisted steel. The Balad pit may sit quiet now, but I'll bet even money those fires are still going elsewhere.

10   All day. Every day. The smoke of consumption, of Empire.

Evaluating the Essay

Discuss or write about your response to Seth Marlin's essay, using some or all of the following questions.

1. What do you understand this essay to be saying about war, empire, and waste? Where does it say it most clearly or memorably?

2. Throughout this chapter, I've promoted the idea that personal essays have two narrators—the now-narrator and the then-narrator. Are they both present in "Smoke of Empire"? Where?

3. What is the main thing you might take away from reading this piece and apply when you write or revise your own personal essay?

4. This piece was written to be heard rather than read, and the writer assumed that it would be heard only once. Imagine this rhetorical situation: You're in the car listening to the radio while driving to campus and you hear Seth reading "Smoke of Empire." Because he's not in the car with you, you don't have to be polite. You don't even know him. You can change the station if what you hear doesn't interest you. What special demands does this situation make on *how* a personal essay is written? How might it affect the writing and organization of a piece?

Using What You Have Learned

Let's revisit the list of things at the beginning of this chapter that I hoped you'd learn.

1. **Use personal experiences and observations to drive inquiry.** The questions that drive our inquiry into how we understand our lives are no less important than the questions that inspire us to explore other subjects. In fact, Montaigne, the first essayist, believed that self-knowledge is the most important knowing of all.

2. **Apply the exploratory thinking of personal essays to academic writing.** Next time you get a writing assignment in another class, start the work by "essaying" the topic—by developing a quick list of questions and responding to them. What you discover might lead to a thesis later.

3. **Identify the characteristics of personal essays in different forms.** If you know what a personal essay looks like, you can write yours in one of these different forms. Some of the most vibrant examples of the genre are podcasts, radio essays, and photographic essays. Though these media can work with almost any form of writing, they seem to lend themselves especially to autobiographical work.

4. **Use invention strategies to discover and develop a personal essay topic.** You can use techniques such as fastwriting and clustering to discover a topic for personal writing. But perhaps more important, you can use such invention techniques to generate *insight*—not just an idea about something to write about, but discoveries about what you think about that topic.

5. **Apply revision strategies that are effective for shaping narratives.** Even if you never write another personal essay, you can use narrative to tell the story of what you first thought about a subject and what you came to understand.

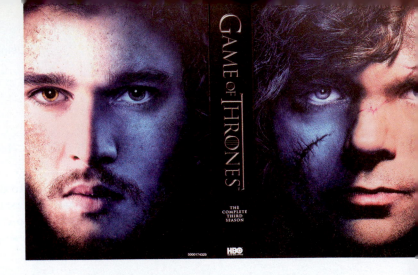

4

Writing a Review

Learning Objectives

In this chapter, you'll learn to

4.1 Use reasons and evidence to support a judgment about something's value.

4.2 Identify the criteria behind a judgment and determine their relevance.

4.3 Identify the characteristics of different forms of the review, including academic applications.

4.4 Use invention and focusing strategies to discover and develop a review essay.

4.5 Apply revision strategies that are effective for shaping reviews.

Writing That Evaluates

Both of my daughters excelled in modern dance, something I knew virtually nothing about. I would go to their performances, the proud dad, and afterwards I'd say, "Oh, that was beautiful. Wasn't that beautiful?" Naturally, this is the proper sentiment for a dad to express. But I also really meant it. Modern dance *can* be extraordinarily beautiful. However, when pressed about exactly why a performance moved me so, I was at a loss for words. I simply didn't know enough about modern dance to have any idea what the *reasons* were behind my judgment. I just knew what I felt.

Not knowing much about certain things rarely stops us from offering our evaluations of those things. We usually just follow our biases and gut feelings. The problem is that this "rationale" is rarely *persuasive*. People hear me gush about a modern dance performance, and in the absence of thoughtful reasons for my evaluation, they think I'm just a proud dad. I want to be both—a proud dad *and* a thoughtful critic. When I offer an evaluation of something, I want people to believe it, and this requires persuasive reasoning. In this chapter, we'll look at five elements of persuasive evaluations:

1. *Judgment(s).* Something is good or bad, useful or not useful, relevant or not relevant, convincing or not convincing, worth doing or not worth doing—or perhaps somewhere in between.

2. *Reasons.* We have reasons for deciding whether something is good or bad or somewhere in between and for all our other judgments. Our reasons usually are based on our criteria and evidence.

3. *Criteria.* These form the basis for deciding whether something is good or bad, useful or not useful, and so on. Our criteria are often implicit and may even be subconscious. The more we know about something—cars, movies, or whatever—the more elaborate and sophisticated our criteria become.

4. *Evidence.* The evidence (specific details, observations, or facts about the thing itself) in support of our reasons is what makes our judgment—and evaluation—persuasive.

5. *Stake.* Someone has a stake in our evaluation when he or she cares about the quality of the thing we're evaluating.

Forming a judgment is the easy part, particularly when it's driven by feeling. There's usually some initial reason, too. "This toaster sucks because it burns my toast every morning." The implied criterion here is pretty straightforward as well: "Good" toasters don't burn the toast. This reasoning is sound, more or less, but there's one big problem: Who really cares about your toaster besides you? However, when an evaluation is an argument (and not just your personal opinion), then you must make others realize that they have a stake in your judgments. Lots of people have toasters. They just don't have *your* toaster. In order to make an argument, then, you have to have something to say about *toasters*: This brand is better than that brand, for example. Similarly, when I praise a particular modern dance performance, no one but my friends and family will care about my judgment if it's just about my daughters. I have to discover criteria about the features of superb modern dance *performances*, criteria that others who care about dance might buy.

Motives for Writing a Review

Once you start thinking about evaluative writing, you'll find it everywhere—the book reviews in the Sunday *Times*, the music reviews in *Spin*, the analysis of websites on Web Sites That Suck. It's probably the most common form of workplace writing, too, for everything from assessing the performance of an employee to evaluating a plan to preserve historic buildings. One motive for reviews is to help people make informed decisions.

The review is a genre of persuasive writing. In a way, it's an aggressive writing form: *You should see this thing the way I see it.* In some cases, the stakes can be high.

4.1

Use reasons and evidence to support a judgment about something's value.

4.2

Identify the criteria behind a judgment and determine their relevance.

The fate of a Broadway show may be in the hands of the theater critic at the *New York Times.* The success of a tech product launch might depend on its reception by the reviewer in *Wired.* Enrollments at a university may be affected by its ranking in the "best" college list of *US News and World Report.* Critics can be arbiters of taste and quality, which is a powerful (and sometimes intoxicating) motive for some.

Evaluative writing is an enormously practical form, relevant in all sorts of situations in and out of school.

For the rest of us, the stakes in writing a review may not be quite as high, but there are many occasions in which our judgments can make a significant difference. Your boss hands you a marketing plan and asks you to evaluate it. Followers of your cooking blog want to know your take on the best kitchen knife. You're writing a letter to the editor on the redesign of a neighborhood park. These are every-day—and fairly common—occasions for the review, and you will want to do it well.

The Review and Academic Writing

We don't usually think of the review as an academic form, although you may be asked to review a film you're shown in an English class or perhaps a performance in a theater class. But reviews are a form of evaluative writing that is among the most common types of writing in all kinds of college classrooms. Here are some examples:

- In English, you might do a rhetorical evaluation of a document, a film, or a story.
- Courses in music, theater, and dance might include a review of performances.
- Courses in art history or photography might call for you to review one or more artworks (see the box "Seeing the Form: Choosing the Best Picture").
- In science and social science classes, you may evaluate the methodology of studies.
- Business writing often involves reviewing proposals or marketing plans.
- Philosophers make arguments, but they also evaluate whether others' arguments are effective.
- In composition, you'll review the writing of your peers.

Seeing the Form

Choosing the Best Picture

When documentary photographer Dorothea Lange encountered Florence Thompson and her family camped by a frozen pea field, she took multiple pictures. One—and only one—of them became famous. Titled "Migrant Mother," it is considered an indelible image of the Depression. If you were charged with evaluating the five shots that Lange took of Thompson and her family, seen here, which would you choose as the best shot? What reasons would you have for making this judgment?

Seeing the Form (*continued*)

Five photographs Dorothea Lange took of Florence Thompson and her family.

4.3
Identify the characteristics of different forms of the review, including academic applications.

Features of the Form

Feature	Conventions of the Review Essay
Inquiry questions	How good is it? What is its value?
Motives	Your basic motive is to make a judgment about something that you may or may not be familiar with, and then, using reasonable criteria and evidence, convince others that your judgment is sensible.
Subject matter	Reviews aren't just about books, films, and performances. Nearly anything is fair game: consumer products, web pages, cars, apps, policies, restaurants, ski areas, college dorms, vacation destinations, and so on. The key is that you evaluate something that interests you and that also might interest someone else.
Structure	Many reviews have the following elements: • *Description.* What does it look like? What are some other key characteristics? • *Back story.* What is the background? What do readers need to know about if they don't know as much as you do? • *Judgments.* What do you think? These judgments don't have to lead to some grand thesis—it was good or bad—but can be a series of assessments given over the course of the review. • *Reasons, evidence.* What are the reasons behind your judgments? And what evidence do you have to support these reasons? • *Criteria.* What is the basis for your reasons? Criteria may be stated explicitly or implied. • *Relevant comparisons.* What category does it belong to? What else is it like, and why is it better or worse?
Sources of information	The raw material of any review is specific evidence drawn from your experience and research on the subject. What specifically influenced your judgment? What did you see? What did you hear? How did it work? What did they say? What were the results? What are the facts? How does it compare? Many review topics (e.g., film, plays, cars, clothes, books) will be most informed by your direct experience with your subject. But research can help any review. You can read about it or ask people what they think of it.

Feature	Conventions of the Review Essay
Language	The review can be tricky, especially if you're an expert on the thing you're reviewing. Be careful of "insider" language—terms, definitions, and so on that people unfamiliar with your topic may not understand.
	Frequently, the "voice" of the reviewer, especially a particular way of saying things, is especially strong. For example, think about successful music or movie reviewers. Often, the persona they project through their writing voice is part of their appeal: sometimes cranky or even snarky, sometimes humorous, frequently clever.

Prose+: Beyond Words

In four frames, cartoonist Tatsuya Ishida offers her review of the book *Fifty Shades of Grey*, a hugely successful erotic novel and now a motion picture.

THAT'S MY STORY AND I'M STICKING TO IT
TATSUYA ISHIDA

READINGS

▶ **Film Review**

One hallmark of a great film is one's willingness to see it again and again, with each viewing yielding some new pleasure. However, holiday films seem like a special category. We see them every year at least in part because of ritual; we watch a certain movie at Christmastime because we always watch that movie at Christmastime. For a lot of people, *A Christmas Story* (1983) is one of those cinematic rituals. The film tells the story of Ralphie, who more than anything wants a Daisy Red Ryder BB gun for Christmas. Unfortunately, everyone in Ralphie's universe is convinced that if he possesses such a weapon, he will surely "shoot his eye out."

What distinguishes *A Christmas Story* from other popular holiday films, according to the late movie critic Roger Ebert, is that the film possesses "many small but perfect moments" that remind us of "a world that no longer quite exists in America." In other words, this isn't simply a great Christmas film. It's a great film by any measure.

Roger Ebert was perhaps the dean of American movie critics. He was a long-time columnist for the *Chicago Sun-Times*, and his website remains a popular resource for all things related to film.

A Christmas Story
Roger Ebert

1   One of the details that "A Christmas Story" gets right is the threat of having your mouth washed out with Lifebuoy soap. Not any soap. Lifebuoy. Never Ivory or Palmolive. Lifebuoy, which apparently contained an ingredient able to nullify bad language. The only other soap ever mentioned for this task was Lava, but that was the nuclear weapon of mouth-washing soaps, so powerful it was used for words we still didn't even know.

2   There are many small but perfect moments in "A Christmas Story," and one of the best comes after the Lifebuoy is finally removed from Ralphie's mouth and he is sent off to bed. His mother studies the bar, thinks for a moment, and then sticks it in her own mouth, just to see what it tastes like. Moments like that are why some people watch "A Christmas Story" every holiday season. There is a real knowledge of human nature beneath the comedy.

3   The movie is based on the memoirs of Jean Shepherd, the humorist whose radio programs and books remembered growing up in Indiana in the 1940s. It is Shepherd's voice on the soundtrack, remembering one Christmas season in particular, and the young hero's passionate desire to get a Daisy Red Ryder 200-shot Carbine Action BB Gun for Christmas—the one with the compass in the stock, "as cool and deadly a piece of weaponry as I had ever laid eyes on."

In a memorable scene from *A Christmas Story*, Ralphie observes firsthand what happens when a warm tongue meets cold metal.

I owned such a weapon. I recall everything about it at this moment with a tactile memory so vivid I could have just put it down to write these words. How you stuffed newspapers into the carton it came in to use it for target practice. How the BBs came in a cardboard tube with a slide-off top. How they rattled when you poured them into the gun. And of course how everybody warned that you would shoot your eye out.   4

Ralphie's life is made a misery by that danger. He finds that nobody in northern Indiana (not his mother, not his teacher, not even Santa Claus) is able to even *think* about a BB gun without using the words "shoot your eye out." At one point in the movie, in a revenge daydream, he knocks on his parents' door with dark glasses, a blind man's cane and a beggar's tin cup. They are shocked, and ask him tearfully what caused his blindness, and he replies coolly, "Soap poisoning."   5

The movie is not only about Christmas and BB guns, but also about childhood, and one detail after another rings true. The school bully, who, when he runs out of victims, beats up on his own loyal sidekick. The little brother who has outgrown his snowsuit, which is so tight that he walks around looking like the Michelin man; when he falls down he can't get up. The aunt who always thinks Ralphie is a 4-year-old girl, and sends him a pink bunny suit. Other problems of life belong to that long-ago age   6

(continued)

(continued)

and not this one: clinkers in the basement coal furnace, for example, or the blowout of a tire. Everybody knows what a flat tire is, but many now alive have never experienced a genuine, terrifying loud instantaneous **blowout.**

7   "A Christmas Story" was released in the Christmas season of 1983, and did modest business at first (people don't often go to movies with specific holiday themes). It got warm reviews and two Genie Awards (the Canadian Oscars) for Bob Clark's direction and for the screenplay. And then it moved onto home video and has been a stealth hit season after season, finding a loyal audience. "Bams," for example, one of the critics at the hip Three Black Chicks movie review Web site, confesses she loves it: "How does one describe, in short form, the smiles and shrieks of laughter one has experienced over more than 15 years of seeing the same great movie over and over, without sounding like a babbling, fanboyish fool who talks too much?"

8   The movie is set in Indiana but was filmed mostly around Toronto, with some downtown shots from Cleveland, by Clark, whose other big hits were "Porky's" and "Baby Geniuses." It is pitch-perfect, telling the story through the enthusiastic and single-minded vision of its hero Ralphie, and finding in young Peter Billingsley a sly combination of innocence and calculation.

9   Ralphie's parents, Mr. and Mrs. Parker, are played by Darren McGavin and Melinda Dillon, and they exude warmth, zest and love: They are about the nicest parents I can remember in a non-smarmy movie. Notice the scene where Mrs. Parker gets her younger son, Randy, to eat his food by pretending he is "mommy's little piggie." Watch the delight in their laughter together. And the enthusiasm with which the Old Man (as he is always called) attacks the (unseen) basement furnace, battles with the evil neighbor dogs and promises to change a tire in "four minutes flat—time me!" And the lovely closing moment as the parents tenderly put their arms around each other on Christmas night.

10   Some of the movie's sequences stand as classic. The whole business, for example, of the Old Man winning the "major award" of a garish lamp in the shape of a woman's leg (watch Mrs. Parker hiding her giggles in the background as he tries to glue it together after it is "accidentally" broken). Or the visit by Ralphie and Randy to a department store Santa Claus, whose helpers spin the terrified kids around to bang them down on Santa's lap, and afterward kick them down a slide to floor level. Or the sequence where a kid is not merely dared but Triple-Dog-Dared to stick his tongue onto a frozen lamp post, and the fire department has to be called. And the deep disillusionment with which Ralphie finally gets his Little Orphan Annie Secret Decoder Ring in the mail, and Annie's secret message turns out to be nothing but a crummy commercial.

11   There is also the matter of Scut Farcas (Zack Ward), the bully, who Ralphie assures us has yellow eyes. Every school has a kid like this, who picks on smaller kids but is a coward at heart. He makes Ralphie's life a misery. How Farcus gets his comeuppance makes for a deeply satisfying scene, and notice the perfect tact with which Ralphie's

mom handles the situation. (Do you agree with me that Dad already knows the whole story when he sits down at the kitchen table?)

In a poignant way, "A Christmas Story" records a world that no longer quite exists in America. Kids are no longer left unattended in the line for Santa. The innocence of kids' radio programs has been replaced by slick, ironic children's programming on TV. The new Daisy BB guns have a muzzle velocity higher than that of some police revolvers, and are not to be sold to anyone under 16. Nobody knows who Red Ryder was, let alone that his sidekick was Little Beaver.   12

So much has been forgotten. There is a moment when the Old Man needs an answer for the contest he is entering. The theme of the contest is "Characters in American Literature," and the question is: "What was the name of the Lone Ranger's nephew's horse?"   13

Victor, of course. Everybody knows that.   14

Inquiring into the Essay

1. **Explore.** Think about the holiday film that you'd like to see every year. Fastwrite for five minutes about the film and your memories of watching it. After the fastwrite, answer this question: What makes this a "good" film? Or think about some other film that you'd like to see every year and do the fastwrite and answer the question.

2. **Explain.** Underline or highlight sentences or passages in which Ebert is telling readers how and why *A Christmas Story* is a great movie. Then summarize in your own words what Ebert is saying about the film, incorporating several words or phrases from the material you underlined or highlighted.

3. **Evaluate.** Ebert uses various kinds of evidence to support his judgment that this is a great movie because of its "small but perfect moments" that get all the details of childhood in America right. He uses personal evidence, evidence from others, and of course lots of evidence from the movie. Find examples of these different kinds of evidence, and assess how effective they are in supporting the reasons Ebert gives for his judgment of the movie.

4. **Reflect.** In evaluative writing, judgments can be as small as brief comments or as big as thesis statements. Is there a thesis statement somewhere in Ebert's review of *A Christmas Story*? If so, where is it? If not, is the lack of a thesis statement a problem? Does every piece of persuasive writing need a thesis?

▶ Video Game Review

The video gaming industry hauls in something like $10 billion a year, so it's no surprise that more writers than ever are penning reviews of the latest releases. These reviews, if they're any good, balance technical information about the game with attention to the experience of playing it. It is a well-described gaming experience, not arcane detail, that will appeal to most readers. That's why Seth Schiesel's review of "Grand Theft Auto IV," a hugely popular video game released in 2008, is such a great example of how to write a review that might make even non–video game players interested in giving it a try.

Even when he doesn't make them explicit, the criteria Schiesel uses to determine the qualities of a good game aren't hard to find. One criterion he clearly uses is what we often look for in film and literature: "fully realized characters." When you think about it, this is a pretty extraordinary accomplishment in a video game. After all, characters in a game such as "Grand Theft Auto IV" must consistently service the action, making things (usually violent things) happen, and this wouldn't seem to provide the time or the situations to develop character. But according to Schiesel, protagonist Niko Bellic is "one of the most fully realized characters video games have yet produced."

Seth Schiesel sidesteps the ethics of producing games such as "Grand Theft Auto IV," which makes efficient killing a key to advancement. But this is a review, not a public argument on the virtues of gaming, and his readers likely aren't interested in such ethical questions. They just want to know whether the game is any good. As you read "Grand Theft Auto Takes on New York," consider what exactly Schiesel sees as being a good video game. On what other criteria does he base his judgment?

Grand Theft Auto Takes on New York
Seth Schiesel

1   I was rolling through the neon deluge of a place very like Times Square the other night in my Landstalker sport utility vehicle, listening to David Bowie's "Fascination" on the radio. The glittery urban landscape was almost enough to make me forget about the warehouse of cocaine dealers I was headed uptown to rip off.

2   Soon I would get bored, though, and carjack a luxury sedan. I'd meet my Rasta buddy Little Jacob, then check out a late show by Ricky Gervais at a comedy club around the corner. Afterward I'd head north to confront the dealers, at least if I could elude the cops. I heard their sirens before I saw them and peeled out, tires squealing.

3   It was just another night on the streets of Liberty City, the exhilarating, lusciously dystopian rendition of New York City in 2008 that propels Grand Theft Auto IV, the ambitious new video game to be released on Tuesday for the Xbox 360 and PlayStation 3 systems.

4   Published by Rockstar Games, Grand Theft Auto IV is a violent, intelligent, profane, endearing, obnoxious, sly, richly textured and thoroughly compelling work of cultural satire disguised as fun. It calls to mind a rollicking R-rated version of Mad

magazine featuring Dave Chappelle and Quentin Tarantino, and sets a new standard for what is possible in interactive arts. It is by far the best game of the series, which made its debut in 1997 and has since sold more than 70 million copies. Grand Theft Auto IV will retail for $60.

Niko Bellic is the player-controlled protagonist this time, and he is one of the most fully realized characters video games have yet produced. A veteran of the Balkan wars and a former human trafficker in the Adriatic, he arrives in Liberty City's rendition of Brighton Beach at the start of the game to move in with his affable if naïve cousin Roman. Niko expects to find fortune and, just maybe, track down someone who betrayed him long ago. Over the course of the story line he discovers that revenge is not always what one expects.   5

Besides the nuanced Niko the game is populated by a winsome procession of grifters, hustlers, drug peddlers and other gloriously unrepentant lowlifes, each a caricature less politically correct than the last.   6

Hardly a demographic escapes skewering. In addition to various Italian and Irish crime families, there are venal Russian gangsters, black crack slingers, argyle-sporting Jamaican potheads, Puerto Rican hoodlums, a corrupt police commissioner, a steroid-addled Brooklyn knucklehead named Brucie Kibbutz and a former Eastern European soldier who has become a twee Upper West Side metrosexual.   7

Breathing life into Niko and the other characters is a pungent script by Dan Houser and Rupert Humphries that reveals a mastery of street patois to rival Elmore Leonard's. The point of the main plot is to guide Niko through the city's criminal underworld. Gang leaders and thugs set missions for him to complete, and his success moves the story along toward a conclusion that seems as dark as its beginning. But the real star of the game is the city itself. It looks like New York. It sounds like New York. It feels like New York. Liberty City has been so meticulously created it almost even smells like New York. From Brooklyn (called Broker), through Queens (Dukes), the Bronx (Bohan), Manhattan (Algonquin) and an urban slice of New Jersey (Alderney), the game's streets and alleys ooze a stylized yet unmistakable authenticity. (Staten Island is left out however.)   8

The game does not try to represent anything close to every street in the city, but the overall proportions, textures, geography, sights and sounds are spot-on. The major landmarks are present, often rendered in surprising detail, from the Cyclone at Coney Island to the Domino Sugar factory and Grand Army Plaza in Brooklyn and on up through the detritus of the 1964–65 World's Fair in Queens. Central Park, the Empire State Building, various museums, the Statue of Liberty and Times Square are all present and accounted for. There is no Yankee Stadium, but there is a professional baseball team known, with the deliciousness typical of the game's winks and nods, as the Swingers.   9

At least as impressive as the city's virtual topography is the range of the game's audio and music production, delivered through an entire dial's worth of radio stations available in almost any of the dozens of different cars, trucks and motorcycles a   10

(*continued*)

(continued)

player can steal. From the jazz channel (billed as "music from when America was cool") through the salsa, alt-rock, jazz, metal and multiple reggae and hip-hop stations, Lazlow Jones, Ivan Pavlovich and the rest of Rockstar's audio team demonstrate a musical erudition beyond anything heard before in a video game. The biggest problem with the game's extensive subway system is that there's no music underground. (Too bad there are no iPods to nab.)

11   The game's roster of radio hosts runs from Karl Lagerfeld to Iggy Pop and DJ Green Lantern. It is not faint praise to point out that at times, simply driving around the city listening to the radio—seguing from "Moanin'" by Art Blakey and the Jazz Messengers to the Isley Brothers' "Footsteps in the Dark" to "The Crack House" by Fat Joe featuring Lil Wayne—can be as enjoyable as anything the game has to offer.

12   Grand Theft Auto IV is such a simultaneously adoring and insightful take on modern America that it almost had to come from somewhere else. The game's main production studio is in Edinburgh, and Rockstar's leaders, the brothers Dan and Sam Houser, are British expatriates who moved to New York to indulge their fascination with urban American culture. Their success places them firmly among the distinguished cast of Britons from Mick Jagger and Keith Richards through Tina Brown who have flourished by identifying key elements of American culture, repackaging them for mass consumption and selling them back at a markup.

13   It all adds up to a new level of depth for an interactive entertainment experience. I've spent almost 60 hours practically sequestered in a (real world) Manhattan hotel room in recent weeks playing through Grand Theft Auto IV's main story line and the game still says I have found only 64 percent of its content. I won't ever reach 100 percent, not least because I won't hunt down all 200 of the target pigeons (known as flying rats here) that the designers have hidden around the city.

14   But like millions of other players I will happily spend untold hours cruising Liberty City's bridges and byways, hitting the clubs, grooving to the radio and running from the cops. Even when the real New York City is right outside.

Inquiring into the Essay

1.   **Explore.** This review doesn't address the ethical questions raised by a game that celebrates "gloriously unrepentant lowlifes" including potheads, gangsters, and "crack slingers." "Grand Theft Auto IV" may be no worse than other violent video games, and unless you've played it, criticism or praise of this particular game is unfair. But in a four-minute fastwrite, explore your own feelings about violent video games. In his review, Schiesel argues that "Grand Theft Auto IV" is "cultural satire." Would that make a difference? Can games such as this one serve a larger, even useful purpose?

2. **Explain.** In your own words, state what Seth Schiesel seems to see as the qualities of a good video game.

3. **Evaluate.** How rhetorically effective is this review for different readers? Assess what parts would work—or wouldn't—for the following categories of readers:

   a. People who have never played a video game in their lives but might consider it.

   b. People who are avid and experienced gamers.

   c. People who, when asked, usually consider playing video games "a waste of time."

4. **Reflect.** Video game reviews are but one type of a growing number of review subgenres, which include reviews of movies, books, blogs, websites, best and worst dressed, and so on. Consider the subgenres of reviews you read or might read. What exactly would you be looking for in a "good" review?

THE WRITING PROCESS

Inquiry Project Writing a Review Essay

Inquiry questions: How good is it? What is its value?

Write a review essay on any subject—a performance, a book, a website, a consumer product, a film, whatever. Just make sure your review has the following qualities (see also the "Features of the Form" box on pages 98–99 for typical features of the review essay):

■ The essay is focused on a specific example of a larger category. (For instance, the film *Maltese Falcon* is an example of forties film noir, *The Curious Writer* is an example of a composition textbook, and Lady Gaga's song "Born This Way" is an example of politically themed contemporary rock music.)

■ The writer's judgments are clearly stated and are supported with reasons and evidence.

■ The evaluation seems balanced and fair. The criteria for judging the value of the subject seem sound.

Prose+

Write and publish your review for an online audience. There are review sites for nearly anything, from the very focused (e.g., birding binoculars) to the quite broad (music, film, TV, *and* video games). For example,

■ For a book review, consider publishing on the Amazon or Barnes & Noble site, or on a site such as Goodreads or LibraryThing.

■ For music, check out the website Music-Critic.

■ For music, movies, TV, apps, or video games, look to sites such as Metacritic.

■ For consumer products, there is Eopinions.

Turn your review into a video project. If you're writing about a consumer product, for example, demonstrate in a short film how it works and how it could work better. (There are a gazillion examples of this on YouTube.) If you're reviewing a movie or television show, put together a short film that incorporates clips, if available online, with your voiceover commentary. Make sure you allow time to learn how to use the basics of your video-editing software.

Add images to your essay. You might, for example, take a series of photographs to demonstrate how something works or to highlight its key features.

What Are You Going to Write About?

Imagine all the things about which you might ask, "How good is it?" From smart-phones to theater performances, movies to college websites, books to dog-training programs—the possibilities are endless. You don't have to start with an opinion about your review subject—and it's better if you don't—but it should be something that interests you.

Get started thinking about what you're going to write about by opening up the possibilities with the following prompts, most of which involve generating ideas. Later, you'll narrow things down to a promising topic and try it out.

4.4

Use invention and focusing strategies to discover and develop a review essay.

Opening Up

Suspend judgment to explore a range of possible review essay topics.

Listing Prompts. Lists can be rich sources of triggering topics. Let them grow freely, and when you're ready, use a list item as the focus of another list or an episode of fastwriting. The following prompts should get you started.

1. Fold a piece a paper into four equal columns. You'll be making four different brainstormed lists. In the first column, write, "Things I Want." Spend two minutes making a quick list of everything you wish you had but don't: a new computer, a classical guitar, a decent boyfriend, and so on.

2. In the next column, write, "The Jury Is Still Out." In this column, make a fast list of things in your life that so far are hard to judge: the quality of the school you attend, this textbook, your opinion about the films you saw last month, how well Susie cuts your hair, and so on.

3. In the third column, write, "My Media." Devote a fast list to particular films, TV shows, books, websites, or musicians you like or dislike; jot down whatever you watch, listen to, or read regularly.

4. Finally, make a list of "Things of Questionable Quality." Try to be specific.

Fastwriting Prompts. Remember, fastwriting is a great way to stimulate creative thinking. Turn off your critical side and let yourself write "badly."

1. Choose an item from any of the four preceding lists as a prompt for a seven-minute fastwrite. Explore your experience with the subject, or how your opinions about it have evolved.

2. Begin with the following prompt, and follow it for five minutes in a fast-write: *Among the things I have a hard time judging is* _____. If the writing stalls, shift subjects by writing, *And another thing I can't judge is* _____.

Visual Prompts. Sometimes the best way to generate material is to see what we think represented in something other than sentences. Boxes, lines, webs, clusters, arrows, charts, and even sketches can help us see more of the landscape of a subject, especially connections that aren't as obvious in prose.

1. On a blank page in your journal, cluster the name of an artist, musician, film, book, author, performance, band, building, academic course or major, restaurant, university bookstore, tablet, computer, food store, or pizza joint. Cluster the name of anything about which you have some sort of feeling, positive or negative. Build a web of associations: feelings, details, observations, names, moments, facts, opinions, and so on. Look for a single strand in your essay that might be the beginning of a review.

2. Draw a sketch of what you think is an *ideal version* of something you need or use often: a computer, a classroom, a telephone, a wallet or handbag, and so on. If you could design such a thing, what would it look like? Use this as a way of evaluating what is currently available and how it might be improved.

Research Prompts. Explore what other critics are saying, look around, or collaborate.

1. Do an Internet or library search for reviews on one of your favorite films, books, sports teams, artists, and so on. Do you agree with the evaluations? If not, consider writing a review of your own that challenges the critics.

2. Take a walk. As you wander on and off campus, look for things to evaluate—downtown architecture, local parks, paintings in the art museum, neighborhoods, coffee shops. You'll be amazed at how much is begging for a thoughtful judgment.

3. Here's an entertaining generating activity: Plan a weekend of movie watching with a few friends. Ask each of them to suggest two or three favorite films, and then obtain a slew of them. When you're thoroughly spent watching the films, discuss which one might be the most interesting to review.

Narrowing Down

Now that you've opened up possibilities for review topics, there are choices to make. Which do you want to write about?

What's Promising Material and What Isn't? My favorite coffee shop in my hometown of Boise, Idaho, is a place called the Flying M. It's a funky place with an odd assortment of furniture: overstuffed couches, worn armchairs, and wobbly tables. On the walls, there's work from local artists, mostly unknowns with talent and unusual taste. There are other coffee places in town, including the ubiquitous Starbucks and another, more local chain called Moxie Java. I don't find much difference in the coffee at any of these places, and they're all rather pleasant. What makes me prefer the Flying M?

I've never really thought about it. That's one of the reasons I liked the idea of reviewing my favorite local coffeehouse when "the Flying M" appeared on one of my lists. The best inquiry-based projects begin when you're not quite sure what you think and want to explore a topic to find out.

- *Is there anything in your lists and fastwrites that you might have an initial judgment about but really haven't considered fully?*

- *As you consider potential subjects for your review, do some clearly suggest the possibility of comparison with other, similar things in that category?*

- *Do any of your potential subjects suggest the possibility of conducting primary research, or research that might involve direct observation?* Can you listen to the music, attend the performance, read the novel, examine the building, visit the website, look at the painting?

- *Does a topic lend itself to demonstration through visuals or video?* Can you download clips, film a demonstration, take pictures, create an infographic?

- *Does someone have a stake in your evaluation of the thing?* Are more people than just you interested in your judgments about its value?

Questions About Audience and Purpose. When people read reviews, they either are actively *seeking information* (they are considering buying the tablet or attending the dance performance) or are *looking for reinforcement* (reasons why what they've already decided to do makes sense). I bought a Ford Escape recently, and now I read every review I see on the car, hoping to feel good about my decision. These two audiences have very different dispositions. The information-seekers are more critical readers than those who seek reinforcement. But what they both share is a stake in the topic under review. They're *interested.* As you consider a review topic, ask yourself whether it's easy to imagine an audience who would care, one way or another, about a judgment about the usefulness or value of the thing you might review.

Trying Out

Let's work with your tentative topic, doing some more-focused work, culminating in a sketch, or a first try at writing it up for an audience.

Focusing the Category. First, let's try focusing your topic in the context of a category. Can you see how your topic fits into broader and narrower categories? An inverted pyramid, as shown in Figure 4.1, is a nice model for this.

Suppose you love the 1940s film classic *The Maltese Falcon*, and you'd like to explore why it's so good. You can evaluate the film as an example of movies generally, but that makes little sense because the category's too broad. However, suppose you list progressively narrower subcategories of film to which *The Maltese Falcon* might belong. You might end up evaluating the film as an example of 1940s film noir. Why is this narrowed focus useful?

1. *It gives you a way of seeing appropriate comparisons.* You're comparing *The Maltese Falcon* not to all Hollywood movies—there are, after all, so many different kinds—but to other 1940s Hollywood crime films that belong to the film noir genre.

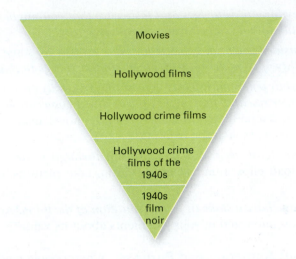

Movies

Hollywood films

Hollywood crime films

Hollywood crime
films of the
1940s

1940s
film
noir

Figure 4.1   An inverted triangle model for focusing a topic

2. *It helps you focus on appropriate criteria.* Just as it would be weird to compare *The Maltese Falcon* with *A Christmas Story* because they are such different types of films, it would be hard to arrive at criteria for such an evaluation. What makes a 1940s crime film "good" will be very different from what makes a family comedy "good."

Try creating an inverted pyramid on your subject, looking for a category that is narrow enough to make comparisons and criteria appropriate.

Fastwriting. Through a focused fastwrite, explore your initial feelings and experiences, if any, about your subject. Use one of the following prompts to launch this exploration. If the writing stalls, try another prompt to keep you going for five to seven minutes.

- *Write about your first experience with your subject.* This might be, for example, the first time you visited the restaurant, or heard the performer, or saw the photographs. Focus on scenes, moments, situations, and people.

- *Write about what you think are important qualities of your subject.* Ideally, this would be what the thing should be able to do well or what effects it should have on people who use it or see it.

- *Write about how the thing makes you feel.* Explore not just your initial good, bad, or mixed feelings about your subject, but also the place from where those feelings arose. Why do you feel anything at all about this thing?

- *Compare the thing you're evaluating with something that's similar.*

Web Research. Try some web searches, gathering as much relevant background information as you can.

- *Search for information on product websites or web pages devoted specifically to your subject.* If your review is on Ford's new electric car, visit the company's website to find out what you can about the vehicle. Visit Green Day's home page or fan site for your review of the band's latest CD.

- *Search for existing reviews or other evaluations on your subject.* One way to do this is to Google the keyword "review" or "reviews" (or "how to evaluate") along with your subject. For example, "laptop reviews" will produce dozens of sites that rank and evaluate the machines. Similarly, there are countless reviews on the web of specific performers, performances, CDs, consumer products, and so on.

Interviews. If possible, interview people about what they think. You may do this formally by developing a survey (see pages 264–268), or informally by simply asking people what they like or dislike about the thing you're evaluating. Also consider whether you might interview someone who's an expert on your subject. For example, if you're evaluating a website, ask people in the technical communications program what they think about it, or what criteria they might use if they were reviewing something similar.

Experiencing Your Subject. This may be the most useful activity of all. Visit the coffeehouse, examine the website, listen to the music, attend the performance, read the book, view the painting, visit the building, look at the architecture, watch the movie. As you do this, gather your impressions and collect information. Take notes. Take pictures. Shoot video.

Thinking About Criteria

You hate something. You love something. You have mixed feelings about it. All of these judgments arise from your criteria, your assumptions about the qualities that make such a thing good. And thinking about your criteria can help you know what to look for.

Refining Criteria for Better Evidence. Consider a process of evaluation something like the one in Figure 4.2.

You see a website and think, "This is really ugly." You look more closely and conclude, "I think there's too much text." You could stop there, of course, but you want to provide a more thorough evaluation. A natural next step, then, would be to consider the criterion behind your reason and judgment. You could simply say, "Good websites don't use too much text," but that doesn't advance your evaluation any further because the criterion is too general and vague. After a little research into what this criterion's really about, you arrive at this: "Good sites break text into readable chunks." Sites that don't have readable chunks give the visual appearance

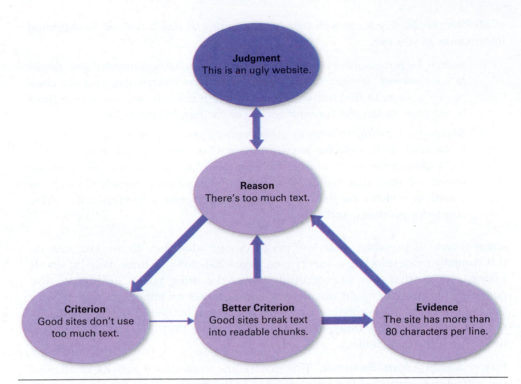

Figure 4.2   A process for refining criteria and using criteria to generate better evidence

of too much text. What's a "readable chunk"? Turns out it is around 80 characters per line. Now you can take another look at your ugly website with a criterion that really helps you support your judgment with better evidence.

This implies a couple things about good criteria in evaluation:

1. The more specific your criterion for evaluation, the better.
2. Identifying criteria is a powerful tool for finding better evidence to support your judgment.

The more you know about something, the more specific your criteria are likely to be. For example, I asked my daughter Becca what criteria she would use to judge a modern dance performance (see the box). I'm unschooled in dance, so I don't understand all of her criteria, but I'm certain I could use some of them the next time I see a modern dance performance, to evaluate what I see.

Considering Criteria and Rhetorical Context. We often don't think about our criteria and whether they're valid; we treat them as self-evident and may assume that our audience would agree with them. But careful reviewers at the very least *consider* the criteria that shape their reactions and decide whether they're fair and sensible. (If you're finding your criteria hard to tease out, or want to know what criteria others might have, try getting some help.

Becca's Criteria

A good modern dance performance has...

1. Interesting features—props, comedy, or music
2. Something improvised
3. Visible expressions of the dancers' enjoyment
4. Interesting variation
5. Good balance in choreography between repetition and randomness
6. Beginning, middle, and end seamlessly joined

In thinking about criteria, you need to think about rhetorical context: audience and purpose. As you saw in Chapter 1, the qualities of "good" writing really depend on the situation: purpose, audience, genre. A main purpose of a review is to give readers potentially useful information. So, if you're evaluating a new type of downhill skis, you'll need to think about skis for whom. An advanced skier fond of deep powder will have different expectations of her skis' performance than will an intermediate skier like me, who falls on his face off groomed runs. For this reason, in thinking about criteria that might guide your evaluation of the thing you're reviewing, you'll find it useful to

First, identify your audience:

- *Who will be using the thing (going to the performance, etc.)?*

Then, take another look at your criteria:

- *Are the criteria that you are thinking in terms of appropriate for your audience?*

Writing the Sketch

A sketch, as the name implies, is a kind of verbal drawing of your topic—an early draft—to see if you should develop it further. Even when you write a sketch with readers in mind, it is hardly polished. You are "essaying" the topic to try it out, and you may not know yet what you think or what you want to say. Your review sketch, however, should include the following:

- A tentative title.

- An effort to help readers understand why they might have a stake in the thing you're evaluating. What's significant about this particular CD, book, performance, place, or product?

- A tentative answer to the inquiry question "How good is it?"

- A few convincing reasons for your judgment that are tied to specific evidence from the thing itself.

▶ **Student Sketch**

Here are some common criteria for a good film:

1. There is someone in the film who we come to like, despite that person's flaws.
2. Characters change. They learn from mistakes.
3. The story ends with some resolution of the conflict.

According to Laura Burns, whose sketch of the Charlize Theron film *Young Adult* follows, that movie doesn't meet any of the three criteria. And yet, she argues, *Young Adult* is a great film. Obviously, Laura is saying that the criteria most of us assume must be met for a film to be good in fact don't have to be met. Because she challenges our assumptions, Laura needs to be particularly persuasive in her review. How persuasive is she in this first attempt?

Recipe for a Great Film: Unlikeable People, Poor Choices, and Little Redemption
Laura Burns

1   Charlize Theron is arguably the most traditionally beautiful woman in film. High, smooth cheekbones, long, thin legs, a delicate nose set at the center of a perfectly proportioned face. This considered, it's remarkable how ugly she can get.

2   *Young Adult* is a movie about unlikeable people making poor life choices which they don't learn from. Theron plays Mavis Gary, an ex-prom queen from Mercury, Minnesota, making her living as a ghostwriter of a teen series in what the Mercurians call the "Mini-apple." From the first sequence of the film, we can tell that Mavis is a mess. She gets wasted, slumps around her apartment in sweats, and guzzles Diet Coke in a way that almost gave me heartburn. Upon receiving a birth announcement email from her now-married ex-prom king, the aptly named Buddy (Patrick Wilson), Mavis decides to pop an old mixtape into her dirty Mini Cooper and win him back.

3   This is, essentially, the entire plot of *Young Adult*. Mavis' trip back to Mercury is a kind of *anti*-hero's journey. On her first night in town, getting wasted in a local dive, she meets her "guide," Matt (the wonderful Patton Oswalt), a former classmate who remains crippled from an assault during high school. Through the course of the film, as she reunites with her parents (Jill Eikenberry & Richard Bekins), insinuates herself into Buddy and his wife Beth's (Elizabeth Reaser) lives, and gets plastered on Matt's home-brewed bourbon, rather than moving towards revelation, Mavis seems to retreat further and further into her past.

4   Unlike *Juno*, writer Diablo Cody's most well-known film, *Young Adult* rejects preciousness in favor of obscenity. It's difficult to make a film about terrible people enjoyable, but Cody

injects just enough silliness to keep us from feeling too badly. Director Jason Reitman rightly focuses on Mavis, and both Theron and Oswalt are brave enough to let us into their characters' grossness and un-likeability. Smartly, Cody refuses to manufacture empathy for her characters, leaving us to boldly accept the ugliness of these people fully.

I don't doubt that *Young Adult* will displease many movie-goers who are used to redemptive stories and characters who are "good at heart." Cody refuses to indulge that expectation. When Mavis dresses to go out (which is often), Theron's extraordinary beauty is obvious. Yet we're never allowed to shake that Mavis is truly ugly at her core—an effective subversion of expectation that is the exemplar of this memorable performance. This isn't a feel-good film, and thank goodness. If Cody and Reitman had tried, I think we might leave the theater feeling worse.

5

Moving from Sketch to Draft

A sketch is an audition. It's a brief performance for an audience that may or may not work out well. In a review, what do you look for in your own performance? To start with, you've got to still care about your topic, of course. This should be a topic you still want to write about. But what else?

Evaluating Your Sketch. Start with a summary of what you think the sketch is saying by finishing the following sentence.

Because of   (reason 1)   and   (reason 2) , I think that   (thing you're evaluating) is   (judgment of value) , and the strongest evidence for this is _____ and _____.

Example: Because of its unusually hefty neck and its thick, solid rosewood body, the Martin 0-28VS acoustic guitar has a bright sound that belies its small size, and the strongest evidence for this is how great it sounds with light fingerpicking and its long sustains.

If you can finish the sentence to your satisfaction, your audition was successful. You know, more or less, where you might be going. (Don't be surprised if you change your mind as you revise.) However, you might have encountered some problems. Maybe you haven't yet arrived at a judgment. Or perhaps you can't come up with two compelling reasons for the judgment you do have. In any case, here are the things you should focus on as you develop your review:

- *Clarify your judgment.* What is the one thing you're trying to say (S.O.F.T.) about the thing you're reviewing?

- *Explain your reasons.* What is behind your evaluation? And are the criteria that these reasons are based on sensible?

- *Provide the back story.* What is it, where did it come from, how does it compare, why is it important, what is the history?

- *Gather evidence.* How will you prove that your reasons are persuasive? What specifically can you point to?

Reflecting on What You've Learned. To get some perspective on what you've learned so far about the thing you're reviewing, fastwrite in your journal or on the computer using the following prompt:

When I first started exploring this, I thought _____, and now I'm beginning to think _____.

Developing

Before you revise your sketch into a draft, generate more material through writing and research. This is almost always necessary.

Talking It Through. Generate more material by having a conversation with me about your topic. Imagine I'm sitting across the table from you, asking you the following questions about the thing you're reviewing. Respond in your journal to each question, in order, fastwriting a response for at least a few minutes. If the writing takes off in response to any one question, run with it. The order of the questions may prove to be a useful organizing principle for your draft, so write as much as you can in this exercise.

Bruce	You
To start with, why are you reviewing this? To whom might it matter and under what circumstances?	
Can you describe it? What does it look like? What is the story behind it? Would you compare it to anything else I might know about?	
Okay, so what do you most want me to know about it? What is it you're saying, exactly?	
Interesting. Why do you say this?	
Surely not everyone thinks this. What do people who disagree with you say? How would you respond to them?	

Consider the following research strategies for developing your draft.

Re-Experience. Probably the single most useful thing you can do to prepare for the next draft is to collect more observations of your subject. Why? You're much more focused now on what you think, what criteria most influence that judgment, and what particular evidence you were lacking in the sketch that will make your review more convincing. You might also consider documenting your research not only with notes but multimedia as well. Could you take pictures to demonstrate a feature or show how the thing you're reviewing is used? Might you include screenshots of the relevant websites? Download images of the thing being used?

Interview. If you haven't already done so, collect the comments, opinions, and observations of others about the subject of your review. If you reviewed a concert or other event, find others to interview who also attended. If you reviewed a film, get some friends to watch the movie with you and jot down their reactions afterward. If it would be helpful to collect data on how people feel, consider designing a brief survey.

Also consider interviewing someone who is an expert on the thing you're reviewing.

Read. Go to the library and go online and search for information about your subject. Try finding:

- *Information about how it's made or designed.*
- *Other reviews on your topic.*
- *Information on relevant people, companies, traditions, local developments— any background that will help readers see the thing you're reviewing in a larger context.*

Drafting

When you've got enough information, start your draft, beginning at the beginning.

Finding an Opening. A comparison of class note taking on paper versus on computers begins:

> The moment of truth for me came in the spring 2013 semester. I looked out at my visual-communication class and saw a group of six students transfixed by the blue glow of a video on one of their computers, and decided I was done allowing laptops in my large lecture class. "Done" might be putting it mildly. Although I am an engaging lecturer, I could not compete with Facebook and YouTube, and I was tired of trying.
>
> The next semester I told students they would have to take notes on paper. Period.*

There's no thesis in this introduction (that will come later), but it clearly establishes the dilemma the essay proposes to explore: Was it a good idea to force students to close their laptops and take notes by hand? But this beginning does more than billboard the essay's purpose. It also

1. Raises questions the reader might want to learn the answers to.
2. Creates a relationship between reader and writer.
3. Gets right to the subject without unnecessary scaffolding.

---

*Carol Holstead, "The Benefits of No-Tech Note Taking," The Chronicle of Higher Education, March 4, 2015.

Here are some other approaches to creating a strong lead for a review:

- Begin with a common misconception about your subject and promise to challenge it.
- Begin with an anecdote that reveals what you like or dislike.
- Help readers realize the relevance of your subject by showing how it's used, what it says, or why it's needed in a familiar situation.
- Provide interesting background that your readers may not know.

Methods of Development. What are some ways to organize your review?

Narrative. If you're reviewing a performance or any other kind of experience that has a discrete beginning and end, then telling a story about what you saw, felt, and thought is a natural move. Another way to use narrative is to tell the story of your thinking about your subject—an approach that lends itself to a delayed-thesis essay, where your judgment comes late in the review.

Comparison/Contrast. Comparison with other items in the same category—say, other science fiction films, electric cars, or laptops—is a common and useful element in reviews. If comparison is especially important to your review, you might structure your essay around it.

Question to Answer. One of the most straightforward methods of structuring a review is to simply begin by raising the question *What makes _____ good?* This way, you make your criteria for evaluation explicit. From there, the next move is obvious: How well does the thing you're evaluating measure up?

Using Evidence. As you compose your draft, keep in mind that the most important evidence in a review is probably your own observations of the thing. These should be specific, and most likely they will draw on *primary research* you conducted by attending the concert, listening to the CD, or visiting the coffeehouse. As illustrated in Figure 4.2, thinking about your criteria can be a tool for finding strong evidence. You may also use evidence from secondary sources: For example, what did another critic say or observe?

Workshopping

When you workshop a review, you're sharing your evaluation of something your peers may have no experience with. Maybe they've never seen the movie, tried the coffee, visited the restaurant, or listened to the music. This has rhetorical implications you should consider as you prepare to discuss your draft:

1. *Context.* Do you provide enough background on the thing you're evaluating: what it is, how it works, why it's significant, what it does, etc.?
2. *Comparisons.* Even if none of your readers have, say, ridden the road bike you're reviewing, most have ridden a bicycle of some kind. Did you establish common ground with readers by exploiting any overlaps between their experience and your review topic?

3. *Definitions.* You can't assume that your peers are familiar with insider jargon. Did you define terms and explain features and so on that readers may not understand?

In workshopping the first draft of your review, your initial focus should be on what peers make of the purpose and meaning of your essay. Above all else, knowing what you're trying to do and say in an essay will help you decide what to cut and what to add in revision. It's the most powerful knowledge you can have for rewriting. This box can help you frame the questions for your workshop group.

Questions for Peer Reviewers	
1. Purpose	Why is this being reviewed? Who has a stake in whether it's good or not?
2. Meaning	In your own words, what exactly is my judgment? In your words, what are my main reasons for this judgment? Are they persuasive? Why or why not?

If you're reviewing something that your peers may be familiar with—and perhaps have strong feelings about—you might consider a workshop for your draft that encourages participants to debate your conclusions, both supporting your judgments and challenging them (see box).

Option for Review Essay Workshop

1. Divide each workshop group into two teams—believers and doubters.
2. Believers are responsible for presenting to doubters why the writer's review is convincing and fair.
3. Doubters challenge the writer's judgments and respond to the believers' claims.
4. The writer observes this conversation without participating.
5. After five minutes, believers and doubters drop their roles and discuss suggestions for revision with the writer.

Reflecting on the Draft. Immediately after your workshop session, fastwrite in your journal (paper or computer) on what you learned about writing an effective review *from reading your peers' drafts.* How might you apply these things to your revision?

Revising

Revision is a continual process—not a last step. You've been revising—"reseeing" your subject—from the first messy fastwriting in your journal. But the things that get your attention vary depending on where you are in the writing process. With your draft in hand, revision becomes your focus through what I'll call "shaping and tightening your draft."

4.5

Apply revision strategies that are effective for shaping reviews.

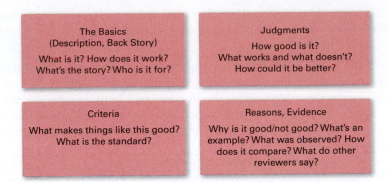

Shaping. You've clarified the purpose and meaning of the piece. Now you want to redesign it around both purpose and meaning.

Analyzing the Information. Shaping involves, among other things, arranging and rearranging information so that it is more effectively organized around your main idea. One way to think about the structure of your review is to look at its information in terms of the elements that reviews typically include:

By analyzing your draft in this way, you can look at whether you've included enough information for each element. While there's no formula for ordering this information, consider the structure of your draft rhetorically. If your audience is familiar with the item you're reviewing, then "the basics" need less emphasis; obviously, the opposite is true if your audience has little knowledge of the item. In either case, the basics are usually presented early in the draft. Similarly, audiences who are familiar with your topic (e.g., they've seen the movie or used the device) may already share your assumptions about your criteria. In that case, you can spend less time explaining them. Others who are unfamiliar with your topic need to learn the criteria you're using, so give them more emphasis. Judgments can appear anywhere in the draft, not just as a thesis in your first paragraph.

To imagine organizing strategies, you can try the "Frankenstein Draft" (Revision Strategy 11.18 in Chapter 11): Cut up your draft with scissors into the different elements mentioned here, and then play with the order. What seems to be most effective? Worry about transitions later.

Other Questions for Revision. Because a review's a form of argument, start by asking yourself, "Is my evaluation clear, and will it be persuasive to readers?" For example, here's a paragraph from Jesse's review of the film *Crank*:

> *Crank* (2006), written and directed by Mark Neveldin and Brian Taylor, is a fast-paced, dark, action comedy. This is not your typical "good guy saves the day" action film though. With a lot of profanity, wild antics and defiance of the law, it is very edgy. It really reminds me of a Grand Theft Auto Vice City. The star of the show even steals a cop's motorcycle and rides it around the city recklessly. But don't be quick to judge this film only by its novel gamer appeal. This movie also had good theatrical performances.

Jesse's evaluation is clear: The film *Crank* is good. And he explains why: strong performances and an "edgy" feel similar to that of the video game "Grand Theft Auto." One way to "resee" an evaluation is to plunge under its surface to see the criteria and assumptions underneath. Jesse works from an assumption that a film that has the feel and look of a familiar video game is a good film. But why? To make his evaluation more compelling to readers, when Jesse revises, he should probably explain that assumption.

Consider starting your rewrite by thinking about the criteria and assumptions behind the judgments you make. Which need to be explicitly addressed because an audience might not agree with them?

Polishing. Shaping focuses on things such as purpose, meaning, and overall design and structure. No less important is polishing—looking more closely at paragraphs, sentences, and words. Are your paragraphs coherent? How do you manage transitions? Are your sentences fluent and concise? Are there any errors in spelling or syntax? The section of Chapter 11 called "Problems with Clarity and Style" on page 388 can help you focus on these issues.

Before you finish your draft, work through the following checklist:

- ✓ Every paragraph is about one thing.
- ✓ The transitions between paragraphs aren't abrupt.
- ✓ The lengths of sentences vary in each paragraph.
- ✓ Each sentence is concise. There are no unnecessary words and phrases.
- ✓ You've checked grammar, particularly verb agreement, run-on sentences, unclear pronouns, and misused words (*there/their*, *where/were*, and so on).
- ✓ You've run your spellchecker and proofed your paper for misspelled words.

▶ Student Essay

Earlier in the chapter, you saw Laura Burns's sketch, a review of the Charlize Theron film *Young Adult*. Here you can see Laura's next draft. Her positive evaluation of the film is nicely captured by the title she chose and the punchy prose that follows it. Like a lot of reviews, "How Not to Feel Good and Feel Good About It" depends on a strong writing voice, and Laura's celebration of "unlikeable people making poor life choices from which they don't learn a thing" is easy to read, even if you don't agree with it. She's added images, too, which makes the essay easy on the eyes.

How to Not Feel Good and Feel Good About It
A Review of *Young Adult*

Laura Burns

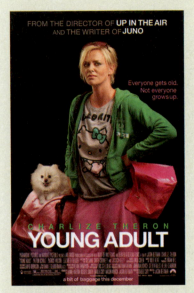

1   Charlize Theron is certainly one of the most beautiful women in film. High, smooth cheekbones, long, thin legs, and a delicate nose set at the center of a perfectly proportioned face. This considered, it's remarkable how ugly she can get.

2   *Young Adult* is a movie about unlikeable people making poor life choices from which they don't learn a thing. Theron plays Mavis Gary, an ex-prom queen from Mercury, Minnesota, making her living in the "Miniapple" (as the Mercurians call Minneapolis) as the ghostwriter of a formerly popular teen book series. From the first sequence of the film, we can tell that Mavis is a mess. She gets wasted, slumps around her apartment in sweats, and guzzles Diet Coke in a way that almost gave me heartburn. Upon receiving a birth announcement email from her now-married ex-prom king beau, the aptly named Buddy (the similarly beautiful Patrick Wilson), Mavis decides to pop an old mix tape into her dirty Mini Cooper and go home to Mercury to win him back.

3   This is, essentially, the entire plot of *Young Adult*. Mavis' trip back to Mercury is a kind of *anti-hero's* journey. On her first night in town, getting wasted in a local dive, she meets her guide, Matt (the wonderful Patton Oswalt), a former classmate who remains crippled from a high school assault by jocks who mistakenly thought he was gay. Through the course of the film, as she reunites with her parents (Jill Eikenberry & Richard Bekins), insinuates herself into the lives of Buddy and his wife Beth (Elizabeth Reaser), and gets plastered on Matt's home-brewed bourbon, rather than moving towards revelation, Mavis seems to retreat further and further into her past.

4   Unlike writer Diablo Cody's most well-known and Oscar-winning screenplay *Juno, Young Adult* rejects preciousness in favor of obscenity. It's difficult to make a film about terrible people enjoyable, but Cody injects just enough silliness to keep us from feeling too badly. Director Jason Reitman (who also paired with Cody on *Juno*) wisely keeps us focused on Mavis through every moment, from the night out to the morning after, and both Theron and Oswalt are brave enough to let us into their characters' grimy inner selves. Smartly, Cody refuses to manufacture empathy for her characters, leaving us to boldly accept the ugliness of these people fully.

I don't doubt that *Young Adult* will displease many movie-goers who are used to redemptive stories and characters who, as *Salon* put it are "good at heart." Cody refuses to indulge that expectation. When Mavis dresses to go out and drink (which is often), Theron's extraordinary physical beauty is obvious. Yet we're never allowed to shake that Mavis is truly ugly at her core—an effective subversion of expectation that is the reason this memorable performance works. This isn't a feel-good film, and thank goodness. If Cody and Reitman had tried, I think we might leave the theater feeling worse.

5

Young Adult is writer Diablo Cody's most mature work yet.

Evaluating the Essay

1. As I've already mentioned, reviews often thrive on the persona—and the voice—of the reviewer. I think Laura has a strong persona in this review. The question is, how is persona communicated in a piece such as this one? What exactly would you point to in her review that reflects an individual voice and character?

2. Describe the structure of Laura's review. Diagram it using the elements of a review: description, back story, judgment, reasons, evidence, and criteria.

Using What You Have Learned

Let's revisit the list from the beginning of this chapter of things I hoped you'd learn about this form of writing.

1. **Use reasons and evidence to support a judgment about something's value.** Of course, it's not news that judgments are supported by reasons and evidence, but now you can think about these things more systematically and, as a result, have tools to analyze not only your own arguments but the arguments of others.

2. **Identify the criteria behind a judgment and determine their relevance.** Knowing to look for assumptions will give you a strong footing when analyzing any argument.

3. **Identify the characteristics of different forms of the review, including academic applications.** Reviews are a method of evaluating virtually anything. Whenever you are asked to evaluate something you can apply the skills you practiced here.

4. **Use invention and focusing strategies to discover and develop a review essay.** In this chapter, you practiced a skill you can apply in nearly any paper you write: how to see your topic *in context*, recognizing its place in an ever-larger scheme of things.

5. **Apply revision strategies that are effective for shaping reviews.** Using a wider range of evidence, requires you to cast a wider net for information as you revise. This is a skill that you'll build on in the next assignments, as you write more and use more outside sources.

5

Writing a Proposal

Learning Objectives

In this chapter, you'll learn to

5.1 Describe a problem of consequence, framing it narrowly enough to explore convincing solutions.

5.2 Identify the wide range of rhetorical situations that might call for a proposal argument.

5.3 Argue effectively for both the seriousness of the problem and the proposed solutions, using strong evidence.

5.4 Use appropriate invention strategies to discover and develop a proposal topic.

5.5 Apply revision strategies that are effective for a proposal.

Writing About Problems and Solutions

Several students sit around the table in my office. We're talking about problems each of us would love to solve. "I've got a short story due at three this afternoon and I've only written three pages," says Lana. Everyone nods sympathetically. "I'd really like to feel better about work," confides Amy, who works as a chef at a local restaurant. "Most days I just don't want to go." Margaret is a history major, familiar with the making and unmaking of nations and other grand narratives of colonialism, war, and social change. Her problem, however, is a bit more local. "I can't get my boyfriend to clean up the apartment," she says.

"What about you?" they ask me.

"The problem I most want to solve today is how to avoid getting scalded in the shower when someone in my house flushes the toilet," I say, getting into the spirit of things.

This conversation had not gone quite the way I expected. I know these students are socially engaged, politically aware, and academically gifted people. When I asked about problems that need solutions, I expected that they might mention local issues such as housing developments that threaten the foothills, the difficulty that nontraditional students have adjusting to the university, or budget cuts that threaten the availability of courses next semester. If they had been thinking on a larger scale—say, nationally or even internationally—perhaps the conversation would have turned to the federal deficit or the conflict in Darfur. Of course, I hadn't asked them to suggest social or economic problems. I had simply asked them what problems most vexed them at the moment.

I should not have been surprised that these problems involved boredom with work, too little time, and a messy boyfriend. These problems are quite real, and they demand attention, *now*. One was easy to solve. Lana would carve out extra time in the afternoon to finish her story—"I already know what I need to do," she said. But Amy and Margaret saw their respective problems—disenchantment with work and a boyfriend who's a slob—not so much as problems to solve as realities they had to live with. In fact, all the students admitted that they rarely look at the world from the perspective of problem solving—the perspective that's at the heart of a proposal.

"What if you did?" I asked.

"Then I guess I'd ask myself if there was an opportunity to learn something," said Amy.

Problems of Consequence

5.1
Describe a problem of consequence, framing it narrowly enough to explore convincing solutions.

While not all problems are equally solvable, the process of seeking and proposing solutions can be rewarding if you see, as Amy did, the opportunity to learn. There's another motivation, too: If the problem is shared by others, whatever you discover may interest them. Part of the challenge is recognizing problems *of consequence*. What makes a problem consequential?

1. It potentially affects a number of people.
2. There may be multiple solutions and people disagree about which is best.

My problem with getting scalded in the shower if somebody flushes a toilet is clearly not consequential; all I need to do is go to Ace Hardware and buy a device for the showerhead. But what about Margaret's problem with her boyfriend? Is that a problem of consequence? Undoubtedly there are lots of people with messy mates, the solution is not at all obvious (just ask Margaret), and there are likely multiple ways of dealing with the problem.

While not all problems are equally solvable, the process of seeking and proposing solutions can be rewarding if you see it as an opportunity to learn.

If a problem is consequential, it's likely that someone has said something about it. Like many other forms of inquiry, problem solving usually requires some research. An important consideration, then, is whether others have said something about the problem that might help us think about the best ways to solve it. On a quick search of the web and several library databases, Margaret found some material that she thought could serve as background for an essay that looks at the problem of a messy mate and proposes some solutions. While Margaret may not succeed in getting her boyfriend to pick up his socks, she will probably learn a few things about how to deal with the problem.

Problems of Manageable Scale

You can't write about solving the problem of radical Islam in five pages. But you probably can write about the potential of reconciliation projects between Sunni and Shiite Muslims in Iraq. Basically, you can't write in five or even twenty pages about how to solve a big problem—there's just too much territory to cover—so an early step in this process is to keep shaving away at your topic until it's a manageable size. You might start by thinking about your topic this way:

- Who's involved? Who are the key actors?
- Why is this a problem? What are some of the causes?
- Where is this a problem? Are there specific places that dramatize either the problem or the solution?
- What are some of the solutions people have already proposed?

Use each of these questions on a subject as you might use a knife to carve a block of wood. The shavings offer potentially workable *pieces* of a larger problem that you can write about. For example, you might localize the problem, or focus on just one of the key actors or proposed solutions.

In other words, when you are choosing a problem to explore in a proposal, the *manageable scale* of the problem is as important as its consequentiality.

Motives for Writing a Proposal

Quite simply, people write proposals to try to argue convincingly to others that a problem is worth tackling and a proposed solution is a good way to tackle it. Your motives for writing a proposal will probably include the following:

- *You care about the problem.* Whether it's something in your personal life (avoiding procrastination, having a more obedient dog, or finding a way to use less water in the garden) or a public issue (protecting bicyclists from traffic, increasing neighborhood police protection, or battling adolescent obesity), you should feel that the problem deserves your attention.

■ *You hope to change something.* Writing a proposal is a way of overcoming powerlessness. Maybe you feel helpless about the daily deluge of scammers and junk messages in your e-mail. You can just complain about it. I do. But you can also research a proposal that might help you—and the many others affected by the problem—to avoid the Nigerian scammers who want to "give" you $8.5 million if you just send them a copy of your passport and $1,750.

■ *You hope to learn something.* A proposal is like all other inquiry projects: You choose a topic because you're motivated to discover things you don't know. This motive alone isn't sufficient, of course. Others must be affected by the problem and have a stake in considering your solution. But if the problem is sufficiently complex and the solutions varied enough, then you stand to learn a lot.

> **Writing a proposal is a way of overcoming powerlessness.**

The Proposal and Academic Writing

Numerous academic situations call for proposal writing and, more generally, writing to solve problems. Here are some such situations you might come across in classes you take:

■ The case-study approach, popular in business, medicine, and some social sciences, is essentially the presentation of a real-world problem for you to solve.

■ Problem-based learning is an approach to inquiry common in the sciences that begins with a messy problem and involves learners in coming up with tentative solutions.

■ In some classes, you'll be asked to write proposals. For example, political science courses may include an assignment to write a policy proposal or an essay that looks at a specific public policy problem—say, the organization of the city government or the state's role in wolf management (a big issue here in Idaho)—and suggests some possible solutions. In a marketing class, you might be asked to draft a proposal for dealing with a particular management problem.

> **5.2**
> Identify the wide range of rhetorical situations that might call for a proposal argument.

Academics in many disciplines write research proposals. These identify a question and then propose a plan for studying it (see "Inquiring into the Details: Writing a Research Proposal"). The research question may relate to a problem (air pollution inversions in the valley, energy inefficiencies in buildings, and so on) or simply to a topic that could be useful to study (use of iPads in the classroom or the effects of birth order). To get grants for their research, academics usually need to submit proposals.

Inquiring into the Details

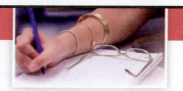

Writing a Research Proposal

A research proposal is a kind of action plan that explains your research question, what you expect might be the answer, how your investigation will contribute to what has already been said on the topic, and how you will proceed.

While the format varies, most research proposals aim to persuade readers that (1) the project is reasonable given the investigator's time and resources, (2) the research question or problem is significant, and (3) the researcher has a good plan for getting the job done.

The following elements are typically included in a research proposal:

- *Title:* Short and descriptive.
- *Abstract:* A brief statement of what you intend to do, including your research question and hypothesis, if you've got one.
- *Background or context:* Why is the project worth doing? What problem does it solve, or how does it advance our understanding of the subject? This key section establishes where your question fits into the ongoing conversation about your topic in your class, in the academic literature, or both. You also want to demonstrate that you've done your homework—you've got a handle on the relevant literature on your topic and understand how you might build on it.
- *Methodology or research design:* How will you try to answer your research question? How will you limit your focus? What information will you need to gather, and how will you gather it?
- *Results:* This isn't a common section of proposals in the humanities, but it certainly is in the sciences. How will you analyze the data you collect?
- *References or works cited:* Almost all research proposals, because they review relevant literature, include a bibliography. Sometimes you may be asked to annotate it.

Because the research proposal is a persuasive document, craft it to keep your reader engaged: Find a good balance between generalities and detail, avoid jargon, and demonstrate your curiosity and eagerness to pursue your question.

Features of the Form

Feature	Conventions of the Proposal
Inquiry questions	What is the problem? What should be done?
Motives	You hope to change a problem related to something that matters to you and others, and there is the potential that you will learn something about the problem and possible solutions.

(continued)

Feature	Conventions of the Proposal
Subject matter	Proposals suggest a best plan of action on any problem of consequence. Proposals could address large problems (the homeless problem in town) or small ones (a boyfriend who doesn't take dirty dishes seriously), as long as others have a stake in solving the problem. Research proposals suggest a plan for studying a problem or other issue.
Structure	Proposals typically address both the problem and the solution, in that order, but may emphasize one or the other. When an audience largely agrees that the problem is significant, a proposal might focus on the solution. When there is disagreement about the significance of the problem, a proposal might focus on why the problem needs attention. Other elements of a proposal include: • *Causes and effects.* These can help establish why the problem needs attention and why the proposed solution will deal with the problem. • *Justifications.* Typically proposals that argue for certain solutions over others offer clear reasons why the proposed solutions are the best ones. • *Evidence.* Evidence from research and experience makes a case for the problem and for the solutions. • *Other perspectives.* If you're writing about a problem of consequence, then other people have said something about it and probably have proposed various solutions. • *Visual rhetoric.* Often, problems and/or solutions can be illustrated with pictures, tables, and graphs; headings and bulleted lists can also be useful.
Sources of information	Writers who have experience with a problem should tap that experience in a proposal. However, if they're not experts, then personal experience alone may not be persuasive evidence. Proposals usually depend on information from research—reading or interviews—on what people who *are* experts on the problem say about it.
Language	Proposals are a form of argument. As with other arguments, the language you use depends largely on the rhetorical situation. Formal proposals intended for an expert audience, such as research or marketing proposals, take a formal tone. Others—for example, a proposal that's a letter to the editor or a blog entry—are much more casual and even personal.

Prose+

The nonprofit group Bluewater Baltimore, formed to prevent pollution in the city's watershed, adopts a "holistic" solution to the problem, one that combines local activism, stream monitoring, and advocacy. That's a pretty abstract idea, until it's captured in a "How We Work" graphic, which you can see below. One way to read this image is as a story, something that seems especially relevant to proposals, since like proposals narrative is about causes and effects. Try analyzing the image as a story: What is the significant event? Who are the characters? How is the rising action and resolution visually represented? How is the image organized in relation to time?

Courtesy of Blue Water Baltimore. WWW.BLUEWATERBALTIMORE.COM.

READINGS

▶ Proposal 1

I teach at a university with a football team that is frequently ranked in the top twenty-five nationally. Our stadium's blue turf is more famous than any one of our academic programs, prompting the university's marketing folks to coin the slogan "Beyond the Blue." In other words, we just want you to know that there is actually teaching and research going on here, not just football. And yet, the games are fun, and the athletic program is the strongest link the university has to the community. The sale of sports paraphernalia—hats, t-shirts, bobble-heads, and dog collars emblazoned with the school colors—funds student scholarships. Is college football really a problem? Buzz Bissinger thinks so. He notes that these are often hugely expensive programs that hemorrhage money in a time of endless tuition hikes. The solution: Ban college football.

Why College Football Should Be Banned

Buzz Bissinger

1   In more than 20 years I've spent studying the issue, I have yet to hear a convincing argument that college football has anything do with what is presumably the primary purpose of higher education: academics.

2   That's because college football has no academic purpose. Which is why it needs to be banned. A radical solution, yes. But necessary in today's times.

3   Football only provides the thickest layer of distraction in an atmosphere in which colleges and universities these days are all about distraction, nursing an obsession with the social well-being of students as opposed to the obsession that they are there for the vital and single purpose of learning as much as they can to compete in the brutal realities of the global economy.

4   Who truly benefits from college football? Alumni who absurdly judge the quality of their alma mater based on the quality of the football team. Coaches such as Nick Saban of the University of Alabama and Bob Stoops of the University of Oklahoma who make obscene millions. The players themselves don't benefit, exploited by a system in which they don't receive a dime of compensation. The average student doesn't benefit, particularly when football programs remain sacrosanct while tuition costs show no signs of abating as many governors are slashing budgets to the bone.

5   If the vast majority of major college football programs made money, the argument to ban football might be a more precarious one. But too many of them don't—to the detriment of academic budgets at all too many schools. According to the NCAA, 43 percent of the 120 schools in the Football Bowl Subdivision lost money on their

programs. This is the tier of schools that includes such examples as that great titan of football excellence, the University of Alabama at Birmingham Blazers, who went 3-and-9 last season. The athletic department in 2008–2009 took in over $13 million in university funds and student fees, largely because the football program cost so much, **The Wall Street Journal** reported. New Mexico State University's athletic department needed a 70% subsidy in 2009–2010, largely because Aggie football hasn't gotten to a bowl game in 51 years. Outside of Las Cruces, where New Mexico State is located, how many people even know that the school has a football program? None, except maybe for some savvy contestants on "Jeopardy." What purpose does it serve on a university campus? None.

The most recent example is the University of Maryland. The president there, Wallace D. Loh, late last year announced that eight varsity programs would be cut in order to produce a leaner athletic budget, a kindly way of saying that the school would rather save struggling football and basketball programs than keep varsity sports such as track and swimming, in which the vast majority of participants graduate. 6

Part of the Maryland football problem: a $50.8 million modernization of its stadium in which too many luxury suites remain unsold. Another problem: The school reportedly paid $2 million to buy out head coach Ralph Friedgen at the end of the 2010 season, even though he led his team to a 9-and-4 season and was named Atlantic Coast Conference Coach of the Year. Then, the school reportedly spent another $2 million to hire Randy Edsall from the University of Connecticut, who promptly produced a record of 2-and-10 last season. 7

In an interview with the **Baltimore Sun** in March, Mr. Loh said that the athletic department was covering deficits, in large part caused by attendance drops in football and basketball, by drawing upon reserves that eventually dwindled to zero. Hence cutting the eight sports. 8

This is just the tip of the iceberg. There are the medical dangers of football in general caused by head trauma over repetitive hits. There is the false concept of the football student-athlete that the NCAA endlessly tries to sell, when any major college player will tell you that the demands of the game, a year-round commitment, makes the student half of the equation secondary and superfluous. There are the scandals that have beset programs in the desperate pursuit of winning—the University of Southern California, Ohio State University, University of Miami, and Penn State University among others. 9

I can't help but wonder how a student at the University of Oregon will cope when in-state tuition has recently gone up by 9% and the state legislature passed an 11% decrease in funding to the Oregon system overall for 2011 and 2012. Yet thanks to the largess of Nike founder Phil Knight, an academic center costing $41.7 million, twice as expensive in square footage as the toniest condos in Portland, has been built for the University of Oregon football team. 10

Always important to feed those Ducks. 11

(continued)

(*continued*)

12   I actually like football a great deal. I am not some anti-sports prude. It has a place in our society, but not on college campuses. If you want to establish a minor league system that the National Football League pays for—which they should, given that they are the greatest beneficiaries of college football—that is fine.

13   Call me the Grinch. But I would much prefer students going to college to learn and be prepared for the rigors of the new economic order, rather than dumping fees on them to subsidize football programs that, far from enhancing the academic mission instead make a mockery of it.

Inquiring into the Essay

1. **Explore.** Here's a sampling of assertions from Bissinger's essay:

    - "College football has no academic purpose."
    - The beneficiaries of college football aren't the students, the athletes, or the school but coaches who pull in salaries in the millions.
    - The vast sums invested in coaches, stadiums, and training facilities often end up being a drain on universities' budgets. This is especially objectionable in an age of tuition increases.

    Choose one of these assertions (or another from the essay you'd like to write about) and fastwrite for five minutes, exploring your own thinking about the claim. If you can, write about what you observe on your own campus.

2. **Explain.** Follow up on your fastwrite in the last step by composing a summary of your own thinking about Bissinger's proposal to ban college football.

3. **Evaluate.** One of Bissinger's key claims is that college football programs often lose big money, and as evidence he cites the NCAA, which reported that 43 percent of the schools in the Football Bowl Subdivision were in the red. Using your own research, evaluate that claim.

4. **Reflect.** A proposal is an argument: There is a problem, here are some solutions, and this is evidence that makes these solutions credible. It's never that simple, of course. For one thing, you have to secure audience agreement that there is a problem in the first place, and if your audience agrees, then there are many possible solutions. Why yours? Finally, some evidence is better than other evidence, and there is the issue of what you *don't* say. Is there a counterargument? Is there inconvenient evidence you ignore? With all this in mind, how would you evaluate Bissinger's proposal that college football should be banned?

▶ Proposal 2

Okay, so this isn't the most scintillating reading, but the topic is certainly relevant to anyone in college, and it's a useful model of the basic elements of many proposals. The problem, of course, is obvious to anyone who has hung around young people clutching red plastic cups: the epidemic of alcohol abuse on college campuses. What might be done? The National Institute on Alcohol Abuse and Alcoholism, drawing on a range of studies, offers a series of recommendations, but first, the author establishes the significance of the problem with a bulleted list of fairly startling facts about college drinking. The recommendations follow, listed in order of relevance to the problem *and* strength of the support from various studies. When writing a proposal, it's easy to think that you're charged with coming up with the *one* best solution. This proposal takes another approach, offering a range of recommendations, but grading each in terms of its potential effectiveness.

Preventing Alcohol-Related Problems on College Campuses—Summary of the Final Report of the NIAAA Task Force on College Drinking

Robert F. Saltz, Ph.D.

College administrators and their prevention staff face numerous challenges when attempting to reduce the prevalence and severity of alcohol consumption and alcohol-related harm on their campuses. For example, drinking, and particularly binge drinking have been shown to be pervasive and persistent behaviors among college students (Wechsler et al. 2000). In addition, until a few years ago research assessing the effectiveness of various prevention approaches in the college setting was scarce, making it difficult to identify effective measures. In recent years, however, several studies have looked more closely at approaches to preventing college drinking. For example, Dowdall and Wechsler (2002), Borsari and Carey (2001), Perkins (2002*a*), and Berkowitz (2004) reviewed or analyzed prevention approaches among college populations. Another important contribution was the final report from the National Institute on Alcohol Abuse and Alcoholism (NIAAA) Task Force on College Drinking (NIAAA 2002), which reviewed epidemiological and intervention research on college drinking and issued recommendations for prevention strategies. This article describes the motivation for focusing on college student drinking and summarizes the Task Force's findings and recommendations.

Why Target College Student Drinking?

Given the all-too-common reports in the press of occasional tragic deaths and of mass celebrations or riots among college students that are accompanied by alcohol consumption, the answer to this question may seem obvious. But these singular events do

(continued)

(continued)

not accurately reflect the actual prevalence of death and injury associated with alcohol use among college students. Based on epidemiological data from a variety of sources, Hingson and colleagues (2002) generated the following estimates of the consequences of college student drinking:

- More than 1,400 college students die annually in alcohol-related events, primarily traffic crashes.
- More than 2 million college students (of a total of 8 million) occasionally drive under the influence of alcohol, and more than 3 million students ride with a drinking driver.
- More than 500,000 students annually suffer unintentional injury under the influence of alcohol.
- More than 600,000 students annually are hit or assaulted by another student who has been drinking.

3   In addition to these acute consequences of drinking, evidence suggests that alcohol consumption can lead to longer term cognitive impairment (Spear 2002; White 2003).

4   The college environment itself (specifically, such factors as peer influence and alcohol availability) may contribute to college students' risk of alcohol-related harm. O'Malley and Johnston (2002) found that although college-bound high school students drink less than their peers, their alcohol consumption surpasses that of their noncollege peers during the college years, only to decrease again after they finish college. In light of these observations, drinking among college students deserves special attention.

The NIAAA Task Force on College Drinking

5   The NIAAA Task Force on College Drinking commissioned several review papers on various aspects of drinking among college students (e.g., drinking patterns and consequences of alcohol consumption). (These reviews are available at www.collegedrinkingprevention.gov.) With respect to prevention research, however, the Task Force found that studies evaluating prevention approaches focused mostly on interventions aimed at individual student drinkers rather than on interventions aimed at entire college populations (i.e., universal interventions).

6   The Task Force's findings regarding the efficacy of individual-level interventions have been reviewed and summarized by Larimer and Cronce (2002), who distinguish between educational or awareness programs, cognitive-behavioral interventions, and motivational enhancement techniques. With one or two exceptions, this review found little evidence to support the effectiveness of purely educational or awareness programs. Newer approaches combining provision of information with other components, such as motivational enhancement, await evaluation and may be found to be more successful.

7   Cognitive-behavioral skills training programs attempt to teach skills relevant to moderating alcohol consumption, including those specific to drinking (e.g., monitor-

ing one's consumption or gauging one's blood alcohol levels) and more general life skills, such as stress management. These programs also can include components such as clarification of values, information, and/or education.

One cognitive-behavioral approach focuses on identifying students' expectancies regarding alcohol's effects, because studies have shown that a substantial portion of alcohol's effects is attributable to such expectancies rather than to alcohol's physiological effects.[*] Research indicates that focusing on expectancies impacts the drinking behavior of students, particularly males.   8

Larimer and Cronce (2002) concluded that the most promising interventions incorporate several components, such as training in drinking skills and life skills, self-monitoring, and challenges to students' expectancies.   9

Brief interventions—which include alcohol information, skills training, and personalized, nonjudgmental feedback to enhance motivation to change—can be effective in both individual and group formats.   10

NIAAA Task Force Recommendations

The NIAAA Task Force summarized its findings and recommendations in a comprehensive report (NIAAA 2002). At the time the report was written, the interventions described above represented nearly all that had been rigorously evaluated with college students. However, the Task Force expanded the scope of the recommendations by including universal prevention efforts that had been evaluated in other community settings and could reasonably be extended to college settings as well as those already adopted by some colleges without being formally tested. The recommendations were organized in four "tiers" based on both the interventions' relevance to college student drinking and the degree to which they are supported by empirical evidence. Although this classification is not universally accepted and may have to be modified in response to more recent research, it can help college administrators and researchers to choose the most promising approaches.   11

Tier 1   Based on the findings described in the previous section, the Tier 1 category included strategies that show evidence of effectiveness with college students, including: 12

- Combinations of cognitive-behavioral skills training with norms clarification and motivational enhancement interventions.
- Brief motivational enhancement interventions.
- Interventions challenging alcohol expectancies.

---

[*] "Alcohol expectancies" is a term often used in scholarship focused on problem drinking. It essentially means the set of beliefs someone has about alcohol's effects. For example, drinkers with social anxiety might believe that drinking with people will make it easier to be around them.

(continued)

(*continued*)

13   *Tier 2*   This category includes strategies that research shows have been successful with general populations and could be applied to college settings, including efforts either to restrict the availability of alcohol or to create an environment supportive of such restrictions. These universal strategies are critical because alcohol-related harm to society can be attributed not only to the heaviest drinkers but also to the large numbers of light and moderate drinkers (Gruenewald et al. 2003). Tier 2 strategies could include approaches involving minimal legal drinking age (MLDA) laws (e.g., increased enforcement of MLDA laws) and other alcohol-related criminal and administrative measures such as:

- Implementation, increased publicity, and enforcement of laws to prevent alcohol-impaired driving.
- Restrictions on alcohol retail outlet density.
- Increased prices and excise taxes on alcoholic beverages.
- Responsible beverage service policies in social and commercial settings.
- Campus and community coalitions of all major stakeholders to implement these strategies effectively.

14   The Tier 2 interventions have not been evaluated on college campuses, at least in part because such measures are challenging to implement and studies are difficult to design. Efficacious community-level prevention interventions, such as the Massachusetts Saving Lives program (Hingson et al. 1996), Communities Mobilizing for Change on Alcohol (Wagenaar et al. 2000), and the Community Trials Project (Holder et al. 2000), however, can guide future college-based efforts.

15   *Tier 3*   Tier 3 consists of strategies with logical and theoretical promise that require more comprehensive evaluation. These strategies could prove effective in future studies, and some already are highly regarded by prevention program professionals and college administrators. The Task Force Report suggested the following Tier 3 strategies:

- Marketing campaigns to correct student misperceptions of peer alcohol use, sometimes called "social norms marketing" or normative education (see Perkins 2002*b*). (This strategy already is widely used; evaluation reports will be available in the near future.)
- Consistent enforcement of campus alcohol policies.
- Provision of safe rides for students who drink too much to drive.
- Regulation of happy hour promotions.
- Information for new students and their parents about alcohol use and campus policies.
- Other strategies to address high-risk drinking, such as offering alcohol-free residence halls and social activities or scheduling classes on Fridays to reduce Thursday night parties.

16   *Tier 4*   Tier 4 strategies include those with "evidence of ineffectiveness," such as simple educational or awareness programs used alone, without any other strategies or

components. The Task Force warned against the use of breathalyzers to give students information about their level of impairment, because this approach has produced negative results (i.e., students have used the information as a challenge to reach higher levels of intoxication).

Future Research and Applications

Although the NIAAA Task Force and others have identified some strategies to prevent college drinking, more research and evaluation are needed to identify more effective approaches for college administrators to add to their repertoire. Additional research needs to focus on how to implement successful universal campus or community interventions. Although researchers have achieved some successes in implementation (at least, judging from the positive examples of Tier 2 strategies), many of these interventions have not been subject to systematic research. Few researchers are developing measures of organizational or community "readiness" based on an underlying theory or hypothesis about what facilitates implementation (see Oetting et al. 1995). Nevertheless, developing general models of organizational or community change that are applicable to alcohol prevention is critically important to the design of reliable strategies that will keep college students safe from harm.

17

References

Berkowitz, A.D. *The Social Norms Approach: Theory, Research, and Annotated Bibliography*. Department of Education, Higher Education Center for Alcohol and Other Drug Abuse and Violence Prevention, 2004. Available online at: www.edc.org/hec/socialnorms/theory.html.

Borsari, B., and Carey, K. Peer influences on college drinking: A review of the research. *Journal of Substance Abuse* 13:391–424, 2001. PMID: 11775073

Dowdall, G.W., and Wechsler, H. Studying college alcohol use: Widening the lens, sharpening the focus. *Journal of Studies on Alcohol* (Suppl. 14):14–22, 2002. PMID: 12022719

Gruenewald, P.J.; Johnson, F.W.; Light, J.M.; et al. Understanding college drinking: Assessing dose response from survey self-reports. *Journal of Studies on Alcohol* 64:500–514, 2003. PMID: 12921192

Hingson, R.; McGovern, T.; Howland, J.; et al. Reducing alcohol-impaired driving in Massachusetts: The Saving Lives Program. *American Journal of Public Health* 86:791–797, 1996. PMID: 8659651

Hingson, R.; Heeren, T.; Zakocs, R.; et al. Magnitude of alcohol-related morbidity, mortality, and alcohol dependence among U.S. college students age 18–24. *Journal of Studies on Alcohol* 63:136–144, 2002. PMID: 12033690

Holder, H.D.; Gruenewald, P.J.; Ponicki, W.R.; et al. Effect of community-based interventions on high-risk drinking and alcohol-related injuries. *JAMA: Journal of the American Medical Association* 284:2341–2347, 2000. PMID: 11066184

(continued)

(*continued*)

Harimer, M., and Cronce, J. Identification, prevention and treatment: A review of individual-focused strategies to reduce problematic alcohol consumption by college students. *Journal of Studies on Alcohol* (Suppl. 14):148–163, 2002. PMID: 12022721

National Institute on Alcohol Abuse and Alcoholism (NIAAA). *A Call to Action: Changing the Culture of Drinking at U.S. Colleges. Final Report of the Task Force on College Drinking*. NIH Pub. No. 02–5010. Rockville, MD: NIAAA, 2002.

O'Malley, P.M., and Johnston, L.D. Epidemiology of alcohol and other drug use among American college students. *Journal of Studies on Alcohol* (Suppl. 14):S23–S39, 2002. PMID: 12022728

Oetting, E.R.; Donnermeyer, J.F.; Plested, B.A.; et al. Assessing community readiness for prevention. *International Journal of the Addictions* 30:659–683, 1995. PMID: 7657396

Perkins, H.W. Surveying the damage: A review of research on consequences of alcohol misuse in college populations. *Journal of Studies on Alcohol* (Suppl. 14):91–100, 2002*a*. PMID: 12022733

Perkins, H.W. Social norms and the prevention of alcohol misuse in collegiate contexts. *Journal of Studies on Alcohol* (Suppl. 14):164–172, 2002*b*.PMID: 12022722

Spear, L.P. Adolescent brain and the college drinker: Biological basis of propensity to use and misuse alcohol. *Journal of Studies on Alcohol* (Suppl. 14):71–81, 2002. PMID: 12022731

Wagenaar, A.C.; Murray, D.M.; Gehan, J.P.; et al. Communities Mobilizing for Change on Alcohol: Outcomes from a randomized community trial. *Journal of Studies on Alcohol* 61:85–94, 2000. PMID: 10627101

Wechsler, H.; Lee, J.E.; Kuo, M.; and Lee, H. College binge drinking in the 1990s: A continuing problem. Results of the Harvard School of Public Health 1999 College Alcohol Study. *Journal of American College Health* 48:199–210, 2000. PMID: 10778020

White, A. Substance use and adolescent brain development: An overview of recent findings with a focus on alcohol. *Youth Studies Australia* 22:39–45, 2003.

Inquiring into the Essay

1. **Explore.** You've been on campus long enough to know that college students drink, and some drink excessively. Fastwrite about what you've seen, heard, or experienced, perhaps starting with one of your first encounters with the drinking scene at your school. Do you think this is an issue, and if so, what do you think should be done about it?

2. **Explain.** What is your takeaway from reading this report? Summarize what you believe to be the central argument. When doing so, try to use some of terms from the article, explaining them in a way that a nonexpert would understand them.

3. **Evaluate.** The report claims that "educational or awareness programs" directed at students have little effect on alcohol abuse. Do you agree or disagree? Why? Which of the recommendations here make the most sense to you?

4. **Reflect.** Like a lot of academic writing, this article uses terms that insiders in the area of scholarship wouldn't need defined: "alcohol expectancies" and "cognitive-behavioral approaches." The rest of us, who aren't experts, can feel befuddled when reading writing like this. Certainly you have had the experience of reading in a genre, like this one, that is unfamiliar to you, in a discourse that makes you feel like an outsider. How do you deal with this, especially when you need to read and try to understand it? What are your reading strategies?

Seeing the Form

A Problem in Pictures

When members of the San Francisco Bicycle Coalition (SFBC) wanted to dramatize the problem of insufficient space for bikes on a city commuter train, they did it with pictures. It was a powerfully simple idea. They took shots of three morning trains, each overloaded with bicycles and nearly empty of passengers. The contrast is obvious. And so is the solution to the problem: Add more space for bicycles on trains. A few months later, transit authorities did just that.

No Space for Bikes:
A photo study of trains bumping cyclists out of SF.

1: Train 134: Sept 22 9:07 AM

2: Train 134: Sept 22 9:07 AM

Seeing the Form (*continued*)

3: Train 230: Sept 24 8:53 AM

4: Train 230: Sept 24 8:53 AM

5: Train 332: Sept 30 8:56 AM

6: Train 332: Sept 30 8:56 AM

Submitted to JBP Oct 2
by Benjamin Damm

THE WRITING PROCESS

5.3
Argue effectively for both the seriousness of the problem and the proposed solutions, using strong evidence.

Inquiry Project   Writing a Proposal

Inquiry questions: What is the problem? What should be done?

Write a proposal to help resolve a problem that you care about. Make sure your proposal does the following (see also the "Features of the Form" box on pp. 131–132 for typical features of proposals):

- Addresses a problem that is of consequence and of a manageable scale, including the problem's causes and effects.
- Provides evidence for the seriousness of the problem and for ways to solve it, justifying these solutions over alternative solutions. You can draw on your experience but should also use outside sources.
- Is appropriate in both form and content to your purpose and audience.
- Includes graphics if relevant.

What Are You Going to Write About?

Perhaps you already have a topic in mind for your proposal. But if you don't, or you want to explore some other possibilities, begin by generating a list of problems you'd like to solve. Don't worry too much about whether they're problems of consequence or about whether you have solutions to the problems. Try some of the generating exercises that follow.

The explosion of "how-to" and "self-help" books and articles is evidence of the popularity of writing that attempts to solve problems.

Opening Up

Play with some ideas about subjects for the proposal assignment. Remember not to judge the material at this stage.

5.4
Use appropriate invention strategies to discover and develop a proposal topic.

Listing Prompts. Lists can be rich sources of triggering topics. Let them grow freely, and when you're ready, use a list item as the focus of another list or an episode of fastwriting.

Open a Word document and make the following table (or jot down these headings in your journal). At the risk of totally ruining your day, brainstorm four lists of problems that you think need to be solved in four arenas: international, national, local, and personal. Jot down anything that comes to mind.

World problems
National problems
Local problems
Personal problems

Fastwriting Prompts. Write fast without stopping, and don't think too much about what you're going to say before you say it. Allow yourself to write "badly."

1. Pick any item from the preceding lists as a launching place for a five-minute fastwrite. Explore some of the following questions:

   - When did I first notice that this is a problem? What, if any, is my experience with it?
   - What's the worst part about it?
   - What might be some of its causes?
   - What moment, situation, or scene is most typical of this problem? Describe it as if you're experiencing it by writing in the present tense.
   - How does this problem make me feel?
   - What people do I associate with it?

2. Depending on how familiar you are with a problem that interests you, do a five-minute focused fastwrite that explores solutions, beginning with the sentence I think one of the ways to deal with _____ is _____. Follow that sentence as long as you can. When the writing stalls, use the following prompt: Another possible solution to the problem of _____ might be _____.

Figure 5.1 Exploring the possible causes of a problem

Visual Prompts. Only a few problems have a single root cause. Use the template in Figure 5.1 to begin thinking about some of the possible causes of a problem. Describe the problem in the middle circle and then build arrows to as many explanations of possible causes as come to mind.

Research Prompts. Reading, observing, and talking to people can be great ways to discover a proposal topic. The following research prompts can help you along.

1. Interview your classmates about what they think are the biggest problems facing them as students. Interview student or faculty leaders or administrators about what they think are the biggest problems facing the university community. Do the same with community leaders.

2. Design an informal survey targeted to a particular group that you're interested in—students, student-athletes, local businesspeople, sports fans, migrant workers, and so on. This group may or may not be one to which you belong. Discover what they believe are the most serious problems they face.

3. Become a student of a local newspaper. In particular, pay attention to the letters to the editor and the local community pages. What seems to be a recurrent problem that gets people's attention? Clip articles, letters, or editorials that address the problem.

4. Google the following phrase: "solution to the problem of." Scan the results for topic ideas.

Narrowing Down

Feeling a little overwhelmed? Seeing problems everywhere? It can be wearing to focus on what's wrong with your life, your university, and your community. But remember that your ultimate goal is to write a proposal that suggests ways these problems might be resolved. You may have already explored some of these solutions, but if you haven't, don't worry—you'll get the chance later. Begin by scrutinizing the material you generated for possible topics.

What's Promising Material and What Isn't? We've talked about some initial judgments you can make. Now look at the material you generated in the fastwrites, lists, research, or clusters, and ask yourself which of the problems listed do you care about the most, or which are you most interested in? Once you've selected some tentative topics for your proposal, narrow them down using the following questions:

- *Does someone aside from you have a stake in finding a solution? Is there an identifiable audience for proposals about solutions?*
- *Is the problem a manageable one?*
- *Have other people said something about the problem and possible solutions?*
- *Which subject offers you the most opportunity for learning?*

Questions About Audience and Purpose. This assignment asks you to craft a proposal appropriate to your audience and purpose. When you have identified an audience for your proposal, consider what exactly might be your purpose with respect to that audience. Do you want to:

- *Inform* them about the problem and explore possible solutions?
- *Advocate* certain solutions as the best ways to solve the problem?
- *Inform and advocate*, dramatizing the problem because your audience may not fully appreciate and understand it, and then persuading them to support the solutions you favor?

These purposes will shape your approach. And which purpose you choose will depend partly on how your audience already thinks and feels about the problem you're tackling and the solutions you offer. Use the chart in Figure 5.2.

Although it might be premature to decide on the *form* your proposal will take, sometimes an awareness of purpose and audience will suggest an appropriate form. Ask yourself this question: Given the problem I'm writing about, which audiences are (1) most affected by it and (2) most likely to contribute to the solution?

Awareness of the problem	If low, increase emphasis on dramatizing the problem.	If high, emphasize proposed solutions.
Initial disposition toward proposed solution	If favorably disposed, emphasize action that needs to be taken to implement solution. Emphasize *pathos* over *logos*.	If unfavorably disposed, offer balanced treatment of possible solutions before stating yours. Emphasize *logos* over *pathos*.
Attitude toward speaker	If positive, emphasize stronger action to solve the problem.	If negative, emphasize the views or experience speaker *does* share with audience.

Figure 5.2   Audience analysis chart. As with other forms of argument, the persuasiveness of a proposal depends on a rhetorical understanding of your audience. This is discussed in more detail in Chapter 6, where I introduce the rhetorical triangle, as well as *ethos, pathos,* and *logos* (see pp. 173–174 for a discussion of those terms). See if you can do a rhetorical analysis on your proposal, and use what you discover to revise your essay.

Next, think about how to best reach one or both of those audiences. For example, suppose that Cheryl's purpose is to advocate for a new nontraditional-student center on campus and her audience is school administrators. Her best approach for getting her message across might be to write her proposal in the form of a letter to the university's president.

Trying Out

Got a topic you want to try? Good. Let's do some focused work on that topic to generate some more material on it. Unless you've got a lot of personal experience with the problem you're considering writing about (and probably even if you do), you need to develop a working knowledge of the topic through some quick research.

Researching to Answer the *So What?* Question. To start with, you need to be able to establish that the problem you're interested in is significant. To do that, you'll need to answer a skeptic's question: *Okay, so what's the big deal about this?* That will be the focus of your initial research.

Using Google, Google Scholar, or library databases, find at least three sources online that show the significance of the problem you're interested in writing about. These sources may

a. Provide statistics or facts that suggest the seriousness of the problem.
b. Relate a story, case study, or anecdote about people who are affected by the problem.
c. Visually illustrate the effects of the problem.
d. Offer assertions by experts who are concerned with the problem.

Giving Your Answer on a PowerPoint. Using what you've learned, prepare a single PowerPoint slide that you would use to answer the question "So what's the big deal about this?" Figure 5.3 is a slide that one of my students, Andrea, developed to dramatize the problem of disappearing honeybees. While it isn't a very effective PowerPoint slide—there's too much text, for one thing—it's a really useful summary of the problem.

Use the material you generate from this exercise to help establish the significance of the problem in your sketch.

Writing the Sketch

Try out a tentative proposal topic by writing a sketch, a relatively brief early draft written with an audience in mind. Your sketch should:

- Have a tentative title.
- Use appropriate evidence (personal experience, facts, statistics, etc.) to dramatize the problem.
- Identify one or more causes of the problem and offer some tentative solutions for addressing those causes.
- Be written with an appropriate audience and purpose in mind.

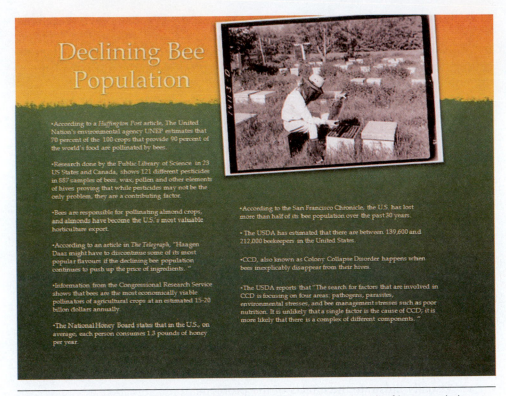

Figure 5.3 Develop a single PowerPoint slide like this one on the crash of bee populations to establish the significance of the problem you're writing about.

You might also develop this sketch in a form that you think would be particularly effective given your purpose and audience. Your sketch might be an essay or a letter, a PowerPoint, a podcast, a web page, or the text of a brochure or ad.

▶ Student Sketch

Loving and Hating Reality TV

Jenna Appleman

1   When I moved into my own apartment without TV or cable, I assumed I'd be watching much less television. My TV consumption had never been a problem—I'd watch *Law & Order* and HBO when I was home, but didn't follow very much else. I prided myself on watching intelligent television, avoiding the low-culture reality series with a sneer. But in the silence of a studio

apartment in the busiest semester of my college career, I needed a way to fill the space and blow off some steam. That's when I started watching reality TV.

There are TV channels dedicated exclusively to reality programming. Bravo houses the various *Real Housewives* series (my gateway), as well as their many spinoffs, E! plays the various Kardashian series, and reality competition shows like *The Biggest Loser* and *The Bachelor* rake in thousands of viewers on primetime. Certainly such success is indicative of something, and there are those who would disagree with my assumptions, but I stand by my initial negative cast on the cultural saturation of reality TV.

Reality television is (theoretically) unscripted and unacted, removing thousands of paying jobs for writers and actors from the market. I also sense that such excessive exposure can be exploitative. One show I have guiltily watched on Lifetime called *Dance Moms* follows a team of very young competitive dancers, between the ages of 7 and 14. Surely having their emotional breakdowns and embarrassing parents on camera at that young age isn't helping their development.

And yet, I watch it. Frequently. But in public, I pretend I don't know the names of the Kardashians and roll my eyes wildly at front page news about the Housewives. For better or worse, I have grown accustomed to the comfort of curling up in bed with my cat and watching a marathon of *Millionaire Matchmaker* after an exhausting day. I watched an episode of *The Bachelor* while I was drafting this proposal, just to have some noise in the background to help me think. I want to hate it, but there's a lot about it I love.

I don't propose that we change the burgeoning culture of reality television entirely. That's far from realistic, and I have a feeling eventually this too will cycle out of popularity. But I do feel that I need to find a way to reconcile how I feel about reality TV with my penchant for it. The first step, I recognize, is admitting that I have a problem.

I don't propose that I stop watching reality television. But I do think it's important to clarify *why* I do—if it's to help me focus on schoolwork, that's a benefit. If I find it calming after a long day, that's okay too. But if I start watching because I simply *must* find out what's happening in these people's lives, if I begin to really stake weight in it, that's when I need a reality check. If I can accept the reasons why, then I can start feeling less guilty about it. I also think I should make a point to also watch other television; the normal kind that employs actors and writers. It would also be good to try to utilize my gym membership and watch these "guilty pleasures" on the cardio machines' TVs while I'm actually doing something physical. I should also recognize the shows that I find particularly exploitative, and avoid them, or at least view them with an intelligent, critical eye in order to form an opinion.

Moving from Sketch to Draft

Return to the inquiry questions behind a proposal: *What is the problem? What should be done about it?* How well does your sketch answer those questions? Is the problem clear, and would a skeptical reader be convinced that it is serious enough to address? Based on what you know now, do the solutions make sense? Explore these considerations in the next section.

Evaluating Your Own Sketch. Proposal sketches, no matter what their form, usually need work in the following areas:

- ■ *Refining the problem.* It's too big and needs to be more focused.
- ■ *Insufficient evidence.* More research is required to establish the seriousness of the problem, identify key causes, and/or support proposed solutions.

For example, Jenna's sketch argued that people watch too much TV. Okay, but might that assertion be easier to write about if it were less general? Which people, exactly, watch too much TV? What do they watch too much of? Violent programs? Advertising? Reality TV? What is "too much"? And finally, what are the consequences of watching that much? All of these questions require research. Jenna might discover that the effects of TV watching are especially problematic for a certain age group, or that certain kinds of advertising—say, snack food commercials aimed at children—are particularly troublesome. So Jenna can refine his problem from "People watch too much TV" to something more focused like "Television commercials for high-calorie snack foods contribute to childhood obesity." Now, that's much easier to work with! Jenna's much clearer about the problem and its consequences, and can now focus his research.

See if you can refine the problem statement in your sketch in similar ways. "Wh" questions (who, which, what, where, when, why) can help you pare down a big problem to something more manageable. Use the example in Figure 5.4 as a guide, applying the "Wh" questions to the problem you discussed in your sketch. Then restate the problem as Jenna did, so that it's more specific.

Figure 5.4 Using "Wh" questions to pare down a problem

Reflecting on What You Learned. The thing I like about sketches is that they are very early drafts—attempts, really—at trying out a topic without a huge investment of time. At least they're not supposed to be huge investments of time. But pretty often I have students who approach nearly every writing assignment as if it requires "perfection" or who have such harsh internal critics that writing is always kind of painful and slow. For these students, sketches are no different. What about you? Do a journal entry in which you fastwrite for a few minutes about your experience writing this sketch. In particular, was it hard for you to accept that your sketch didn't meet your usual standards for writing something to hand in? What are your "usual standards," and do they get in the way of drafting and revising?

Developing

If you refined the problem you're exploring, stating it more clearly and concretely, then you've made it much easier to develop your draft. Developing your draft is a process that will require research.

Research. But what kind of research will you need to do? What are you looking for? The table below shows some key elements of proposals and questions to think about for each. Consider these questions as guides for your research.

Element	Questions for Research
Problem	What's the evidence that it's serious? Who does it affect and under what circumstances?
Effects and causes	What will happen if nothing is done? Why is it happening? Why does this matter?
Solutions	What should be done? How do these proposals address key causes and effects?

Where should you look to find the evidence to answer these questions?

- **Exploit local publications.** If you've chosen a topic of local interest, then sources such as the local daily newspaper, government reports, and university policies may be important sources for your proposal. Some of these sources, such as local newspapers and government documents, may be available in online databases at your library.

- **Interview experts.** In Chapter 4, you practiced interview skills. Here's a chance to put them to use again. One of the most efficient ways to collect information for your revision is to talk to people who have knowledge about the problem. These may be experts who have researched the problem or people who are affected by it.

■ *Search for experiences with similar solutions elsewhere.* If your proposal calls for an education program on binge drinking, what other universities might have tried such a program? What were their experiences? Search for information using keywords that describe the problem you're writing about ("binge drinking"), and try adding a phrase that describes the solution ("binge drinking education programs"). Also check library databases that might lead you to articles in newspapers, magazines, and journals on the problem and its solutions.

A word of advice about solutions: Researching and thinking about solutions can be a bit like following a horse race: You might favor one solution until another one suddenly races up from behind as you learn more. In an inquiry project, that's normal. Make sure that the solutions you end up writing about are consistent with your own experience and with your values about the best ways to solve problems.

Focusing on the Justifications.
In my part of the country, everyone has an opinion about wolves. Many people hate them. Wolf packs were reestablished in the West under the Endangered Species Act, and in recent decades wolves have extended their range well beyond the national parks and into ranching and agricultural areas. The problem is that some wolves kill livestock. What does one do with a wolf pack that won't stop killing sheep? Some popular solutions include: (1) Nothing—they were here first; (2) capture them and relocate them away from populated areas; (3) kill them.

Each of these solutions has problems of its own—and advocates and critics who will energetically argue over them. If you're working on an essay that focuses on a problem that affects people (and isn't that the definition of a problem?), then you will discover controversies over what to do about it. One thing your draft should not do is pretend that these controversies don't exist. On the contrary, your draft should not only justify the solutions you prefer, but also identify the solutions you've rejected and show why your solutions are better.

You've done some research on the problem and solutions. Develop your draft by focusing on the justifications for your solutions:

■ Why are they the best solutions?

■ How do they effectively address the causes and effects of the problem?

■ What is evidence that they will work?

■ What might critics say? Why are they wrong?

These *justifications* for your solutions will be a key part of your draft.

Drafting

As you think about how to organize your draft, consider some of the suggestions below.

Methods of Development.
As mentioned earlier in the chapter, a proposal often moves from problem to solution, and some proposals, like the research proposal,

need to follow a specific form. But if the form of your proposal has not been specified, you can organize it in a number of ways. One way to think about how to organize your draft is to imagine the questions typical readers of a proposal, or a problem-solution paper, might ask and the order in which they might ask them:

- What's the big deal?
- Who says it's a big deal besides you?
- What's at stake?
- What causes the problem? What are its effects?
- What solutions have other people proposed? Are they justified?
- Which solution do you prefer? How do you justify it?
- What are the potential problems with the solution you like?
- Why do you still like it?
- If we do this, is everything going to be okay? Is there anything you're asking us to do?

You might play with the order in which you deal with these questions in your draft, but you will likely have to address all of them somewhere.

Using Evidence. You will answer the preceding questions with evidence that you've gathered from research (reading, interviewing, observing) and experience. Like much else, the evidence you use depends on your intended audience. In other words, choosing the strongest evidence in a proposal is an exercise in audience analysis:

- How much does your audience know about the problem?
- Is your audience likely to favor your idea, oppose it, or have no opinion?
- What kind of evidence is most likely to convince your audience?

The *amount* of evidence you need to provide depends on whether your audience is likely to be predisposed to agree or disagree with the solutions you propose. Obviously, if readers will need convincing, you will need to offer more justification. The *types* of evidence you provide depend on your assessment of what your audience will be most likely to believe. As you compose your draft, consider who your readers will be and the kinds of evidence they will find most persuasive.

Workshopping

Because a proposal is a form of argument, your workshop is a chance to test its persuasiveness with readers. One key thing to consider before the session is how much your peers already know regarding the problem you're writing about. The less they know, the more work your draft needs to do in these areas:

1. Convince readers of the seriousness of the problem.
2. Provide a context for the problem: who's involved, who's affected, what's been tried, how long it's been going on, what will happen if nothing is done.

Questions for Peer Reviewers	
1. Purpose	After reading the draft, what do you think is at stake? If nothing is done to solve the problem, what might be the consequences?
2. Meaning	In your own words, how does the essay answer the inquiry question *What should be done?* Play the doubting game for a moment: What potential problems do you see with the solution I'm proposing?

3. Persuade peers that your proposal is fair and reasonable. That means not only providing convincing evidence to support your solution, but also considering the arguments of critics of your approach.

In addition to these concerns, when you workshop the first draft of your proposal, you should focus on what peers make of the purpose and meaning of your essay, using their responses to guide your revision. The "Questions for Peer Reviewers" box can help you frame these questions for your workshop group.

Reflecting on the Draft. Following your workshop, make an entry in your journal that follows these prompts:

- If I were going to write this over again, the one thing I think I'd do would be....
- The most important thing I've learned so far about writing a proposal....
- The most difficult part of the process for me has been....
- The biggest question I have about the draft is....

Revising

5.5
Apply revision strategies that are effective for a proposal.

Revision is a continual process—not a last step. You've been revising—"reseeing" your subject—from the first messy fastwriting in your journal. But the things that get your attention vary depending on where you are in the writing process. With your draft in hand, revision becomes your focus through what I'll call "shaping and tightening your draft."

Shaping. Shaping involves, among other things, arranging and rearranging information so that it is organized around the main idea or question.

Analyzing the Information   One way to think about the structure of your proposal is to see the information you've collected as being in categories. In a proposal, remember that these categories typically include the categories shown in Figure 5.5.

This isn't a recipe for organizing your draft, but a way to look at whether you've included enough information in each category. Try using the "Frankenstein Draft" strategy (Revision Strategy 11.18 in Chapter 11). Cut up your draft with scissors into pieces that fall into the categories mentioned here—problem, solution, evidence, and so on—and then play with the order. Worry about transitions later.

Problem	Causes and Effects	Solutions and Justifications
What is it? Why is it important? What is at stake? Who's involved?	What causes it? What's the impact? What will happen? Why does it happen?	What should be done? Why is this the best solution?

Evidence	Other Perspectives
What are the facts? What do experts say? What are your experiences and observations?	What is the controversy? What do others propose? Who has a different perspective?

Figure 5.5   Structuring your review

Other Questions for Revision   Proposal drafts also have some fairly typical weaknesses at this stage in the process, most of which can be addressed by repeating some of the steps in this chapter or selecting appropriate revision strategies in Chapter 11. Here are some questions to consider as you decide which of these strategies might be most helpful.

✓ Have you done enough to dramatize the problem if you're writing for an audience that may not be aware of it? Should you do more to establish how your readers have a stake in solving the problem?

✓ How well have you justified your solutions? Is there enough evidence? Is it appropriate evidence for your audience?

✓ Have you overemphasized one solution at the expense of the others? Would your proposal be more balanced and persuasive if you considered alternative solutions, even if you ultimately reject them?

Polishing.   Shaping focuses on things such as purpose, meaning, and design. No less important is looking more closely at paragraphs, sentences, and words. Are your paragraphs coherent? How do you manage transitions? Are your sentences fluent and concise? Are there any errors in spelling or syntax? The section of Chapter 11 called "Problems with Clarity and Style" on page 388 can help you focus on these issues.

Before you finish your draft, work through the following checklist:

✓ Every paragraph is about one thing.

✓ The transitions between paragraphs aren't abrupt.

✓ The lengths of sentences vary in each paragraph.

✓ Each sentence is concise. There are no unnecessary words or phrases.

✓ You've checked grammar, particularly verb agreement, run-on sentences, unclear pronouns, and misused words (*there/their, where/were,* and so on).

✓ You've run your spellchecker and proofed your paper for misspelled words.

▶ Student Essay

Jenna watches reality TV and feels guilty about it. But that's not the problem that interests her. She can see the appeal of programs such as *American Idol*, and she'd like to continue to watch them from time to time, but she would really like to watch reality shows that follow an ethical code of conduct. Jenna proposes that reality TV producers agree to a code that would minimize the emotional and physical injuries inflicted on participants, which she thinks is a problem on many of the shows.

Avoidable Accidents: How to Make Reality TV Safer

Jenna Appleman

1   When I moved into my own apartment without TV or cable, I assumed I'd be watching much less television. My TV consumption had never been a problem—I'd watch *Law & Order* and HBO when I was home, but didn't follow very much else. I prided myself on watching intelligent television, avoiding the low-culture reality series with a sneer. But in the silence of a studio apartment in the busiest semester of my college career, I needed a way to fill the space and blow off some steam. That's when I started watching reality TV.

2   There are TV channels dedicated exclusively to reality programming. Bravo houses the various *Real Housewives* series (my gateway), as well as their many spinoffs; E! plays the various Kardashian series; there are kid-centered shows like *Toddlers and Tiaras* on TLC and *Dance Moms* on Lifetime; and reality competition shows like *The Biggest Loser* and *The Bachelor* rake in thousands of viewers on prime time. Reality TV dominates American programming.

3   How dominant is it? According to the Nielson ratings for the week I'm writing this, seven of the top ten shows on cable were reality programs. *Jersey Shore* and *Pawn Stars* were one and two ("Top 10s"). On TV, *American Idol* is a perennial viewer favorite, often the most-watched program.

4   Yet my instinctive guilt about watching these shows is indicative of a pressing problem. "People are attracted to reality television because they know it has real consequences," said reality blurred editor Andy Dehnart. "You get the sense this is a real human being who could be hurt or injured" (Dehnart). And in August 2011, Russell Armstrong, the husband of Beverly Hills *Real Housewives'* Taylor Armstrong, committed suicide. While A[r]mstrong's suicide is an extreme example, injuries on reality TV programs are rampant. A brawl on *Survivor* in 2010 resulted in a dislocated shoulder and broken toe. In 2011, an athlete on the reality show *Jump City* fell doing a stunt and shattered his wrist. Injuries on shows like *So You Think You Can Dance* are common.

5   Not only are contestants injured but viewers "inspired" by the programs are also at risk. Recently, for example, the American Medical Association warned that viewers of the TV show *Extreme Makeover,* now off the air, might have had a distorted understanding of the risk of

plastic surgery: "Heavily edited and selected scenes from reality TV have lulled the public into thinking there are no real risks or complications in these procedures. It's easy for viewers to forget that these are real people, who face the real risks—not just the benefits—of surgery" (216). All of this is a brash reminder that reality television is just that—*real*.

"These shows are Roman coliseums that we visit virtually," writes Matt Seitz of Salon. "Participants in contact sports have corner men and doctors on hand to nurse their wounds, and determine if they are fit enough to step in the ring in the first place." So, too, then, should the participants of reality television shows.

6

To lower the risks to participants and viewers of watching reality TV, I propose the following:

7

1. Possible candidates for a reality television show should be pre-screened, to ensure that they are fit emotionally and physically to withstand the rigors of a reality set.
2. Candidates with substance abuse, physical abuse, self-destructive behaviors, among others, would not be permitted to participate on the show *unless* they are provided with the following:
   a. Active counseling throughout the filming process
   b. Guaranteed after-care once filming ceases
   For example, *Hoarders* on A&E provides healthcare services during and after filming to the subjects it follows.
3. *All* participants should be provided with free after-care and counseling once filming wraps, for at least three months.
4. All participants should have immediate and total access to medical care, with the show absorbing all medical costs incurred during filming.
5. No footage of participants under the influence of alcohol should be used *if* the alcohol had been provided by producers.
6. Only non-incidental footage of minors should be used.
7. If a show focuses on minors (such as *Toddlers and Tiaras* and *Dance Moms*), counselors with training in adolescent and child psychology should be present during *all filming* and available to children before and after the conclusion of filming.
8. All participant contracts should be public.

An ethical code like this would admittedly be hard to implement and impossible to require. Further, as NPR's Linda Holmes writes, "there is . . . no solution for people who want to watch *The Real Housewives Of Beverly Hills* without guilt . . . you have to live with the fact that it exploits emotionally charged situations" (Holmes). Nonetheless, having an adoptable ethical code for reality television producers, and public knowledge of which shows abide by the code, would at least put a modicum of power back in the hands of the viewer. We would be given the ability to make informed choices about which programs we choose to watch—"to shop for ethical television the same way [we] might shop for ethically produced goods of any other kind, and to provide the financial incentives [for producers]," as Holmes says.

8

I will probably never stop feeling guilty for watching reality television, particularly the more exploitative shows. However, if I were given the option to watch reality programs that I could feel comfortable indulging in, knowing that there were an ethical code in place, I would

9

(continued)

(continued)

like to think I'd choose those shows. Such a code wouldn't cure the problem, but at least it would empower viewers and encourage them to support less destructive programming.

Works Cited

D'Amico, Richard. "Plastic Surgery Is Real, Not Reality TV." *Virtual Mentor: American Medical Association Journal of Ethics*, vol. 9, no. 3, Mar. 2007, pp. 2150-218.

Dehnart, Andy. "Real Housewives Cast Member Russell Killed Himself." *Reality Blurred*, 16 Aug. 2011, www.realityblurred.com/realitytv/2011/08/the-real-housewives-russell-dead/.

Holmes, Linda. "Ethical 'Reality': A Proposed Code for Producers to Live By." *NPR*, 31 Aug. 2011, www.npr.org/sections/monkeysee/2011/08/31/140082930/ethical-reality-a-proposed-code-for-producers-to-live-by.

Seitz, Matt Zoller. "Reality TV: A Blood Sport That Must Change." *Salon*, 18 Aug. 2011, www.salon.com/2011/08/18/reality_tv_blood_sport/.

"Top 10s and Trends: TV" *Nielsen*, 13 Feb. 2012, www.nielsen.com/us/en/top10s.html. Accessed 20 Feb. 2012.

Evaluating the Essay

1. A key part of a persuasive proposal is establishing the seriousness of the problem. Are you convinced that reality stars are at risk on these programs? If not, what would you suggest about strengthening that part of the essay?

2. Suppose Jenna were considering incorporating visuals—images, video, graphics, and tables—into the essay. What visuals would you suggest?

3. What's your evaluation of the solution that she proposes? Is it convincing? Why or why not?

Using What You Have Learned

Let's revisit the list from the beginning of this chapter of things I hoped you'd learn about this form of writing.

1. **Describe a problem of consequence, framing it narrowly enough to explore convincing solutions.** A fundamental problem with early drafts in any genre is that they're not focused enough; the writer takes a landscape shot when she needs to take a close-up. This is especially true with research-based writing such as proposals, where you're dealing with a lot of information. See if you can apply some of the things you learned here to, for example, a research essay.

2. **Identify the wide range of rhetorical situations that might call for a proposal argument.** There are all kinds of proposals—marketing proposals, business plans, grant proposals, policy proposals, and so on—but they are

all in the service of the same question: What should be done? As you write for other college classes, you will probably have assignments that aren't called proposals but essentially ask you to answer this question.

3. **Argue effectively for both the seriousness of the problem and the proposed solutions, using strong evidence.** Among other things, the proposal relies more heavily on research than does the review, and in subsequent assignments you'll be drawing on what you learned here, especially your understanding of what is appropriate evidence to support a claim.

4. **Use appropriate invention strategies to discover and develop a proposal topic.** You've gotten considerable practice with fastwriting, clustering, listing, and so on. But with each assignment, you've cast a wider net for information. The proposal, for example, asks you to generate considerably more information from outside sources than, say, the profile or personal essay do. Invention isn't just trying to get what's already in your head out on paper or screen. Invention also includes using techniques for *finding* information and thinking about what you make of it. This skill will become increasingly important in later assignments.

5. **Apply revision strategies that are effective for a proposal.** In this chapter, you've spent time considering not only how to convince someone that a problem you care about is something he or she should care about, too, but also crafting proposals that are persuasive. Reviews, proposals, public arguments, and research essays are among the most reader-based forms, and it becomes even more important in revising these forms to imagine readers who may not think much like you do.

Writing an Argument

Learning Objectives

In this chapter, you'll learn to

6.1 Understand the connection between inquiry and persuasion, and apply inquiry strategies for exploring and developing an argument topic.

6.2 Distinguish between causal, factual, and definitional arguments, and develop an essay that uses one of those three approaches to persuasion.

6.3 Identify the key elements of argument—reasons, claims, and evidence—and apply them in both reading and writing.

6.4 Develop a question that is focused enough to lead to a strong claim and convincing evidence.

6.5 Use audience analysis and logical methods to help guide revision of an argument.

Writing to Persuade People

When you teach, it pays to check your assumptions at the door. This semester, Hailie, a student in my first-year writing class, was a member of the debate team. Successful debaters are typically deeply committed to going all in on the proposition they're supporting—doubt and uncertainty don't win points in these contests. Inquiry-based investigations, as you know by now, begin with questions, not answers, and at least initially, welcome complexity and even uncertainty. You write about a topic not because you know what you think but because you want to find out what you think. I thought Hailie would struggle with this ("Just give me a side to argue!"), and that she would see little connection between inquiry and argument.

I was wrong.

"How do you decide on a topic that you want to argue?" I asked her one day in conference.

"It interests me," she said. "It's something I want to learn about."

"But don't you quickly jump over the exploration phase and rush to some kind of judgment about what you think?" I said.

"Um, no, not really. I always explore the topic first," she said. "That's the most interesting part."

It was obvious to me that Hailie saw no conflict between the initial motive of inquiry—to find out—and the motive of argument—to prove. Cementing the connection between the two is a major theme of this chapter, and let's begin by recognizing that all persuasion begins with inquiry.

> **Persuasive essays such as the op-ed are a great way to participate in public debates that affect your campus and community, and even your nation.**

Motives for Writing an Argument

Obviously, we use persuasion all the time to try to get others to see things our way. Today, my wife, Karen, and I politely argued about what movie to see tonight. But that's not the kind of argument that I'm talking about here because, really, *who cares* (other than Karen and me) what movie we choose tonight? Instead, I'm talking about arguments in which people *have some kind of stake.* In inquiry-based argument, that's where inquiry first finds a home: in a community that seeks answers but that can't agree on which answer is best.[1] The investigator may belong to that community or not (you don't have to be a college football player to be interested in whether amateurism is corrupted by money), but either way, as Hailie knows, the inquiry begins with an exploration into what that community cares about, what it already believes, and what others have to say about issues of common concern.

While a writer may have feelings, one way or another, about what the community *should* think, it would be irresponsible not to inquire first into the debate, and this is often wonderfully complicated. So the formula for argument is **not** this:

Pick an issue + take a side + line up evidence
that supports that side.

The formula for inquiry-driven argument is more like this:

Identify communities with a stake in the question + explore what
those communities believe + craft a case, supported by evidence,
for the best answer.

---

[1]This focus on community as the basis for identifying what is worth arguing draws from rhetoric expert Sharon Crowley, and especially her work on argumentative writing, as well as pedagogies developed by composition scholar Michelle Payne.

Writing Beyond the Classroom

Public Argument in a Digital Age

An argument with Northwest Airlines over whether they owe you a lunch voucher after your flight was cancelled is typical of everyday uses of persuasion. But arguing well—and ethically—is an important civic duty in a democratic society. A few thousand years ago, the Greeks and Romans created schools of rhetoric where people could learn the art of speaking persuasively in public settings.

These days, probably more than ever, argument is a vibrant part of civic life in the United States, particularly on the Internet. Here are a few of the many genres of public argument available to you for persuading people to think or do something you consider important:

- *Op-ed essays:* These essays, ubiquitous in newspapers, remain among the most common brief argumentative essays for a general audience.
- *Letters to the editor:* Like op-ed essays, these appear in print or online publications; they're often a response to a previous contribution.
- *Blogs:* One of the newest forms of public argument is the blog. Hosted by such online sites as Wordpress or Google's "Blogger," the so-called blogosphere has grown so explosively that no one really knows how big it is.
- *Photo essay:* Over one hundred years ago, Jacob Riis used photographs of immigrants' squalid conditions in New York City tenements to incite a public outcry—and policy change—on how we treat the poor.
- *YouTube:* It's not just a forum for videos of weird cat tricks.
- *PowerPoint:* Former vice president Al Gore's slide presentation "An Inconvenient Truth" made the point that there really can be power in PowerPoint.

For example, college students (a community) are plagued by loan debt. There's considerable debate about whether, at certain income levels, this debt should be forgiven or reduced (answers). After investigating this issue, what do you believe is the best approach, and why? Many athletes and fans of the Olympics (several communities) are concerned about the impact of corporate sponsorship on the Games' guiding principles. Some think this sponsorship is an inevitable part of the modern Olympics, while others think there should be some restrictive sponsorship policies (answers), and still others believe that the Games should return to its simple roots, without all the fanfare. What is the answer that will best address these communities' concerns, and why? The central motive for argument, then, is not simply to offer evidence to support your point of view but to first investigate a wide range of ideas to determine what might be best for the communities with a stake in the debate.

We argue not to *win* but to *learn*. This is a distinction that philosopher Daniel Cohen believes is subverted by the most common way we tend to think about argument—that it is a war. Arguments *can* involve conflict, but they are rarely combat—despite the frequent use of war metaphors such as "finding ammunition" or "attacking a position." Far more often, the motives for arguing are more benign, including learning something (even if we "lose") and actually feeling good about it.

The Argument and Academic Writing

Proposals, reviews, and analytical essays (discussed in the next chapter) are all types of arguments you might write in college. What distinguishes them from the argumentative essay you will write here? One difference is the kind of questions (and the claims that arise from them) that each genre typically emphasizes. For example, a proposal (Chapter 5) asks policy questions—what should be done? A review (Chapter 4) asks an evaluative question—how good is it? Argumentative essays like the one you will write tend to focus on three kinds of questions:

- What's the cause? (e.g., Deforestation of the Amazon has led to the decimation of native cultures.)

- What's true? (e.g., The evidence suggests voter ID legislation suppresses the African-American vote.)

- What is it and how should it be classified? (e.g., Russia's behavior in Ukraine re-creates its Cold War foreign policy.)

These three types of questions are relevant to all kinds of writing assignments you'll encounter in your college classes, including things like position papers, opinion pieces, persuasive essays, and cause-effect essays. If you can learn to identify the kind of question a writing assignment involves, you will know the genre of argument your instructor expects and the type of claims that arise from it.

In general, academics value argument not because they're argumentative (though some are), but because it's the way that they "make knowledge," which is the central business of the university. Scholarly communities make discoveries through contesting what was once assumed to be true. Reasoned argument supported by research is the engine behind academic inquiry.

Fundamental to academic argument is an idea that isn't always obvious to newcomers to college: "Facts" can be contested. While it often seems that the facts we take for granted are immutable truths—as enduring as the granite peaks I can see through my office window—things often aren't immutable at all. Our knowledge of things—how the planet was formed, the best ways to save endangered species, the meaning of a classic novel, how to avoid athletic injuries—is entirely made up of ideas that are *contested*. And the primary tool for shaping and even changing what we know is argument.

Features of the Form

Feature	Conventions of the Argument Essay
Inquiry questions	What is true? What's the cause? How should it be defined and classified?
Motives	We hope to convince others to think as we do. Sometimes, however, we first need to convince ourselves, and argument is an invitation to *explore* as well as to persuade. A fundamental motive is discovery.
Subject matter	Any topic is fair game, but one thing is essential: Others must have a stake in the issue. An audience should be persuaded that whatever claim you're making matters.
Structure	Like any form of writing, the design of arguments depends on the situation. However, outlines for arguments developed by rhetoricians share some of these features: • Background on the issue, especially what people seem to agree on. What's the controversy as most people understand it? • The inquiry question. • Claims and supporting reasons and evidence. • Acknowledgement of counterarguments and analysis of their significance. • Closing that refines the claim, summarizes it, or returns to the beginning to affirm how the argument addresses the issue.
Sources of information	Experts on your topic, sources of reliable data on your topic, your experiences and observations, and the stories of others can all potentially be evidence for your argument.
Language	Who is the audience? Arguments for expert audiences are often formal. Arguments for the general public are much less formal, with relatively relaxed rules of evidence and casual language. The balance of appeals should be appropriate to the audience.

Prose+

Editorial cartoons such as this one are a popular form of argument, and one reason they're effective is a quality that comics share: By simplifying things, they amplify those things. Cartoonist Joe Heller notes that when we render something more abstractly—in this case, taking a coal mine and superimposing a graveyard and smoke—the details that were eliminated make the details that remain more apparent. Cartoons that make an argument, however, also have features typical of any argument: a claim (often implied) and reasons. The cartoon strip here, for example, combines drawings with very few words to make a pretty unambiguous claim: Wind power is preferable to nuclear, oil, and coal energy. The reason offered? The problems associated with wind power are relatively benign.

What Is Argument?

We've already distinguished an argumentative essay from a proposal and a review. Each works from a different inquiry question and claim. But let's bore more deeply into the question of what we mean by argument, starting first with another popular misconception.

Argument Has More Than Two Sides

TV talk shows stage "discussions" between proponents of diametrically opposed positions. Academic debating teams pit those for and those against. We are nurtured on language such as *win or lose, right and wrong*, and *either...or*. It's tempting to see the world this way, as neatly divided into truth and falsehood, light and dark. Reducing issues to two sides simplifies the choices. But one of the things that literature—and all art—teaches us is the delightful and nagging complexity of things. Huck Finn is a racist, and in *Huckleberry Finn* there's plenty of evidence in his treatment of Jim that confirms this. Yet there are moments in the novel when we see a transcendent humanity in Huck, and we can see that he may be a racist, *but.*...It is this qualification—this modest word *but*—that trips us up in our apparent certainty. Rather than *either...or*, can it be *both...and*? Instead of two sides to every issue, might there be thirteen?

Here's an example:

One side: General education requirements are a waste of time because they are often irrelevant to the students' major goal in getting a college education—getting a good job.

The other side: General education requirements are invaluable because they prepare students to be enlightened citizens, more fully prepared to participate in democratic culture.

It's easy to imagine a debate between people who hold these positions, and it wouldn't be uninteresting. But it *would* be misleading to suggest that these are the only two possible positions on general education requirements in American universities.

One of the reasons why people are drawn to arguing is that it can be a method of discovery, and one of the most useful discoveries is that of a side to the story that doesn't fall neatly into the usual opposed positions. The route to these discoveries is twofold: *initially withholding judgment* and *asking questions*.

For instance,

What might be goals of a university education other than helping students get a good job and making them enlightened citizens?

Is it possible that a university can do both?

Are general education courses the only route to enlightenment?

Are there certain situations in which the vocational motives of students are inappropriate?

Are there certain contexts—say, certain students at particular schools at a particular point in their education—when general education requirements should be waived or modified?

As often happens with two-sided arguments, all of these questions, and others, tend to unravel the two sides of the argument and expose them for what they are: *starting points* for an inquiry, in this case, into the question *What good are general education requirements?*

Inquiry Arguments Begin with Exploration

Oh, how tempting it is to simply build an argument from what you already think! It seems so much more efficient, allowing you to leap over the messy, exploratory part of the process and get right to the point—you know, the point that you started with, the one you just *know* is true. But this shortcut comes with a serious cost: You'll learn less. Inquiry is about discovery, and as you know, this means beginning with questions, not answers, and taking the time to listen to what others have said about your topic.

So you begin with a question—"What good are general education requirements?"—and before you make any claims about it, you do some research on who has a stake in the answer to the question (see Figure 6.1).

You don't have an argument until you identify the areas of disagreement. The discovery phase of an inquiry-based argument explores the range of existing beliefs among communities with a stake in your question. For the question about the effectiveness of general education requirements, several stakeholders are obvious, none more so than students. Educators also have an investment in the

6.1

Understand the connection between inquiry and persuasion, and apply inquiry strategies for exploring and developing an argument topic.

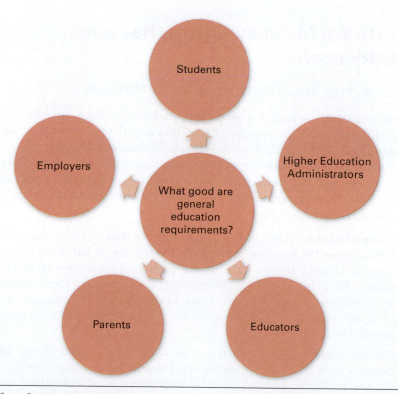

Figure 6.1 Stakeholder analysis

question. Parents of college students are probably less apparent stakeholders, but many feel strongly that their children not "waste" time with "unnecessary" courses. And finally, do people who hire college graduates care whether potential employees have taken courses in a range of subjects?

You still don't really have an argument to make yet. That will emerge when you find the points of disagreement among stakeholders. One way to do that is to work through a series of questions:

1. *Do the stakeholders agree on the facts?* (e.g., Is it true that most college students would prefer not to take general education courses?) If it isn't true, then perhaps there's a factual argument you might make.

2. *Do they agree on what key terms mean?* (e.g., Is there confusion about what is meant by "general education"?) If there isn't confusion, should you make a definitional claim?

3. *Do they agree on the causes?* (e.g., General education makes students "well-rounded" citizens.) Is there a causal argument lurking here?

Once you've identified which one of the three types of argument you might want to make, then comes the hunt for a claim that you can get behind.

What Do We Mean by Claims, Reasons, and Evidence?

Claims: What You Want People to Believe

6.2

Distinguish between causal, factual, and definitional arguments, and develop an essay that uses one of those three approaches to persuasion.

"I have a headache" is simply a statement, and not a claim, because no one is likely to disagree with it. "Headaches can be caused by secondhand smoke" is a statement that is also a claim (a causal one) because reasonable people might agree or disagree with it. Exploration into your topic will help you identify the areas of disagreement, and from one of these areas you can work towards discovering a particular kind of claim, which is linked, of course, to what kind of question you're posing: factual, definitional, or causal.

- **Factual claims.** One of the most controversial debates these days is a factual one: Do humans cause global warming? What does the evidence suggest is true? It isn't hard to see plenty of examples of factual arguments. Here in the Pacific Northwest, for example, some people can't agree whether removing dams is the best way to help endangered salmon, or if the state government would be a better manager than the feds of public lands.

- **Causal claims.** Closely related to factual claims, causal claims address a disagreement about why something is happening, or what caused it. Following the midterm elections in 2014, there were plenty of causal arguments about why the Democrats did so poorly and the Republicans did so well.

■ ***Definitional claims.*** Is gay marriage an equal-rights issue or a moral one? Is a corporation a "person"? What does it mean to be a "feminist"? Does talking on your cell phone in a nice restaurant constitute rude behavior? All of these questions try to pin down the meanings and classifications of things that a dictionary can't help with.

Reasons: The "Because…" Behind the Claim

I asked my first-year students what they thought of general education, or "core," classes at our university. It provoked a lively debate. Here's what one of them said:

> I am all for the rant about higher education costing a fortune. The core classes are a joke, to be quite honest. Who hasn't had math, science, and history in high school?

This student makes the definitional claim that "core classes are a joke." She gives a reason: Students have already studied math, science, and history in high school. This is the "because" behind her claim. But notice that behind this reason there's an unstated assumption: Math, science, and history classes in high school are equivalent to university core classes in these subjects. Is this true? It may be. But it's certainly debatable, and because this assumption is never addressed, the claim that core classes are a joke is built on a pretty weak foundation.

Reasons—either stated or implied—hold up your claim. Your claim is *what* you believe is true, and your reasons are *why* you believe it is true. A claim and a reason can be linked with the word "because." So, stating its assumption explicitly as part of the reason, we could restate the claim and reason above as "Core classes are a joke *because* their content is similar to what most students learn in high school."

6.3

Identify the key elements of argument— reasons, claims, and evidence— and apply them in both reading and writing.

Evidence: Testing the Claim

The phrase "building an argument" implies that it's a construction job that is merely about assembling the parts—claim, reasons, evidence—according to some preconceived plan concocted by a mastermind who has it pretty much figured out. But an inquiry-based argument is actually nothing like that. It's when writers start looking at evidence that the building is most likely to crumble because evidence is the element of argument that is most likely to shatter assumptions. But you should let evidence mess things up.

Examining evidence is a *test* of a claim; evidence is just as likely to revise what you think as it is to confirm it … *if you let it*. That's the hard part: allowing information to change your mind. For one thing, it's inconvenient. But it's also essential because the motive of argument is to learn something. This learning begins by seeing the landscape of a controversy when figuring out what kind of argument you want to make, and continues by looking at evidence that challenges what you already think.

Look at the best evidence you can find, which will likely come from the following sources:

- Expert testimony (statements by authorities on the topic)
- Reliable data (facts from credible sources)

Seeing the Form

The "Imagetext" as Argument

While model Kate Moss is likely disturbed by the appropriation of her image by advocates in the pro-anorexia ("pro-ana") movement, Moss's picture—along with those of other celebrities such as Calista Flockhart, Mary-Kate Olsen, and Keira Knightley—appear as "thinspiration" on websites that argue that eating disorders are a "lifestyle choice," not a disease. Some of these images (though not this one) are digitally altered to make the models seem even thinner than they really are. In an article on the "imagetexts" used by these controversial websites, Robin Jensen notes that in their new context, pictures like this one of Kate Moss are in effect given a "frame" quite different from the one originally intended. In this way, the meaning of the picture is manipulated to make an argument that serves the purpose of the pro-ana movement. In a sense, this is like quoting someone out of context, and raises a similar ethical question: Is it fair?

Kate Moss in ultra-thin pose.

- Observation and personal experience (what you see and what has happened to you)
- Stories, case studies, anecdotes (the narratives of others that help you dramatize an issue or support a point)

Keep in mind that the kind of evidence that is persuasive will depend on the disposition of your audience—readers who are skeptical about your claim will be harder to convince—and also on the discourse community you're writing in. Obviously, appropriate evidence in a biology article will be different from appropriate evidence in a philosophy article. For the purposes of this assignment, you're probably writing for peers (or a general audience) and, generally speaking, as you move from an expert audience to one that is less so, the rules of evidence get looser.

Analyzing What Makes a *Good* Argument

The simplest method of making an argument is perfected in the third grade: You're wrong and I'm right. So there. Aristotle had problems with this, as does everyone else who lines up behind reason and civility. However, there is considerably less agreement about what actually makes an argument effective. Let's look at three ideas about this: classical argument and two more-contemporary approaches—Toulmin and Rogerian arguments.

Classical Argument: Ethos, Pathos, Logos

Plato thought that we arrive at Truth through dialogue—a back and forth between two parties who are interested in discovering what it all means. Aristotle thought Truth-finding is the business of science. But he also argued that there is a real need for people to sort out disagreements, and that a method exists for doing this. Aristotle's ideas about argument proved durable, and so when we talk about argument, we often focus on how we can use ethos (the appeal of the writer's or speaker's credibility), pathos (the appeal to emotion), and logos (the appeal to reason) to try to persuade a receptive audience. (See Figure 6.2 for a representation of the balance among these appeals.) Aristotle also proposed a structure for how to make a persuasive argument, and it includes a lot of the things we usually associate with persuasive writing:

- **Introduction:** Dramatize the issue to engage reader interest, identify common ground between writer and audience, and lay out the claim (ethos and pathos).
- **Narration:** Provide the background so that readers know what's at stake (logos).
- **Confirmation:** Return to your claim and offer persuasive evidence (usually examples) to support that it's the best answer (logos).

Disposition of Audience	*Ethos*	*Pathos*	*Logos*
Resistant	Most important	Less important	Most important
Neutral	Important	Important	Important
Receptive	Less important	Most important	Less important

Figure 6.2 Audience and the balance of ethos, logos, and pathos

- **Refutation and concession:** Refrain from pretending that your answer is the only one or that it can't be critiqued. What are some of the opposing views (logos)?
- **Conclusion:** Reach back into the essay to reaffirm why your claim is best. Leave a strong impression (ethos and pathos).

While classical argument remains a go-to method, it has drawbacks. For one thing, it can seem formulaic—a dutiful march through a series of logical steps that can seem predictable. It's also easy to imagine that the classical method is less suited to inquiry-based arguments. Will writers be tempted to lock down their thinking, sidestepping complexity and uncertainty, in their determination to prove a point to an already receptive audience?

Toulmin's Approach: What Do You Need to Believe Is True?

Stephen Toulmin, an English philosopher, was interested in practical argument. He worried that classical approaches rely too much on formal logic divorced from real-world situations. What may be most powerful about the Toulmin method is that it offers not *an approach to composing* an argument but *a method of analyzing* an argument—one you've drafted or one you've been asked to read.

For our purposes, we'll simplify the Toulmin approach a bit. First, he suggested that arguments about any subject include:

- claims
- evidence
- warrants
- backing

In an argument, the *claims* are supported by *grounds* (reasons) or *evidence* (examples, observations, statistics, etc.). The most significant aspect of Toulmin's approach is the idea that claims and evidence are linked together by *warrants*—or assumptions about the way things are. If the claim *Michelle must have a lot of*

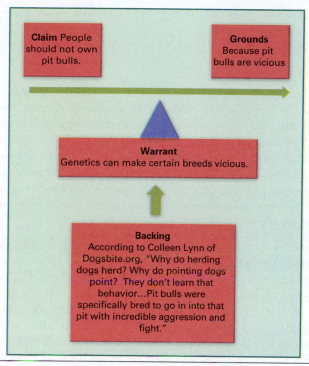

Figure 6.3 The relationship among claims, grounds, warrants, and backing

money is based on the evidence of the half-dozen credit cards in her purse, the person making the claim assumes there's a correlation between the number of credit cards one has and wealth. That's a warrant. To believe the claim based on this evidence, you would have to also believe the assumption. Essentially, then, a warrant is the answer to the question *What do you need to believe is true in order to accept the validity of a claim based on grounds or evidence?*

For example, what do I have to believe is true to accept the claim that people shouldn't own pit bulls on the grounds that they are a vicious breed (see Figure 6.3 above)? I'd have to believe that viciousness is a genetic trait that all dogs of a certain breed share. That's a warrant (there are probably more). If I were going to make the case against pit bulls, I think I'd feel obligated to find some evidence that backs that warrant.

Rogers: Accurately Restating and Refuting Opposing Claims

The Rogerian approach is especially appealing for inquiry arguments because it accommodates the complex issues of stakeholders whose positions are less clear. It's also a method of argument that encourages writers to bend over backwards to understand what those stakeholders believe, especially those with whom writers might disagree.

How might you analyze this letter writer's argument?

Dear Editor,

As part of my required humanities class, I was forced to see the art exhibit "Home of the Brave" at the university gallery. As a combat veteran, what I saw there deeply offended me. I saw so-called "art" that showed great American military leaders such as General Petraeus with skulls superimposed on their faces, and a photo of a man with an American flag wrapped around his head and lashed with a plastic tie at his neck. It's popular to say these days that we should support the troops. Apparently, a group of artists who haven't defended our freedom feel free to use that freedom to be unpatriotic. I wonder if they would feel differently if they had to pay the real cost for freedom of speech.

Most arguments like this don't provoke an analytical response at first. We react emotionally: "This guy is so full of it!" or perhaps, "It's about time someone spoke up about the cost of freedom!" This letter, like many that raise controversial issues, triggers a whole set of deeply held beliefs about things such as patriotism, freedom of speech, and the purpose of art. These are things that *should* provoke discussion—and that inevitably trigger feelings. But without involving the head as well as the heart, it's impossible to have a civil discussion—one that will lead to new understanding. We need to understand not only what we ourselves believe, but also what the other guy believes. To see how this might work, try Exercise 6.1, based on some of American psychologist Carl Rogers' ideas about argument.

Exercise 6.1

Argument as Therapy

Carl Rogers was a therapist and one of the most famous experts on argument theory. Not surprisingly, he thought that when people feel really, really strongly about something, reason just doesn't work well. Instead, he believed, a prerequisite to entering into an argument with someone else about a value-laden topic is to first listen and "say back" what you understand him or her to be saying. Let's do that here.

STEP ONE: Summarize what you understand to be the letter writer's basic argument. What claim is he making, and what seem to be the (implied) reasons behind it? You might use this as a template for your summary:

> *Because of* _____ *and* _____, *the letter writer argues that* _____.

STEP TWO: Now fastwrite for a few minutes in your notebook, exploring your own take on the validity of the claim and the reasons.

STEP THREE: Finally, write a brief analysis of the argument that includes the following:

1. Begin with your understanding of the letter writer's argument and include something about the circumstances that might lead someone to make such claims.
2. Analyze the soundness of the reasons behind the argument. Do you agree or disagree with them? Is there a different way of thinking about them?
3. State your own position (e.g., What would you say about the relationship between art and politics?), including the reasons behind it.

Of all the models for argument discussed here, Rogerian may be most suited to inquiry arguments because it seems to invite complexity. Consider the structure of a typical Rogerian argument:

■ What's the issue (history, context, stakeholders, etc.)?

■ What are the perspectives on the issue? What are the perspectives of those with whom I don't agree?

■ What is sensible about my opponents' views?

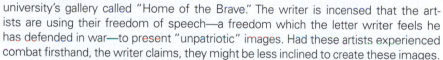

One Student's Response

Rebecca's Journal

EXERCISE 6.1

The letter writer, a combat veteran, found himself "deeply offended" by a collection of artwork in his university's gallery called "Home of the Brave." The writer is incensed that the artists are using their freedom of speech—a freedom which the letter writer feels he has defended in war—to present "unpatriotic" images. Had these artists experienced combat firsthand, the writer claims, they might be less inclined to create these images.

In fact, it is partly the letter writer's experience of combat himself that has led to this intense reaction. The process of going to war is traumatic and singular—one a person can't understand unless they've experienced it first-hand. However, the artwork in the exhibition is not claiming to understand war from the perspective of a soldier, but rather to explore the issues from the artists' unique viewpoint in a creative way. The letter writer's argument that the artists might feel differently if they had been in combat is accurate—surely they would. However, such an argument doesn't invalidate the right of American citizens to express themselves and their diverse opinions through words and images.

I think this discussion is an important one, although I wish the letter writer had used it to spark debate. The vast disparity of experience in artist and audience is what makes art so valuable, encouraging reactions, discussions, and perhaps new understanding. I disagree with the letter writer that the artwork is unpatriotic—in fact, I think the artistic expression of a unique viewpoint is one of the greatest uses of freedom of speech. I also think that the artists could have something valuable to learn from the letter writer as a combat veteran, and I think such a meeting of opposing minds is one of the greatest reactions to art there is.

- What is my view?
- What are the reasons and evidence that supports it?
- How might my ideas *complement* the ideas of others in addressing the issue?

As you can see, this method of argument takes a *both/and* view rather than an *either/or* view, and as a result it's more likely that writers of Rogerian arguments will accept complexity rather than suppress it.

Avoiding Logical Fallacies

An important way to evaluate the soundness of an argument is to examine its logic and, in particular, look for so-called logical fallacies that may lead writers' reasoning astray. Aristotle was one of the first to point out many of these, and a quick search on the web using the term "logical fallacies" will reveal dozens and dozens of them that plague public argument. Many have indecipherable Latin names, testifying to their ancient origins.

Here are ten of the most common logical fallacies. They cover about 90 percent of the ways in which writers stumble when making an argument.

1. *Hasty generalization:* We're naturally judgmental creatures. For example, we frequently make a judgment about someone after just meeting him or her. Or we conclude that a class is useless after attending a single session. These are generalizations based on insufficient evidence. Hasty generalizations *might* be true—the class might turn out to be useless—but you should always be wary of making them.

2. *Ad hominem:* When arguments turn into shouting matches, they almost inevitably get personal. Shifting away from the substance of an argument to attack the person making it, either subtly or explicitly, is another common logical fallacy. It's also, at times, hard to resist.

3. *Appeal to authority:* We all know that finding support for a claim from an expert is a smart move in most arguments. But sometimes it's a faulty move because the authority we cite isn't really an expert on the subject. A more common fallacy, however, is when we cite an expert to support a claim without acknowledging that many other experts disagree on the point.

4. *Straw man:* One of the sneakiest ways to sidetrack reason in an argument is to misrepresent or ignore the actual position of an opponent. Unfortunately, the "straw man" fallacy thrives in many political debates: "I can't support this proposal for universal health care," says politician A. "It's clear that politician A doesn't really take the problem of American health care seriously," says politician B. Huh?

5. *False analogy:* Analogies can be powerful comparisons in argument. But they can also lead us astray when the analogy simply doesn't hold. Are A and B *really* similar situations? For example, when a critic of higher education argues that a public university is like a business and should be run like one, are the two really analogous? Fundamentally, one is nonprofit and the other is designed to make money. Is this really a useful comparison?

6. ***Post hoc or false cause:*** Just because one thing follows another thing doesn't necessarily mean one *causes* the other. It might be coincidence, or the cause might be something else entirely. For example, if you're really keen on arguing that losing the football coach was the cause of the team's losing record, you might link the two. And it's possible that they are linked, but it's also just as possible that the injury to the quarterback was one of the real reasons for the losing record.

7. ***Appeal to popularity:*** In a country obsessed with polls and rankings, it's not hard to understand the appeal of reasoning that argues that because something is popular, it must be good or true. Advertisers are particularly fond of this fallacy, arguing that because their brand is most popular, it must be the best. In fact, the brand might not be the best at all. The majority's opinion can be wrong.

8. ***Slippery slope:*** I love the name of this one because it so aptly describes what can happen when reasoning loses its footing. You might start out reasonably enough, arguing, for example, that a gun control law restricts the rights of some citizens to have access to certain weapons, but pretty soon you start sliding toward conclusions that simply don't follow, such as that a gun control law is the beginning of the end of gun ownership in the country. Now, you might really believe this is true, but logic isn't the route to prove the truth of your view.

9. ***Either/or fallacy:*** In a black-and-white world, something is right or wrong, true or false, good or bad. But ours is a colorful world with many shades. For instance, while it might be emotionally satisfying to say that opponents of the war in Afghanistan must not support the troops there, it is also possible that the war's opponents are against the war *because* they're concerned about the lives of American servicepeople. Rather than *either/or*, it might be *both/and*. We see this fallacy often in arguments that suggest that there are only two choices and that each is opposite to the other.

10. ***Begging the question:*** This one is also called *circular reasoning*, because it assumes the truth of the arguer's conclusion without bothering to prove it. An obvious example of this would be to say that a law protecting people from Internet spam is good because it's a law, and laws should be obeyed. But why is it a good law?

Exercise 6.2

Find the Fallacies

Identifying common logical fallacies in other people's arguments can provide explanations for that gut feeling you have that something just isn't right with certain claims. In other words, fallacies can be a powerful analytical tool. Use the section on ten logical fallacies above to analyze the argument by Khalid Sheikh Mohammed in "The Language of War Is Killing" later in this chapter on page 183.

READINGS

▶ # Factual Argument: Is it true that ___?

We all have that moment in a conversation when we begin with, "Is it true that ___?" Sometimes the question is fun and frivolous: Is it true that your heart stops when you sneeze? (I believed this in the eighth grade.) Is it true that no two snowflakes are alike? But when there are people who have a stake in the answer to the question, then you have a factual argument. For example, climate change and whether it is influenced by human activity is the factual controversy of the day. Another controversy is one that matters a lot to anyone who is facing the prospect of student debt and rising college tuition costs: Does it pay to go to college? In the essay that follows, David Leonhardt has an answer to that question.

Is College Worth It?

David Leonhardt

1   Some newly minted college graduates struggle to find work. Others accept jobs for which they feel overqualified. Student debt, meanwhile, has topped $1 trillion.

2   It's enough to create a wave of questions about whether a college education is still worth it.

3   A new set of income statistics answers those questions quite clearly: Yes, college is worth it, and it's not even close. For all the struggles that many young college graduates face, a four-year degree has probably never been more valuable.

4   The pay gap between college graduates and everyone else reached a record high last year, according to the new data, which is based on an analysis of Labor Department statistics by the Economic Policy Institute in Washington. Americans with four-year college degrees made 98 percent more an hour on average in 2013 than people without a degree. That's up from 89 percent five years earlier, 85 percent a decade earlier and 64 percent in the early 1980s.

5   There is nothing inevitable about this trend. If there were more college graduates than the economy needed, the pay gap would shrink. The gap's recent growth is especially notable because it has come after a rise in the number of college graduates, partly because many people went back to school during the Great Recession. That the pay gap has nonetheless continued growing means that we're still not producing enough of them.

6   "We have too few college graduates," says David Autor, an M.I.T. economist, who was not involved in the Economic Policy Institute's analysis. "We also have too few people who are prepared for college."

7   It's important to emphasize these shortfalls because public discussion today—for which we in the news media deserve some responsibility—often focuses on the

undeniable fact that a bachelor's degree does not guarantee success. But of course it doesn't. Nothing guarantees success, especially after 15 years of <u>disappointing economic growth</u> and <u>rising inequality</u>.

When experts and journalists spend so much time talking about the limitations of education, they almost certainly are discouraging some teenagers from going to college and some adults from going back to earn degrees. (Those same experts and journalists are sending their own children to college and often obsessing over which one.) The decision not to attend college for fear that it's a bad deal is among the most <u>economically irrational</u> decisions anybody could make in 2014.

The much-discussed cost of college doesn't change this fact. According to a <u>paper</u> by Mr. Autor published Thursday in the journal Science, the true cost of a college degree is about *negative* $500,000. That's right: Over the long run, college is cheaper than free. Not going to college will cost you about half a million dollars.

Mr. Autor's paper—building on <u>work by</u> the economists Christopher Avery and Sarah Turner—arrives at that figure first by calculating the very real cost of tuition and fees. This amount is then subtracted from the lifetime gap between the earnings of college graduates and high school graduates. After adjusting for inflation and the time value of money, the net cost of college is negative $500,000, roughly double what it was three decades ago.

This calculation is necessarily imprecise, because it can't control for any preexisting differences between college graduates and nongraduates—differences that would exist regardless of schooling. Yet <u>other research</u>, comparing otherwise similar people who did and did not graduate from college, has also found that education brings a <u>huge return</u>.

In a similar vein, the new Economic Policy Institute numbers show that the benefits of college don't go just to graduates of elite colleges, who typically go on to earn graduate degrees. The wage gap between people with only a bachelor's degree and people without such a degree has also kept rising.

Tellingly, though, the wage premium for people who have attended college without earning a bachelor's degree—a group that includes community-college graduates—has not been rising. The big economic returns go to people with four-year degrees. Those returns underscore the importance of efforts to reduce the college dropout rate, such as those at the University of Texas, which Paul Tough described in a recent Times Magazine <u>article</u>.

But what about all those alarming stories you hear about indebted, jobless college graduates?

The anecdotes may be real, yet the conventional wisdom often <u>exaggerates the problem</u>. Among four-year college graduates who took out loans, <u>average debt</u> is about $25,000, a sum that is a tiny fraction of the economic benefits of college. (My own student debt, as it happens, was almost identical to this figure, in inflation-adjusted terms.) And the unemployment rate in April for people between 25 and 34 years old with a bachelor's degree was a mere 3 percent.

(continued)

(continued)

16   I find the data from the Economic Policy Institute especially telling because the institute—a left-leaning research group—makes a point of arguing that education is not the solution to all of the economy's problems. That is important, too. College graduates, like almost everyone else, are suffering from the economy's weak growth and from the disproportionate share of this growth flowing to the very richest households.

17   The average hourly wage for college graduates has risen only 1 percent over the last decade, to about $32.60. The pay gap has grown mostly because the average wage for everyone else has fallen—5 percent, to about $16.50. "To me, the picture is people in almost every kind of job not being able to see their wages grow," Lawrence Mishel, the institute's president, told me. "Wage growth essentially stopped in 2002."

18   From the country's perspective, education can be only part of the solution to our economic problems. We also need to find other means for lifting living standards—not to mention ways to provide good jobs for people without college degrees.

19   But from almost any individual's perspective, college is a no-brainer. It's the most reliable ticket to the middle class and beyond. Those who question the value of college tend to be those with the luxury of knowing their own children will be able to attend it.

20   Not so many decades ago, high school was considered the frontier of education. Some people <u>even argued</u> that it was a waste to encourage Americans from humble backgrounds to spend four years of life attending high school. Today, obviously, the notion that everyone should attend 13 years of school is indisputable.

21   But there is nothing magical about 13 years of education. As the economy becomes more technologically complex, the amount of education that people need will rise. At some point, 15 years or 17 years of education will make more sense as a universal goal.

22   That point, in fact, has already arrived.

23   *Source:* http://nyti.ms/1hsxnlG

Inquiring into the Essay

1. **Explore.** You've made the decision to go to college. But did you have any doubts? Spend four or five minutes fastwriting your response to that question.

2. **Explain.** Here's the common perception: College graduates these days have a really hard time finding a job. Here's Leonhardt's claim: "But from almost any individual's perspective, college is a no-brainer." Can you explain what Leonhardt says in his essay that reconciles what seem like two contradictory perspectives?

3. **Evaluate.** Using Toulmin's argument model (see page 174) to analyze "Is College Worth It?" For example, Leonhardt argues that excessive talk about

the "limitations of education" discourages some students from enrolling, which he calls "among the most economically irrational decisions anybody could make...." That's a claim. The grounds to make that claim is that despite high tuition and debt, college graduates still make significantly more money than people with only a high school education. What are the assumptions that make the grounds persuasive support for the claim? In other words, what do you have to believe is true about what is meant, say, about the "limitations of education"?

4. **Reflect.** Think about what evidence is most persuasive in a factual argument (see pages 172–173 for types of evidence). Think about what evidence is most persuasive in an evaluation argument like a review. Are they different? Why?

▶ Definition Argument: What should we call it?

Because the sanctioned mass killing that we call war is so horrific, so counter to our moral instincts, we traumatize the language we use to talk about it, too. We have to define war in a way that makes "sense," that makes it less horrific. It's hard to imagine that one of the chief planners of the September 11, 2001, attacks on New York and Washington, DC, might invoke George Washington as his hero. In the excerpt that follows, Khalid Sheikh Mohammed, a commander for al Qaeda who has been in custody since 2003, argues that, like Washington, Islamic extremists are just fighting for their independence. The language of war, says Mohammed, is universal, and that language is killing.

This partial transcript of Mohammed discussing his role in the 9/11 attacks, the murder of journalist Daniel Pearl, and the hotel bombings in Bali was released by the U.S. Department of Defense and later appeared in *Harper's Magazine*.

The Language of War Is Killing
Khalid Sheikh Mohammed

I'm not making myself a hero when I said I was responsible for this or that. You know very well there is a language for any war. If America wants to invade Iraq, they will not send Saddam roses or kisses. They send bombardment. I admit I'm America's enemy. For sure, I'm America's enemy. So when we make war against America, we are like jackals fighting in the night. We consider George Washington a hero. Muslims, many of them, believe Osama bin Laden is doing the same thing. He is just fighting. He needs his independence. Many Muslims think that, not only me. They have been oppressed by America. So when we say we are enemy combatants, that's right, we are. But I'm

(continued)

(continued)

asking you to be fair with many detainees who are not enemy combatants. Because many of them have been unjustly arrested. You know very well, for any country waging war against their enemy, the language of the war is killing. If man and woman are together as a marriage, the others are kids, children. But if you and me, two nations, are together in war, the others are victims. This is the way of the language. You know forty million people were killed in World War I. Many people are oppressed. Because there is war, for sure, there will be victims. I'm not happy that three thousand have been killed in America. I feel sorry even. Islam never gives me the green light to kill people. Killing, in Christianity, Judaism, and Islam, is prohibited. But there are exceptions to the rule. When you are killing people in Iraq, you say, We have to do it. We don't like Saddam. But this is the way to deal with Saddam. Same language you use I use. When you are invading two thirds of Mexico, you call your war "manifest destiny." It's up to you to call it what you want. But the other side is calling you oppressors. If now we were living in the Revolutionary War, George Washington would be arrested by Britain. For sure, they would consider him an enemy combatant. But in America they consider him a hero. In any revolutionary war one side will be either George Washington or Britain. So we considered American Army bases in Saudi Arabia, Kuwait, Qatar, and Bahrain. This is a kind of invasion, but I'm not here to convince you. I don't have to say that I'm not your enemy. This is why the language of any war in the world is killing. The language of war is victims. I don't like to kill people. I feel very sorry kids were killed in 9/11. What will I do? I want to make a great awakening in America to stop foreign policy in our land. I know Americans have been torturing us since the seventies. I know they are talking about human rights. And I know it is against the American Constitution, against American laws. But they said, Every law has exceptions. This is your bad luck—you've been part of the exception to our laws. So, for me, I have patience. The Americans have human rights, but enemy combatant is a flexible word. What is an enemy combatant in my language? The Ten Commandments are shared between all of us. We are all serving one God. But we also share the language of War. War started when Cain killed Abel. It's never gonna stop killing people. America starts the Revolutionary War, and then the Mexican, then the Spanish, then World War I, World War II. You read the history. This is life. You have to kill.

Inquiring into the Essay

1. **Explore.** Does Mohammed have a point when he compares Islamic extremists who fight for "freedom" to American revolutionaries such as George Washington, who fought for independence? Fastwrite on this question in your journal for five minutes, exploring what you think. When you're done, skip a line and compose a one-sentence answer to this question: *What surprised you most about what you said in your fastwrite?*

2. **Explain.** Are there examples of the logical fallacy of false analogy? Find one and explain why it's false.

3. **Evaluate.** Use the model of classical argument (see page 173) to analyze Mohammed's argument. In particular, evaluate how he uses ethos, pathos, and logos to address an audience that is quite likely to be resistant to his appeal.

4. **Reflect.** The September 11 attacks have, understandably, made many Americans very emotional about terrorism and terrorists. What did you notice about your emotional reaction to Mohammed's argument in "The Language of War Is Killing"? Did you find it difficult to read the transcript analytically, as the previous questions asked you to do?

▶ Causal Argument: What's the Cause?

A few weeks ago, my neighbor state of Oregon joined Colorado and Washington in legalizing recreational marijuana. Leading up to all of these votes was a fury of causal arguments offered by both sides of the debate, all addressing the question "What's going to happen if we do this?" Naturally, in those few states that have made the move, the argument has changed to "What *has* happened here since legalization?" The jury, as they say, is out; it's still fairly early in this social experiment. But in Colorado, where implementation of the laws first started, this new debate is building.

Kevin Sabet, writing in the newspaper *The Washington Times*, weighed in fairly early, within a month of implementation of the law, on the effects of legalization in Colorado, arguing that "legalization's worst enemy is itself." He then goes on to detail what he believes will be the negative effects. It's interesting to consider these early predictions now that we're getting some data on the effects of Colorado's law. Does this new information confirm, complicate, or challenge Sabet's claims? Read the essay, do some Googling, and see what you think. Sabet is a former White House drug policy adviser.

Colorado Will Show Why Legalizing Marijuana Is a Mistake

Kevin Sabet

On Jan. 1, Colorado made history as the first jurisdiction in the modern era to license the retail sales of marijuana. 1

To be sure, there were no bloody fistfights among people waiting in line and, as far as we know, no burglaries or robberies. Legalization advocates cheered. 2

While it is true that most people who use marijuana won't become addicted to heroin or otherwise hurt society as a result, Colorado's experiment with legal pot can be called anything but successful. 3

What didn't make the news were some troubling developments. 4

(continued)

(continued)

5   Multimillion-dollar private investing groups have emerged and are poised to become, in their words, "Big Marijuana"; added to a list of dozens of other children, a 2-year-old girl ingested a marijuana cookie and had to receive immediate medical attention; a popular website boldly discussed safe routes for smugglers to bring marijuana into neighboring states; and a marijuana-store owner proudly proclaimed that Colorado would soon be the destination of choice for 18- to 21-year-olds, even though for them marijuana is still supposed to be illegal.

6   Popular columnists spanning the ideological spectrum, in The New York Times, The Washington Post and Newsweek/Daily Beast, soon expressed their disapproval of such policies as contributing to the dumbing down of America.

7   Colorado's experience, ironically, might eventually teach us that legalization's worst enemy is itself.

8   This raises the question: Why do we have to experience a tragedy before knowing where to go next?

9   Sadly, the marijuana conversation is one mired with myths. Many Americans do not think that marijuana can be addictive, despite scientific evidence to the contrary.

10   Many would be surprised to learn that the American Medical Association (AMA) has come out strongly against the legal sales of marijuana, citing public health concerns. In fact, the AMA's opinion is consistent with most major medical associations, including the American Academy of Pediatrics and American Society of Addiction Medicine.

11   Because today's marijuana is at least five to six times stronger than the marijuana smoked by most of today's parents, we are often shocked to hear that, according to the National Institutes of Health, one in six 16-year-olds who try marijuana will become addicted to it; marijuana intoxication doubles the risk of a car crash; heavy marijuana use has been significantly linked to an 8-point reduction in IQ; and that marijuana use is strongly connected to mental illness.

12   Constantly downplaying the risks of marijuana, its advocates have promised reductions in crime, flowing tax revenue and little in the way of negative effects on youth. We shouldn't hold our breath, though.

13   We can expect criminal organizations to adapt to legal prices, sell to people outside the legal market (e.g., kids) and continue to profit from other, much larger revenue sources, such as human trafficking and other drugs.

14   We can expect the social costs ensuing from increased marijuana use to greatly outweigh any tax revenue—witness the fact that tobacco and alcohol cost society $10 for every $1 gained in taxes.

15   Probably worst of all, we can expect our teens to be bombarded with promotional messages from a new marijuana industry seeking lifelong customers.

16   In light of the currently skewed discourse on marijuana, these are difficult facts to digest. In one fell swoop, we have been promised great things with legalization. However, we can expect to be let down.

17   Voters in other states should watch Colorado closely and engage in a deep conversation about where they want this country to go. Buyer, beware.

18   *Source:* http://www.washingtontimes.com/news/2014/jan/17/sabet-marijuana-legalizationsworst-enemy/

Inquiring into the Essay

1. **Explore.** In a fastwrite, explore your reaction to this statement: "Fairness dictates that policymakers either need to play nanny and ban everything that's bad for us—from sugar-laden soda to fat-filled fast food—or they need to allow Americans to make adult decisions about what they want to put in their bodies. Making cigarettes, beer, and whiskey legal, while banning joints and hash brownies, unfairly favors the makers of certain harmful products."[2]

2. **Explain.** Using the Rogerian approach discussed earlier (pp. 175–176), "say back" what you understand to be Sabet's argument. Summarize his argument, including his main claim (or S.O.FT.) and some of the reasons he offers to support it.

3. **Evaluate.** This article was written within a few weeks of the implementation of Colorado's marijuana law. Do some research on whether the reasons Sabet offers to support his claims are backed by the most recent evidence on the law's effects. How would you evaluate his argument based on what you discovered?

4. **Reflect.** What would you say is your feeling about the question of legalization of recreational marijuana at this moment—oppose, neutral/not sure, supportive? How do you suppose your view influenced your reading of the essay compared to the reading by someone with a different view? What does this imply about how an audience's disposition towards an issue might affect how you make an argument?

---

[2]Shane, Scott. "Why Colorado and Washington Were Wise to Legalize Pot." *Entrepreneur*, 20 Jan. 2014, www.entrepreneur.com/article/230942.

THE WRITING PROCESS

Inquiry Project Writing an Argument

Inquiry questions: What is true? What should it be called? What is the cause?

Write an essay in which you make a factual, causal, or definitional claim about an issue or controversy that interests you. You are writing for an audience of nonexperts. Make sure your essay includes the following:

- *Claims* that are supported by clear reasons.
- *Relevant evidence* from your research, observations, and personal experience to support your claims and reasons.
- A strong sense of *what is at stake* for your readers. Why should they care as much as you do about the issue?
- At least some attention to *counterarguments*. What are other ways of looking at the issue, and why did you reject them?

What Are You Going to Write About?

Gun control, abortion rights, and other hot-button public controversies often make the list of banned topics for student essays. This is not because they aren't important public debates. Instead, the problem is much more that the writer has likely already made up his or her mind and sees the chance to ascend a soapbox.

Now, I have my own favorite soapboxes; people with strong convictions do. But as you think about subjects for your essay, consider that the soapbox may not be the best vantage point for practicing inquiry. If you've already made up your mind, will you be open to discovery? If you just want to line up ducks—assembling evidence to support an unwavering belief—will you be encouraged to think deeply or differently? Will you be inclined to filter the voices you hear rather than consider a range of points of view?

The best persuasive essays often emerge from the kind of open-ended inquiry that you might have used for writing the personal essay. What do you want to understand better? What issue or question makes you wonder? What controversies are you and your friends talking about? Be alert to possible subjects that you might write about *not* because you already know what you think, but because you want to find out what you think. Or consider a subject that you might have feelings about but feel uninformed on, lacking the knowledge to know exactly what you think.

The best argument essays make a clear claim, but they do it by bowing respectfully to the complexity of the subject, examining it from a variety of perspectives, not just two opposing poles.

Opening Up

Play around with some ideas first by using some of the following triggers for thinking-through-writing in your journal. Suspend judgment. Don't reject anything. Explore. Remember that your goal is to come up with a factual, causal, or definitional argument, so always be on the lookout for those types of arguments as you generate ideas.

Listing Prompts. Lists can be rich sources of triggering topics. Let them grow freely, and when you're ready, use a list item as the focus of another list or an episode of fastwriting. The following prompts should get you started.

1. In your journal, make a quick list of issues that have provoked disagreements between groups of people in your hometown or local community. What about on campus?

2. Think about these important areas of your life: school, family, work, hobbies, relationships. Title columns with each of these words in your journal or on your computer, and then make a fast list of whatever comes to mind when you think of controversial issues in each category. (See "One Student's Response: Rebecca's Journal" on the following page.)

3. Try brainstorming lists from the inquiry questions. Quickly complete the following seed sentences. See if you can generate five of each.

   - I wonder if _____ causes _____?
   - I wonder how people define _____?
   - Is it true that _____?

4. Jot down a list of the classes you're taking this semester. Then make a quick list of topics that prompt disagreements among people in the fields that you're studying. For example, in your political science class, did you learn that there are debates about the usefulness of the Electoral College? In your biology class, have you discussed global warming? In your women's studies class, did you read about Title IX and how it affects female athletes?

Fastwriting Prompts. Remember, fastwriting is a great way to stimulate creative thinking. Turn off your critical side and let yourself write "badly." Don't worry too much about what you're going to say before you say it. Write fast, letting language lead for a change.

1. Search online for the Harper's Index, a monthly list of interesting statistics that often tell a story about the way things were, are, or will become.

   Here are a few examples:

   Percentage of all Americans who consider themselves part of the top 1 percent of U.S. earners: 13
   Percentage of Hispanic Americans who do: 28
   Percentage of 27- to 45-year-old women who have at least four sexual fantasies per week: 35
   Percentage of 18- to 26-year-old women who do: 27

One Student's Response

Rebecca's Journal

LISTS OF POSSIBLE ARGUMENT TOPICS

1. **Issues:** Gay marriage, rent control, cat calling
   on the street (or in restaurant jobs!), cleanliness, encouraging diversity vs. affirmative action, underage drinking, abortion rights
2. **School:** funding for the arts
3. **Family:** retirement/money issues, distance between family members, aging
4. **Work:** survival job vs. dream job, bad economy
5. **Hobbies:** too much work, NYC too expensive
6. **Relationships:** too much work, how to meet people?
7. **Cultural trends:** Twitter/Facebook/Tumblr/other social media, going to movies, drinking/clubbing, gossip

Fastwrite about one of these facts. In your fastwrite, explore the following questions:

- Is this surprising?
- Does this fact seem true? If so, what would explain it? If not, what makes me skeptical?
- What is my personal experience with this? Does it remind me of any stories, people, situations?
- What might be the cause?

2. Use something from your lists in the preceding section for a focused fastwrite.

3. In a seven-minute fastwrite, explore the differences between your beliefs and the beliefs of your parents. Tell yourself the story of how your own beliefs about some question evolved, perhaps moving away from your parents' positions. Can you imagine the argument you might make to help them understand your point of view?

Visual Prompts. Think about words whose meanings are contested or raise questions for you. For example: feminism, attractiveness, intelligence, manhood, redneck. In your journal, choose one of these words as a nucleus for a cluster. Then build branches, free-associating names of people, ideas about, personal observations, common definitions, memories, facts, places, questions, and so on.

Let your cluster grow as many branches as possible; when one dies out, start another. Are you growing an idea about a definition argument?

Research Prompts. By definition, argument essays deal with subjects in which people beyond the writer have a stake. And one of the best ways to collect ideas about such issues is to do a little quick and dirty research. Try some of the following research prompts:

1. Read the letters to the editor in your local paper a few days in a row. What issues have people riled up locally? Is there one that you find particularly interesting?

2. Do a Google search for terms or phrases on an issue that interests you, such as "global warming Greenland glaciers" or "pro-anorexia websites." Did you find any results that make you curious or make you feel something about the issue, one way or another?

3. Your Facebook friends may list groups that support or oppose social causes. Browse some of them to see if one inspires an argument topic.

Narrowing Down

Remember that the task here is to discover a topic that might inspire one of these three types of arguments: *factual, causal,* or *definitional*.

6.4

Develop a question that is focused enough to lead to a strong claim and convincing evidence.

What's Promising Material and What Isn't?   First, you must be interested in the topic, even if you know little about it. Also consider some of the following as you make your choice:

- *Evidence.* Do you think you'll be able to find facts, statistics, comments from experts, or stories about people affected by the issue?

- *Disagreement.* A topic lends itself to argumentative writing if it leads to disagreement among reasonable people.

- *Inquiry.* Do you already have strong feelings about what you think about a topic? If so, using another topic will provide more opportunities for learning and discovery.

   To help narrow down towards an essay topic that might lead to the *type* of argument we're focusing on here, review the ideas you generated and consider which of the following observations seem relevant to the potential topics you have so far.

Argument Type	Initial Observations on a Topic
Factual	No one seems to agree on the facts!
Causal	It seems like there is a cause/effect relationship that might explain the problem.
Definitional	Different people seem to call this issue, problem, or phenomenon really different things.

Questions About Audience and Purpose. In the beginning of the chapter, I emphasized that we make public arguments only about issues in which certain people have a stake. Who are those people? What audiences might care that the issue is addressed? To whom does it matter? For each potential topic, map out potential stakeholders in a mind map like the one in Figure 6.4. If you can, break each audience down further, identifying more specific groups of stakeholders in each target audience.

Looking at your mind map, identify which of these audiences has the most at stake in the answer to the question you're posing. In Figure 6.4, a causal argument that asks, "Does Facebook use cause depression?", it isn't hard to see that Facebook users are the most important stakeholders. Is this group likely to have existing attitudes about the answer to the question you're asking? What are those attitudes? Are there secondary audiences, perhaps those not directly affected by the issue but who can influence the solution to the problem? For example, certainly psychologists who treat adolescent depression would be keenly interested in the answer to the question about Facebook's relationship to depression. They're also a group in a position to do something about it.

Keeping all of this in mind, can you imagine at this point the audience you are most interested in reaching in your argument? What might be your purpose in doing so?

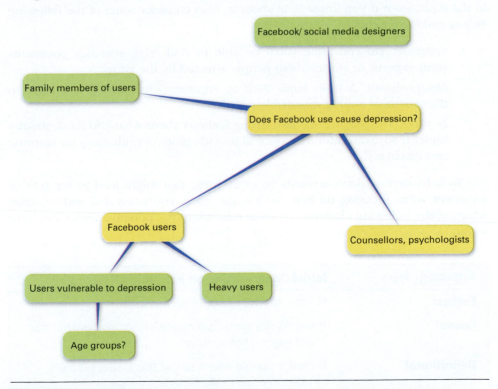

Figure 6.4 Audience analysis

Trying Out

Okay, you've got a tentative topic and inquiry question for your argument essay: *Does Facebook use cause depression?* At this point, you're thinking that your claim might be that, yes, it does. This isn't a bad start. But your opening question is still pretty broad. What *aspects* of Facebook use might you focus on? After all, users have all kinds of ways of interacting with the site. The question also begs the question of which users you might be talking about. Certainly not everyone. And are you talking about certain kinds of depression? Like a lot of research-based projects, the argument essay should pose a question that will help you make the decision about what information to look for and what to ignore. It should be focused enough that you can wade into a creek rather than a raging river of information. If you think your question might be too general, try the following activity to cut it down to size.

Kitchen Knives of Thought. Try the following steps in your journal:

STEP ONE: Write your tentative argument question at the top of a page of your notebook, and circle or underline every general or vague term.

Does Facebook use cause depression?

STEP TWO: "Wh" questions (who, what, which, when, where, why) are the kitchen knives of thought. They can help you cut abstractions and generalities down to size. For each circled word in your inquiry question, find an appropriate "Wh" question that might help you make your research question more specific. Then jot down a quick list of ideas to answer the question you pose. For example,

1. *What* **kinds** of Facebook use?
   - Number of friends
   - Online interactions—rejection, being blocked, etc.
   - Authoring or reacting to certain posts on emotional state

2. *Which* **users**?
   - Adolescent
   - Heavy users
   - Users with existing emotional problems

3. *What* **kinds** of depression?
   - Major, possibly leading to treatment or hospitalization
   - Minor, affecting self-esteem
   - Suicidal

STEP THREE: Restate your inquiry question, making it more specific and focused.

Do social interactions on Facebook cause major depression among heavy users?

Research Considerations. While writing this argument essay does involve some research, it isn't exactly a research paper. A research paper is a much more extended treatment of a topic that relies on more-detailed and scholarly information than is usually needed for an argument essay.

To develop a working knowledge of the topic for your argument essay, focus your research on the following:

1. *The back story:* What is the history of the controversy? (When did it begin, who was involved, how was the issue addressed, and what were the problems?)

2. *Popular assumptions:* What do most people currently believe is true about the issue?

3. *The evidence:* Which particular people have said which particular things that seem to support your claim or provide backing for your assumptions?

4. *Opposing arguments:* Who offers a counterargument that you might need to consider?

Interviews. While both the web and the university library are great sources of information on your topic, often the best way to learn about it—and get some good quotes for your essay—is to find someone to talk to. Your reading will probably give you the best clues about who to contact. Who is often quoted in news stories? Who has been writing or blogging about the issue? You might also be able to find someone on your own campus. If you're writing, say, about measures that attempt to protect students from date rape on your campus, someone in the criminal justice department or in Student Affairs can tell you more about the issue in a few minutes than you might learn in a couple hours online.

Writing the Sketch

Now draft an exploratory sketch with the following elements:

- It has a tentative title.
- It raises a causal, definitional, or factual question.
- It presents and analyzes several contrasting points of view on the question.
- It offers a tentative answer to the question that includes a few reasons that support the claim, as well as supporting evidence: an anecdote or story, a personal observation, data, an analogy, a case study, expert testimony, other relevant quotations from people involved, a precedent.
- It includes a Works Cited or References page listing the sources used.

▶ **Student Sketch**

Rebecca Thompson takes up a causal question: Do social media (things meant to connect us) actually undermine communication between users? At this point, she's inclined to argue that social media like Twitter enhance communication, but she concedes that there are many critics who believe that sites such as Facebook do harm by undermining our social relationships rather than enhancing them, as Rebecca starts to argue here. Her sketch is the seed of an argument: There's a claim, reasons that support it, evidence, and consideration of another point of view. We'll see later in the chapter how the argument develops from here.

Twitter a Profound Thought?

Rebecca Thompson

Facebook Chat. iPhone texting. Checking in on FourSquare. Twitter hashtags. Tumblr blogging. These days, there's no limit to the ways we can talk to each other. Suddenly, talking and listening is much more complicated. But is this a good thing?   1

I use social media regularly. I use my email, Facebook, Twitter, and iPhone in all areas of my life, from connecting with high school friends now scattered across the country, to networking and advertising projects I'm involved in, to keeping updated on news stories. When Hurricane Irene struck the East Coast, I was out of town. I kept tabs on my friends via Facebook, and followed the news stories by following the hashtag #HurricaneIrene on Twitter. It was a relief to be connected, even from far away. "At its core, it is about connections and community," said Mailet Lopez, the founder of the networking site I Had Cancer, to *Forbes* magazine. "Social networking provides an opportunity beyond physical support networks and online forums…because with a social network, people can connect based on whatever criteria they want, regardless of location."   2

Yet detractors argue that social media does the opposite of what Lopez claims—it encourages *disconnectivity*. By focusing more on the kind of communication based around gadgets and the internet, critics argue that social media deconstructs traditional methods of conversation and undermines interpersonal relationships. "Technology is threatening to dominate our lives and make us less human," writes Paul Harris, referencing Sherry Turkle's book *Alone Together*. "Under the illusion of allowing us to communicate better, it is actually isolating us from real human interactions in a cyber-reality that is a poor imitation of the real world."   3

While there is certainly truth to this claim, I argue that social media sites have the potential, if used to their best advantage, to facilitate communication and networking. Because I can respond to emails and texts on the go, I can plan ahead. I can keep in touch with my friends studying abroad when phones aren't an option. I get lost a *lot* less. Even the Pope has spoken of the benefits of the internet, social networking, and media. "Search engines and social networks have become the starting point of communication for many people who are seeking advice, ideas, information and answers," he said. "In our time, the internet is becoming ever more a forum for questions and answers…In concise phrases, often no longer than a verse from the Bible, profound thoughts can be communicated."   4

Works Cited

Harris, Paul. "Social Networking under Fresh Attack as Tide of Cyber-Skepticism Sweeps US." *The Guardian*, 22 Jan. 2011, www.theguardian.com/media/2011/jan/22/social-networking-cyber-scepticism-twitter.

John, Tracey. "New Social Network Connects Cancer Survivors, Patients, and Supporters." *Forbes*, 25 Aug. 2011, www.forbes.com/sites/traceyjohn/2011/08/25/new-social-network-connects-cancer-survivors-patients-and-supporters/#16baa1804ac5.

Shariatmadari, David. "Pope Benedict Praises Twitter-like Forms of Communication." *The Guardian*, 24 Jan. 2012, www.theguardian.com/world/2012/jan/24/pope-benedict-twitter-communication.

Moving from Sketch to Draft

A successful sketch points the way to the next draft. But how can you get your sketch to point the way, particularly for an essay that makes an argument? One of the most useful things you can ask yourself about your sketch is this: *What is the balance between explaining what I think and presenting evidence to support it?* If your sketch is mostly what writing expert Ken Macrorie once called "explainery," then the most important thing you might do is refocus on research. Gather more information on your topic. Test your ideas against your current opinions.

Evaluating Your Own Sketch. There are some other, more specific ways of evaluating your sketch. For example, answering these questions should give you some guidance:

- **Is the question you started with narrow enough?** Does it use specific terms rather than general terms ("society," "people," etc.)? When you did some research, were you either overwhelmed with information or unsure of where to look? If you conclude that your question still isn't focused enough, try "Kitchen Knives of Thought," earlier in this chapter.

- **Does the sketch point to a S.O.F.T.?** What seems to be the main claim you're making based on the evidence you've gathered so far?

- **Is that claim linked to one or more reasons?** Remember that claims are built on reasons (e.g., Twitter played a key factor in the success of Egypt's "Arab spring" *because* the regime couldn't control it.).

Reflecting on What You've Learned. Based on your experience so far with developing an argument essay, make an entry in your journal that explores the following questions:

- What's the difference between a fact and an opinion? Between a claim and an opinion?

- Consider what you've always thought about making arguments. How has that changed since you started working on this project?

Developing

Writing for Your Readers. You've read and written about an issue you care about. Now for the really hard part: getting out of your own head and into the heads of your potential readers, who may not care as much about your issue as you do. One way to do this is to imagine what someone in your target audience might say to you if you were telling him or her about the topic. Figure 6.5 suggests just such a conversation in three parts:

6.5
Use audience analysis and logical methods to help guide revision of an argument.

- **Backstory.** What does someone who is familiar or unfamiliar with the issue need to know to appreciate that he or she has a stake in it?

- **Concessions, Qualifications, and Complications.** People disagree. Questions have many possible answers. What have other people said?

- **Reason-Evidence Loop.** At the heart of your argument is circling this loop enough times to convince your questioner to believe your claim. (See Figure 6.5.)

This is not necessarily a scheme for structuring your essay—just for identifying the key parts of an argument that make it persuasive to readers. Which of these parts are underdeveloped or even missing from your sketch?

Another element of argument is the way the writer comes across to readers—his or her ethos. In the writing you've done so far on your topic, how do you think you might come off to an audience? Is your tone appealing, or might it be slightly off-putting? Do you successfully establish your authority to speak on this issue, or is the persona you project in the sketch somewhat unconvincing, perhaps too emotional or not fair enough?

As we develop convictions about an issue, one of the hardest things to manage in early argument drafts is creating a persuasive persona (ethos). Another is finding ways to establish connections with our audience; this does not merely involve connecting writer and readers, but also includes creating some common ground between readers and *the topic*. There are many ways to do this, including the following:

1. Connecting your readers' prior beliefs or values with your position on the topic.

2. Establishing that readers have a *stake*, perhaps even a personal one, in how the question you've raised is answered; this may be self-interest, but it may also be emotional (remember the advertiser's strategy).

3. Highlighting the common experiences readers may have had with the topic and offering your claim as a useful way of understanding that experience.

4. Being reasonable. Do you devote time to looking at points of view that you may not share?

Researching the Argument. The key to developing your draft is research. Though you might be able to use some of the information you gathered for your sketch, chances are that your focus or claims are shifting as you learn more. That

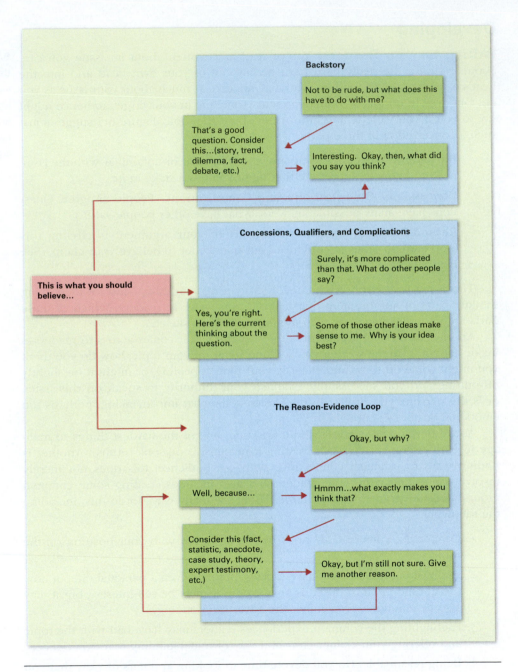

Figure 6.5 The reason-evidence loop

means going back to the research well. In particular, you need enough information on the following:

- Evidence that supports your claims. Not just anything will do. Which evidence is most *persuasive*? You may have to look hard to find this evidence.
- Counterarguments from sources that take a view different from yours.
- Background information that establishes the *context* of the issue you're writing about. What's the debate? Who's involved? How long has this been going on? Why does it matter?

More Looking in the Library.   One of the most useful things you can do to prepare for the draft is to spend forty-five minutes at the campus library searching for new information on your topic. Consider expanding your search from current newspapers and periodicals to books or government publications. In addition, you can refer to online almanacs such as Infoplease, the CIA's online World Factbook, and statistical information available from sources such as the U.S. Census Bureau's American Fact Finder—a wonderful resource that draws on the Bureau's massive database of information on U.S. trends.

Face-to-Face Interviewing.   Try some interviews if you haven't already. People who are somehow involved in your topic are among the best sources of new information and lively material. An interview can provide ideas about what else you should read or who else you might talk to, as well as the quotations, anecdotes, and case studies that can make the next draft of your argument essay much more interesting. After all, what makes an issue matter is how it affects people. Have you sufficiently dramatized those effects?

Using the Web to Obtain Interviews and Quotes.   The Internet can also be a source for interview material. Look for e-mail links to the authors of useful documents you find on the web and write to them with a few questions. Interest groups, newsgroups, or electronic mailing lists on the web can also provide the voices and perspectives of people with something to say on your topic. Remember to ask permission to quote them if you decide to use something of theirs in your draft. For leads on finding web discussion groups on your topic, visit Google Groups or Yahoo Groups, which allow you to search for online discussion groups on virtually any topic, or Catalist, the official catalog of electronic mailing lists, which has a database of about 15,000 discussion groups.

Finding Images.   When appropriate, look for images to dramatize your claims or your evidence. Images are easy to find using search engines such as Google Image Search. But any images you use must be specifically relevant to your argument. If you do use online images in your essay, make sure to give the source credit in the text and the bibliography.

Drafting

Designing Your Argument Rhetorically. The argument essay is one of those forms of writing that are plagued by organizing formulas. The claim must go in the first paragraph. The reasons behind the claims should be topic sentences, followed by evidence. The conclusion should restate the claim. But take a look at any published arguments, and you'll see how far this formula is from the way arguments are actually written.

On the other hand, arguments do typically have the features that we've discussed: a question, a claim that addresses it, reasons, evidence, counterclaims. Just don't ever imagine that you should march through these features in some strict order. You need to decide the design of your argument. And what will help you most in doing this is thinking about audience, especially:

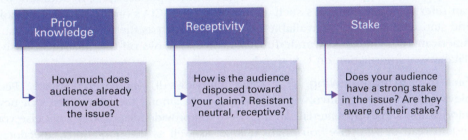

Prior knowledge	Receptivity	Stake
How much does audience already know about the issue?	How is the audience disposed toward your claim? Resistant neutral, receptive?	Does your audience have a strong stake in the issue? Are they aware of their stake?

This rhetorical awareness of your audience has implications for what information you include—and especially what you emphasize—in your draft:

- **Prior knowledge.** If your audience knows little about your topic, then you'll spend more time with background and context than you might if they largely understand the issue.

- **Receptivity.** Audiences that are already inclined to strongly agree are less critical. They probably need less evidence to be convinced of your position than neutral readers do. A resistant audience is the toughest sell: Strong evidence, and lots of it, are key.

- **Stake.** Neutral audiences—the kind you're most likely to encounter—have little awareness that your topic matters to them. You have to make it matter, and make it matter quickly.

Methods of Development. Earlier in this chapter, we explored three models for argument: classical, Toulmin, and Rogerian. Each of these is typically associated with certain ways of structuring an argument (for structures of classical and Rogerian arguments, see pages 173 and 177). While there is no formula for organizing an argument, there are some ways of developing parts—and sometimes all—of your essay.

Narrative. Telling a story is an underrated way of developing an argument. Can you imagine a way to present your topic in an extended story, perhaps by focusing on the experience of a particular person or group of people, in a particular place, at a particular time? Obviously, the story must somehow be logically linked to your claim.

There are other ways to use narrative, too. Anecdotes, or brief stories that illustrate an idea or a problem, are frequently used in argument essays. One effective way to begin your essay might be to tell a story that highlights the problem you're writing about or the question you're posing.

Question to Answer.   Almost all writing is an attempt to answer a question. In the personal essay and other open forms of inquiry, the writer may never arrive at a definite answer, but an argument essay usually offers an answer. An obvious method of development, therefore, is to begin your essay by raising the question and end it by offering your answer.

Are there several key questions around which you might organize your draft, leading to your central claim at the end?

Problem to Solution.   This variation on the question-to-answer structure can be particularly useful if you're writing on a topic readers may know very little about. In such cases, you might need to spend as much time establishing what exactly the problem is—explaining what makes it a problem and why the reader should care about it—as you do offering your particular solution.

Effect to Cause or Cause to Effect.   At the heart of some arguments is the *relationship* between causes and effects; often what is at issue is pinpointing such a relationship. Once a relationship is pinpointed, solutions can be offered. Sadly, we know the effects of terrorism, but what are its causes? If you were to argue, as some do, that Islamic radicalism arose in response to U.S. policies in the Middle East, including its policies toward Israel and the Palestinians, then you would be arguing from effect to cause. As the solution, you might go on to propose a shift in foreign policy. Some arguments can be organized simply around an examination of causes and effects.

Combining Approaches.   As you think about how you might organize your first draft, you don't necessarily have to choose among these various methods of development. In fact, most often they work well together.

Using Evidence.   All writing relies on evidence—that is, on specific information that has some relationship to the general ideas expressed. For some of these relationships, see "Inquiring into the Details: What Evidence Can Do" on the following page. Although all these relationships are possible in an argumentative essay, especially common is the use of evidence to support ideas that the writer wants the reader to believe. What *kind* of evidence to include is a rhetorical issue. To whom are you writing, and what kind of evidence will they be most likely to believe?

Generally speaking, the narrower and more specialized the audience, the more particular they will be about the types of evidence they'll find convincing. As you continue on in your chosen major, you'll find that the types of evidence that help you make a persuasive argument will be more and more prescribed by the

Inquiring into the Details

What Evidence Can Do

Usually we think of using evidence only to support an idea or claim we're making. But evidence can be used in other ways, too. For example, it can do the following:

- *refute* or challenge a claim with which you disagree
- *show* that a seemingly simple assertion, problem, or idea is actually complex
- *complicate* or even contradict an earlier point you've made
- *contrast* two or more ways of seeing the same thing
- *test* an idea, hypothesis, or theory

field. In the natural sciences, the results of quantitative studies count more than case studies; in the humanities, primary texts count more than secondary ones.

The important thing for this argument essay, which you're writing for a more general audience, is that you attempt to *vary* your evidence. For example, rather than relying exclusively on anecdotes, include some quotes from an expert as well.

Workshopping

Workshops on argument drafts can be lively affairs. People have opinions, and other people may disagree with those opinions. Facts can be contested with counterfacts. As you prepare to share your draft, I'd encourage you to ask peers to speak to two separate issues:

1. Do you agree with my argument? What are your feelings about it?
2. No matter what your disposition is toward the argument in my draft, can you help me make it better?

Both discussions are important. But it may be hard to get to the second discussion if your workshop group is consumed by a debate over the issue itself.

As always, focus your peer review on the central concerns of a first draft: purpose and meaning. You can use the following box.

Questions for Peer Reviewers	
Purpose	What is the question driving my argument? At what point in the draft do you first understand the question? Is that early enough?
Meaning	Do you understand the claim I'm making? Are the reasons I'm taking this position clear? Which do you find most convincing? Least convincing? What questions do you have that I haven't answered?

Reflecting on the Draft. After having spent time choosing an argument topic and developing and drafting your argument, what do you now understand about making effective arguments that you didn't when you started? If you were to make a single PowerPoint slide explaining that, what would it say?

Revising

Revision is a continual process—not a last step. You've been revising—"reseeing" your subject—from the first messy fastwriting in your journal. But the things that get your attention vary depending on where you are in the writing process. With your draft in hand, revision becomes your focus through what I'll call "shaping and tightening your draft."

Shaping. In your draft, you made a tentative commitment to your topic, hoping that you could shape it into something that might have meaning for someone other than you. Fundamentally, you've been trying to figure out *what you're trying to say* and then rebuild your essay so that it is both clear and convincing. In an argument essay, you also want it to be convincing.

Shaping focuses first on the largest concerns of purpose and meaning—which you've already looked at if you workshopped your draft—and on the next-to-largest concerns of information and organization. It starts with knowing what your essay is about—your inquiry question and maybe your claim—and then revising to make every element of the draft focused on that question or assertion.

This chapter includes some useful tools that should help you shape the next draft, and in particular examine your reasoning strategies.

1. **Toulmin and Rogers.** A helpful technique for revising the first draft of your argument essay is to use a method of analyzing argumentative reasoning, such as Toulminian or Rogerian logic (see pages 174–175). Toulmin logic is particularly powerful for detecting the warrants or assumptions that might be lurking behind your reasons and claims. Are these assumptions valid? Should they be addressed in the revision?

2. **Logical fallacies.** Did you get yourself on any slippery slopes or beg a question? Find out by looking at the "Avoiding Logical Fallacies" section earlier in this chapter.

3. **Rhetorical analysis.** We've talked about Aristotle's elements of persuasion: ethos, pathos, and logos. Is there an effective emphasis on each of these in your draft, and have you used them in proportions appropriate for your topic and audience?

Polishing. When you are satisfied with the shape of your draft, focus on paragraphs, sentences, and words. Are your paragraphs coherent? How do you manage transitions? Are your sentences fluent and concise? Are there any errors in spelling or syntax?

▶ Student Essay

One of the things I really like about Rebecca Thompson's causal argument "Social Networking Social Good?" is that even though she's a fan of social networking, she readily concedes that there are downsides to it. Rebecca could have quickly nodded to critics of her position in a sentence or two. But instead she explores the case against social media in some detail, quoting extensively from people who worry that social media undermine conversations and personal relationships. Rebecca agrees with some of this. But she argues that, overall, media such as Facebook and Twitter have made her life better. Acknowledging opposing viewpoints is an important move in argumentative essays. But writers of these essays rarely take these viewpoints seriously. Because Rebecca recognizes the complexity of her topic, and tries to deal with it in her essay, the claim she makes seems more persuasive.

Social Networking Social Good?

Rebecca Thompson

1   Facebook Chat. iPhone texting. Checking in on FourSquare. Twitter hashtags. Tumblr blogging. OkCupid matchmaking. These days, there's no limit to the ways we can talk to each other. Suddenly, the basic human foundation of communication—talking and listening—has become much more complicated. It's incontrovertible that our society has changed in response to technological and media advancements. The day-to-day functions of our lives are different than they were even five years ago. We read differently (on Kindle or Nook), we watch differently (on Netflix, Hulu, or OnDemand), we hear differently (earbuds and surround sound), we even learn differently (smart boards, smart phones, Google). Despite the major advancements in rapid response, worldwide networking, as well as major shifts in the arts and sciences, many are concerned that there are major downfalls to the way that we, as a society, have begun to use social networking and media devices. Yet overall the explosion of social networking has provided unforeseen benefits, too. We can now find comfort in the company of strangers, erase the distance between far-flung friends, and most important, participate in conversations that spread new knowledge.

2   I use social media, like e-mail, Facebook, Twitter, and Wordpress, in all areas of my life, from connecting with high school friends now scattered across the country, to networking and advertising projects I'm involved in, to keeping updated on news stories. When Hurricane Irene struck the East Coast, I was out of town. I kept tabs on my friends via Facebook, and followed the news stories by following the hashtag #HurricaneIrene on Twitter. It was a relief to be connected, even from far away. Similarly, following the devastating tornado in Missouri in May 2011, so-called "small-media efforts" (such as Facebook, local radio, and Twitter) were the ones that led most mainstream media to the scene. Facebook groups formed instantaneously and expanded exponentially, featuring posts from families searching for survivors as well as complete strangers offering prayers and support. As one poster wrote, "On one hand,

my heart is just aching for your loss and devastation . . . [O]n the other hand, seeing everyone pulling together reminds me how resilient the human spirit is" (Mustich).

In instances of catastrophe like Hurricane Irene and the tornados in the Midwest, social networking is put to effective use in networking relief efforts, gathering and spreading crucial information, and sharing messages of support. Few would argue the positive effects of these technological advances. However, social media also functions on a more personal level, connecting people on a one-on-one basis, often inviting them into the most clandestine parts of their lives. "At its core, it is about connections and community," said Mailet Lopez, the founder of the networking site I Had Cancer, to *Forbes* magazine. "Social networking provides an opportunity beyond physical support networks and online forums . . . because with a social network, people can connect based on whatever criteria they want, regardless of location" (John).

Thousands of anonymous viewers can read about the inner workings of thousands of other social media users, following their Twitter, subscribing to their blogs, mapping their location on FourSquare. This is a new phenomenon, thanks to the rapid developments in speed and accessibility in the technology, and is often cited as a cause of heightened disconnectivity and impersonality in human relationships. For some, though, social networking's seemingly impersonal associations actually provide great personal comfort. During the time her husband suffered from debilitating cancer and treatment, writer Lee Ann Cox chronicled her struggles on Twitter, her own "defiant cry to be seen, to testify, bearing witness to suffering in 140 characters or less." Cox tweeted about the mundane, the terror, and the absurdities of handling her husband's condition, and though she had followers, the simple act of tweeting in and of itself was her therapy. "Maybe I did get something I needed from Twitter," she writes. "With no one's permission, I gave myself a voice . . . I needed to say these things and imagine some heart in the Twittersphere absorbing my crazed reality" (Cox).

Social media critics see the downside of Cox's experience, arguing that rather than encouraging communication and interpersonal relationships, it diminishes them. These critics worry that social media deconstructs traditional methods of conversation and undermines interpersonal relationships. I have certainly sat in a room with four of my friends, all of us checking our iPhones and laptops, barely speaking. I've had more communication with some people on Facebook than I have with them in real life. I'm sure that the authors of certain blogs I follow have more "blog friends" than real friends. Certainly, this kind of distance makes communication easier. If there's an awkward pause in a conversation, pull out your phone. If you're too shy to actually talk to a boy you're interested in, poke him on Facebook. The risk that online conversations might impoverish actual conversations is real. However, as Susan Greenfield, director of the Royal Institution of Great Britain, put it:

Real conversation in real time may eventually give way to these sanitized and easier screen dialogues, in much the same way as killing, skinning and butchering an animal to eat has been replaced by the convenience of packages of meat on the supermarket shelf. Perhaps future generations will recoil with similar horror at the messiness, unpredictability and immediate personal involvement of a three-dimensional, real-time interaction. (qtd. in Mackey)

(continued)

(continued)

6   Greenfield's gruesome image exemplifies the lowered stakes of communication, and therefore, repercussions, online. In 2011, the *Oxford English Dictionary* put the term "cyberbullying" into its lexicons. With increasing anonymity, access to personal information, and expanded public forums, social media has opened the door to new forms of cruelty—and not just for kids. Take the Dharun Ravi case. He used his webcam to tape his college roommate Tyler Clementi in a homosexual encounter with another student, and then shared it online with his friends. Clementi subsequently committed suicide. The case is unusual because it was based primarily on records of online interaction. Both the prosecution and defense used mountains of electronic evidence, including numerous tweets (some of which were tampered with), Facebook posts (including Clementi's final status update), text messages, screenshots, e-mails, and web chats. The sheer volume of evidence on social networking tools is beyond the scope of any other major bullying case in recent history. In many ways, this is a boon to the judicial process, as records of the students' online interactions are prime evidence for both the prosecution and defense. On the other hand, it is disturbing to note how the deteriorated relationship between these two boys "played out on social media with curiously few face-to-face exchanges" (Clayton).

7   Ravi's ability to quickly disperse the contraband video highlights is another inherent problem in social media. In mere seconds, an online post can be captured, saved, reposted, and shared. While a great boon for marketing and the quick dissemination of crucial information (such as in the case of a major natural disaster or a political event), there exists no system to judge the veracity and reliability of viral posts. The most viral video of all time is a 30-minute documentary made by the organization Invisible Children about Ugandan leader Joseph Kony, which received over 100 million hits in under a week when it was first posted in March 2012. However, after that first week had passed and certain critics began to look deeper, deep flaws in the message of the video emerged. "To call [Kony2012's] campaign a misrepresentation is an understatement," writes Angelo Izama, quoted in Time's "Global Spin" blog (Tharoor). The organization itself, Invisible Children, is under fire for its practices as an NGO. Most concerning to critics, though, is the extreme simplification and digestibility of the message itself. In this telling, to simply "know" about Kony . . . would be enough to bring him down," writes Ishaan Tharoor in "Global Spin." "That quest takes place in a world of moral simplicity, of good and evil, of innocence and horror . . . justice is about much more than manhunts and viral video crusades" (Tharoor).

8   I recall seeing the Kony post on Facebook, and watched a few minutes before closing it down. I almost reposted, but then figured I should perhaps watch the whole 30 minutes before showing my support to my friends and followers. Upon reading the criticism of the documentary, now nearly as viral as the video itself, it seems to me that knowledge has been disseminated, albeit in a non-traditional way. Social networking allows for great diversity of opinion, and also opens the door to conversation. "Knowledge consists of a network of people and ideas that are not totally in sync, that are diverse, that disagree," states David Weinberger in an interview with Salon's Thomas Rogers. "Books generally have value because they encapsulate some topic and provide you with everything you know, because when you're reading it you cannot easily leap out of the book to get to the next book. The Web only has value because it contains difference" (Rogers).

9   Weinberger elucidates precisely the problems with, and the importance of, social media and the way knowledge is shared. It has inherently changed our tools of communication and

of functioning in modern society—we can't go back now. "Ask anybody who is in any of the traditional knowledge fields," states Weinberger.

> She or he will very likely tell you that the Internet has made them smarter. They couldn't do their work without it; they're doing it better than ever before, they know more; they can find more; they can run down dead ends faster than ever before...Now we have a medium that is as broad as our curiosity. (qtd. in Rogers)

I agree that social networking tools have the potential, if used to their best advantage, to facilitate communication, networking, and the spread of knowledge. It's made functioning on a day-to-day basis much easier. Because I can respond to emails and texts on the go, I can plan ahead. I can keep in touch with my friends studying abroad when phones aren't an option. I get lost a lot less. Even the Pope has spoken of the benefits of the Internet, social networking, and media. "Search engines and social networks have become the starting point of communication for many people who are seeking advice, ideas, information and answers," he said. "In our time, the Internet is becoming ever more a forum for questions and answers...In concise phrases, often no longer than a verse from the Bible, profound thoughts can be communicated" (Shariatmadari).

10

Works Cited

Clayton, Mark. "Rutgers Spycam Case: Why It's Not Open and Shut." *The Christian Science Monitor*, 22 Feb. 2012, www.csmonitor.com/USA/Justice/2012/0222/Rutgers-spycam-case-why-it-s-not-open-and-shut.

Cox, Lee Ann. "Losing My Husband, 140 Characters at a Time." *Salon*. 24 Jan. 2012, www.salon.com/2012/01/24/losing_my_husband_140_characters_at_a_time/.

Harris, Paul. "Social Networking under Fresh Attack as Tide of Cyber-Skepticism Sweeps US." *The Guardian*, 22 Jan. 2011, www.theguardian.com/media/2011/jan/22/social-networking-cyber-scepticism-twitter.

John, Tracey. "New Social Network Connects Cancer Survivors, Patients, and Supporters." *Forbes*, 25 Aug. 2011, www.forbes.com/sites/traceyjohn/2011/08/25/new-social-network-connects-cancer-survivors-patients-and-supporters/#16baa1804ac5.

Mackey, Robert. "Is Social Networking Killing You?" *The Lede*, New York Times, 25 Feb. 2009, nyti.ms/1brNxMi.

Mustich, Emma. "Joplin Rescue Effort's HQ: Facebook." *Salon*, 23 May 2011, www.salon.com/2011/05/23/missouri_twister_support/.

Rogers, Thomas. "Are We on Information Overload?" *Salon*, 1 Jan. 2012, www.salon.com/2012/01/01/are_we_on_information_overload/.

Shariatmadari, David. "Pope Benedict Praises Twitter-like Forms of Communication." *The Guardian*, 24 Jan. 2012, www.theguardian.com/world/2012/jan/24/pope-benedict-twitter-communication.

Tharoor, Ishaan. "Why You Should Feel Awkward About the 'Kony2012' Video." *Time*, 8 Mar. 2012, world.time.com/2012/03/08/why-you-should-feel-awkward-about-the-kony-2012-video/.

Evaluating the Essay

1. Rebecca claims that, overall, social media offer "comfort," eliminate "the distance between far-flung friends," and contribute to the creation of "new knowledge." Do you agree?

2. Use the rhetorical concepts of ethos, pathos, and logos to analyze the effectiveness of the essay. If the claim is that social networking, despite its potential shortcomings, is beneficial, what are the reasons Rebecca uses to support the claim? Which do you find most convincing? Least convincing?

Using What You Have Learned

Let's return to the learning objectives I outlined in the beginning of the chapter.

1. **Understand the connection between inquiry and persuasion, and apply inquiry strategies for exploring and developing an argument topic.** The object of argument is not winning but learning—discovery remains the heart of the process. When you receive assignments that ask you to make an argument, consider writing about topics about which you may not already have a strong opinion, and use the writing process—especially at the invention stage—to discover what you think. A practical advantage of this is that you can write about nearly anything if it interests you.

2. **Distinguish between causal, factual, and definitional arguments, and develop an essay that uses one of those three approaches to persuasion.** You now have three ways of identifying argument types: causal, factual, and definitional. When other writing situations call for argument or persuasion, return to your understanding of these argument types. What type does this writing task require? Once you know that, you'll also know the type of question that will drive your essay and what your argument will need to prove.

3. **Identify the key elements of argument—reasons, claims, and evidence—and apply them in both reading and writing.** Making and recognizing a claim in an argument isn't hard. But most of us aren't so good at crafting reasons for what we believe and using evidence to make those reasons persuasive. You will find this understanding powerful, not just in school, where you make arguments all the time, but in life, too, where we also make arguments all the time.

4. **Develop a question that is focused enough to lead to a strong claim and convincing evidence.** This is a consistent theme in *The Curious Writer*. Inquiry begins with questions. But not just any questions. They must be questions that are sufficiently focused, and that help you to know more explicitly what you need to know. Here you've learned three more *types* of inquiry questions that lead arguments, and also used new strategies for refining your inquiry question.

5. **Use audience analysis and logical methods to help guide revision of an argument.** Audience analysis *begins* the process of developing an argument. Who cares? Why do they care? What do they currently think? Understanding what others, especially stakeholders, believe is (to borrow from Rogers) an act of empathy, of listening. This is an essential part of civil discourse as well as a key part of making a persuasive argument.

7

Writing an Analytical Essay

Learning Objectives

In this chapter, you'll learn to

7.1 Apply the methods of analysis to a subject whose meanings aren't apparent.
7.2 Use evidence from primary sources to argue effectively for a convincing interpretation.
7.3 Use appropriate invention strategies to discover a topic for an analytical essay.
7.4 Apply revision strategies that are effective for the analytical essay.

Writing to Interpret

On the top of a bookcase in my campus office, there's a plastic leg from a mannequin, and on its pointed foot are spurs. My students, at least the ones who notice it, think this is weird, and a few of them ask, "Hey, what's with the leg?" In other words, they are asking, "What does that mean?" Think how often we ask that question when we encounter something whose meanings aren't immediately apparent. On the other hand, consider how much more often we see things whose meanings are settled for us. The stop sign on the exit from the parking lot outside my office doesn't have ambiguous meanings at all. It tells me to stop, and I stop. No analysis needed.

We make the move to interpret things like a mannequin's leg in a professor's office—and not the stop sign outside it—because one has ambiguous meanings and the other does not. If you think about it, there is no

209

shortage of things in everyday life with ambiguous meanings: tattooed eyeballs, Facebook profile pictures, Lady Gaga, advertisements for men's cologne, the zombie craze, retro eyewear, the Honey Boo Boo reality TV show, misogynistic rap lyrics, the evolution of the Apple logo, motorcycle riders, a Langston Hughes poem. When we write to interpret, the challenge is to try to untangle the meanings of things like these, not to find *the* explanation but to offer a convincing argument for a few possible meanings. This is an analytical act that is central to academic study and is also something—in a less systemized fashion—that human beings do every day. In this chapter, we'll explore some of these analytical methods.

Motives for Writing an Analytical Essay

7.1

Apply the methods of analysis to a subject whose meanings aren't apparent.

Fortunately, traffic signs have fairly settled meanings for most American drivers, at least until they start driving in another country. It's hard to think of an interpretive activity with higher stakes, something I discovered recently upon encountering my first Scottish traffic circle. Social situations and observations, while less risky, involve interpreting meanings that help us make our way in the world. Last week, Sean wrote an essay that examined the complicated gender dynamics of whether a man opens a door for a woman. Consumer culture offers endless opportunities for interpretation. Analyzing advertising is a popular classroom activity, but beyond that, it is interesting to interpret the meanings behind changes in fashion, or the evolution of brands like Apple's iconic apple image. Entertainment media—film, TV, YouTube, etc.—are ripe for interpretation. How might we interpret the meaning of Bart Simpson's ragged haircut or the pleasures of watching zombies being dismembered in shows like *The Walking Dead*? Whether the stakes are high (the meaning of gender to transgender people filling out college applications) or relatively low (the meaning of landscape in Leslie Silko's novel *Ceremony*), interpretation is one of the most important ways we make judgments about what we see and what those things might mean. Interpreting things thoughtfully has the potential to make a real difference in our lives. As I write this, controversy over a grand jury's failure to indict an officer who killed a black teenager in Ferguson, Missouri, has raised, among other things, interesting questions about the militarization of the police. How are we to interpret the symbolism of police officers riding in Mine Resistant Ambush Protected vehicles (MRAPs) rather than Ford police cruisers? Depending on how you see it, this choice of vehicle is reassuring or disturbing. Figuring out how you sort out the meanings of things like this is an act of interpretation.

To fully appreciate what authors are saying or what effects they're trying to create in an essay, poem, or story, you often need to look closely, and in doing so, you see beyond the obvious.

The Analytical Essay and Academic Writing

No term is used more often than "critical thinking" to describe the goals of a college education. This term means a lot of things, of course, but it certainly involves what Gregory Fraser and Chad Davidson call an "analytical frame of mind." This is the kind of thinking that you'll use whenever you take a class that asks you to interpret something: In art, you might interpret a medieval painting; in English, a story by Alice Walker; in sociology, the indoctrination rituals of street gangs; in nursing, the meaning of certain kinds of informal talk among nurses about doctors; and in biology, data on the flight patterns of bees. All of these disciplines have their own theories that determine analytical methods, of course. A scientist might use statistical theories to interpret data. An anthropologist might use theories related to cultural ecology. A literary critic might use feminist theory. For many of these disciplines, no matter what theories inform it, critical analysis is in the service of an argument that answers the question *What might it mean?*

But what method of analysis might you use here? When we analyze a picture, a poem, a fashion trend, an advertisement, or a representation of an animated character on TV, we're doing *qualitative* analysis. We examine things that aren't easily measured. There are lots of methods for doing qualitative analysis, but they all typically involve two general moves, which you can imagine are like analyzing a metaphorical iceberg:

1. Looking closely at the thing (text, image, trend, brand, character, etc.) you're trying to interpret. What does it look like, how often do you see it, where do you see it?

2. Looking underneath the thing at what isn't readily seen—what is it trying to sell, what is its context, what larger ideas does it seem to promote?

Seeing what's in front of you

- **Frequency:** How often do you see it?

- **Comparison:** What is it like and unlike?

- **Location:** Where do you see it?

- **Relations:** What is its relationship to other parts?

Looking at what's underneath

- **Context:** Historical, social, genre.

- **Convention:** What are the usual meanings assigned to this?

- **Ideology:** What are the ideas this seems to be promoting?

If you're analyzing a short story, what's visible are the words in front of you. What images recur in the text? How is this character unlike that character? How does one scene in the story connect with another scene? The work of analysis always begins with the tip of the iceberg, the part above water. But it's underneath, the less visible ideas and meanings, that can give what you see above water more meaning. When analyzing a short story, we might first ask *when* was this story written—in what historical period—and *how* might this period influence what the story is trying to do? Is the story trying to challenge certain commonly held ideas about, say, family, or nature, or race?

Try applying this two-part method of analysis to the following Depression-era photograph.

Exercise 7.1

Interpreting an Image

Lewis Hines, a documentary photographer who was best known for his crusading work against child labor in the early twentieth century, in 1920 took the photograph on page 213, which is titled "Power House Mechanic Working on a Steam Pump." Keeping in mind the historical context of the image—the nation was in a titanic shift from a primarily rural economy to an industrial one—as well as Hines's interest in using photography as a form of social commentary, what would be your analysis of this image? Account for both what you actually see in the photograph—significant details in the image—and the less apparent, "submerged" meanings that you think are in it. The "Inquiring into the Details: Five Methods of Analysis feature on page 221 will also help you analyze various elements of the composition of the photo.

Generate

STEP ONE: In your notebook, begin with a narrative-of-thought fastwrite: *The first thing I notice in the picture is…. And then I notice… And then… And then….* When the writing stalls, return again to look at the image.

Judge

STEP TWO: Review your fastwrite, looking at things you noticed in the picture that strike you—perhaps in conjunction with other details there—as potentially significant, that might hint at what the photograph is suggesting about industrialization, workers, work, masculinity, and so on.

STEP THREE: Compose a four- to six-sentence caption for the photograph that captures your interpretation. Make sure that you link that interpretation to specific evidence in the photograph.

7.2

Use evidence from primary sources to argue effectively for a convincing interpretation.

Analytical essays are built around a main idea, claim, or interpretation you are making about a text.

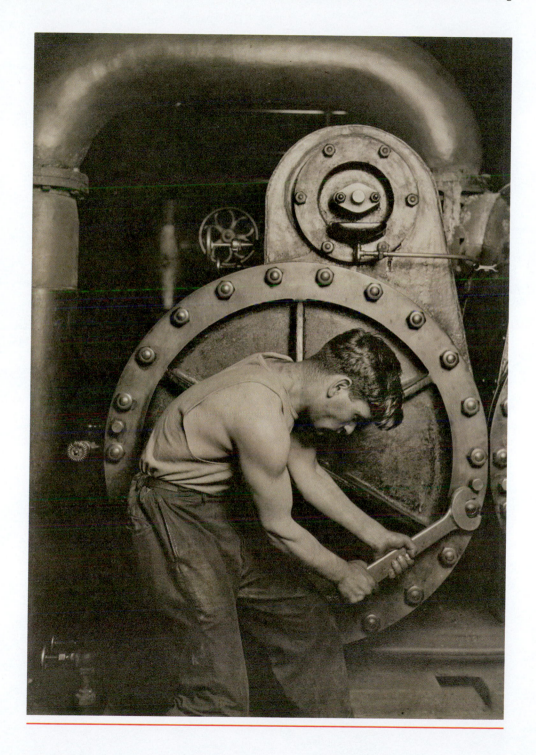

Features of the Form

Feature	Conventions of the Analytical Essay
Inquiry question	What might it mean?
Motives	We turn to forms such as the analytical essay whenever the meaning of something is unsettled. This analysis requires that we examine it more closely to identify patterns, and then find convincing reasons about why those patterns are significant to understanding the meaning of the thing.
Subject matter	While analytical essays are a common assignment in English, focusing on literary texts, they also might explore film, art, popular culture, social behaviors, or any other subject matter whose meanings are unsettled.
Structure	There are three elements in most analytical essays: 1. Identifying *specific* features of the object being analyzed (e.g., characters in a story, elements of an image, etc.) that raise a question about meaning. 2. Exploring how those features are the tip of the iceberg of less apparent and larger themes or ideas. 3. Finding reasons, drawn from evidence in the object itself, to support this interpretation.
Sources of information	This depends on what's being analyzed. An interpretation of a story, for example, would draw evidence from the story itself: lines, passages, scenes, characters. Analytical essays, at least initially, are written *inductively*, through close analysis and observation of the object of study. This yields specific information that influences any interpretation. In addition, analytical essays might include information from other critics or analysts who have contributed to the conversation about possible interpretations.
Language	The tone of an analytical essay, as for most essays, depends on the audience. Formal essays, the kind assigned in literature classes, rarely use the first person, focusing readers' attention on the argument, not the writer. Less-formal response essays might use much more casual language.

READINGS

▶ ## Literary Analysis

"There are a lot of hidden meanings in poems." I suppose there is some truth to this characterization of poetry—poems can certainly have ambiguous meanings—but the implication is that poets stealthily scatter these "hidden meanings" for readers to find, that these are already cast with a certain significance, and that the job of readers is to hunt the meanings down and report what they find, hoping they get the meanings "right."

Thankfully, poetry (and, for that matter, all other literary texts) is a lot more interesting than this. Yes, meaning is waiting to be found. But readers aren't miners, they're meaning-makers. We each bring our own histories and perceptions to our encounters with literature, and we have access to tools (like literary theories or analytic methods) that help make some of the less visible patterns emerge. Bart Brinkman's brief analysis of the N. Scott Momaday poem "The Shield That Came Back" is a nice example of how this meaning-making works. Momaday, a Kiowa, is one of our greatest Native American writers, and this poem, drawing on myth, history, and allegory, is typical of much of his work.

The Shield That Came Back
N. Scott Momaday

Turning Around tested his son Yellow Grass. "You must kill thirty scissortails and make me a fan of their feathers."
"Must I make the whole fan?" asked Yellow Grass. "Must I do the beadwork too?" Yellow Grass had never made a fan.
"Yes. You must do the beadwork too—blue and black and white and orange."
"Those are the colors of your shield," said Yellow Grass.
Yellow Grass fretted over the making of his father's fan, but when at last it was finished it was a fine, beautiful thing, the feathers tightly bunched and closely matched, their sheen like a rainbow—yet they could be spread wide as a disc, like a shield. And the handle was beaded tightly. The blue and black and white and orange beads glittered in every light. And there was a long bunch of doeskin fringes at the handle[']s end.
When Turning Around saw the fan he said nothing, but he was full of pride and admiration. Then he went off on a raiding expedition to the Pueblo country, and there he was killed. After

1

(continued)

(*continued*)

> that, Yellow grass went among the Pueblos and redeemed his
> father's shield. But the fan could not be found.
> When he was an old man Yellow Grass said to his grandson
> Handsome Horse, "You see, the shield was more powerful than
> the fan, for the shield came back and the fan did not. Some things,
> if they are very powerful, come back. Remember that. For us, in
> this camp, that is how to think of the world."

On "The Shield That Came Back"
Bart Brinkman

1 N. Scott Momaday's "The Shield that Came Back," from the poetry sequence, "In the Presence of the Sun: A Gathering of Shields[,]" takes as one of its central metaphors the Plains Indian warrior shield. Made from the thick chest skin of a male buffalo, the warrior shield is painted with talismanic—often animal—symbols, such as birds and deer. It was commonly believed that the design on the shield, rather than the shield itself, would protect the warrior. In making the shield a prominent metaphor in his poem, Momaday places "The Shield that Came Back" within a long Indian tradition, drawing on one of its most important cultural markers. But the shield is also suggestive of Western tradition. The shield has been a prominent Western image at least as far back as the depiction of Achilles' shield in the Iliad and has resonated through much of the literature of the West. In suggesting both Indian and Western traditions, the shield as central metaphor and Momaday's poem in general signals its need, and the need of the Modern American Indian, to negotiate both of these traditions.

2 For a poem ostensibly about a shield, however, there is a disproportionate emphasis on a fan. It is, in fact, one of the jobs of the poem to work out the identification between the fan and the shield. The poem opens with Turning Around's instructions to his son Yellow Grass that, "'You must kill/thirty scissortails and make me a fan of their feathers.'" The fan that Yellow Grass is to make—which will require a great amount of skill and effort both in hunting the scissortails and weaving together their feathers—will resemble his father's shield. As Yellow Grass tells Turning Around, of the blue and black and white and orange beadwork, "'Those are the colors of your shield.'" And the "tightly bunched and closely matched" feathers of the fan "could be spread wide [as] a disc, like a shield." In its shape and color, the fan is patterned after the shield, just as the son is patterned after the father.

3 After Turning Around is killed on a raiding expedition to the Pueblo country, Yellow Grass retrieves his father's shield "[b]ut the fan could not be found." The poem does not reveal what happened to the fan, whether it was lost, stolen, or kept close

to the father, but much later, when Yellow Grass was an old man, he told the story of the shield to his grandson Handsome Horse, with the explanation "'You see, the shield was more powerful than the fan, for the shield came back and the fan did not. Some things,/ if they are very powerful, come back. Remember that. For us, in/ this camp, that is how to think of the world." The moral to Yellow Grass's story is that tradition is powerful and will come back to protect them. It is important for his grandson to remember that "in this camp" as they struggle through a marginalized existence encapsulated by Western tradition.

But the poem offers a means of resisting Yellow Grass's moral. The fan can be   4
seen as not only an excellent imitation of the shield, but as its successor, an object in its own right and one that is lauded by the father. Although the shield returns, it is no longer necessary because Turning Around is now dead. But the fan, as a successor to the shield, is lost in the world, just as Yellow Grass as successor to his father is also lost. The son cannot be protected by his father's shield, but must recover his own fan just as his camp cannot be protected by tradition but must identify with it to make something new. The poem (which is itself not unlike the fan in its imitation and transformation of the past) suggests that, rather than looking back to traditional ways to be saved, one must use traditional ways to look forward. This is the way that the modern American Indian can survive in the face of Western tradition and begin to draw that tradition into its own.

Inquiring into the Poem

1. **Explore.** This will be most useful *before* you read Brinkman's interpretation of the Momaday poem: On the left page of your notebook, jot down at least five lines or passages that you believe were key to your understanding of the poem. These may include details that seem important, names, or moments in the narrative. On the right page, do a narrative-of-thought fastwrite about what you first noticed, and then what, and then…. Whenever the writing stalls, look left at a detail or passage you collected and fastwrite about why you found it interesting or significant.

2. **Explain.** Brinkman writes, "The poem … suggests that, rather than looking back to traditional ways to be saved, one must use traditional ways to look forward." Explain what you understand this to mean.

3. **Evaluate.** Do some quick online research on the significance of the warrior shield in Native American cultures. Use what you learn to evaluate Brinkman's claims about the significance of the shield.

4. **Reflect.** When you studied poetry in high school, you developed certain routines for writing analytical papers. What were they? Was your experience analyzing Momaday's poem different from what you're used to doing when you're asked to interpret poetry?

▶ Ad Analysis

Students of marketing often worship at the altar of Apple, whose "brand strategy" has helped make it the "world's most valuable company," according to *Forbes* magazine. Its advertising successes make Apple's promotion campaigns the subject of intense interest among people who analyze marketing. Even those of us who don't share that interest may own at least one Apple product, and it's interesting to consider what sold us on an "i" device or, perhaps more important, what keeps us going back for more. Analysts often point to "Apple's emotional branding"—how its marketing (like most advertising) is heavy on pathos, making us *feel* part of the "Apple experience." The company's television advertising is an important part of this effort, and in December 2013 Apple released its "Misunderstood" ad. Critics were divided on the commercial's effectiveness. In the blog essay that follows, Alex Soojung-Kim Pang, an expert on the social implications of new technologies, analyzes "Misunderstood" and finds himself at odds with its critics. See the ad for yourself on YouTube, and then consider Pang's argument.

What Does Apple's "Misunderstood" Advertisement Mean?

Alex Soojung-Kim Pang

1   "In its latest ad, with an 'if you can't beat em, join 'em' message, Apple isn't carving aspirational ground, it's caving to people's vices," Jennifer Rooney <u>declares</u>. She's talking about "Misunderstood," the Apple Christmas commercial that's become a kind of Rorschach test: Everyone seems to find their own moral from it. (You can find the 2013 ad on YouTube).

2   It focuses on a teenage boy who's going with his family to the grandparents' house (they live just outside Thornton Wildertown, near Walden Pond, by the looks of things) for Christmas.

3   Families gather, cousins go skating, snowmen are built, the tree is decorated, dinner made—and the teen seems focused on his phone. Then, on Christmas Day, he plays the video he's been shooting. He hasn't been disengaged; he's been watching the whole time. You can even watch "Harris Family Holiday" (hereafter "HFH") for yourself.

4   Some people quite like it: The Verge, for example, <u>thought it was charming</u>; *Entertainment Weekly* called it a "<u>merry little cry</u>." Emma Mustich describes it as a "<u>completely beautiful surprise</u>." Rooney's objection is that "while he was creating, he

wasn't really living the day, he was a mere voyeur during it." That "life is better through video. Don't live life, tape it." Gizmodo <u>saw it as fundamentally antisocial, too</u>. "He's not letting anything come between him and his iPhone, not even the memories he cares enough about to record," Brian Barrett writes. "He's experiencing the holidays at an anthropological remove." (By the way, when did "anthropological" become an epithet? Aren't anthropologists some of the most astute observers around? Isn't this like as insulting as calling an athlete "ninja-like"?)

But I'm not so sure.   5

I saw the exact opposite of an equally controversial advertisement: the <u>Facebook</u>   6
<u>Home</u> ad, in which a young woman escapes the droning tedium of Thanksgiving with her family by vicariously enjoying the lives of her much cooler, kite-surfing, nightclubbing friends.

"Misunderstood," in contrast, doesn't celebrate technology's ability to let us escape   7
from boring family events. It shows how we might use it to participate.

Maybe I've watched too many Akira Kurosawa movies, and so I assume that com-   8
plicated backstories can be revealed in just a few seconds (watch *Seven Samurai* to see how he was the master of revealing a whole village's life histories in an amazingly sparse manner). But while I'm sure the Apple ad wizards want us to assume that the teen could be any kid with an iPhone, the ad raised all kinds of questions for me. What if the kid is <u>on the autism spectrum</u>, or extremely shy (notice he never speaks, and rarely makes eye contact)? What if he's an exchange student? Thirty years earlier, would he have done the same thing with a Betamax camcorder (you can imag[in]e Spielberg at a family gathering acting like this)?

This last came to mind because "HFH" is actually *really good*. It's not just the   9
work of a teen playing around: It's the work of someone who spends plenty of time watching people, and who had a <u>good eye</u> for the little scenes and artifacts and vignettes that capture a mood *and* will hold a viewer's attention. In other words, it's not the equivalent of <u>two minutes of selfies</u>. (And indeed people have argued about whether <u>photography</u> makes you more engaged with the world, or creates a distance from it.)

In other words, I see this kid and I don't see an ordinary tech-absorbed slacker.   10
I come away with the sense that there's a backstory here, which makes me less willing to project my own anxieties about kids today with their damn smartphones onto it.

Further, as Jason <u>Morehead observes</u> in Patheos, "I'm not so sure that someone   11
making a video like this teen's is quite as detached" as critics think. The video backs this up. It has tons of action shots: Clearly the kid is sledding with his cousins, watching the little ones, noticing little moments of affection and goofiness—he's not always off to the side, and he's certainly *not* staying inside, blasting the latest from Norwegian death metal rappers Maülhammer and playing *GTA V* while everyone else is out being

(continued)

(*continued*)

human. In this respect, the ad cheats a little—you have to see "HFH" to realize that the original commercial has obscured his participation.

12   Finally, I sympathized with the kid because I do something like this myself. At events at <u>my kids' school</u>, I often bring my good camera and take lots of pictures. Of course I help put up tents or serve soup or what have you—I sign up for real jobs—but at some point I usually grab the XE-1 and go wandering.

13   People by now either appreciate it or put up with it. It means that we have a far better record of school events than we used to. I like providing for the collective memory: Lots of the pictures are now in school publications, brochures, fundraising letters, and so on.

14   But it also gives me an excuse to both wander around and watch people, while also providing a little buffer from socializing *too much*.

15   In a school full of business development and VC parents who never really turn it off, being able to take pictures lets me be involved and useful on my terms.

16   Maybe I don't wonder about the "Misunderstood" teen's backstory that much, after all.

Inquiring into the Ad

1. **Explore.** Watch Apple's "Misunderstood" commercial on YouTube. Critics of the ad claim it exemplifies one of the worst things about technology like smartphones: It isolates us from others. Apple implicitly addresses this concern in the ad. Explore your own experience with this isolation, and the extent to which the commercial speaks to that experience. Do you buy what Apple is selling? What is it selling (beyond iPhones)?

2. **Explain.** Video, like writing, has a grammar. There are certain conventions—use of camera angles, framing, integration of music, cuts from scene to scene, use of lighting, and so on—that are intended to have certain effects on the viewer. Based on your own experience as a viewer of video and film, how are some of these conventions handled in the Apple ad? Which do you find particularly effective?

3. **Evaluate.** Here's what we see on the surface of the ad: An American family of multiple generations gathers on a snowy day for Christmas in a suburban home. An apparently distracted teenager appears to be a marginal participant, spending most of his time staring at his iPhone. But then he surprises everyone with a touching video he made of the family's time together. What's under the surface of this ad? In particular, *what ideas does it seem to be selling* about technology, about families and family relationships, about an American holiday like Christmas?

4. **Reflect.** Suppose your instructor asked you to analyze the Apple ad using one or more of the approaches to analysis in the "Inquiring into the Details: Five Methods of Analysis." Which method do you think might yield the most interesting results?

Inquiring into the Details

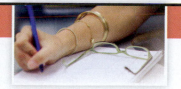

Five Methods of Analysis

We casually interpret the meanings of things all the time, especially in social situations: "That guy is always wearing a long black trench coat. He must be some kind of trench coat mafia loner dude." We observe and quickly interpret, and then the analysis is over. However, thoughtful analysis—in an effort to arrive at a more considered judgment about something—looks more methodically at how we interpret something, and most importantly *why* we interpret something the way we do. Frequently, the object of analysis is not just social behavior but texts, and I mean "texts" in the broadest sense as anything that can be "read": writing, transcripts, TV commercials, film, advertisements, etc.

As you can imagine, there are a range of methods for doing this analysis. Below are five common approaches used in a range of disciplines. You can learn more about each method by searching online. You might consider using one or more of these methods in your own analysis.

Method	Approach	Examples
Content Analysis	Counts the frequency of content in a text (certain words, phrases, ideas, themes, images, references, information types, comments, categories, etc.) and infers what they might mean. What does the text actually contain?	Recurring images in student anxiety dreams, violent images in "Grand Theft Auto," use of personal anecdote in *The Curious Writer*.
Rhetorical Analysis	Examines the effectiveness of ethos, pathos, and logos in a particular communication situation. How does the text work? What makes it persuasive? Also involves analyzing purpose, audience, and genre to investigate how they influence a text's composition.	Persuasiveness of ads for men's cologne, analysis of Dr. King's "I Have a Dream" speech, effectiveness of a website on academic honesty.
Semiotic Analysis	Identifies "signs" (in texts and social situations) that are assigned certain implied social meanings in particular contexts. What does it mean? What ideas is it selling? Who will benefit?	Significance of wearing baseball caps with stickers, the evolution of the Apple logo, the cultural meaning of Bart Simpson's haircut, analysis of ads for Mercedes-Benz automobiles.

(continued)

Inquiring into the Details *(continued)*

Method	Approach	Examples
Critical Analysis	Identifies patterns in a text that, when seen in relationship to each other, imply certain themes or ideas. Applying a context (historical, theoretical, traditional) can help tease out these patterns.	Feminist analysis of female characters in "Tomb Raider," light and dark motifs in Hawthorne's *Scarlet Letter*.
Genre Analysis	Analyzes the "family resemblances" that constitute genre. These might include certain conventions, structures, discourses, and rhetorical assumptions.	The convention of the "jump scare" in horror movies (see the essay by Bryan Bishop). Analysis of introductions to academic articles in criminal justice.

▶ Film Analysis

If you've ever watched a horror movie, you've been victim to a "jump scare," though you probably didn't know what it is called. The evil one is dead and gone, and all seems well again, until suddenly a withered hand is thrust upward from the fresh grave and grabs an ankle, and the musical soundtrack crescendos. The jump scare is a *convention* of the horror genre, a technique that is used again and again. Genre analysis often examines these conventions, describing how they work and why. "Why Won't You Die?!" is exactly this kind of analysis, exploring how jump scares work (and why they don't when they don't) and why the technique seems to be making a comeback in the horror genre.

"Why Won't You Die?!" The Art of the Jump Scare

Bryan Bishop

1   *An alarm clock glows in the darkness: 3:18AM. All is silent… until a low, steady creak groans through the house.*

2   *A young woman turns on the bedside lamp, squinting across the room. Shadows gather around vague outlines of furniture. Nothing moves. Then, voices. Murmuring. Somewhere down the hall.*

She pads into the living room on bare feet. The television must have been left on, but there's a problem with the signal. The picture flickers, briefly coalescing around the shape of a shadowy figure, only to break apart into digital noise.   3

Moving closer, she reaches out towards the TV. With every step, the image becomes clearer; it's almost as if the figure can see her…   4

CLICK! She turns the television off. Exhales.   5

That's when a pair of hands shoot out from the screen, wrapping around her face.   6

The audience screams.   7

If you've ever watched a horror film, you've seen a jump scare. It's that moment when a character thinks they're safe, only to have a demon appear suddenly behind them. The final coda when it feels like the movie's wrapping up—but the killer comes back for one last jump. A mix of tension, cinematic sleight-of-hand, and score, it's one of the most basic building blocks of horror movies, and it excels at one thing: catching the audience off guard, and jolting the hell out of them.   8

'80s slasher films drove the jump scare into the ground, and the technique eventually became a cliché in its own right—with moviegoers often watching *for* the surprise rather than being shocked themselves. In the last few years, however, we've seen the technique make a comeback with audiences. Movies like the *Paranormal Activity* series, which rely almost exclusively on the jolt of the jump scare, have pulled in impressive grosses and spawned multiple sequels.   9

How do these scares work, and what's behind the recent uptick in audience interest? Lock your doors and turn off the lights; let's go check out that noise in the basement and find out.   10

"What makes a jump scare work is classic misdirection." C. Robert Cargill is one of the screenwriters of this year's *Sinister*, and a film critic who's written for *Ain't It Cool News* and *Film.com*. "A good jump scare is a magic trick," he says. "It's 'I'm going to get you to look over here while I'm doing this,' and then out of nowhere—bam!—something's going to get you."   11

In fact, a well-done jump scare breaks down the same way Michael Caine describes illusions in *The Prestige*, with three distinct steps. First there's the pledge: a character is introduced into a situation where danger is present. They hear a rattling in the kitchen, or voices when they're home alone. Then comes the turn, where the character finds a reasonable explanation, or the immediate threat is somehow removed. Everything seems alright, and the audience lets its guard down. That's when the filmmakers execute the prestige, hitting an unsuspecting audience with the actual scare—usually accompanied by a shrieking music cue or sound effect.   12

Film history is littered with them (see some of our favorites below), but one only needs to look at the original *A Nightmare On Elm Street* for a textbook example. Tina wanders through her nightmare, stalked by … *something*. Just when her fear builds to a crescendo, however, the danger dissipates. The noises stop—she thinks she's going to be okay. We relax. And that's when Krueger strikes.   13

(continued)

(continued)

14   While we may associate the technique with modern horror movies, it's actually been with us almost as long as genre films themselves. Director Jacques Tourneur used it 70 years ago in *Cat People*, using the arrival of a bus to craft a scare that still plays today. Other filmmakers tried their own riffs in subsequent decades. Showman William Castle even brought the jump scare into the real world in 1959 with *The Tingler*, rigging seats in theaters to vibrate during a key sequence in the movie.

15   Alfred Hitchcock, however, put it front and center with *Psycho*. In the film's climax, Vera Miles searches for Mrs. Bates, knowing that she has mere moments before Norman discovers she's poking around his house. In the basement she finds the old woman sitting in a chair, seemingly ending the nightmare once and for all. But when Miles spins her around, she discovers something horrific—that nobody was expecting back in 1960.

16   The jump scare hit a wall in the '80s. At first slasher films used it to great effect; the original *Friday the 13th* features what could be considered the definitive "killer returns" scare, when a young Jason emerges from the lake to attack the heroine. As knock-offs rolled out, however, the technique became less and less of a surprise, and was soon as rote and obvious as the now-parodied genre conventions themselves.

17   It wasn't that the horror movies of the era were bad as a whole—though to be fair, for every *Evil Dead II* there's also a *Silent Night, Deadly Night Part II*. Instead, it was a matter of repeating the same gags in movies that weren't actually frightening anymore.

18   If you look at the best horror films, Cargill says, "the common thread is almost all of them have amazing characters." From the original *The Texas Chainsaw Massacre* to *Poltergeist*, the characters pull the audience in, and the more you care, the more anxious you'll be that something bad's going to happen to them. Many horror flicks of the '80s stepped off that path, instead presenting a parade of lookalike characters that not only weren't developed, but could be straight-up obnoxious. "When you put five kids out in the woods and they're all douchebags, you don't care that they're getting killed," he says. "In fact you kind of enjoy it, it's kind of cathartic. It becomes more comedy than it is tragedy." The result were movies that were more like gory rollercoaster rides rather than something that would keep audiences up at night.

19   Compounding the problem was a general lack of inventiveness with the scares themselves. Instead of setting the audiences up with clever misdirection, some filmmakers would try to cheat the system, relying on just the third element of the jump scare formula—having a cat randomly leap on-screen with an accompanying music hit, for example. As horror entered its self-reflective phase in the 1990s, movies like *Scream* called out the clichés directly. While that twist may have imbued them with new short-term life, it also pulled back the curtain, making them even less effective in the long run. Worst of all was the constant recycling of some gags, none of which has received more screen time than the dusty "mirror scare." That particular trick, where a character closes a medicine cabinet or mirrored door to reveal a monster just behind them, is so played out it's become a meme unto itself. When a movie trick gets its own supercut, it's not surprising—or scaring—anyone.

20   That's not to say the basic principles behind the jump scare aren't sound, however. The key is in the execution, and as a result filmmakers today have to be just as

cognizant of audience expectations as they do of any other element. "When we sat down to write the script," Cargill says of *Sinister*, "the first thing I did is I composed a list of all the tropes and clichés that appear in all the mainstream horror movies that people are tired of." The audience's built-in scare awareness can even be used to a movie's advantage. In *Sinister*, Cargill says, they at times used tropes to suggest the film was going in one direction—only to hit viewers from a different angle altogether.

With such incredible longevity—the jump scare has appeared in everything from *Jaws* to *Seven*—it's clear audiences appreciate a well-tuned jump. Mary Beth Oliver, Professor and Co-Director of the Media Effects Research Laboratory at Penn State University's College of Communications, thinks the reasons behind it are twofold. "I do believe that there's a tendency for some people to simply enjoy the actual adrenaline rush of the scare itself right then and there," she says, comparing it to a ride. On the other hand, she suggests, being scared heightens the physiological state of the audience—intensifying emotions they feel during the movie, and making any dramatic payoffs at the end that much more satisfying. In that sense, being scared may actually make the story in a horror movie stronger.   21

That notion of catharsis is also in play when it comes to the found footage set-up of the *Paranormal Activity* series. The conceit is as straightforward as it was back in *The Blair Witch Project*: bad things happened to some people with cameras, and here's what they recorded. In found footage movies, however, there's often little emphasis on character or traditional dramatic narrative. The *PA* movies are basically made up of creepy vignettes, which use the jump scare formula for almost every interesting beat. One might think that such an exercise would fall flat, but they've been enormously successful thus far.   22

The key may be the found footage approach itself. "Some research," Oliver says, "has wrestled with the idea that we tend to find fascination in things that are violent and frightening when we feel threatened ourselves." By playing off our lack of privacy in a world of Facebook oversharing and YouTube videos, the films may be appealing to underlying fears without the audience even realizing it.   23

Cargill sees the aesthetic intensifying scares by placing the movies in a world audiences are familiar with—and where they could be the victims. "I think the reason why they work right now is because audiences feel like they're watching something genuine," he says. "And it allows that audience to put themselves in the mindset that what they're watching could actually happen."   24

There's also an inherent tension in the format itself. Let's face it; you buy your ticket knowing terrible things are going to happen to these people, you just don't know *when*. Without a traditional story to guide your expectations, it becomes a voyeuristic waiting game. When you're anticipating a scare around every corner, even the slightest movement in the background is enough to ratchet up the tension.   25

Of course, *Paranormal Activity* didn't invent the idea of found footage; it's been percolating in the horror world since 1980's *Cannibal Holocaust*, with recent standouts like the Spanish film *REC* breaking through to broader audiences. The *PA* franchise has gotten Hollywood's attention, however, cementing the approach as a viable subgenre—and bringing its own set of tropes and audience expectations to the table.   26

Inquiring into the Essay

1. **Explore.** To go to a horror movie is to *expect* to be scared, writes Bishop. Why in the world would we choose to be scared? There is scholarship that suggests certain personality types are drawn to the horror genre. Are horror lovers more—or less—empathetic? Other research explains attraction to horror as "sensation-seeking" behavior, and there's particular pleasure in seeing bad things resolved at the end of the movie. Explore your own ideas about the appeal (or repulsion) of the horror genre. Think about your own reactions and those of people that you know. What do you think about why some people might choose to be scared?

2. **Explain.** The "key" to a good jump scare, Bishop notes, is in the "execution." What does he believe are the elements of a properly executed jump scare? Why is the convention now more popular?

3. **Evaluate.** How would you evaluate the organization of this essay? Go through it, paragraph by paragraph, and make a note of what each one seems to be saying or doing. Map the basic pieces of Bishop's argument. Can you imagine another way it might have been organized?

4. **Reflect.** Many of us don't hesitate to throw around the word "genre" from time to time, especially when we're talking about film. But how exactly do we distinguish one genre from another? For example, what's the difference between the horror film genre and the action film genre? What are the types of conventions or rhetorical features you might look for in making the distinction?

THE WRITING PROCESS

Inquiry Project: Writing an Analytical Essay

Inquiry Question: What might it mean?

Write an analytical essay about something that is open to interpretation. By now you know there is a world of possibilities for this. You might analyze literary works, films or television programs, advertisements, video games, speeches, fashion trends, photographs, brands, etc. Whatever you choose as an object for analysis must be *suggestive*: that is, there must be meanings that are not obvious. The ad might explicitly be selling luxury cars, but it's also selling some ideas about wealth or privilege. The poem might seem to be about the "road not taken," but this isn't necessarily what we usually think the poem means. The Apple vs. PC commercial is obviously trying to promote Macs, but it also draws on certain cultural ideas about "hipness." The local newspaper's coverage of football injuries seems balanced, but a content analysis suggests it isn't. In general, your analytical essay should do the following three things:

1. Describe the object of your analysis and then identify the patterns, elements, passages, references, or features that interest you.
2. Examine how these elements are connected to certain larger themes, ideas, ideologies, representations, historical contexts, or traditions.
3. Finally, argue for a particular interpretation, a particular answer to the question: What might this mean?

Prose+

- Consider producing an infographic to represent your interpretation. This genre is particularly useful for analyses that involve the frequency of certain elements or that might involve other statistical patterns.
- Build a web page around an analytical essay focused on a literary text, embedding video or audio of interviews with the author of the work and links to the works of other critics who comment on it. You might also add images, including those that you think echo the interpretation you're arguing for. Other features might include a bibliography with links to the sources you used, a list of other works by the author or artist, a sidebar that highlights an important passage, etc.
- Develop a PowerPoint or Pages presentation for your analytical essay, or as a supplement to it. This would be especially effective if you're analyzing a visual work, because you can include close-ups of significant features that are key to your interpretation. But a slide presentation can be effective for conventional literary analysis, too. Consider developing slides that provide background on the work, a statement of your thesis, and key passages or quotes from criticism that you're using as evidence.

What Are You Going to Write About?

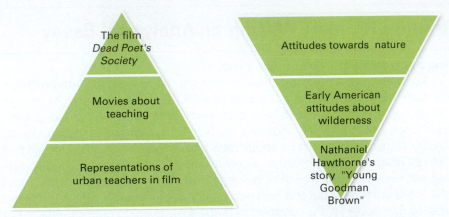

In the conversation between what a text says and what it might be saying, you discover fresh understandings of what you read.

When generating ideas for subjects, you can start big (deductively) with large themes about society that interest you and work down to find specific examples of things that might help you explore those themes. Or you might start small (inductively) with a particular film, poem, advertisement, or other object that you find interesting because it has unsettled meanings. We'll work both ways in the exercises that follow.

Opening Up

Listing Prompts.

1. Let's start small by brainstorming specific things that might invite interpretation.

Cultural trends	Great songs	Favorite movies	Favorite books, stories, essays	Memorable pictures, paintings, images

In each column, generate a fast list of things that come to mind. What cultural trends do you find hard to explain, what songs do you find strangely moving, what films or TV shows capture your interest? Are there books you love, paintings or photographs you remember?

2. Now let's go big, and generate three different lists of ideas about society that you think are important. In your journal, make a fast list of values, beliefs, or ideas that you think are *endangered* (e.g., public education, respect for elders, race relations, etc.). Then make a list of things that come to mind under the heading "This I Believe." Make another list under the heading "This I Used to Believe." We'll work with these lists in the subsection "Visual Prompts."

Fastwriting Prompts. Remember, fastwriting is a great way to stimulate creative thinking. Turn off your critical side and let yourself write "badly."

1. Choose one of the items in a column from step 1 of the "Listing Prompts" subsection to write about. If possible, re-experience the thing you'd like to interpret: Reread the poem, skim the stories, watch the film, listen to the song, study the ad. When you're finished, write a narrative-of-thought fastwrite: *When I first watched/read/observed this, I thought…. And then I thought… And then….* If you get some traction on some idea in this fastwrite, focus on that.

2. Choose an idea, value, or belief from your lists in step 2 of the listing subsection. Write fast about the idea, using this phrase as an opening prompt: *The best example of why I think this is important is….*

Visual Prompts. Visual thinking might help you play with ideas about how to analyze the work you're studying. Try these prompts to explore your response to a literary work:

1. Return to the fastwriting activities you tried earlier, and focus on the ideas, values, themes, and beliefs you generated in step 2. Make one of these the center of a cluster. Now build branches, identifying any times, places, people, and things you associate with that idea or value. Grow branches in your cluster that make what you're thinking more concrete (and less abstract).

2. Make a visual map of a story, if that's what your potential topic is about. Begin by placing at the center of a blank page a brief description of what you believe is the most significant moment in the story. This might be a turning point, or the point of highest tension, or perhaps the moment when the main character achieves his or her desires and dreams. Consider that moment the destination of the story. Now map out events or details in the narrative that threaten to lead the protagonist away from that destination and those that appear to lead the protagonist toward it.

Research Prompts. Analysis often involves working with primary sources: the poem, novel, essay, photograph, or painting. Sometimes, especially if the work isn't a text, you have to observe the object, performance, or behavior. If you're considering a subject like these for your analytical essay, then you need to go out and look. This fieldwork might include

1. Attending a performance (e.g., watching the modern dance, going to see the drama, etc.)

2. Observing a behavior (e.g., observing how people behave in a certain social situation)

3. Going to a museum (e.g., browsing paintings)

4. Seeing the films or shows (e.g., an evening watching zombie films)

On the other hand, if you're considering analyzing a literary text, you can research your favorite authors' work online, but you can also research top-ten lists of short stories, poems, and essays. There are annual "Best of" collections published every year in your university library.

7.3

Use appropriate invention strategies to discover a topic for an analytical essay.

Inquiring into the Details

Common Literary Devices

Many key concepts provide useful frameworks for analyzing literature. The key is to see the following ideas as an angle for viewing an essay, story, or poem much as you might approach a subject from different camera angles. Each provides a different way of seeing the same thing. In addition, each becomes a platform from which to pose a question about a text.

■ *Plot and significant event:* Plot is what happens in a story and what moves it forward. One way of thinking about plot is to consider this: What are the key moments that propel the story forward? Why do you consider them key? How do they add tension to the story? In an essay, these moments often give rise to the question the writer is exploring. In short stories, there is often a significant event that happens inside or outside of the story, and the entire narrative and its characters act or think in response to that event.

■ *Characters:* Imagine a still pond upon which small paper boats float. Someone throws a rock—big or small—into the pond, and the ripples extend outward, moving the boats this way and that. Depending on the size of the ripples, some of the boats may list or capsize, sinking slowly. Characters in a short story are like those boats, responding in some way to something that happened, some significant event that is revealed or implied. They move almost imperceptibly, or quite noticeably, or even violently. Is there logic to their responses? How exactly are the characters changed? How do they relate to each other?

■ *Setting:* Where a story takes place can matter a lot or a little, but it always matters. Why? Because where a story takes place signals things about characters and who they are. A story set in rural Wyoming suggests a certain austere ranching culture in which the characters operate. Even if they're not ranchers, they must somehow deal with that culture. Similarly, a story set in Chicago's predominantly black South Side introduces a set of constraints within which characters must operate. In some cases, setting might even become a kind of character.

■ *Point of view:* In nonfiction essays, point of view is usually straightforward—we assume the narrator is the author. But in fiction, it's much more complicated; in fact, *how* a story is told—from what perspective—is a crucial aesthetic decision. Telling a story from the first-person point of view in the present tense gives the story a sense of immediacy—the feeling that it's happening *now*—but at the same time limits our understanding of the other characters, because we can't get into their heads. So-called omniscient narrators can introduce a feeling of distance from the action, but they are also gratifyingly godlike because they can see everything, hovering above all the action and even entering characters' minds at will. Why might an author have chosen a particular point of view? Is the narrator trustworthy? What might be his or her biases, and how might they affect the telling?

- ■ **Theme:** One way to understand a story or essay is to consider that everything— character, point of view, and setting—contributes to a central meaning. In a good story, everything is there for a purpose—to say something to the reader about what it means to be human. In essays, this theme may be explicit, because essays both show *and* tell. Short stories, and especially poems, are often short on explanation of theme, operating with more ambiguity. The writer hopes the reader can *infer* certain ideas or feelings by paying close attention to what he or she *shows* the reader. To get at the theme, begin with the simple question *So what?* Why is the author telling this story or sharing this experience? What significance are we supposed to attach to it?

- ■ **Image:** Stories and poems ask us to see. When I read them, I imagine that their writers take my face in their hands and gently—or sometimes brutally—direct my gaze. What are they insisting that I look at, and how do they want me to see it? Images that recur may also be significant.

Narrowing Down

Now that you've opened up possibilities for analysis topics, there are choices to make. Which do you want to write about? First thing, naturally, is that you should pursue a subject that interests you. But also consider the following:

1. Returning to the iceberg metaphor that opened this chapter, might your potential subject have both obvious, visible meanings as well as less obvious, more submerged meanings?

2. Is the object of your analysis specific enough? If you started with a larger theme about society, did you manage to anchor it to *particular representations of that theme*? In other words, if you are interested in representations of manhood, how might manhood be implicated in the evolution of the action figure (doll?) GI Joe?

What's Promising Material and What Isn't? Try out a possible topic for your analytical essay by doing some more-focused writing and by thinking about it. First, generate some thinking-through-writing.

- ■ **First thoughts?** Interpretation is inspired by this question: *What might it mean?* And that's not a bad question to start with. Spend some time rereading, observing, or studying the work you've tentatively chosen, and if you're using a double-entry journal, collect notes (e.g., key passages, lists of observations, descriptions, etc.) on the left-facing page of your journal. Then, on the right, fastwrite for as long as you can, exploring and speculating about possible interpretations. When the writing stalls, pick up on something in your notes on the left page. This writing should be very open ended; you don't need to come to conclusions yet.

Now judge what you've generated:

- Can you refine your question? Analysis asks that you look closely at something and discover connections between it and the world of ideas. Imagine, for example, a bottomless bucket full of ideas about how people act and think in the world. Undoubtedly, there are ideas in that bucket that help to describe some of the implied meanings in the object of your analysis. You just have to figure out what those ideas are.

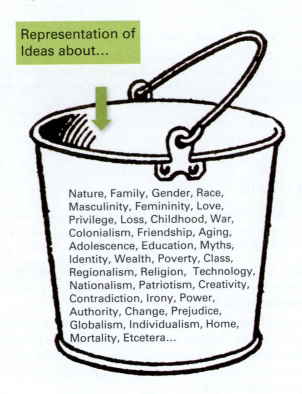

Representation of Ideas about...

Nature, Family, Gender, Race, Masculinity, Femininity, Love, Privilege, Loss, Childhood, War, Colonialism, Friendship, Aging, Adolescence, Education, Myths, Identity, Wealth, Poverty, Class, Regionalism, Religion, Technology, Nationalism, Patriotism, Creativity, Contradiction, Irony, Power, Authority, Change, Prejudice, Globalism, Individualism, Home, Mortality, Etcetera...

Try to tease out some of these connections by completing this sentence as many times as you can, each time focusing on some different aspect or element of the thing you're analyzing:

The (name an aspect or element of your subject) ___ seems to be representing certain ideas about ___ .

For example,

The slow, shuffling gait of zombies in shows like The Walking Dead *seems to be representing certain ideas about human vulnerability—civilization is threatened by the apocalypse but it will come at us slowly and relentlessly.*

Consider doing some online research to generate ideas to help complete these interpretive statements.

Questions About Audience and Purpose. One basic rhetorical question is this: Is your audience familiar with the work you're interpreting? If not, should you provide background so that they share enough knowledge of it to appreciate your analysis? This might include things like

- **Background on the work.** When was it published or created? How was it received? What was it compared to?

- **Summary or description.** What is the basic plot? What happens? What does it say? What does it look like?

- **Background on the author.** Significance in literary, design, or artistic circles? How the thing being analyzed fits into the body of the author's work?

Another key rhetorical consideration is finding ways to interest readers in the work you're analyzing, especially if they're unfamiliar with it. Why should they care about your analysis of N. Scott Momaday's poem or your interpretation of the "jump scare" convention in horror films? Think about ways in which the thing you're studying is relevant to understanding everyday experience. That's not so hard with your interpretations of horror films, since many of us watch them. But a poem? Make it interesting. Why is this poem important? How does it speak to how we might live and feel? How does it speak to you?

Writing the Sketch

We'll begin again with an early draft, a sketch that represents an initial attempt to discover what you want to focus on and what you might have to say about the work (or works) you've chosen.

Develop your sketch with the following things in mind:

- It should have a tentative title.

- It should be at least 500 to 600 words long.

- Write it with the appropriate audience in mind. Are you writing for readers who are familiar or unfamiliar with the object of your analysis?

- It should both describe a few key elements of the thing you're analyzing and offer some tentative interpretations of what those elements mean.

▶ Student Sketch

Hailie, a student in my first-year writing course last semester, brings her university debate skills to her analysis of the Meghan Trainor song "All About That Bass," a tune that is ostensibly a celebration of female body types that don't conform to a skinny ideal. However, in writing her sketch, Hailie discovers that she's troubled by the lyrics, and begins to build an argument that suggests that Trainor's good intentions go awry.

All About That Hate

By Hailie Johnson-Waskow

1   Meghan Trainor's breakout hit *All About That Bass* is a spirited attempt to create an anthem for women that society has deemed 'overweight'. However, Trainor's song falls desperately short of achieving the message of equality and acceptance that it was initially tasked with. In a feigned attempt at feminism Trainor has created a false dichotomy with her song; pitting the 'skinny girls' against the 'big girls.' This leads to her promotion of a culture that uses criticism to find self-solace.

2   The central message of the song is seen strongly in the chorus, and, not surprisingly, the opening line when Trainor claims she is "… all 'bout that bass, no treble." Trainor told Billboard magazine in December 2012, "You know how the bass guitar in a song is like its 'thickness,' the 'bottom'? I kind of related a body to that." This analysis alone seems to create the separation between thick and thin. The phrase 'all about that' encourages the acceptance of one body type while actively discouraging another. Trainor attempts to make larger bodies acceptable by pushing the small into the 'no treble' category. Further, it is interesting to note that the bass and treble are both music scores. The bass are round and thick while the treble clefs are tall and skinny. This symbolism is made by no coincidence and further enforces the skinny/fat dichotomy. Because she is ''bout' larger body types but says 'no' to other types she creates two separate groups. She argues that you must be part of one of these groups, you are either larger or smaller, and indicates that those who are smaller are lesser. The symbolism of the bass and treble create the basis for Trainor's work.

3   Immediately following the chorus, which opens the song with the repeated line "I'm all 'bout that bass, 'bout that bass, no treble," Trainor begins her first verse by proclaiming "Yeah it's pretty clear, I ain't no size two." This only further entrenches the idea that smaller women, specifically the particularly small at a size two, are unacceptable. This line is followed by the statement "But I can shake it, shake it like I'm supposed to do." By implying that women who are smaller cannot do what society expects of them, Trainor bluntly states that smaller women are inadequate. This idea of inadequacy and unacceptability is discussed further when Trainor states "I'm bringing booty back/Go ahead and tell them skinny b****** that." By explicitly calling smaller women an obscenity associated with rudeness, hostility, etc. Trainor places women who do not resemble herself into a specific category. This category seems to be marked by inferiority. She seems to continue her message of negativity toward women who are smaller than herself.

4   Although Trainor claims that she initially set out to create a song that encouraged the acceptance of all women, she has created a song that perpetuates bullying in order to achieve happiness. Trainor encourages the acceptance of larger bod[y] types but she is only able to do this by bringing down those who are not like herself. Thus, "All About That Bass" should be critically analyzed to ensure that those looking for happiness never bring others down to achieve it.

Moving from Sketch to Draft

How well does your sketch lead you to assertions about the meaning of the thing you're analyzing? Does it have a clear focus?

Evaluating Your Own Sketch. Among the key concerns in evaluating this early draft of your analytical essay is whether you've discovered a workable focus and whether you're beginning to get some clear idea of what you're trying to say. One of the best things you can do at this point is to use your sketch to craft a tentative thesis *or* the question that will be the focus of the next draft.

- **Thesis.** On the back of your sketch, in a sentence or two (but no more), state the main thing you're trying to communicate in answer to the question *What does it mean?*

- **Inquiry question.** Compose a question that reflects what you want to focus on in your interpretation. A relationship? The significance of certain recurring elements? An analysis based on a certain context—when the work was written or a tradition or theory?

Reflecting on What You've Learned. At the beginning of this chapter, I talked about some of the basic elements of analysis (see p. 211) and said that a close examination of *evidence* leads to inferences about what the evidence might mean. This in turn leads to an *interpretation* that you think makes sense, and, drawing on the evidence, an *argument* that convinces someone else of the soundness of your interpretation. How well did you incorporate those three elements into your sketch? What needs more development in the next draft? What do these elements tell you about the act of interpretation? Does the analytical essay encourage a kind of thinking that can be distinguished from the thinking encouraged by other forms of writing?

Developing

To develop your sketch into a draft, work on two fronts:

1. Closer analysis of the primary work or phenomenon
2. Research in secondary sources on the context of the thing you're writing about: what other critics say, theories that guide the analysis, relevant background on the work or situation

Analysis. Interpretation is an inductive process. By looking closely at the specifics, you develop ideas about patterns in the work that might be significant. If you're studying a text, for example, then your analysis must be grounded in what exactly you see in the poem, story, or essay. In literary analysis, you might focus on common devices such as setting and characters (see "Inquiring into the Details: Common Literary Devices" earlier in this chapter on p. 230). What exactly is the setting? What exactly do the characters say and when do they say it? What you look at will depend, of course, on your thesis or inquiry question. This evidence is the foundation of any analytical essay, because it helps writers discover the reasons that support a particular interpretation.

Research. Any significant work of art—a painting or novel or a cultural artifact such as reality TV or Facebook profile pictures—exists in context. These contexts include:

- **Historical.** When was it created? Is it part of a tradition? In what ways does the work or performance reflect the politics and culture of its time?

- **Biographical.** Who created the work? What does its author say about it or about his or her aesthetic intentions?

- **Critical.** What do other critics who have studied the work or phenomenon say about it?

- **Methodological.** Look at the five approaches to analysis in the "Inquiring into the Details: Five Methods of Analysis" feature earlier in this chapter on page 221. Is one of these methods relevant to your project? If so, do some further research online about the basics of the relevant method so that you can apply it to your project.

Drafting

Because an analytical essay is an argument, your draft needs to make an argument. If you're writing a formal analytical paper, then your thesis—the interpretation that is at the heart of your argument—should be stated explicitly pretty early in your paper. In a less formal analytical essay (see "Why Won't You Die?!" earlier in the chapter), the thesis isn't necessarily a fixture of the introduction. You might instead work your way to it, like the unraveling of a ball of string. The question that is driving your essay, however, should be clear in the beginning (e.g., What does the popularity of zombies in American film say about us?).

Methods of Development. Like most writing, there is no formula for structuring your analytical essay, but if you're writing for an audience that is relatively unfamiliar with your subject, you should probably assume that your draft needs to answer a series of questions in roughly the following order:

- What do you find particularly interesting in the work or phenomenon that inspired your analysis? (Show something specific.)

- What's the question that interests you? (Make sure your thesis answers that question.)

- Can you summarize or describe what you're analyzing?

- What have other critics or experts said about it? (Include interpretations that differ from yours.)

- What's a reason behind your interpretation? What's the evidence that led you to see it?

- What's another reason? And the evidence?

- Can you tell me again what your close analysis or observation helped you to see about the meaning of the work or phenomenon?

Here are some of the other ways you might organize your analytical essay:

Narrative.   An entirely different approach is to use your question as the starting point for a story you tell about how you arrived at an answer. This approach is more essayistic in the sense that it provides the story of *how* you came to know rather than reports *what* you think. A narrative essay might also involve relevant autobiographical details that influenced your analysis. For example, what feelings or experiences did you *bring* to the reading of the text?

Question to Answer.   Because the assignment is designed around a question you're trying to answer about the topic, the question-to-answer approach is an obvious choice. Consider spending the first part of your essay highlighting the question you're interested in. The key is to convince readers that yours is a question worth asking, and that the answer might be interesting to discover.

Compare and Contrast.   Analytical essays often benefit from this method of development. The approach might be to compare and contrast certain elements within the work. In a story there might be several characters, symbols or metaphors, plot developments, and so on—or you might compare the work to others by the same or even different authors. Note that these comparisons have to be relevant to the question you're asking.

Combining Approaches.   Frequently, an analytical essay uses several or even all of the methods of development mentioned here: question to answer, comparison and contrast, and narrative. Consider how you might put them all to work, especially in certain sections of your draft.

Using Evidence.   You need to consider two main kinds of evidence in an analytical essay: evidence that comes from so-called *primary* sources—especially the work itself, but also letters or memoirs by the author; and evidence that comes from *secondary* sources—books, articles, and essays by critics who are writing about the work or author. Primary sources are generally more important. In more-personal literary responses, however, your personal associations, anecdotes, stories, or feelings may be used as evidence, if they're relevant to the question you're posing.

Workshopping

As you now know, an analytical essay argues for a particular interpretation of a text or phenomenon. As you prepare to share your draft, you'll want to look for some of these weak links in your argument; consider asking peer reviewers whether you've avoided them:

- **Insufficient evidence.** Remember that this is a form of writing that works mostly with *primary sources*—the short story, the film(s), the ad, the first-hand observations, etc. Most of the information in your essay should be your close examination of the primary sources you're focusing on.

- **Broad focus.** Even lengthy analytical essays should look only at the *particular aspects* of the primary source that most contributed to the writer's interpretation.

- **General interpretation.** After all your analysis, you're not going to write something like "zombies are everywhere in film and are an interesting cultural phenomenon" as your thesis. That might be a setup for your thesis, which must be an interpretation with a much sharper edge: *The rise of the zombie in American film is testimony to the growing cultural nightmare that there are no safe places anymore, especially with the spread of nuclear weapons.*

In addition to these concerns, when you workshop the first draft of your analytical essay, you should focus first on what peers make of the purpose and meaning of your essay, both of which guide your revision. The following box can help you frame these questions for your workshop group.

Questions for Peer Reviewers	
1. Purpose	After reading the draft, can you explain back to me why I think the topic I chose to analyze is significant? Do I convince you that it might be significant to you, too?
2. Meaning	In your own words, how does the essay answer the inquiry question *What does it mean?* What evidence do you find most convincing in support of this interpretation? Least convincing?

Reflecting on the Draft. Take a look at the draft before you and circle the passage that you think is the best in the essay so far. Now circle the passage that you think is weakest.

In your notebook, fastwrite for five minutes about both passages. What seems to be working in the better passage? What problems do you notice about the weaker one? Does either one address the question you're writing about? If so, how? If not, how might it? When you compare the two passages, what do you notice about the differences? How might you make the weaker passage more like the stronger one? How might you make the rest of the essay stronger?

Revising

Revision is a continual process—not a last step. You've been revising—"reseeing" your subject—from the first messy fastwriting in your journal. But the things that get your attention vary depending on where you are in the writing process. With your draft in hand, revision becomes your focus through what I'll call "shaping and tightening your draft."

7.4

Apply revision strategies that are effective for the analytical essay.

Shaping. When we shape a draft, the focus is on design—the order of information, the chain of reasoning, the coherence of paragraphs, and the paragraphs' contributions to the whole composition. In an analytical essay, some of the basic units of reasoning are the moments of analysis in your essay, or those places where you actually work with a primary source to tease out its implications.

Here's an example from an analytical essay I once wrote on how American Indian writers seem to use memory in their fiction, poetry, and nonfiction. My focus here was on Sherman Alexie's work, and his character Thomas-Builds-the-Fire, who appears in several of the writer's stories.

> I think that the implications of this—that tribal memory and personal memory merge—are profound. Perhaps that's why nobody wants to listen to the stories of Thomas Builds-the-Fire in Spokane/Coeur d'Alène writer Sherman Alexie's recent works, *Reservation Blues* and *Tonto and the Lone Ranger Fistfight in Heaven*, Thomas, whose stories came to him before he "had the words to speak" (*Reservation* 73), tells stories that many of the Indians on the Spokane reservation refuse to hear, "stealth stories" that work their way into dreams and into "clothes like sand, [that] gave you itches that could not be scratched" (15). I wonder if the antipathy to Thomas's stories is really resistance to the hegemonic power of someone else's story to structure and contain individual experience and memory. Is that why Victor and Junior, two Spokanes who are adrift, unable to find the symmetry between personal past, history, and legend that Momaday discovers in *Rainy Mountain*, "tried to beat those stories out of Thomas, tied him down and taped his mouth shut" (*Reservation* 15).

(Marginal labels: Interpretation, Evidence)

Notice how the analysis here is *layered*. An interpretation is introduced and then explicated with evidence, which then leads to an elaboration of the initial interpretation and ends with some supporting evidence.

Examine your own paragraphs in a similar way. Take a highlighter and use two different colors, one for interpretation (assertion) and the other for evidence. Look to see if your analysis is layered—working back and forth from your ideas about a work or phenomenon and the evidence from the text or your observations—and if not, revise to encourage that quality in the paragraphs or passages of your draft.

Polishing. Shaping focuses on things such as purpose, meaning, and design. No less important is looking more closely at paragraphs, sentences, and words. Are your paragraphs coherent? How do you manage transitions? Are your sentences fluent and concise? Are there any errors in spelling or syntax?

Before you finish your draft, work through the following checklist:

✓ Every paragraph is about one thing.
✓ The transitions between paragraphs aren't abrupt.
✓ The lengths of sentences vary in each paragraph.
✓ Each sentence is concise. There are no unnecessary words or phrases.
✓ You've checked grammar, particularly verb agreement, run-on sentences, unclear pronouns, and misused words (*there/their, where/were*, and so on).
✓ You've run your spellchecker and proofed your paper for misspelled words.

▶ **Student Essay**

To fully appreciate Hailie's sketch about the Meghan Trainor song "All About That Bass," (see page 234), I watched the music video on YouTube, something I recommend before you read the revision of the piece below. Here, Hailie's analysis is richer and more fully developed. Like any strong analysis, the essay looks more closely at the visible elements of her study object—in this case, the lyrics of the Trainor song—and then teases out a network of implications that aren't readily apparent.

All About That Hate: A Critical Analysis of "All About That Bass"

By Hailie Johnson-Waskow

1   Meghan Trainor's breakout hit *All About That Bass* is a spirited attempt to create an anthem for women that society has deemed 'overweight.' However, Trainor's song falls desperately short of achieving the message of equality and acceptance that the artist initially intended. In a feigned attempt at feminism Trainor has created a false dichotomy with her song; pitting the "skinny girls" against the "big girls" which promotes the solace of one group at the expense of another. She then encourages male approval as the only way of measuring self-worth. Overall, Trainor's piece will never have the ability to be a song that all may use as an anthem for body acceptance.

2   When one initially listens to Trainor's song, the first thing noticed is that it does not sound much like the other popular songs of its time. "All About That Bass" has a very '50s/'60s doo-wop feel. Watching the music video cements the idea that this was an intentional move on the artist's part. The music video for the song features the artists in scenes you would expect from the '50s/'60s and wearing clothing that would also seem to reflect this time period. Specifically, the use of pastel colors throughout the video indicates that Trainor uses this time period to symbolize antiquated notions, specifically that larger girls are not attractive. She does this very purposefully to create humor in the idea that larger girls are unacceptable in society. She effectively shows that this prejudice toward larger women is out of date and that society must move forward. This creates the message that, in the 21st century, it is necessary to accept women of larger body types. However, another listen to Trainor's lyrics shows that she does not effectively argue for the acceptance of larger body types.

3   The central message of the song is seen strongly in the chorus, and, not surprisingly, the opening line when Trainor claims she is "... all 'bout that bass, no treble." Trainor told Billboard magazine in December 2012, "You know how the bass guitar in a song is like its 'thickness,' the 'bottom'? I kind of related a body to that." This analysis alone seems to create the separation between thick and thin. The phrase 'all 'bout that' encourages the acceptance of one body type while 'no treble' actively discourages another. Further, it is interesting to note that the bass

and treble are both music notation. The bass are round and thick while the treble clefs are tall and skinny. This symbolism is no coincidence and further enforces the skinny/fat dichotomy. Because she is "'bout' larger body types but says 'no' to other types she creates two separate groups. She argues that you must be part of one of these groups, you are either larger or smaller, and indicates that those who are smaller are lesser, a theme Trainor develops in the rest of her song.

Immediately following the chorus, which opens the song with the repeated line "I'm all 'bout that bass, 'bout that bass, no treble," Trainor begins her first verse by proclaiming "Yeah it's pretty clear, I ain't no size two." This only further entrenches the idea that smaller women, specifically the particularly small at a size two, are unacceptable. This line is followed by the statement "But I can shake it, shake it like I'm supposed to do." By implying that women who are smaller cannot do what society expects of them, Trainor bluntly states that smaller women are inadequate. This idea of inadequacy and unacceptability is discussed further when Trainor states "I'm bringing booty back/Go ahead and tell them skinny b****** that." By explicitly calling smaller women an obscenity, Trainor marks women who do not resemble her as inferior. She seems to continue her message of negativity toward women who are smaller than her.

But Trainor does not stop at critiquing smaller women. In both verses of her song she sings, "You know I won't be no stick-figure, silicone Barbie doll." This "stick-figure, silicone Barbie doll" symbolizes another category of women she has create[d]; women who participate in plastic surgery of any type. She signals this with the use of the word 'silicone' which is what many assume is used in most of these procedures. She implies that these women are fake or not authentic by calling them Barbies, reducing them to no better than plastic dolls. This association with a doll further indicates that Trainor believes women who use plastic surgery to be idiotic, or empty-minded like a doll. By associating this "Barbie doll" with the derogatory "stick-figure" she also argues that those who are smaller can only get that way through plastic surgery rather than exercise or a healthy diet.

However, one of the largest ways that she hopes to achieve acceptance is arguably even more flawed. There are several lines in this song including "But I can shake it, shake it like I'm supposed to do/'Cause I got that boom boom that all the boys chase" and "Boys they like a little more booty to hold at night" implying that self-acceptance comes only through male approval. The first example uses the phrase "shake it like I'm supposed to do" [and] displays subservience to men in order to feel good about oneself. It also argues that a woman is 'supposed to do' certain things for a man that make women slaves to male approval. This line enforces the patriarchy that modern feminism has made great strides to eliminate. The next example "Boys they like a little more booty to hold at night" also perpetuates the idea of male superiority. It takes a shot where many women find trouble already: their sexuality. Trainor suggests that a woman may only feel attractive when she has the 'right amount of booty to hold at night.' This leaves women struggling to find acceptance and relying on whether or not a man finds them sexually attractive. Essentially, it leaves a woman's confidence up to a man, which only supports the ridiculous notion that men are superior to women.

The other problem with these lines is one that is especially troubling in a song that encourages acceptance: Lyrics that encourage women to find acceptance through men are incredibly

(continued)

(continued)

heteronormative and sexist. The ideas presented in this song make the assumption that all listeners are heterosexual women. If a listener is a homosexual woman she quickly learns that she will never achieve body acceptance because she does not have any desire to be with a man. This further pushes listeners of this type into the periphery simply because they do not fit Trainor's mold. This assumption also hurts any male listeners. Trainor makes the assumption that only women struggle with body acceptance but that could not be further from the truth. While many will argue that wom[e]n's struggle with body acceptance is more difficult, it is important to remember that any struggle is important to consider. Instead the male listener is completely ignored in this message of acceptance and, instead, told he should be telling women whether or not their bodies are fit for society. The narrowness of Trainor's message of equality in body types undermines its goals.

8   With lines like "Every inch of you is perfect from the bottom to the top" it is clear that Trainor had the chance to achieve greatness but never was able to do so. Trainor should have created an anthem for all body types; of any gender and any sexuality. Instead she created a disappointing, dangerous song. Although Trainor claims that she initially set out to create a song that encouraged the acceptance of all women, she has created a song that perpetuates criticism in order to achieve happiness. Trainor encourages the acceptance of larger bod[y] types but she is only able to do this by bringing down those who are not like herself. Furthermore, the only way that those of her body type are able to achieve happiness is through the approval of men. This song then pushes numerous people to the periphery by insisting that they fit into what Trainor considers acceptable. "All About That Bass" is never able to achieve a message of true body acceptance.

Evaluating the Essay

1. Hailie's argument is clear: "All About That Bass" masquerades as liberation but ultimately just cooks up another variety of discrimination. After reading her essay and watching the video, what is your analysis?
2. Compare the sketch with this revision. What moves does Hailie make in the second draft of the essay, and do they make it more persuasive?

Using What You Have Learned

1. **Apply the methods of analysis to a subject whose meanings aren't apparent.** I hope the answer is obvious by now. The act of interpretation is a fundamental part of making sense of the world; it's also an essential academic skill. In the future, you'll be asked to interpret data, field observations, historical narratives, case studies, and many other primary sources. Interpretation is a method of thought you can't practice enough.

2. **Use evidence from primary sources to argue effectively for a convincing interpretation.** The last three chapters—the proposal, the argument, and now the analytical essay—are all persuasive forms of writing. In some ways, you build arguments in all three forms in very similar ways. But with an analytical essay, you've composed an argument that works with a particular kind of evidence: primary sources. This is a more scholarly approach to argument that builds on the foundations of persuasive writing you've developed in previous chapters.

3. **Use appropriate invention strategies to discover a topic for an analytical essay.** Though research has been part of the invention toolbox since the first assignment chapter on the personal essay, it has become increasingly important as we move towards writing on subjects outside our experience and knowledge. Because it relies on close reading and observation, the analytical essay is mostly research. By now it should be apparent that research (reading, interviewing, observing) *is* an invention strategy—a source of discovery—not just a move to build support for what you already know.

4. **Apply revision strategies that are effective for the analytical essay.** Research is, of course, not only an invention strategy but a revision strategy, especially with a form such as the analytical essay. When we "do research," particularly on the web, it often seems haphazard—looking here and there unsystematically, hoping to stumble into something usable. In the final two chapters, I hope you see that revising with research is, well, strategic. There are certain *categories* of information that you should look for. For example, in this chapter we talked about researching in terms of context: historical, biographical, critical, and methodological. Various forms of writing—and types of inquiry questions—give you guidance about types of information to research as you draft and revise. Look at your future research-based assignments rhetorically: What are the features of this kind of writing, and are there recognizable categories of information that are typically present?

8

Research Techniques

Learning Objectives

In this chapter, you'll learn to

8.1 Identify the "research routines" you've typically used, and practice new ones appropriate to college-level research.

8.2 Refine and improve the effectiveness of search terms.

8.3 Apply research strategies for developing "working knowledge" and "focused knowledge" on your topic.

8.4 Use a method to analyze and evaluate research sources.

8.5 Understand and apply new note-taking strategies that will help you analyze sources while you're researching.

Methods of Collecting

This chapter should tell you everything you need to know about finding what you need in the university library and on the web. It is particularly useful for collecting information for research essays, but research is a source of information that can make *any* essay stronger. Every assignment in *The Curious Writer*, therefore, includes suggestions for research as you're searching for a topic and writing your draft. Research also can be an especially useful revision strategy for any essay.

Use this chapter much as you would a toolbox—a handy collection of tips and research tools that you can use for all assignments. Refer to it whenever you discover a topic that raises questions that research can help answer, or whenever it would be helpful to hear what other people say about the things you're thinking about.

Research in the Electronic Age

The digital revolution has profoundly changed the way we do research, and it's mostly a wonderful thing. It's extraordinary, for example, how much information I can access on any topic from right here at my desk. But research in the electronic age has also created some new challenges. For example,

- An extraordinary amount of information, while more accessible than ever, is really, really bad, at least for academic research.

- The information that is accessible online is as disorganized as a hoarder's closet.

What this means is (1) that you need to spend more time critically evaluating what you find when searching online, (2) that the quality of the search terms you use will make a big difference in how easy it is to find reliable and relevant information, (3) that the library, which exists in part to *organize* information so it's easier to find, is more important than ever. In this chapter, I'll cover each of these points and offer some advice about how to develop your research skills.

> There's strong evidence that college undergraduates use some pretty standard "research routines" when given a paper assignment, no matter what the assignment says.

Research Routines

You've probably written research papers before. (My daughter Julia started writing them in the seventh grade.) And like anything you've done before, you have certain routines that you invoke when faced with a familiar task, often without thinking about them. For most of us, one of these research routines is to simply Google your topic. Another is to harvest the results from only the first page or so that appears. But as a college researcher, you need to be much more flexible and sophisticated than this. You need to look wider and deeper for information. Unlearning old routines begins with identifying what those routines are. Start this process by reflecting on what kind of researcher you are: "fast surfer," "broad scanner," or "deep diver."[1]

> **8.1**
> Identify the "research routines" you've typically used, and practice new ones appropriate to college-level research.

Fast Surfer

- I prefer to read only the sources that are written at a level that I can understand.

- If I don't find much on my topic when I search, I usually assume that there isn't much written about it.

- I always feel I'm under a lot of time pressure when I do research.

---

[1]Heinstrom, Jannica. "Fast Surfing, Broad Scanning, and Deep Diving: The Influence of Personality and Study Approach on Students' Information-Seeking Behavior." *Journal of Documentation*, vol. 60, no. 2, 2005, pp. 228-47.

- I pretty much limit myself to searching in the kinds of sources that I'm familiar with.
- I just look for what I need and little more.

Broad Scanner
- I search for a range of sources on my topic, a process that I don't necessarily plan but that develops slowly as I work.
- I often find my best sources accidentally.
- I'm pretty careful about evaluating the reliability of the relevant sources I do find.

Deep Diver
- I'm more interested in getting the highest-quality sources than in finding a lot of sources.
- I'm very open to changing my mind about what I think about my topic.
- I spend some time planning my research because I want my search to be thorough.

Depending on the research task, "fast surfing" might be just fine. But typically, academic researchers are "deep divers," whose habits of mind you should strive to emulate. "But wait," you might say. "I'm already pretty good at doing research. I did okay in high school." Researchers use the term "information literacy" to describe people's skills at finding and evaluating information, and one of the things researchers find over and over about the information literacy of college students is that college students are overconfident about their research abilities.

There's strong evidence that college undergraduates use some pretty standard "research routines" when given a paper assignment, no matter what the assignment says. One of these routines, according to the study group Project Information Literacy, is writing a thesis and making an outline early on in the process. In some cases, this isn't a bad approach. But if your goal is discovery—and that, after all, is the motive behind academic inquiry—then dreaming up a thesis before you've done much research defeats the purpose of doing research in the first place. You might have other routines as well, such as consulting Wikipedia, waiting until the night before the paper is due to begin doing any writing, or relying exclusively on Google and skimming only the first few sources that appear.

I'm a lousy dancer. I pretty much do the same moves over and over again and try not to be self-conscious. Similarly, writers who keep using the same routines never discover new moves that will help them adapt to new demands. In Chapter 1 and Chapter 2, you thought about your writing and reading habits, some of which you may have developed in high school, or simply by accident. To be conscious of your process is to get control over it and to see the *choices* you might make in particular writing or reading situations. Research is a process, too. And you'll find that many of the research routines you brought with you to college may not serve you well. But how can you know what you need to *unlearn* if you don't think about your process? Reflect often on what you're noticing about your ways of doing research. You'll then learn more dance moves, whatever the music.

Power Searching Using Google

Say I'm researching why people believe in alien abduction. For better or worse, most of us start our research at Google. So I type the following in the search window:

8.2

Refine and improve the effectiveness of search terms.

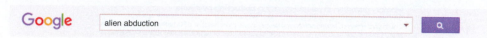

I get 5.87 million hits. Okay, that's a lot of stuff to scroll through. If you're like most people, you'll harvest just the first few relevant results on the opening page or two. But that would squander the power of the search engine and ignore lots of even better potential sources. But how do you find those sources?

Add a word or two:

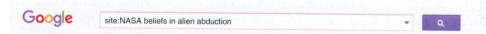

That's a little better: Now I get less than a million results. I might refine the search further by adding some words and putting a few terms in quotation marks. The quotes tell Google that I want documents with that exact phrase. Still, I'd like fewer and better results, from sources I am likely to trust. Here's where some of the more advanced commands can help. Suppose I want to get information from a particular site—say, NASA. What does the federal government's space agency have to say about belief in alien abduction? To do this, I begin with the word *site* and the name of the website:

Ninety-seven hits! This more focused search produced more reliable sources.

You can also search for particular kinds of documents such as the formats pdf, jpg, doc, etc., by beginning your query with *filetype: (jpg, doc, pdf, etc., and search terms)*. To summarize, then: To use Google efficiently, play with terms, including searching for an exact phrase using quotation marks; and focus your search by using the *site, filetype,* and *related* operations.

Google Scholar. Perhaps the most useful thing you can do is to try Google Scholar, to see if there is any scholarly work published on your topic. You will be amazed at the things that academics research, including belief in alien abduction, and the results you get will produce sources with the highest quality for an academic essay. *To use Google Scholar, the first thing you should do is link with your university library using a setting in Preferences.* Once you do this, the results will allow you to retrieve documents from your campus library without having to pay for them. To do this, open Google Scholar, open "scholar preferences," and scroll down to "library links."

Search windows from Google, Inc.

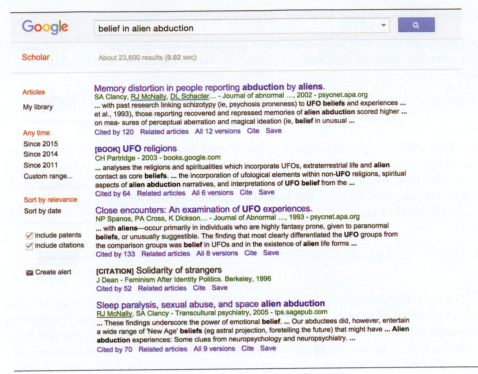

Figure 8.1 Google Scholar search for *belief in alien abduction*

Source: Google, Inc.

Enter the name of your university or college. Click on your school, and then you may have to enter your login credentials. Now you will see links to your own library on your results pages when a document is available (see the screenshot in Figure 8.1).

Notice, too, that if you do find a relevant article, you can quickly discover who has cited it (leading you to other potentially useful sources) and "related" work. It's hard to overstate how useful this site is for college research.

Power Searching in the Library

Many of us just search electronic card catalogs and library databases using our web-searching routines. And to some extent, that is sufficient. But you're going to search far more efficiently if you understand things called "controlled language searches" and "Boolean operators." Library databases often use both, so they're good to know, and they are less complicated than they sound.

Combining Terms Using Boolean Searching. George Boole, an eighteenth-century mathematician, came up with a system for using words like AND, OR, and NOT to help researchers craft logical search queries. Searches still use these words, though it isn't always obvious. Remember that I did a keyword search on *alien abduction* using Google in the previous section? What wasn't obvious is that Google assumes there is an AND between the two terms even if I don't type it; in other words, Google searches for online documents that contain *all* the terms I type in the search window. On the other hand, if I typed *alien OR abduction*, I would be telling Google to find materials that contain *either* term. In that case, by using the operator *OR*, I would be *telling* Google to broaden the search. Another Boolean convention you might want to try using is NOT, which excludes a term (e.g., *alien* AND *abduction* NOT *ufos*). Many databases also allow you to use quotation marks around exact phrases. What you end up with is a way to join a bunch of keywords using the operators to get better results. For example, you might search using the following string:

alien AND *abduction* AND *stories* NOT *ufos*

When I did that search on my university library's websites, I ended up with fifty-nine hits—both books and articles—and the great majority were relevant.

Using Controlled Language Searches. Mostly, we search using keywords—terms that we come up with, usually through trial and error, that we think will give us the best results. But in libraries there's another option: controlled language searches. These are the preferred words that librarians use to organize and find information. But how would you know what those authorized terms are? There are two ways to find out:

1. *Consult the Library of Congress Subject Headings.* This is the standard that reference librarians use to identify which terms to search with to yield the best results on any topic. You can search the LCSH online (authorities.loc .gov). Enter in your keywords, and voilà, there's a list of preferred headings you might use to search library databases. I found out that *alien abduction* is the favored search term, but I also discovered twenty variations, some of which I hadn't thought to use in a database search. For example,

   - Alien abduction in literature
   - Alien abduction-prevention-case studies
   - Alien abduction-psychological aspects
2. *Do a keyword search.* Sometimes you can also find the authorized terms by doing a keyword search in your library's database and looking at the results to see if the *LCSH* or other preferred vocabulary is listed in one of the relevant results.

Developing Working Knowledge

Every day we make decisions about how much we need to know about something. Twenty-five years ago, I decided I wanted to know enough to tune up my car, which I did badly. Later, I decided I wasn't interested in keeping up with the changes in electronic ignitions and fuel injection, so now I leave car repair to Davey at State Street Auto. A scholar is someone who, like Davey, has committed his or her professional life to keeping up with the knowledge in his or her field. College professors possess *expert knowledge* of their disciplines. In a way, we are all experts on at least one thing: ourselves. Five hundred years ago, the French philosopher

8.3

Apply research strategies for developing "working knowledge" and "focused knowledge" on your topic.

Michel de Montaigne argued that it is most important to be a "scholar of the self." Having this expertise can help us in writing insightful personal essays. But if our research projects lead us into unfamiliar territory—and inquiry projects almost always do—then we need to know something about our subjects. But how much?

How much we need to know about a subject is, in part, a personal choice, but a college education does at least two things: It challenges you to develop new knowledge about things that will make you a better citizen and a more productive professional; and it teaches you *how* to better acquire the new knowledge that you might seek by choice. A research project is driven by both goals—you'll be challenged to go beyond superficial knowledge about a meaningful topic, and you'll learn some of the methods for doing that.

You will not end up a scholar on anorexia, college dating, the medical effects of music, or whatever topic you're researching. But you will go way beyond superficial knowledge of your subject; and when you do, it will be like opening a door and entering a crowded room of intelligent strangers, all deep in conversation about your topic. At first, you simply listen in before you speak, and that process begins with a *working knowledge*.

All of us know how to develop a working knowledge of something, especially when we need to. For example, I recently developed a working knowledge of podcasting software for a course I was teaching. Now I can knowledgeably talk, for a few minutes without repeating myself, about how to use Audacity to edit digital recordings. An audio expert would be unimpressed, but someone unfamiliar with the software might find it informative. As a researcher, you've got to know enough about your topic in order to come up with a strong research question, and this begins with two simple questions:

1. What is known about my topic? (Question of fact)
2. What *is* it? (Question of definition)

Exploring the answers to these questions will give you some essential background on your topic, and this background will help you develop a more focused and interesting research question.

A Strategy for Developing Working Knowledge

It's hard to beat using the Internet as a quick-and-dirty way to develop working knowledge about nearly any topic. But the library can play an important role, too. Combine the two to develop a good working knowledge of your topic, efficiently. There are many ways to do this, but Figure 8.2 shows a sequence of research steps I recommend, and Figure 8.3 includes examples of specific sources.

Refine the Research Question. With a working knowledge of your topic, you're now ready to craft a stronger research question, which will guide your investigation over time and lead to some kind of judgment. It's hard to overstate how important this step is; a good question is the difference between a successful research project and one that flounders.

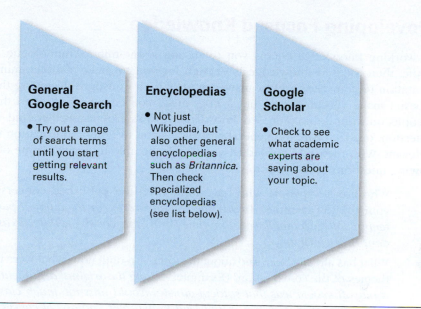

Figure 8.2 A recommended sequence of research steps for developing working knowledge

Source	Examples
General Encyclopedias	Encyclopedia.com, Columbia Encyclopedia, Wikipedia, Oxford Reference, Encyclopedia Britannica
Specialized Encyclopedias	Encyclopedia of Psychology, Encyclopedia of World Art, Encyclopedia of Sociology, Encyclopedia of the Environment, Encyclopedia of Women and Sports, Encyclopedia of African American Culture and History, Encyclopedia of Democracy, Encyclopedia of Science and Technology, Encyclopedia of Children, Adolescents, and the Media
Google (or other search engines)	Google, Mamma, Dogpile
Google Scholar	Google Scholar

Figure 8.3 Examples of sources that will help you develop a working knowledge of your topic

Now is also a good time to begin building a "working bibliography." (See the "Inquiring into the Details: The Working Bibliography" feature on page 257 for tips on how to do that.)

Developing Focused Knowledge

If working knowledge equips you to sustain a one-minute monologue on your topic, then focused knowledge is enough for you to make a fifteen-minute presentation to your class and to answer most of their questions. Knowing this much doesn't make you an expert, but it does make you far more informed than most people on your topic. Focused knowledge grows from a well-crafted research question, one that isn't too general and allows you to *ignore* information that isn't relevant. With focused knowledge, you should be able to answer some of the following questions about your topic.

- Who are key people who have influenced the published conversation on your topic? (Example: *Among the key advocates for the current playoff system in college football were longtime Penn State coach Joe Paterno and President Barack Obama.*)

- What has already been said about the topic? Up until now, what were the major themes of the conversation? (Example: *Among the original arguments against a playoff system was that student-athletes would miss too much class. Others added that such a system would lead to the "NFL-ization" of college football, extending the season and compounding the academic problems of student-athletes, who already spend as many as forty hours a week on football.*)

- What is at stake for people? Why is the research question significant? (Example: *Thousands of student-athletes in the United States are wedged between two conflicting goals for college football: the public hunger for big-time entertainment and the athletes' desire to complete a degree.*)

Library Research: A Strategy for Developing Focused Knowledge

While the web is an intoxicating source of information, academic research still fundamentally depends on library work. Much of this work you can do online. Libraries offer database indexes to magazines, journals, and books that are accessible from your computer at home or at school, and in some cases you can retrieve and print out full-text articles.

But there are still reasons to walk into the university library. Here are six:

1. That's where the books are.
2. Some of the best articles on your topic aren't available as full-text PDFs.
3. Browsing the stacks in your topic's subject area will lead you to books you won't find any other way.
4. You can read current periodicals not yet online.
5. The reference room has books and other resources that aren't available anywhere else.
6. Reference librarians are irreplaceable.

So, you'll want to go to the library—online and on foot—but you won't want to waste your time there. The two best ways to avoid wasting time are to have a good research question, one that will allow you to focus your efforts, and to have a handful of good search terms to try. Don't forget to use "controlled language searches," or searches that use the terms librarians have chosen to organize access to materials on every subject (see pp. 248–249). As you recall, you discover these terms in the *Library of Congress Subject Headings*. Find this online (search for "Library of Congress Authorities") or look for bound copies in the library, which librarians often call the "big red books."

Where should you begin? When you developed working knowledge, you started with more-general sources such as encyclopedias and then shifted to more-specialized sources such as Google Scholar, trying to dive down a little ways into your subject. Now it's time to dive more deeply. For focused knowledge, you can start anywhere—really—especially because you've already got some background knowledge on your research question. The key is to cover a lot of ground.

Searching for Books.

Searching for Books. Every library has an online index for books (also available at computers in the library, naturally), and by using the right search terms, you'll get an instantaneous list of relevant books on your topic and their "call numbers," which will help you find them in the stacks. Your results will also tell you if the book is checked out, missing, or unavailable at your college library. If any of these apply to a book you're really hankering for, don't despair. You've got several options:

- *Recall.* Make an online request that the book be returned (usually in a few weeks) by the person who has checked it out.

- *Interlibrary loan.* This is a wonderful, underutilized service, often provided by campus libraries at no charge to students. You can request, usually on-line, a call-out to a large network of university libraries for the book (or article) you need. It is then delivered to you, sometimes within days.

- *Check another library.* If your campus library doesn't have it, check the community library's index online.

The book search form on your university's website, like most search portals, has simple and advanced options. The advanced page is pretty cool because it makes it easy to do a Boolean search on your topic. You can also put "limiters" on the terms, allowing you to control the results for things such as author, title, date, and so on. Learning to use the Advanced Search will really pay off after enduring the initial, brief learning curve.

Searching for Periodicals and Newspapers.

Searching for Periodicals and Newspapers. It's hard to imagine a research question or topic that isn't covered by periodicals. You'll also want to check those databases, which are organized into four broad categories:

1. General subject databases, or indexes to periodicals across disciplines.
2. Specialized databases, or indexes that are discipline-specific.
3. Genre-specific databases such as Newspaper Source.
4. Government document databases.

Quite often, general subject databases include periodicals that may not be considered scholarly, including magazines such as *Discover, Newsweek*, and *Psychology Today*. These databases are a good place to start. To drill down further, use specialized databases, which are much more likely to produce the most interesting results on your research question because they are written by specialists in the fields of interest. They will also produce articles that can be a chore to understand if you don't know the jargon. That's when your working knowledge of your topic will really pay off. Also consider databases that warehouse certain types of content—plays, government documents, dissertations, and so on. You can see examples of all of these databases in Figure 8.4.

Database Type	Examples
Interdisciplinary/general subject databases	Academic Search Premier, Academic One File, JSTOR, ArticleFirst, Project Muse, MasterFILE Premier, WorldCat, Web of Science, ProQuest Central
Discipline-specific databases	ABI/INFORM (business), AnthroSource, America: History and Life, ArtSTOR, Applied Science and Technology, Biography Index, BioOne, Communication and Mass Media, ERIC (education), Health Reference Center, MLA Bibliography (languages and literature), Philosopher's Index, PsycINFO, Sociological Abstracts, Worldwide Political Science Abstracts
Genre-specific databases	National Newspaper Index, Newspaper Source, New York Times Index, Dissertation Abstracts International, Book Review Digest, Literature Criticism Online, Play Index
Government documents	Fed in Print, GPO Monthly Catalog, LexisNexis Government Periodicals Index

Search Type	Examples
General search engines	Google, Ask, Yahoo!, Bing
Metasearch engines	Dogpile, Clusty, SurfWax, Mamma
Subject directories	Yahoo!, About.com, Google, botw.org
Academic search engines or directories	Google Scholar, www.academicindex.net
Search engines for particular content	Yahoo Video Search, Google Books, Google Blogs, Google Images, www.newslink.org, www.internetarchive.org (audio, video, education, etc.), www.usa.org (federal government)

Figure 8.4 Database types and search types

Web Research: A Strategy for Developing Focused Knowledge

Web research for inquiry projects should be motivated by the following principles:

1. Maximize coverage.

2. Maximize relevant results.

3. Find stable sources.

4. Find quality sources.

Later in this chapter, I'll elaborate on what I mean by stable, quality sources, but examples would include: web pages and documents with .edu, .gov, or .org domains; those that are routinely updated; and those that might include a bibliography of references that document claims.

On the other hand, depending on your topic, you might seek a range of types of sources. For instance, suppose you're writing about green design and a blog from an architect in Texas has an interesting proposal for using turbines powered by passing cars on a highway in Austin. The proposal is interesting, and other sites refer to the blogger's idea. While this isn't a conventional academic source, the architect's blog is certainly a relevant and useful one for your essay.

Consider other types of online content as well: images, video, podcasts, discussion boards, and so on. For example, iTunes includes iTunesU, a remarkable collection of lectures, interviews, and video clips on a range of subjects, uploaded from universities around the United States.

The challenge is to find this stuff. Though Google is the dominant player in everyday research, Google is just the beginning, and good academic researchers shouldn't limit themselves to a single search service. Try some of the alternative search portals or directories listed in Figure 8.4.

Advanced Internet Research Techniques. In a previous section, you saw how to use some advanced search techniques on Google. Don't forget to use these techniques as you probe more deeply for sources relating to your research question. There are also a few other things you should try, and one of the most productive might be to use multiple search tools. Google is only one of many search portals, and there's evidence that using several search engines *will* produce unique results. In addition, there are "metasearch" tools that search multiple services at once. It's worth your time to try some of these tools. Here are a few suggestions:

Search Engines
- Ask
- Bing
- Hotbot
- Lycos
- Yahoo! Search

Metasearch Engines
- Dogpile
- Mamma
- SurfWax

Finally, you might also try using some specialized search tools (sometimes called "vertical" search engines) that focus on particular topics and kinds of content. Google Scholar is one of these tools. To find more, visit Noodletools and click on "Choose the Best Search."

Evaluating Library Sources

8.4

Use a method to analyze and evaluate research sources.

One of the huge advantages of finding what you need at the campus library is that nearly everything there was chosen by librarians whose job it is to make good information available to academic researchers. Now that many of the university library's databases are available online, including those of full-text articles, there really is no excuse for deciding to exclusively use the web pages you downloaded from the Internet as sources for your essays.

In general, the more specialized the audience for a publication, the more authoritatively scholars view the publication's content. Academic journals are at the bottom of this inverted pyramid because they represent the latest thinking and knowledge in a discipline, and most of the articles are reviewed by specialists in the field before they are published. At the top of the inverted pyramid are general encyclopedias and general-interest magazines such as *Newsweek* and *Time*. These have broader audiences and feature articles that are written by nonspecialists. They are rarely peer-reviewed. As a rule, then, the lower you draw from the inverted pyramid, the more authoritative the sources are from an academic point of view. Here are some other guidelines to consider:

- *Choose more-recent sources over older ones.* This is particularly good advice, obviously, if your subject is topical; the social and natural sciences also put much more emphasis on the currency of sources than do humanities disciplines.

- *Look for often-cited authors.* Once you've developed a working knowledge of your topic, you'll start noticing that certain authors seem to be mentioned or cited fairly frequently. These are likely to be the most listened-to authors, and may also be considered the most authoritative on your topic.

- *If possible, use primary sources over secondary sources.* In literary research, primary sources are the original words of writers—their speeches, stories, novels, poems, memoirs, letters, interviews, and eyewitness accounts. Secondary sources are articles that discuss those works. Primary sources in other fields might be original studies or experiments, firsthand newspaper accounts, marketing information, and so on.

Inquiring into the Details

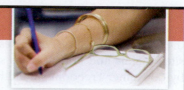

The Working Bibliography

A working bibliography lists sources you've collected that you think will be helpful when you draft your essay. These may include annotations or brief summaries of what the source says that you find relevant to your research question. Consider the following examples:

TOPIC: RELATIONAL AGGRESSION

PRINT SOURCES

Simmons, Rachel. *Odd Girl Out: The Hidden Culture of Aggression in Girls.* Houghton Mifflin Harcourt, 2002.

Simmons argues that the "secret world of girls' aggression"—the backstabbing, the silent treatment, the bartering of friendship for compliance to a group's "rules"—can be just as bad as the less subtle aggression of boys. Her basic thesis is that girls in American culture are supposed to be "nice" and therefore have no outlet for their anger except for exploiting the one thing they do covet: relationships. Because my essay focuses on the popularity phenomenon in high school—How does it affect girls when they become adults?—Simmons's chapter on parents of these girls seems particularly useful because it shows how the parents' responses are often shaped by their own experiences in school.

WEB SOURCES

"What Is Relational Aggression?" *The Ophelia Project,* 22 Sept. 2003, www .opheliaproject.org/issues/issuesRA.shtml.

The page defines relational aggression by contrasting it with physical aggression. It argues that most research, naturally, has focused on the latter because of the need to limit physical injury between children. But girls tend to avoid physical aggression and instead indulge in actions that harm others by disrupting their social relationships, like giving someone the silent treatment. The Ophelia Project is a nonprofit group created in 1997 by parents who wanted to address the problem.

Evaluating Web Sources

Everyone knows to be skeptical of what's on the web. But skepticism is even more crucial when using web sources for college writing. Because it's dominated by commercial sites, much of the World Wide Web has limited usefulness to the academic researcher; and although very few online authors are out to fool researchers with fake scholarship, many have a persuasive purpose. Despite its "educational" mission, for example, the purpose of the Consumer Freedom website is to promote industry views on laws relating to food and beverages. That doesn't make the information it offers useless, but a careful researcher would be wary of the site's claims and critical of its studies. At the very least, the information provided by Consumer Freedom should be attributed as a proindustry view.

Imagine, as you're researching on the web, that you've been dropped off at night in an unfamiliar neighborhood. You're alert. You're vigilant. And you're careful about whom you ask for directions. You can also be systematic about how you evaluate online sources. In general, follow these principles:

- *Favor governmental and educational sources over commercial ones.* These sites are more likely to have unbiased information. How can you tell which sites are institutional when it's not obvious? Sometimes the domain name—the abbreviation *.edu, .org,* or *.gov* at the end of an Internet address—provides a strong clue, as does the absence of ads on the site.

- *Favor authored documents over those without authors.* There's a simple reason for this: You can check the credentials of authors if you know who they are. Sometimes sites provide e-mail links so you can write to authors, or you can do a search on the Internet or in the library for other materials they've published.

- *Favor documents that are also available in print over those available only online.* Material that is published in both forms generally undergoes more scrutiny. An obvious example is newspaper articles, but some articles from journals and magazines are also available electronically and in print.

- *Favor web sources that document their claims over those that don't.* This well-known academic convention is strong evidence that the claims an online author is making are supported and verifiable.

- *Favor web pages that have been recently updated over those that haven't changed in a year or more.* Frequently at the bottom of a web page there is a line indicating when the information was posted to the Internet and/or when it was last updated. Look for that line.

An Evaluation Checklist for Web Sources

1. **Relevance.** Is this web source relevant to my research question?
2. **Authors.** Are there any? If so, can I trust them? Are they recognized experts on the subject? Do they have a bias? Do they say sensible things? If there aren't authors, are there other things about the source that make it credible?
3. **Source.** What's the domain: .edu, .gov, .org? If it's a commercial site, is it still useful because of its author, content, or relevance?
4. **Verifiability.** Can you contact the authors? Is there a bibliography of references? Do other, credible sites refer to this one?
5. **Stability.** How long has the website been around, and how often is it updated?

Research with Living Sources: Interviews, Surveys, and Fieldwork

Sometimes the best way to get information about something is to ask someone. Sometimes the best way to see what happens is to go out and look. And sometimes the best way to find out what people think or believe is to invite them to tell you. While we often assume that research means reading, much research also involves interviews, observations, and surveys. Consider whether your research project can benefit from collecting information from these sources (see Figure 8.5).

Interviews

Tethered as we are these days to the electronic world of the web and the increasingly digital university library, it's easy to forget an old-fashioned source for research: a living, breathing human being. People are often the best sources of information because you can have a real conversation rather than the imagined one simulated by the double-entry notebook. Some kinds of writing, such as the profile, fundamentally depend on interviews; with other genres, such as the personal essay or the research paper, interviews are one of several sources of information. But interviews can be central to bringing writing to life, because when we put people on the page, abstract ideas or arguments suddenly have a face and a voice. People on the page make ideas matter.

> Tethered as we are these days to the electronic world of the web and the increasingly digital university library, it's easy to forget an old-fashioned source for research: a living, breathing human being.

The face-to-face interview often yields much better material than the online interview, so we'll look at face-to-face interviews first. But we'll also consider the convenience and usefulness of online interviews.

Interviews
- Find a local expert
- Interview people affected by the problem

Field observations
- Photograph, record, and collect
- Observe and describe

Surveys
- Determine attitudes
- Collect comments
- Describe a population

Figure 8.5   Selecting a research method

Arranging Interviews. Whom do you interview? Basically, there are two kinds of interviews: (1) the kind in which the interviewee is the main subject of your piece, as in a profile; (2) the kind in which the interviewee is a source of information about another subject.

The interviewee as a source of information is the far more common type of interview, and it usually involves finding people who either are experts on the topic you're writing about or have been touched or influenced in some way by it. For example, Tina is writing a research essay on the day-care crisis in her community. Among those affected by this crisis are the parents of small children, their day-care teachers, and even the kids themselves; all are good candidates for interviews about the problem. The appropriate experts were a little more difficult to think of immediately. The day-care teachers might qualify—after all, they're professionals in the area—but Tina also learned of a faculty member in the College of Health and Social Sciences who specializes in policies related to child care. Interviewing both types of people—experts and those affected by the crisis—gives Tina a much richer perspective on the problem.

How do you find experts on your topic? Here are a few strategies for locating potential interviewees:

- *Check the faculty directory on your campus.* Many universities publish an annual directory, which may be online, of faculty and their research interests. In addition, your university's public information office might have a similar list of faculty and their areas of expertise.

- *Cull a name from an online discussion group.* Use a specialized search engine such as Google Groups to search by topic and find someone appropriate who might be willing to do an e-mail interview.

- *Ask your friends and instructors.* They might know faculty who have a research interest in your topic or someone in the community who is an expert on that topic.

- *Check the phone book.* The familiar *Yellow Pages* can be a gold mine. For example, want to find a biologist who might have something to say about the effort to bring back migrating salmon? Look in the phone book for the number of the regional office of the U.S. Fish and Wildlife Service and ask to speak to the public information officer. He or she may be able to help you find the right expert.

- *Check your sources.* As you begin to collect books, articles, and Internet documents, note their authors and affiliations. I get calls or e-mails from time to time from writers who came across my book on lobsters, posing questions I love to try to answer because no one else in Idaho gives a hoot about lobsters. Google searches of authors who are mentioned in your sources may produce e-mail addresses or websites with e-mail links that you might query.

- *Check the Encyclopedia of Associations.* This resource—another underused book and database in your university's reference room—lists organizations in the United States with concerns as varied as promoting tofu and saving salmon.

Conducting the Interview. The kinds of questions you ask fundamentally depend on what type of interview you're conducting. In a profile, your questions will focus on the interview subject. To some extent, this is also the focus of your questions when you interview nonexperts who are *affected* by the topic you're writing about. For example, Tina is certainly interested in what the parents of preschoolers *know* about the day-care crisis in her town, but she's also interested in the feelings and *experiences* of these people. Wanting to gather this kind of information leads to some of the questions you may have used in a profile, but with more focus on the subject's experience with your topic:

- What was your first experience with _____? What has most surprised you about it?
- How does _____ make you feel?
- Tell me about a moment that you consider most typical of your experience with _____.

More often, however, your motive in an interview will be to gather information. Obviously, this motive will prompt you to ask specific questions about your topic as you try to fill in gaps in your knowledge. But some more general, open-ended questions may also be useful to ask. For example:

- What is the most difficult aspect of your work?
- What do you think is the most significant popular misconception about _____?
- What are the significant current trends in _____?
- If you had to summarize the most important thing you've learned about _____, what would that be?
- What is the most important thing other people should know or understand?
- What do you consider the biggest problem with _____?
- Who has the power to do something about that problem?
- What is your prediction about the future? Ten years from now, what will this problem look like?

Once you have a list of questions in mind, be prepared to ignore them. Good interviews often take turns that you can't predict, and these journeys may lead you to information and understandings you didn't expect. After all, a good interview is like a good conversation: It may meander, speed up or slow down, and reveal things about your topic and your interview subject that you didn't expect to discover. But good interviewers also attempt to control an interview when the turns it's taking aren't useful. You do this through questions, of course, but also with more-subtle tactics. For example, if you stop taking notes, most interview subjects notice, and the astute ones quickly understand that what they're saying has less interest to you. A quick glance at your watch can have the same effect.

E-mail interviews produce a ready-made text with both your questions and the subject's answers. This is pretty wonderful. Live interviews, on the other hand, require more skill. It's thus usually a good idea to use a tape recorder (with your subject's permission), but not to rely exclusively on it, especially because machines can fail and batteries can expire unexpectedly. *Always take notes.* If nothing else, your notes will help you know where on the tape you should concentrate later, transcribing direct quotations or gathering information. Note taking during interviews is an acquired skill; the more you do it, the better you get, along the way inventing all sorts of shorthand for commonly occurring words. Practice taking notes while watching the evening news.

Most of all, try to enjoy your interview. After all, you and your interview subject have something important in common—an interest in your topic—and this usually produces an immediate bond that transforms an interview into an enjoyable conversation.

Using the Interview in Your Writing. Putting people on the page is one of the best ways to bring writing to life. This is exactly what information from interviews can do—give otherwise abstract questions or problems a voice and a face. One of the most common ways to use interview material is to integrate it into the lead or first paragraph of your essay. By focusing on someone involved in the research question or problem you're exploring, you immediately capture reader interest. For example, here's the beginning of a *Chronicle of Higher Education* essay titled "What Makes Teachers Great?"[2] Quite naturally, the writer chose to begin by profiling someone who happened to be a great teacher, using evidence from the interviews he conducted.

> When Ralph Lynn retired as a professor of history at Baylor University in 1974, dozens of his former students paid him tribute. One student, Ann Richards, who became the governor of Texas in 1991, wrote that Lynn's classes were like "magical tours into the great minds and movements of history." Another student, Hal Wingo, the editor of *People* magazine, concluded that Lynn offered the best argument he knew for human cloning. "Nothing would give me more hope for the future," the editor explained, "than to think that Ralph Lynn, in all his wisdom and wit, will be around educating new generations from here to eternity."

This is a strong way to begin an essay, because the larger idea—the qualities that make a great teacher—is then grounded in a name and a face. But information from interviews can be used anywhere in an essay—not just at the beginning—to make an idea come to life.

Information from interviews can also provide strong evidence for a point you're trying to make, especially if your interview subject has expertise on the topic. But interviews can also be a *source* of ideas about what you might want to say in your essay. The essay on great teaching, for instance, offers seven qualities that great teachers embrace in their classrooms—things such as "create a natural critical learning environment" and "help students learn outside of class." All of these claims grew from interviews with sixty professors in a range of disciplines.

---

[2]Bain, Ken. "What Makes Teachers Great?" *The Chronicle of Higher Education*, 9 Apr. 2004, pp. B7-B9.

The principal advantage of doing interviews is that you ask the questions that you're most interested in learning the answers to. Rather than sifting through other sources that may address your research questions briefly or indirectly, interviews generate information that is often relevant to and focused on the information needs of your essay. In other words, interviews are a source of data that can also be sources of theories or ideas on your topic. And this is often the best way to use interview material in your essay.

The Online Interview

My phone doesn't ring much anymore, but I hear the "ding" of incoming messages on my computer all day long. I hear from people by e-mail, text, and Facebook, and I mostly like staying in touch with people that way, at least until I get compulsive about checking for messages. Obviously, online contact with people is convenient, and it also opens up new possibilities for researchers who want to contact people for interviews.

Finding People Online. There are lots of ways to find people online, including these:

- *Through organizational affiliation.* If in your research you discover that a key researcher works at a particular university, agency, or business, then you can search the institution online and sometimes find an e-mail address for that researcher.

- *Through a web document.* It isn't unusual for a web document or page you're using in your research to include a contact link or even the e-mail addresses of the authors or other institutional contacts.

- *Through a search function.* This is the most obvious move. Google the name and institution of the person you want to interview, or search on Facebook.

- *Through discussion groups and listservs.* It's great if you have identified in your reading the name of someone you'd like to interview, but what about *locating* people who are involved in the topic you're researching? One way to do this is to find online discussion groups that focus on your topic. Say you were researching campus sustainability. A quick search on Yahoo! Groups will yield a list of online groups around the world that are interested in the same thing you are, and often people with the expertise or experiences you're looking for. Search online discussion groups by topic using one or more of the following portals:

  BoardReader (http://boardreader.com)
  BoardTracker (http://www.boardtracker.com)
  Google Groups (http://groups.google.com)
  Yahoo! Groups (http://groups.yahoo.com)

Contacting Someone for an Online Interview. Once you find the e-mail address of someone who seems like a good interview subject, proceed courteously and cautiously. One of the Internet's haunting issues is its potential to violate privacy. Be especially careful if you've gone to great lengths in hunting down the e-mail address of someone involved with your research topic; she may not be keen on receiving unsolicited e-mail messages from strangers. It would be courteous to approach any potential interview subject with a short message that asks permission to conduct an online interview. In this message, briefly describe your project and why you think she might be a good source. You will be much more likely to get an enthusiastic response to your request if you can demonstrate your knowledge of her work on or experience with your topic.

Let's assume your initial contact has been successful and your subject has agreed to answer your questions. Your follow-up message should ask a limited number of questions—say, four or five—that are thoughtful and, if possible, specific. Keep in mind that while the e-mail interview is conducted in writing rather than through talking, many of the methods for handling oral interviews still apply.

Surveys

The survey is a fixture in American life. We love surveys. What's the best economical laptop? Should the president be reelected? Who is the sexiest man alive? What movie should win Best Picture? Some of these are scientific surveys with carefully crafted questions, statistically significant sample sizes, and carefully chosen target audiences. In your writing class, you likely won't be conducting such formal research. More likely it will be like Mike's—fairly simple—and although not necessarily statistically reliable, your informal survey will likely be more convincing than anecdotal evidence or your personal observation, particularly if your survey is thoughtfully developed.

Defining a Survey's Goals and Audience. A survey is a useful source of information when you're making some kind of claim regarding "what people think" about something. Mike observed that his friends all seem to hate pennies, and he wanted to generalize from this anecdotal evidence to suggest that most people probably share that view. But do they? And which people are we really talking about? As we discussed this in his writing group, Mike pointed out that his grandfather grew up during the Great Depression and has a very different perspective on money than Mike does. "So your grandfather would probably pick up a penny in the parking lot, right?" I asked. "Probably," Mike said.

Quickly, Mike not only had a survey question but also began to think about qualifying his claim. Maybe younger adults—Mike's generation—in particular share this attitude about the lowly penny. To confirm this, Mike's survey had both a purpose (to collect information about how people view pennies) and an audience (students on his campus). If he had the time or inclination, Mike could conduct a broader survey that included older Americans, but for his purposes the quad survey would be enough.

Two Types of Survey Questions. There are typically two broad categories of survey questions: open ended and structured. Figure 8.6 shows the advantages and disadvantages of each for your survey.

Question Type	Examples	Advantage(s)	Disadvantage(s)
Open ended	Brief response, essay question	May get surprising answers. More insight into respondents' thoughts and ideas.	Take more time. Can't easily be measured.
Structured	Multiple choice, true/false, Likert, ranking	Easier to analyze responses. Don't take much time.	Must know enough to provide appropriate choices.

Figure 8.6   Question Types: Advantages and Disadvantages

Generally speaking, you should limit the number of open-ended questions you use since they are more demanding on the respondents. But don't hesitate to use them if you hope to open a window on the thinking of your survey audience. These responses might not reveal a pattern, but they often provide interesting anecdotal evidence you can use in your essay.

Crafting Survey Questions.   To begin, you want to ask questions that your target audience can answer. Don't ask a question about a campus alcohol policy that most students in your target audience have never heard of. Second, keep the questions simple and easy to understand. This is crucial because most respondents resist overly long survey questions and won't answer confusing ones. Third, make sure the questions will produce the information you want. This is a particular hazard of open-ended questions. For example, a broad open-ended question such as "What do you think of the use of animals in the testing of cosmetics?" will probably produce a verbal shrug or an answer of "I don't know." A better question is more focused: "What do you think about the U.S. Food and Drug Administration's claim that animal testing by cosmetic companies is 'often necessary to provide product safety'?"

Such a question could be an open-ended or structured question, depending on the kind of responses you're seeking. Focusing the question also makes it more likely to generate information that will help you compose your essay on the adequacy of current regulations governing animal testing. Also note that the question doesn't necessarily betray the writer's position on the issue, which is essential—a good survey question isn't biased or "loaded." Imagine how a less neutral question might skew the results: "What do you think of the federal bureaucrats' position that animal testing for cosmetics is 'often necessary to provide product safety'?" An even more subtle bias might be introduced by using the term *federal government* rather than *Food and Drug Administration* in the original question. In my part of the world, the Rocky Mountain West, the federal government is generally not viewed favorably, no matter what the issue.

Keep the number of survey questions to a minimum. It shouldn't take respondents long—no more than a few minutes at most—to complete your survey, unless you're lucky enough to have as your respondents a captive audience such as a class.

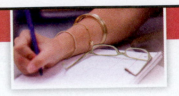

Inquiring into the Details

Types of Survey Questions

These are a few of your options when deciding what type of questions to ask in a survey.

1. **Limited choice**

   Do you believe student fees should be used to support campus religious organizations?

   ____ Yes

   ____ No

   ____ I'm not sure

   At what point in the writing process do you usually get stuck?

   ____ Getting started

   ____ In the middle

   ____ Finishing

   ____ I never get stuck

   ____ Other: _____

2. **Scaled response (Likert)**

   The Student Film Board should show more foreign films.

   ____ Strongly agree

   ____ Agree

   ____ Neither agree nor disagree

   ____ Disagree

   ____ Strongly disagree

3. **Ranking**

   Which of the following do you consider important in designing a classroom to be conducive to learning? Rank them from 1 to 5, with the most important a 1 and the least important a 5.

Comfortable seating	
Natural light from windows	
Carpeting	
Effective soundproofing	
Dimmable lighting	

4. **Open ended**

   Describe three things you learned in this course.

   What steps do you think the university should take to increase attendance at women's soccer games?

Finally, consider beginning your survey with background questions that establish the identity of each respondent. Typical information you might collect includes the gender and age or, with student-oriented surveys, the class ranking of the respondent. Depending on your topic, you might be interested in particular demographic facts, such as whether someone has children or comes from a particular part of the state. All of these questions can help you sort and analyze your results.

Conducting a Survey: Paper or Electronic?

After you mull over the purpose of your survey, you need to decide whether you'll distribute it electronically or on paper. These days, free online software like the popular SurveyMonkey allows users to easily create basic digital surveys. You can distribute the survey to a targeted list of recipients by e-mail or by posting it on a blog, website, or even social media like Facebook and Twitter. In addition, a program like SurveyMonkey helps you analyze the results and filter, compare, and summarize the data with charts and graphs. Web-based surveys are also cheaper than paper surveys. Why wouldn't you want to go digital instead of using old-fashioned paper surveys? A couple of reasons:

- With paper, you can target an audience much more easily, particularly if you can locate those potential respondents in a specific time or place. For example, if you want to survey your school's football fans, distributing your survey on game day at the tailgate party will give you direct access to your survey audience.

- Not everyone has easy Internet access.

- The free versions of the online software may limit the number of responses you can gather.

- Response rates to electronic surveys can be lower than response rates to paper surveys.

Despite these drawbacks, a web-based survey is often the best choice for an undergraduate research project, particularly if you can find ways to target your audience, make a personal appeal for a response, and send out a reminder or two.

Testing the Survey.

Whether you're using an online or a paper survey, *if you can, test it first*. Invariably, this testing turns up problems: A survey is too long, a question is poorly worded, the response rate to a particular question is low, and so on. You won't be able to test your draft survey nearly as thoroughly as the experts do, but you also shouldn't put your faith in an untested survey. Instead, ask as many people as you can to try it out and describe their experience answering your questions. Was there any confusion? How long did it take? Don't forget to also ask yourself whether the survey is generating relevant information.

Finding the Target Audience.

Once you're confident in the design of your survey, plan how you'll distribute it. There are several options:

1. *If paper, distribute it in an appropriate location.* Begin by asking yourself whether your target audience tends to gather in a particular location. For example, if you're surveying sports fans, then surveying people by the main gate at the football stadium on Saturday might work. If your target audience is first-year

college students and your university requires freshman English composition, then surveying one or more of those classes would be a convenient way to reach that audience. In some situations, you can leave your survey forms in a location that might garner responses from your target audience. For example, a student at my university wanted to survey people about which foothill's hiking trails they liked best, so she left an envelope with the forms and a pencil at several trailheads.

2. *If online, find appropriate sites.* You can reach respondents online in the following ways:
   - E-mail
   - Social media like Facebook or Twitter
   - Listservs, discussion groups
   - Posting a survey link on a blog or web page

Using Survey Results in Your Writing. The best thing about conducting an informal survey is that you're producing original and interesting information about your topic's local relevance. This kind of information can be an impressive element of your essay and will certainly make it more interesting.

Because analysis of open-ended questions can be time consuming and complicated, consider the simplest approach: As you go through the surveys, note which responses are worth quoting in your essay because they seem representative. Perhaps the responses are among the most commonly voiced in the entire sample, or perhaps they are expressed in significant numbers by a particular group of respondents.

In a more detailed analysis, you might try to nail down more specifically the *patterns* of responses. For example, perhaps you initially can divide the survey results into two categories: people who disagree with the university's general education requirements and those who agree with them, Group 1 and Group 2. The next step might be to further analyze each of these groups, looking for patterns. In particular, pay attention to responses you didn't expect, responses that might enlarge your perspective about what people think about your topic.

Your analysis of the responses to direct questions will usually be pretty simple—probably a breakdown of percentages. In a more sophisticated analysis, you might try to break the sample down, if it's large enough, into certain categories of respondents—men and women, class ranking, those with high or low test scores, and so on—and then see if any response patterns correlate to these categories. For example, perhaps a much higher percentage of sampled freshmen than seniors agreed that a good job is the most important reason to go to college.

What might this difference mean? Is it important? How does it influence your thinking about your topic, or how does it affect your argument? Each of these questions involves interpretation of the results, and sample size is the factor that most influences the credibility of survey evidence.

Fieldwork: Research on What You See and Hear

There are a lot of inquiry projects that might benefit from direct observation and description, especially if you're researching something that has a local angle and there might be something relevant to learn. Would your essay on farmer's markets, for instance, benefit from listening to and observing people at the Saturday market downtown?

There are two kinds of fieldwork:

1. *Participant observation.* You are involved as an active participant in the thing you're researching.

2. *Direct observation.* You unobtrusively observe the settings or phenomena.

Because you're not doing formal scholarship for this project, whichever method you use as your approach will probably be informal rather than carefully planned and methodologically strict. What you *are* trying to do that is common to all fieldwork is look for patterns in what you see. In particular, you might want to describe what is either *typical* (e.g., a common behavior, complaint, attitude, problem, etc.) or *exceptional* (e.g., significant differences, nonconformance, unusual circumstances, etc.). Remember, too, that you're not limited to recording these observations with a notebook and pen alone. You might also digitally record, videotape, and photograph the things you see for analysis later.

The Ethics of Fieldwork. Because fieldwork often involves research on people, you should always be careful to protect the privacy and wishes of your subjects. For a relatively informal project such as this one—something that isn't likely to be published—there are fewer ethical concerns, but there are some principles that should guide you. The least complicated ethical situation is direct observation in a public setting. In this case, you don't need an invitation from anyone to observe unless you directly approach the people you're observing. Sometimes, though, especially when you're a participant-observer, you'll be actively seeking permission to watch, record, and interview. How should you handle those situations?

- Make your study subjects aware of the purpose of your project.
- Preserve the anonymity of the people you observe unless they give you permission to use their names.

Note-Taking Strategies. Write down and document in detail what you see and hear. This includes descriptions of behaviors, activities, settings, conversations, and people's movements, etc. This is the raw data you'll analyze for patterns. In addition to looking for things that seem "typical" and "exceptional," consider the following frames for analysis:

- What evidence confirms, contradicts, or qualifies the theories and claims you've read about in your research?
- What do people do or say during moments of particular significance?
- What "artifacts" seem important? What things do people use?
- *How* do the people you observe talk about themselves or the activity they are participating in?

Using Field Research in Your Writing. The observations and descriptions you gather from the field can be powerful additions to your research project. For example,

- *Give your topic a face.* Use a description of an individual who is affected by the problem you're writing about, as a way to dramatize the problem's impact.
- *Make a scene.* Help your readers *see* what you're writing about.
- *Incorporate images.* Even a written research essay can benefit from pictures, which can be included in the text and analyzed.
- *Develop a multimodal essay.* Might your research project be transformed into an audio documentary or a video podcast? Could you create an online slide show?

Writing in the Middle: Note-Taking Techniques

8.5

Understand and apply new note-taking strategies that will help you analyze sources while you're researching.

Like most students, when I wrote undergraduate research papers I never did any writing until the end—usually late at night with all of my sources fanned out across my desk like cards at a blackjack table. I'm going to propose an alternative scenario that will work much better, and it looks something like this: It's not the night before but *weeks* before the paper is due, and I'm writing like mad in my notebook *as* I'm reading an article. I'm not exactly writing my paper—instead, I'm using writing to think about what I'm reading, to understand the source, and to *converse* with it.

Throughout *The Curious Writer*, I've promoted what's termed "dialectical thinking"—moving back and forth between suspending judgments and making judgments—and this method is particularly useful when writing about what you read. One way to do this as you research is to use the "double-entry journal."

Whatever method you use for "writing in the middle," these actions are key:

1. You write as—or immediately after—you read something that's relevant to your project.
2. You use the writing to talk to yourself and *to the source* about what you understand it to be saying, what you find particularly interesting, how you might agree or disagree, and what questions the source raises.
3. You carefully jot down bibliographic information so you can build your list of references as you research.

The double-entry journal makes a great research notebook. On the left-facing page, you collect passages, ideas, statistics, summaries, and so on from the source, and on the right-facing page, you explore what you make of what you've collected. You can do this in a paper notebook or in a Word document using columns. In the section that follows, you can see how the double-entry journal might work for you.

Double-Entry Journal

In the sample double-entry journal in Figure 8.7, notice how the writer collects material in the left column and then explores in the right column, looking left whenever the writing stalls to find traction on something else in from the source.

Page	Source Notes	First Thoughts
140	"Carl Sagan suggested that the 'pay dirt' of space alien abduction accounts is not in what they might tell us about alien visitation but in what they might tell us about ourselves."	Really interesting article that summarizes the research, as of 1996, on alien abduction memories. Point seems to be the ways in which these don't necessarily tell us anything about aliens but a lot about ourselves. But what? I think the evidence here suggests that it isn't necessarily some kind of psychiatric problem, but how vulnerable we are to suggestion. The stop sign case, for example. Even when the visual clearly has a yield not a stop sign, the mere suggestion it's a stop sign made people confidently believe it. But maybe the most interesting thing here to me is the dynamic of having a memory of something that is challenged, which is a kind of threat, and as a result we believe even a false memory more strongly. We believe what we want to believe and then actively seek out information that reinforces it, particularly in the face of challenge.
141	"the misinformation effect" Describes "classic experiment" to demonstrate this: a pedestrian accident in which slide shows yield sign but respondents "subtly" told was stop sign. Majority claimed stop sign was there with "high degree of confidence."	
142	"... humans can cook up false memories ..." But why aliens? ✓ variety of sources in popular culture of "true" abduction stories ✓ most reported under hypnosis, and this makes it seem more "real" to the abductee because it evokes "strong visual imagery" ✓ when belief is challenged, holder of belief clings to it more strongly ✓ reinforced by other "support groups" of believers	The thing about hypnosis being the source of most abduction reports, and how this might deepen an abductee's belief in it, is also something I need to look into more.
	Clark, Steven E., and Elizabeth F. Loftus. "The Construction of Alien Abduction Memories." *Psychological Inquiry*, vol. 7, no. 2, 1996, pp. 140-43.	

Figure 8.7   A sample double-entry journal

Research Log

Another method of note taking that exploits dialectical thinking is the research log. Rather than using opposing pages, you'll layer your notes and responses, one after another. This is a particularly useful method for those who prefer to compose with a keyboard rather than a pencil. Here's how it works:

1. Begin by taking down the full bibliographic information on the source, something you may already have in your working bibliography.

2. Read the article, book chapter, or web page, marking up your personal copy as you typically do, perhaps underlining key facts or ideas or information relevant to your research question.

3. Your first entry in your notebook or on the computer will be a fastwrite, an open-ended response to the reading under the heading What Strikes Me Most. As the title implies, you're dealing with first thoughts here.

4. Next, take notes on the source, jotting down summaries, paraphrases, quotations, and key facts. Title this section Source Notes.

5. Finally, follow up with another episode of fastwriting. Title this The Source Reconsidered. This is a *more focused* look at the source; fastwrite about what stands out in the notes you took. Which facts, findings, claims, or arguments shape your thinking now?

Using What You Have Learned

Let's return briefly to the learning outcomes listed at the beginning of the chapter.

1. **Identify the "research routines" you've typically used, and practice new ones appropriate to college-level research.** You have "research routines," too, often learned in high school; while some of these routines might still serve you well, many may not, particularly in college. This "unlearning" is an essential part of developing your abilities, not just in academic tasks, but also in anything you want to do that is guided by habits you rarely examine.

2. **Refine and improve the effectiveness of search terms.** The ability to refine search terms will make your academic—and your everyday—research more efficient and it will become even more important as the amount of information continues to expand on the web and in library databases.

3. **Apply research strategies for developing "working knowledge" and "focused knowledge" on your topic.** Any research project is a developmental process. If you don't know much about a topic, then you need to learn enough quickly to come up with a strong research question. From there, you can mine more deeply into your topic, developing "focused" knowledge

with more-advanced research strategies. This is a process you can use for nearly any research project.

4. **Use a method to analyze and evaluate research sources.** There are a lot of methods for doing this, and in this chapter you learned just one. But the key is that you actually *use* a method, one that will consistently help you to find credible sources. As we do more and more research online, it's hard to overstate what an essential skill such a method is.

5. **Understand and apply new note-taking strategies that will help you analyze sources while you're researching.** Whatever note-taking system you use, the important thing is that you do some writing *as* you do your research. This will help you to think about what you're reading as you begin to build your essay.

Using and Citing Sources

Controlling Information

The first college paper that really meant something to me was an essay on whaling industry practices and their impacts on populations of humpback and sperm whales. Writing from the place of itchy curiosity and strong feelings is a wonderful thing. It will motivate you to read and learn about your topic, and when it comes to writing the draft, you might find that you have little trouble enlisting the voices of your sources to make your point. More often, however, you've chosen a topic because you don't know what you think or feel about it—the inquiry-based approach—or you've been assigned a general topic that reflects the content of a course you're taking. In these cases, writing with sources is like crashing a party of strangers that has been going on for a long time. You shyly listen in, trying to figure out what everyone is talking about, and look for an opening to enter the conversation. Mostly you just feel intimidated, so you hang back feeling foolish.

This kind of writing situation is really a matter of control. Will you control the outside sources in your research essay, or will they control you? Will you enter the conversation and make a contribution to it, or will you let others do all the talking? The easiest way to lose control is simply to turn long stretches of your paper over to a source, usually one with long quotations. I've seen a quotation from a single source run more than a full page in some drafts. Another way to lose control is to do what one of my colleagues calls a "data dump." Fill the truck with a heavy load of information, back it up to the paper, and dump in as much as you can, without analysis, without carefully selecting what is relevant and what isn't, without much thought at all. The writer in this situation sees his or her essay as a hole that must be filled with information.

When you introduce a voice other than your own, make it clear what this new voice adds to the conversation you have going about your topic.

Using and Synthesizing Sources

The appropriate use of sources is also a matter of control. Writers who put research information to work for them see outside sources as serving a clear purpose. There are at least five of these purposes:

Purpose	Description
Support a claim or idea	The motive we usually imagine for using information in academic writing.
Provide background	What does your audience need to know about your topic to understand why your inquiry question is significant?
Answer a question	Periodically asking relevant questions—and answering them with information from research—creates a structure built on reasoning.
Complicate things	This is the most counterintuitive use of information. Why would you use information that might *not* support your thesis? Because things are *always* complicated, and that's what makes them interesting.

9.1

Use sources effectively and control sources so they don't control you.

Let's see how this works in an actual passage. In an essay that asks, "Why Did God Make Flies?", writer Richard Conniff argues that the answer might be as a punishment for human arrogance. In the middle of the essay, he draws on research to provide some background for this claim by establishing the long and sometimes unhappy relationship between the housefly and human beings.

The true housefly, *Musca domestica*, does not bite. (You may think this is something to like about it, until you find out what it does instead.) *M. domestica*, a drab fellow of salt-and-pepper complexion, is the world's most widely distribut- ed insect species and probably the most familiar, a status achieved through its pro- nounced fondness for breeding in pig, horse, and human excrement. In choosing at some point in the immemorial past to concentrate on the wastes around human habitations, *M. domestica* made a major career move. Bernard Greenberg of the University of Illinois at Chicago has traced human representations of the housefly back to a Mesopotamian cylinder seal from 3000 B.C. But houseflies were probably with us even before we had houses, and they spread with human culture.*

Here Conniff demonstrates exquisite control over outside sources, marshal- ling them in the service of his larger point. But he does this by not simply quot- ing extensively or going on and on explaining the relevant information, but also by *finding his own way of saying things*. For example, rather than writing that the housefly's fondness for associating with people had significant ecological implications for the insect, Conniff writes that it was "a major career move." We usually think that a *narrator* is something we only encounter in storytelling. But there is always a narrator, even in the most formal academic writing. There is always a guiding hand that leads readers through information, and though that presence may not be explicit (there is no "I"), readers always know when it's missing. We sense narrators when, as Conniff did in the excerpt, they find their own way of saying things. But we also sense them in the questions they ask and when they ask them. You need to be the narrator of your own work, whether it's a personal essay or a research paper. But how do you take on that role?

The Research Writer as Narrator

The narrator in literature is often a commanding presence, particularly when it's apparent in the point of view of a character. In research writing, the narrator's presence may be more subtle. Sometimes the genre exerts some control over how present the narrator is. For example, much academic writing discourages the use of the first person, or the use of personal experience as evidence. But that doesn't mean there is no narrator in academic writing; a guiding hand in writing is always necessary. If you don't use first person or talk about yourself, how else can you be that guiding hand in your writing? Here's how:

- **Control of research question.** You are drawn to particular questions for particular reasons, often because they are related in some way to something you've learned, experienced, or observed.
- **Control of sources.** The research question is like the bouncer at the club door. Based on what you're interested in, some people get in and some get turned away. Depending on your purpose for writing, some sources are in- vited into the conversation you're creating and others are not; among those who are invited, some talk a lot and some talk a little.

---

*Conniff, Richard. "Why God Created Flies." *Audubon*, July 1989, pp. 82-95.

- **Control of context.** One of the most important choices you will make is whether stories will be any part of your examination of a research topic. Will you use case studies and other evidence to show how the topic affects certain people in certain times and places? Genre may influence this decision, of course. But typically, one of the reasons we're interested in researching a topic is its impact on people.

- **Control of voice.** While first person or self-disclosure may not be an option for a research assignment, finding your own way of saying things (as Conniff did in the excerpt above) gives your writing your signature and your voice.

The Narrator as Synthesizer

Effective narrators in research writing don't just dump information into their writing. They *synthesize* it—put it to work to accomplish some purpose. This begins with deciding what outside information to use and what not to use, a decision that begins by considering its relevance, the authority of the source, and the usefulness of the information.

Once the narrator of a research essay identifies a source as a strong candidate to include, the synthesis begins by swarming (think angry bees) that information, circling around it to establish its relevance, significance, and meaning to the research question (see Figure 9.1). You can begin this synthesizing in your research notebook and later export it to the draft. What this means, ultimately, is that whenever you invite a source into your own writing, the invitation is always on your terms. *Your* voice is always there to direct readers' attention.

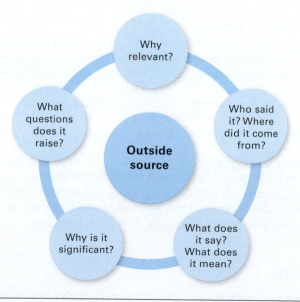

Figure 9.1 Swarming a Source

The Note Taker's Triad: Summary, Paraphrase, and Quotation

Swarming around information with your own thinking is essential when you import that information into your own writing. But so is getting your facts straight. Are you fairly and accurately describing or representing what someone else said? Are the data accurate? Is the context clear? Typically, there are three note-taking strategies we use when borrowing information: summarizing, paraphrasing, and the ever-popular quoting. We'll look at each strategy a little more closely in the following sections.

Summarizing

9.2

Practice summarizing, paraphrasing, and quoting and apply these to your own work.

A summary is usually much shorter than the original. For example, consider the following summary of the earlier paragraph about the relationship between house-flies and human beings:

> The common housefly is among the "most familiar" insects because it found its long partnership with human beings, one that goes back thousands of years, extremely beneficial.

Can you see how the summary captures the main idea of the longer para-graph? Also note that when the summary uses language from the original—the phrase "most familiar"—the writer is careful to use quotation marks. Finally, the summary uses original language that breaks from the source, describing the rela-tionship between people and flies as a "long partnership."

Tips for Crafting a Summary

1. Academic articles in the social sciences often include abstracts, or ready-made summaries of a study. Books frequently explain their purpose in a preface or introduction. Start there. Then check the concluding chapter.
2. If your aim is to summarize a passage of a longer work, remember to look for the author's most important ideas where he or she is most likely to put them: in the first and last sentences of paragraphs or in a concluding paragraph.
3. Summary has little to do with your opinion. Try, as best you can, to capture your understanding of the *source's* meaning or argument.
4. Typically, a summary includes the name(s) of the author(s) or the title of the work, usually attached to a verb that characterizes its nature: So-and-so *argues, finds, explains, speculates, questions,* and so on.

Paraphrasing

Of the three forms of note taking, paraphrasing requires the most attention and the greatest care. Your goal is to craft a restatement, in your own words, of what an original source is saying, in roughly the same length as the original.

Here's a paraphrase of the earlier paragraph on houseflies.

Houseflies, according to Richard Conniff, have had a long partnership with human beings. They are also among "the world's most widely distributed insect species," two factors that explain our familiarity with *Musca domestica*, the housefly's Latin name. This partnership may have been cultivated for thousands of years, or certainly as long as humans—and their animal companions—have produced sufficient excrement in which the flies could breed. Ironically, these pests have benefited enormously from their "fondness" for human and animal wastes, and unwittingly we have contributed to their success at our own expense.

Tips for Crafting a Paraphrase

1. Make sure to find your own way of saying things, quoting phrases that you borrow from the source.
2. Try the "look away" strategy. Carefully read the passage several times, then set it aside. Compose your paraphrase without looking at the passage, trusting that you'll remember what's important. Then check your paraphrase against the passage, changing or quoting any borrowed language and refining your prose.
3. Like summary, introduce paraphrased material in your essay by attributing the author or the work.

Quoting

When should you turn to quotation in your essay? There are two main situations:

1. When the source says something in a distinctive way that would be lost by putting it in your own words.
2. When you want to analyze or emphasize a particular passage in the source, in which case the exact words of the author are necessary to do so.

For instance, the excerpt from "Why Did God Make Flies?" is eminently quotable because Richard Conniff, its author, writes with such a lively voice. Consider this sentence:

The true housefly … is the world's most widely distributed insect species and probably the most familiar, a status achieved through its pronounced fondness for breeding in pig, horse, and human excrement.

What is it about this sentence that seems so quotable? Maybe the way it goes along with fairly straightforward exposition until the second half of the sentence, when suddenly the fly seeks status and feels fondness for you know what.

When you bring someone else's voice into your own writing, it's usually a good idea to introduce the source and provide some justification for making such a move. For instance, you might introduce the preceding quote by saying something like this:

Richard Conniff, whose popular studies of invertebrate animals have made even leeches lovable, observes that the familiarity of the housefly is no accident. He writes….

It's even more important in academic writing to follow up quoted text with your own commentary. What would you like the reader to notice about what the quotation says? What seems most relevant to your own research question or point? How does the quotation extend an important idea you've been discussing or raise an important question? What does it imply? What do you agree with? What do you disagree with? In other words, when you introduce a voice other than your own, make it clear what this new voice adds to the conversation you have going about your topic.

Tips for Handling Quotations

Integrate quoted material into your essay in the following ways:

1. **Separate it.** There are two ways to do this. Provide an introductory tag that ends in a comma or a colon. *According to Carl Elliott (82), the new drug pushers "are officially known as 'pharmaceutical sales representatives' but everyone calls them 'sales reps.'"* Or, *Carl Elliott (82) observes that drug salespeople are easy to spot: "Drug reps today are often young, well groomed, and strikingly good looking. Many are women...."*

2. **Embed it.** Integrate quoted material into your own sentence similar to this:

   Carl Elliott calls drug reps "the best dressed people in the hospital."

3. **Block it.** Extended quotations (40 or more words in APA style and more than four lines in MLA) should be indented five spaces in both APA and MLA style in a block. Quotation marks, except those used in the source, are omitted. For instance:

   Carl Elliott, in "The Drug Pushers," highlights the perks doctors have historically received:

   > *Gifts from the drug industry are nothing new, of course. William Helfand, who worked in marketing for Merck for thirty-three years, told me that company representatives were giving doctors books and pamphlets as early as the late nineteenth century. "There is nothing new under the sun," Helfand says, "There is just more of it." The question is: Why is there so much more of it just now? And what changes occurred during the past decade to bring about such a dramatic increase in reps bearing gifts? (86)**

Citing Sources and Avoiding Plagiarism

Of all the rules some of my students believe were invented to torture composition students, requirements that they carefully cite their sources in research papers may cause the most anguish. They rarely question these requirements; they seem like divine and universal law. But as a matter of fact, these aren't rules at all but conventions, hardly as old as the Greeks, and historically quite new. For many centuries, writers freely borrowed from others, often without attribution, and the appropriation of someone else's words and ideas was considered quite normal and

---

*Elliott, Carl. "The Drug Pushers." *The Atlantic*, Apr. 2006, pp. 82+.

acceptable. This is still the attitude of some non-Western cultures; some students, for example, are quite puzzled in their English as a Second Language classes when they have to cite a source in their research essays.

This convention of explicitly acknowledging the source of an idea, quotation, piece of data, or information with a footnote or parenthetical citation and a bibliography entry arose in the past 150 years. It began when mostly German universities began promoting the idea that the purpose of research is not simply to demonstrate an understanding of what already is known, but to *make a contribution of new knowledge*. Further, researchers are to look for gaps in existing scholarship—questions that haven't yet been asked—or to offer extensions of what has already been posed by someone else. Knowledge making became the business of the research writer, and, like gardeners, scholars should see themselves as tending a living thing, a kind of tree that grows larger as new branches are grafted onto existing limbs.

Just as a child clambering up a tree in the park is grateful for the sturdy limbs under his or her feet, research writers acknowledge the limbs they are standing on that have helped them to see a little more of their subjects. That's why they cite their sources. This is an act of gratitude, of course, but it also signals to readers on whose authority the writer's claims, conclusions, or ideas are based. Citation helps readers locate the writer's work on a specific part of the tree of knowledge in a discipline; it also gives a useful context of *what has already been said* about a question or a topic.

> Citation helps readers locate the writer's work on a specific part of the tree of knowledge in a discipline; it also gives a useful context of *what has already been said* about a question or a topic.

Student writers cite for exactly the same reasons: not because it's required in most college research writing, but because it makes their research writing more relevant and more convincing to the people who read it.

There are quite a few conventions for citing, and these conventions often vary by discipline. Humanities disciplines such as English often use the Modern Language Association (MLA) conventions, while the social sciences use the American Psychological Association (APA) methods. Both of these documentation styles are detailed later in this chapter. Although there are differences between the two styles, the purpose of each is the same: to provide a way to acknowledge those from whom you have borrowed ideas and information.

Avoiding Plagiarism

Modern authors get testy when someone uses their work without giving them credit. This is where the concept of intellectual property comes from, an idea that emerged with the invention of the printing press and the distribution of multiple copies of an author's work. In its most basic form, plagiarism is stealing someone else's words, ideas, or information. Academic plagiarism, the kind that gets a lot of ink these days, especially with the rise of the Internet, usually refers to more-specific misdeeds. Your university probably has an academic honesty or plagiarism policy posted on its website

> Intentional plagiarism stems from an intellectual laziness and dishonesty that, sooner or later, are bound to catch up with the person doing it.

or in a student handbook. You need to look at it. But it probably includes most or all of the following forms of plagiarism:

1. Handing in someone else's work—a downloaded paper from the Internet or borrowed from a friend—and claiming that it's your own.

2. Using information or ideas from any source that are not common knowledge and failing to acknowledge that source.

3. Handing in the same paper for two different classes.

4. Using the exact language or expressions of a source and not indicating through quotation marks and citation that the language is borrowed.

5. Rewriting a passage from a source using substitutions of different words but retaining the same syntax and structure of the original.

Most plagiarism is unintentional. The writer simply didn't know or pay attention to course or university plagiarism policies. Equally common is simple carelessness. How can you avoid this trap? Check out the "Tips for Avoiding Plagiarism" box.

9.3

Understand and identify plagiarism to avoid it in your own work.

Intentional plagiarism, of course, is a different matter. Many websites offer papers on thousands of topics to anyone willing to pay for them. College instructors, however, have tools for identifying these downloaded papers. The consequences of handing in papers bought online are often severe, including flunking the course and even expulsion—an academic Hades of sorts. Moreover, even if a person is not caught committing this academic crime, intentional plagiarism stems from an intellectual laziness and dishonesty that, sooner or later, are bound to catch up with the person doing it. So, just don't go there.

Inquiring into the Details

A Taxonomy of Copying

My colleague Casey Keck, a linguist, has studied how students paraphrase sources and ways to describe students' brushes with plagiarism. Casey notes that there are four kinds of borrowing. The **bolded** words and phrases in each of the following examples are copied from the original source:

1. *Near copy:* About half of the borrowed material is copied from the source, usually in a string of phrases. The bolded phrases are lifted verbatim from an essay titled "What Is College For?"

   Example: Students shouldn't necessarily go to college just to focus on a particular job but also to prepare for **the complexities of a world that needs rigorous analyses** and **to create joy for ourselves and others.**

2. *Minimal revision:* Less than half but more than 20 percent is copied from the original. Notice that the quotation marks appropriately signal at least one borrowed phrase from the original.

   Example: Martin says David Foster Wallace **defined** what it means to go to college as learning to avoid being "a slave to your head" and being **brave enough to risk what they think they know.**

3. *Moderate revision:* Less than 20 percent is copied from the original, and mostly individual words are mentioned only once in the paraphrase.

   Example: Martin says that college is the search for a **calling**, but this isn't necessarily a professional one. It includes a willingness to try new things and risk both **failure** and **growth**.

4. *Substantial revision:* Though the paraphrase might include a few general words that are used a few times in the original text, there are no copies of phrases or unique words that appear in the source.

   Example: According to Martin, college is an opportunity to reimagine ourselves—to break with old ways of thinking, and find delight in something other than the usual "distraction" and "entertainment."

Tips for Avoiding Plagiarism

- **Don't procrastinate.** Many careless mistakes in citation or handling of source material occur in the rush to finish the draft in the wee hours of the morning.

- **Be an active note taker.** Work in the middle of the process to take possession of the material you read, particularly by exploring your responses to sources *in your own words* and *for your own purposes*.

- **Collect bibliographic information first.** Before you do anything else, take down complete publication information for each source, including the page numbers from which you will borrow material.

- **Mark quoted material clearly.** Whenever you quote a source directly, make sure that it's obvious in your notes.

- **Be vigilant whenever you cut and paste.** The great usefulness of cutting and pasting passages in electronic documents is also the downfall of many research writers. Is the copied material directly borrowed, and if so, is it properly cited?

Exercise 9.1

The Accidental Plagiarist

Most instances of plagiarism are accidental. The writer simply isn't aware that he or she has plagiarized. Here's a low-stakes exercise that can test your understanding of how to avoid the simplest—and most common—types of accidental plagiarism. If you get this wrong, the grammar police won't accost you in the middle of the night, throw you against the wall, and make you spell difficult words. You'll just learn something.

Using the words and ideas of others in your own writing is essential to most research essays and papers. Doing this without plagiarizing isn't exactly like walking through a minefield, but you do have to step carefully. For example, Beth is exploring the question "What might explain the high rate of divorce in the early years of marriage?" She's interested in divorce because she just went through one. In her research, Beth encounters Diane Ackerman's book *The Natural History of Love* and finds the following paragraph:

> "Philandering," we call it, "fooling around," "hanky-panky," "skirt chasing," "man chasing," or something equally picturesque. Monogamy and adultery are both hallmarks of being human. Anthropologist Helen Fisher proposes a chemical basis for adultery, what she calls "The Four-Year Itch." Studying the United Nations survey of marriage and divorce around the world, she noticed that divorce usually occurs early in marriage, during the couple's first reproductive and parenting years. Also, that this peak time for divorce coincides with the period in which infatuation normally ends, and a couple has to decide if they're going to call it quits or stay together as companions. Some couples do stay together and have other children, but even more don't. "The human animal," she concludes, "seems built to court, to fall in love, and to marry one person at a time; then, at the height of our reproductive years, often with a single child, we divorce them; then, a few years after, we remarry once again."*

Beth thought this was pretty interesting stuff, and in her draft she summarized the paragraph in the following way:

> According to Diane Ackerman, a hallmark of being human is "monogamy and adultery," and she cites the period right after infatuation subsides—about four years for most couples—as the time when they call it quits.

STEP ONE: In small groups, analyze Beth's summary. Does Beth plagiarize the original passage, and if so, do you have ideas about how she could fix it? Revise the summary on a piece of newsprint and post it on the wall.

STEP TWO: Discuss the proposed revisions. How well do they address any plagiarism you see in Beth's summary?

STEP THREE: Now compare the following paraphrases of the same Ackerman passage. Which has plagiarism and which seems okay?

---

*Ackerman, Diane. *A Natural History of Love*. Random House, 1994.

PARAPHRASE 1

Divorce may have a "chemical basis," something that may kick in after four years of marriage and ironically when partners are reaching their highest potential for having children. Researcher Helen Fisher calls it "The Four-Year Itch," the time that often signals a shift from infatuation into a more sober assessment of the relationship's future: Are they going to stay together or "call it quits"? Most end up deciding to end the relationship.

PARAPHRASE 2

When infatuation fades and couples are faced with the future of their relationship, biochemistry may help them decide. According to researcher Helen Fisher, "divorce usually occurs early in marriage, during the couple's first reproductive and parenting years" (Ackerman 165). She suggests that this is often about four years into the relationship, and argues that humans may be designed to behave this way because the pattern seems so entrenched (Ackerman 166).

STEP FOUR: In class, discuss which paraphrase seems acceptable and which does not. Note that the problems are pretty subtle.

STEP FIVE: Now practice your own *summary* of the following passage, applying what you've learned so far in the exercise about ways to avoid plagiarism when using the words and ideas of other people. This passage from Ackerman's book follows the passage you worked with earlier.

> Our chemistry makes it easy to follow that plan, and painful to avoid it. After the seductive fireworks of first attraction, which may last a few weeks or a few years, the body gets bored with easy ecstasy. The nerves no longer quiver with excitement. Nothing new has been happening for ages, why bother to rouse oneself? Love is exhausting. Then the attachment chemicals roll in their thick cozy carpets of marital serenity. Might as well relax and enjoy the calm and security some feel. Separated even for a short while, the partners crave the cradle of the other's embrace. Is it a chemical craving? Possibly so, a hunger for the soothing endorphins that flow when they're together. It is a deep, sweet river, just right for dangling one's feet in while the world waits.

MLA Documentation Guidelines

The professional organization in charge of academic writing in literature and languages, the Modern Language Association (MLA), promotes one of the two common methods of citing sources that you should be familiar with. The second method, the American Psychological Association (APA) system, is described in the next section. Your English class will most likely use the MLA system.

    The guidelines presented in this section are based on the eighth edition of the *MLA Handbook*.

9.4
Cite sources using MLA and APA documentation styles.

You must cite a source in your paper in the following situations:

1. Whenever you quote from an original source.

2. Whenever you borrow ideas from an original source, even when you express those ideas in your own words by paraphrasing or summarizing them.

3. Whenever you borrow from an original source factual information that is not common knowledge—that is, facts that are widely known and about which there is no controversy.

Citing Sources

The foundation of the MLA method of citing sources *in your paper* is putting the last name of the author and the page number of the source material in parentheses as closely as possible to the borrowed material. For example,

Researchers believe that there is an "infatuation chemical" that may account

for that almost desperate attraction we feel when we're near someone special

(Ackerman 164).

The parenthetical citation tells a reader two things: the source of the information (for example, the author's name) and where in the work to find the borrowed idea or material. A really interested reader—perhaps an infatuated one—who wanted to follow up on this citation would then refer to the Works Cited at the end of the paper, which would list the work by the author's last name and include all the pertinent information about the source:

Ackerman, Diane. *A Natural History of Love*. Random House, 1994.

Here's another example of a parenthetical author/page citation in another research paper. Note the differences from the previous example:

"One thing is clear," writes Thomas Mallon, "plagiarism didn't become a truly sore

point with writers until they thought of writing as their trade. . . . Suddenly his

capital and identity were at stake" (3-4).

The first thing you may have noticed is that the author's last name—Mallon—was omitted from the parenthetical citation. It didn't need to be included because it had already been mentioned in the text. *If you mention the author's name in the text of your paper, then you only need to parenthetically cite the relevant page number(s).* This citation also tells us that the quoted passage comes from two pages rather than one.

Where to Put Citations. Place the citation as close as you can to the borrowed material, trying to avoid breaking the flow of the sentences, if possible. To avoid confusion about what's borrowed and what's not—particularly in passages longer than a sentence—mention the name of the original author *in your paper*. Note that in the next example, the writer simply cites the source at the end of the paragraph, not naming the source within the text. Doing so makes it hard for the reader to figure out whether Blager is the source of the information in the entire paragraph or just part of the paragraph:

> Though children who have been sexually abused seem to be disadvantaged in many areas, including the inability to forge lasting relationships, low self-esteem, and crippling shame, they seem advantaged in other areas. Sexually abused children seem to be more socially mature than other children of their same age group. It's a distinctly mixed blessing (Blager 994).

In the following example, notice how the ambiguity about what's borrowed and what's not is resolved by careful placement of the author's name and parenthetical citation in the text:

> Though children who have been sexually abused seem to be disadvantaged in many areas, including the inability to forge lasting relationships, low self-esteem, and crippling shame, they seem advantaged in other areas. According to Blager, sexually abused children seem to be more socially mature than other children of their same age group (994). It's a distinctly mixed blessing.

In this latter version, it's clear that Blager is the source for one sentence in the paragraph, and the writer is responsible for the rest. Generally, use an authority's last name, rather than a formal title or first name, when mentioning him or her in your text. Also note that the parenthetical citation is placed *inside* the period of the sentence (or last sentence) that it documents. That's almost always the case, except at the end of a block quotation, where the parenthetical reference is placed after the period of the last sentence.

Inquiring into the Details

Citations That Go with the Flow

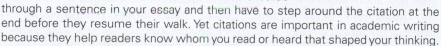

There's no getting around it—parenthetical citations can be like stones on the sidewalk. Readers stride through a sentence in your essay and then have to step around the citation at the end before they resume their walk. Yet citations are important in academic writing because they help readers know whom you read or heard that shaped your thinking.

(continued)

Inquiring into the Details (*continued*)

However, you can minimize including citations that trip up readers and make your essay more readable by doing the following:

- Avoid lengthy parenthetical citations by mentioning the name of the author in your essay. That way, you usually have to include only a page number in the citation.
- Try to place citations where readers are likely to pause anyway—for example, at the end of a sentence or right before a comma.
- Remember that you *don't* need a citation when you're citing common knowledge or referring to an entire work by an author.
- If you're borrowing from only one source in a paragraph of your essay and all of the borrowed material comes from a single page of that source, don't bother repeating the citation over and over again with each new bit of information. Just put the citation at the end of the paragraph.

The citation can also be placed near the author's name, rather than at the end of the sentence, if it doesn't unnecessarily break the flow of the sentence. For example:

Blager (994) observes that sexually abused children tend to be more socially mature than other children of their same age group.

When You Mention the Author's Name. It's generally good practice in research writing to identify who said what. The familiar convention of using attribution tags such as "According to Fletcher,…" or "Fletcher argues that…" and so on helps readers attach a name to a voice, or an individual to certain claims or findings. When you mention the author of a source, you can drop his or her name from the parenthetical citation and just include the page number. For example,

Robert Harris believes that there is "widespread uncertainty" among students about what constitutes plagiarism (2).

You may also list the page number directly after the author's name.

Robert Harris (2) believes that there is "widespread uncertainty" among students about what constitutes plagiarism.

When There Is No Author. Occasionally, you may encounter a source for which the author is anonymous—where the article doesn't have a byline or for some reason the author hasn't been identified. This isn't unusual with pamphlets, editorials, government documents, some newspaper articles, online sources, and short filler articles in magazines. If you can't parenthetically name the author, what do you cite?

Most often, cite the title (or an abbreviated version, if the title is long) and the page number. If you choose to abbreviate the title, begin with the word under which it is alphabetized in the Works Cited. For example:

According to the *Undergraduate Catalog*, "the athletic program is an integral part of

the university and its total educational purpose" (7).

Here is how this publication would be listed at the back of the paper:

Works Cited

Undergraduate Catalog, Boise State University 2014-2015. Boise State U, 2014.

For clarity, it's helpful to mention the original source of the borrowed material in the text of your paper. When there is no author's name, refer to the publication (or institution) you're citing or make a more general reference to the source. For example:

An article in *Cuisine* magazine argues that the best way to kill a lobster is to plunge

a knife between its eyes ("How to Kill" 56).

or

According to one government report, with the current minimum size limit, most

lobsters end up on dinner plates before they've had a chance to reproduce ("Size

at Sexual Maturity" 3-4).

Works by the Same Author. Suppose you end up using several books or articles by the same author. Obviously, a parenthetical citation that merely includes the author's name and page number won't do, because it won't be clear *which* of several works the citation refers to. In this case, include the author's name, an abbreviated title (if the original is too long), and the page number. For example:

One essayist who suffers from multiple sclerosis writes that "there is a subtle

taxonomy of crippleness" (Mairs, *Carnal Acts* 69).

The Works Cited list would show multiple works by one author as follows:

Works Cited

Mairs, Nancy. *Carnal Acts*. Beacon Press, 1996.

- - -. *Voice Lessons*. Beacon Press, 1994.

It's obvious from the parenthetical citation which of the two Mairs books is the source of the information. Note that in the parenthetical reference, no punctuation separates the title and the page number, but a comma follows the author's name. If Mairs had been mentioned in the text of the paper, her name could have been dropped from the citation.

Also notice that the three hyphens used in the second bibliographic entry are meant to signal that the author's name in this source is the same as in the preceding entry.

When One Source Quotes Another. Whenever you can, cite the original source of material you use. For example, if an article on television violence quotes the author of a book and you want to use the quote, try to hunt down the book. That way, you'll be certain of the accuracy of the quote, and you may also find other usable information.

Sometimes, however, finding the original source is not possible. In those cases, use the term *qtd. in* to signal that you've quoted or paraphrased a quotation from a book or article that you found elsewhere. In the following example, the citation signals that Bacon's quote was culled from an article by Guibroy, not Bacon's original work:

> Francis Bacon also weighed in on the dangers of imitation, observing that "it
>
> is hardly possible at once to admire an author and to go beyond him" (qtd. in
>
> Guibroy 113).

Personal Interviews. If you mention the name of your interview subject in your text, no parenthetical citation is necessary. On the other hand, if you don't mention the subject's name, cite it in parentheses after the quote:

> Instead, the recognizable environment gave something to kids they could
>
> relate to. "And it had a lot more real quality to it than, say, *Mister Rogers* . . . ,"
>
> says one educator. "Kids say the reason they don't like *Mister Rogers* is that it's
>
> unbelievable" (Diamonti).

Regardless of whether you mention your subject's name, you should include a reference to the interview in the Works Cited. In this case, the reference would look like this:

> Works Cited
>
> Diamonti, Nancy. Personal interview. 5 Nov. 1999.

Several Sources in a Single Citation. Suppose two sources contributed the same information in a paragraph of your essay. Or perhaps even more common is when you're summarizing the findings of several authors on a certain topic—a fairly common move when you're trying to establish a context for your own research question. You cite multiple authors in a single citation in the usual fashion, using author name and page number, but separating each with a semicolon. For example,

> A whole range of studies have looked closely at the intellectual development of
>
> college students, finding that they generally assume "stages" or "perspectives" that
>
> differ from subject to subject (Perry 122; Belenky et al. 12).

If you can, however, avoid long citations, because they can be cumbersome for readers to get through.

Sample Parenthetical References for Other Sources. MLA format is pretty simple, and we've already covered some of the basic variations. You should also know five additional variations, as follow:

AN ENTIRE WORK

If you mention the author's name in the text, no citation is necessary. The work should, however, be listed in the Works Cited.

> Leon Edel's *Henry James* is considered by many to be a model biography.

A VOLUME OF A MULTIVOLUME WORK

If you're working with one volume of a multivolume work, it's a good idea to mention which volume in the parenthetical reference. The following citation attributes the passage to volume 2, page 3, of a work by Baym and more than three other authors. The volume number always precedes the colon, which is followed by the page number:

> By the turn of the century, three authors dominated American literature: Mark
>
> Twain, Henry James, and William Dean Howells (Baym et al. 2: 3).

A LITERARY WORK

Because so many literary works, particularly classics, have been reprinted in so many editions, it's useful to give readers more information about where a passage can be found in one of these editions. List the page number and then the chapter number (and any other relevant information, such as the section or volume), separated by a semicolon. Use arabic rather than roman numerals, unless your teacher instructs you otherwise:

> Izaak Walton warns that "no direction can be given to make a man of a dull capacity
>
> able to make a Flie well" (130; ch. 5).

When citing classic poems or plays, instead of page numbers, cite line numbers and other appropriate divisions (book, section, act, scene, part, etc.). Separate the information with periods. For example, (*Othello* 2.3.286) indicates act 2, scene 3, line 286 of Shakespeare's work.

AN ONLINE SOURCE

Online sources frequently don't have page numbers. So how can you cite them parenthetically in your essay? Most of the time, you won't include page numbers, particularly when you're citing web pages.

Rarely, digital documents include paragraph numbers. If so, use the abbreviation *par.* or *pars.*, followed by the paragraph number or numbers you're borrowing material from. For example:

In most psychotherapeutic approaches, the personality of the therapist can have a big impact on the outcome of the therapy ("Psychotherapy," par. 1).

Sometimes the material has an internal structure, such as sections, parts, chapters, or volumes. If so, use the abbreviation *sec., pt., ch.,* or *vol.* (respectively), followed by the appropriate number.

In many cases, a parenthetical citation can be avoided entirely by simply naming the source in the text of your essay. A curious reader will then find the full citation to the article in the Works Cited page at the back of your paper. For example:

According to Charles Petit, the worldwide effort to determine whether frogs are disappearing will take somewhere between three and five years.

Finally, if you don't want to mention the source within your text, parenthetically cite the author's last name (if any) or article title:

The worldwide effort to determine whether frogs are disappearing will take somewhere between three and five years (Petit).

Format

The Layout. A certain fussiness is associated with the look of academic papers. The reason for it is quite simple—academic disciplines generally aim for consistency in format so that readers of scholarship know exactly where to look to find what they want to know. It's a matter of efficiency. How closely you must follow the MLA's requirements for the layout of your essay is up to your instructor, but it's really not that complicated. A lot of what you need to know is featured in Figure 9.2.

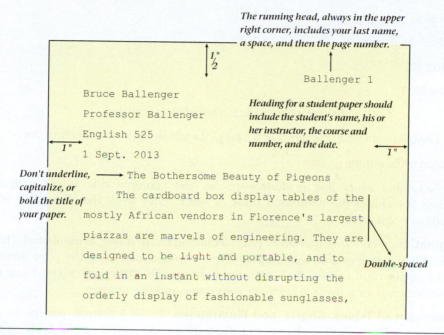

The running head, always in the upper right corner, includes your last name, a space, and then the page number.

$\frac{1}{2}$"

Ballenger 1

Bruce Ballenger

Professor Ballenger

English 525

1 Sept. 2013

Heading for a student paper should include the student's name, his or her instructor, the course and number, and the date.

1"

1"

Don't underline, capitalize, or bold the title of your paper. → The Bothersome Beauty of Pigeons

The cardboard box display tables of the mostly African vendors in Florence's largest piazzas are marvels of engineering. They are designed to be light and portable, and to fold in an instant without disrupting the orderly display of fashionable sunglasses,

Double-spaced

Figure 9.2 The basic look of an MLA-style paper

Printing. Compose your paper on white, 8½" × 11" printer paper. Make sure the printer has sufficient ink or toner.

Margins and Spacing. The old high school trick is to use big margins. That way, you can meet your page length requirements with less material. Don't try that with this paper. Create one-inch margins for every side. The running heads for page numbers (e.g. Ballenger 1) are a half inch from the top and always flush right. Indent the first line of each paragraph five spaces, and blocked quotes ten spaces. *Double-space all of the text, including blocked quotes and Works Cited.*

Title Page. Your paper doesn't need a separate title page. Instead, begin your paper with the first page of text. One inch below the top of the page, type your name, your instructor's name, the course number, and the date (see Figure 9.2). Below that, type the title, centered on the page. Begin the text of the paper below the title.

Julie Bird

Professor Ballenger

English 102

1 June 2013

Nature as Being: Landscape in Silko's "Lullaby"

Leslie Marmon Silko, the author of "Lullaby," is a Native American writer from the

Laguna Pueblo culture. . . .

Note that every line is double-spaced. The centered title is not italicized (unless it includes the name of a book or some other work that should be italicized) or boldfaced.

Pagination. Make sure that every page, including the first one, is numbered. That's especially important with long papers. Type your last name and the page number in the upper right corner, flush with the right margin: Ballenger 3. Don't use the abbreviation *p.* or a hyphen between your name and the number.

Placement of Tables, Charts, and Illustrations. In MLA format, papers do not have appendixes. Tables, charts, and illustrations are placed in the body of the paper, close to the text that refers to them. Number illustrations consecutively (Table 1 or Figure 3), and indicate sources below them (see Figure 9.3). If you use a chart or illustration from another text, give the full citation. Place any table caption above the table, flush left. Captions for illustrations or diagrams are usually placed below them.

Handling Titles. The MLA guidelines about the style of titles are, as the most recent *Handbook* observes, "strict." The general rule is that the writer should capitalize the first letters of all principal words in a title, including any that follow dashes. The exceptions are articles (*a, an,* and *the*), prepositions (*for, of, in, to*), and coordinating conjunctions (*and, or, but, for*). These exceptions apply *only if*

Table 1 Percentage of Students Who Self-Report Acts of Plagiarism

Acts of Plagiarism	Never/Rarely	Sometimes	Often/Very Freq.
Copy text without citation	71	19	10
Copy paper without citation	91	5	3
Request paper to hand in	90	5	2
Purchase paper to hand in	91	6	3

Source: Scanlon, Patrick M., and David R. Neumann. "Internet Plagiarism Among College Students." *Journal of College Student Development,* vol. 43, no. 3, May-June 2002, p. 379.

Figure 9.3 Example of format for a table

the words appear in the middle of a title; capitalize them if they appear at the beginning or end.

The rules for italicizing a title or putting it in quotation marks are as follows:

1. *Italicize the Title* if it is a book, play, pamphlet, film, magazine, TV program, CD, website, newspaper, or work of art.

2. "Put the Title in Quotes" if it is an article in a newspaper, magazine, or encyclopedia; a short story; a poem; an episode of a TV program; a song; a lecture; or a chapter or essay in a book.

Here are some examples:

The Curious Researcher (Book)

English Online: The Student's Guide to the Internet (CD-ROM)

"Once More to the Lake" (Essay)

Preservation Idaho (Website)

"Psychotherapy" (Encyclopedia article)

Idaho Statesman (Newspaper)

"One Percent Initiative Panned" (Newspaper article)

According to the current guidelines (the *MLA Handbook*, eighth edition), titles should be italicized and not underlined. For instance, your Works Cited page would list the book title Bombproof Your Horse as *Bombproof Your Horse*. (And yes, that's "horse" not "house.")

Language and Style

Names. Though it may seem by the end of your research project as if you're on familiar terms with some of the authors you cite, it's not a good idea to refer to them by their first names. Typically, initially give the full names of people you cite, and then only their last names if you mention them again in your essay.

Ellipsis Dots. Those are the three (always three unless you're omitting material that comes at the end of a sentence, where they join a period) dots that indicate you've left out a word, phrase, or even whole section of a quoted passage. It's often wise to use them because you want to emphasize only certain parts of a quotation rather than burden your reader with unnecessary information, but be careful that you preserve the basic intention and idea of the author's original statement. The ellipsis dots can come at the beginning of a quotation, in the middle, or at the end, depending where it is you've omitted material. For example,

"After the publication of a controversial picture that shows, for example, either

dead or grieving victims . . . , readers, in telephone calls and in letters to the editor,

often attack the photographer for being tasteless. . . ."

Quotations. Quotations that run more than four lines long should be blocked, or indented five spaces from the left margin. The quotation should be double-spaced and quotation marks should be omitted. In an exception from the usual convention, the parenthetical citation is placed *after* the period at the end of the quotation. A colon is a customary way to introduce a blocked quotation. For example,

> Gary Price and Chris Sherman, in *The Invisible Web*, contend that much of the Internet, possibly most, is beyond the reach of researchers who use conventional search engines:
>
> > The problem is that vast expanses of the Web are completely invisible to general-purpose search engines like AltaVista, HotBot, and Google. Even worse, this "Invisible Web" is in all likelihood growing significantly faster than the visible Web that you're familiar with. It's not that search engines and Web directories are "stupid" or even badly engineered. Rather, they simply can't "see" millions of high quality resources that are available exclusively on the Invisible Web. So what is this Invisible Web and why aren't search engines doing anything about it to make it visible? (xxi)*

Preparing the Works Cited Page

The Works Cited page ends the paper. Several other lists of sources may also appear at the end of a research paper, though these are much less common in college research essays. An Annotated List of Works Cited not only lists the sources used in the paper, but also includes a brief description of each. A Works Consulted list includes sources that may or may not have been cited in the paper but shaped the writer's thinking. A Content Notes page, keyed to superscript numbers in the text of the paper, lists short commentaries or asides that are significant but not central enough to the discussion to be included in the text of the paper.

The Works Cited page is the workhorse of most college papers. The other source lists are used less often. Works Cited is essentially an alphabetical listing of all the sources you quoted, paraphrased, or summarized in your paper. If you have used the MLA format for citing sources, your paper has numerous parenthetical references to authors and page numbers. The Works Cited page provides complete information on each source cited in the text for the reader who wants more details. (In APA format, this page is called References and is only slightly different in how items are listed.)

---

*Price, Gary, and Chris Sherman. *The Invisible Web: Uncovering Information Sources Search Engines Can't See.* Information Today, 2001.

If you've been careful about collecting complete bibliographic information—author, title, editor, edition, volume, place, publisher, date, page numbers—then preparing your Works Cited page will be easy. If you've recorded that information on notecards, all you have to do is put them in alphabetical order and then transcribe them into your paper. If you've been careless about collecting that information, you may need to take a hike back to the library.

Format

Alphabetizing the List. Works Cited follows the text of your paper on a separate page. After you've assembled complete information about each source you've cited, put the sources in alphabetical order by the last name of each author. If a work has multiple authors, alphabetize by the last name of the first author listed. If a source has no author, then alphabetize it by the first key word of the title. If you're citing more than one source by the same author, you don't need to repeat the name for each source; simply use three hyphens followed by a period (---.) in place of the author's name in subsequent listings.

Indenting and Spacing. Type the first line of each entry flush left, and indent subsequent lines of that entry (if any) five spaces. Double-space between each line and each entry. For example:

Works Cited

Bianchi, William. "Education by Radio: America's Schools of the Air." *TechTrends: Linking Research & Practice to Improve Learning*, vol. 52, no. 2, Mar.-Apr. 2008, pp. 36-44.

Campbell, Gardener. "There's Something in the Air: Podcasting and Education." *EDUCAUSE Review*, vol. 40, no. 6, Nov.-Dec. 2005, pp. 32-47.

Checho, Colleen. *The Effects of Podcasting on Learning and Motivation: A Mixed Method Study of At-Risk High School Students*. 2007. U of Nevada, Reno, PhD dissertation. *ProQuest*, search.proquest.com/docview/304844571.

Davis, Anne, and Ewa McGrail. "'Proof-Revising' With Podcasting: Keeping Readers in Mind as Students Listen to and Rethink Their Writing." *The Reading Teacher*, vol. 62, no. 6, 2009, pp. 522-29.

Grisham, Dana L., and Thomas Devere Wolsey. "Writing Instruction for Teacher Candidates: Strengthening a Weak Curricular Area." *Literacy Research and Instruction*, vol. 50, no. 4, 2011, pp. 348-64.

Klaus, Carl H. *The Made-Up Self: Impersonation in the Personal Essay*. U of Iowa P, 2010.

"What Is Educational Podcasting?" *RECAP*, recap.ltd.uk/podcasting/info/ podcasting.html. Accessed 7 July 2012.

Citing Books. You usually need three pieces of information to cite a book: the name of the author or authors, the title, and the publication information. If you're citing an e-book, however, some additional information may be required. See below.

CITING A BOOK IN PRINT	CITING AN E-BOOK
1. Author(s)	1. Author(s)
2. *Title*	2. *Title*
3. Edition and/or volume (if relevant)	3. Edition and/or volume (if relevant)
4. Name of publisher (provide complete name, but omit business words or abbreviations like Inc. or Company)	4. If also in print, include publisher name and date for the print edition
5. Date of publication	5. Name of site where e-book was accessed
	6. URL for the e-book
SAMPLE CITATION: BOOK IN PRINT	**SAMPLE CITATION: E-BOOK**
Donald, David H. *Lincoln.* Simon and Schuster, 1995.	Browne, Francis F. *The Every-day Life of Abraham Lincoln.* Browne & Howell, 1913. *Project Gutenberg,* www.gutenberg.org/ebooks/14004.

Title. Titles of books are italicized, with the first letters of all principal words capitalized, including those in any subtitles. Titles that are not italicized are usually those of works found within larger works, such as poems and short stories in anthologies. These titles are set off by quotation marks. Titles of religious works are italicized when you are discussing a specific edition (for example, the Authorized King James Version of *The Bible*). (See the guidelines in the earlier "Handling Titles" subsection.)

Edition. If a book doesn't indicate an edition number, then it's probably a first edition, a fact you don't need to cite. Look on the title page. Signal an edition like this: *2nd ed., 3rd ed.*, and so on.

Publisher and Date. Look on the title page to find out who published the book. Include the complete publisher name in your citation but omit business words and abbreviations like Inc. or Company: for example, *St. Martin's Press Inc.* would be cited as *St. Martin's Press.* Also when an academic or university press is the publisher, use the abbreviation P or UP: for example, *Yale UP* or *U of Chicago P.*

The date a book is published is usually indicated on the copyright page. If several dates or several printings by the same publisher are listed, cite the original publication date. However, if the book is a revised edition, give the date of that edition. One final variation: If you're citing a book that's a reprint of an original edition, give both dates. For example:

Stegner, Wallace. *Recapitulation*. 1979. U of Nebraska P, 1986.

This book was first published in 1979 and then republished in 1986 by the University of Nebraska Press.

Page Numbers. You don't usually list the page numbers of the part of a book you used as a source. The parenthetical reference in your paper specifies those page numbers. But if you use only part of a book—an introduction or an essay—list the appropriate page numbers following the publication date. Use periods to set off the page numbers. If the author or editor of the entire work is also the author of the introduction or essay you're citing, list her by last name only the second time you give her name. For example:

Lee, L. L., and Merrill Lewis. Preface. *Women, Women Writers, and the West*, edited

by Lee and Lewis, Whitston Publishing, 1979, pp. v–ix.

Website Name and URL. When citing a book or reference source that you found online, list the name of the site and the URL.

If your online source does not have a publication date or is the type of source that is updated frequently (like some online encyclopedias and dictionaries), include an access date at the end of your citation: for example, *Accessed 21 Sept. 2016.*

Sample Book Citations

A BOOK BY ONE AUTHOR

Keen, Sam. *Fire in the Belly*. Bantam Books, 1991.

In-Text Citation: (Keen 101)

A BOOK BY TWO AUTHORS

Ballenger, Bruce, and Barry Lane. *Discovering the Writer Within*. Writer's Digest, 1996.

In-Text Citation: (Ballenger and Lane 14)

A BOOK WITH MORE THAN TWO AUTHORS

If a book has more than two authors, list the first and substitute the term *et al.* for the others.

Belenky, Mary Field, et al. *Women's Ways of Knowing*. Basic Books, 1973.

In-Text Citation: (Belenky et al. 21-30)

SEVERAL BOOKS BY THE SAME AUTHOR

Baldwin, James. *Going to Meet the Man*. Dial Press, 1965.

---. *Tell Me How Long the Train's Been Gone*. Dial Press, 1968.

In-Text Citation: (Baldwin, *Going* 34)

A COLLECTION OR ANTHOLOGY

Crane, R. S., ed. *Critics and Criticism: Ancient and Modern*. U of Chicago P, 1952.

In-Text Citation: (Crane xx)

A WORK IN A COLLECTION OR ANTHOLOGY

The title of a work that is part of a collection but was originally published as a book should be italicized. Otherwise, the title of a work in a collection should be enclosed in quotation marks.

Bahktin, Mikhail. "Marxism and the Philosophy of Language." *The Rhetorical Tradition*, edited by Patricia Bizzell and Bruce Herzberg, St. Martin's Press, 1990, pp. 928-44.

In-Text Citation: (Bahktin 929-31)

Jones, Robert F. "Welcome to Muskie Country." *The Ultimate Fishing Book*, edited by Lee Eisenberg and DeCourcy Taylor, Houghton Mifflin, 1981, pp. 122-34.

In-Text Citation: (Jones 131)

AN INTRODUCTION, PREFACE, FOREWORD, OR PROLOGUE

Scott, Jerrie Cobb. Foreword. *Writing Groups: History, Theory, and Implications*, by Anne Ruggles Gere, Southern Illinois UP, 1987, pp. ix-xi.

In-Text Citation: (Scott ix-xi)

Rich, Adrienne. Introduction. *On Lies, Secrets, and Silence*, by Rich, W. W. Norton, 1979, pp. 9-18.

In-Text Citation: (Rich 12)

A BOOK WITH NO AUTHOR

American Heritage Dictionary of the English Language. 5th ed., Houghton Mifflin Harcourt, 2011.

In-Text Citation: (*American Heritage Dictionary* 444)

AN ENCYCLOPEDIA

> "Passenger Pigeon." *Encyclopædia Britannica*, www.britannica.com/animal/
>
>   passenger-pigeon. Accessed 26 June 2012.

> *In-Text Citation:* ("Passenger Pigeon")

> "City of Chicago." *Encyclopædia Britannica*, 15th ed., vol. 6, Encyclopædia
>
>   Britannica, 2010, pp. 397-98.

> *In-Text Citation:* ("City of Chicago" 397)

A BOOK WITH AN INSTITUTIONAL AUTHOR

When an organization or corporation is both the author and publisher of a work, start your citation with the title of the work and list the organization only as the publisher.

> *Employee Benefits Handbook.* Hospital Corporation of America, 2015.

> *In-Text Citation:* (*Employee Benefits* 5-7)

A BOOK WITH MULTIPLE VOLUMES

Include the number of volumes in the work at the end of the citation.

> Baym, Nina, et al., eds. *The Norton Anthology of American Literature.* 5th ed.,
>
>   W. W. Norton, 1998. 2 vols.

> *In-Text Citation:* (Baym et al. 2: 3)

If you use one volume of a multivolume work, indicate which one, along with the page numbers, followed by the total number of volumes in the work.

> Anderson, Sherwood. "Mother." *The Norton Anthology of American Literature,* edited
>
>   by Nina Baym et al., 5th ed., vol. 2, W. W. Norton, 1998, pp. 1115-31. 2 vols.

> *In-Text Citation:* (Anderson 1115)

A BOOK THAT IS NOT A FIRST EDITION

Check the title page to determine whether the book is *not* a first edition (2nd, 3rd, 4th, etc.); if no edition number is mentioned, assume it's the first. Put the edition number right after the title.

> Ballenger, Bruce. *The Curious Researcher.* 8th ed., Pearson, 2014.

> *In-Text Citation:* (Ballenger 194)

Citing the edition is necessary only for books that are *not* first editions. Do cite revised editions (*rev. ed.*) and abridged editions (*abridged ed.*).

A BOOK PUBLISHED BEFORE 1900

For a book this old, it's usually unnecessary to list the publisher.

Hitchcock, Edward. *Religion of Geology.* Glasgow, 1851.

In-Text Citation: (Hitchcock 48)

A TRANSLATION

Montaigne, Michel de. *Essays.* Translated by J. M. Cohen, Penguin Classics, 1958.

In-Text Citation: (Montaigne 638)

GOVERNMENT DOCUMENTS

Because of the enormous variety of government documents, citing them properly can be a challenge. Because most government documents do not name authors, begin an entry for such a source with the level of government (United States, or Illinois State, etc.)—unless it is obvious from the title—followed by the sponsoring agency, the title of the work, and the publication information. Look on the title page to determine the publisher. If it's a federal document, then the *Government Publishing Office* is usually the publisher.

United States, Department of Commerce, Census Bureau. *Statistical Abstract of the United States: 2012.* Government Publishing Office, 2012.

In-Text Citation: (United States, Dept. of Commerce, Census Bureau 77)

A BOOK THAT WAS REPUBLISHED

A fairly common occurrence, particularly in literary study, is to find a book that was republished, sometimes many years after the original publication date. In addition, some books first appear in hardcover, and then are republished in paperback. To cite, put the original date of publication immediately after the book's title, and then include the more current publication date, as usual, at the end of the citation. Do it like so:

Didion, Joan. *Slouching Towards Bethlehem.* 1968. Farrar, Straus and Giroux, 1992.

In-Text Citation: (Didion 31)

Badke, William. *Research Strategies: Finding Your Way through the Information Fog.* 5th ed., iUniverse, 2014. *Google Books,* books.google.com/books?id=TGfZAgAAQBAJ&num=13.

In-Text Citation: (Badke)

Citing Periodicals. These days, you're more likely to find an article through a library database or on the web than in a print journal or magazine. Citation of each type of source is quite similar, with the differences listed in the table below.

PRINT ARTICLE	ARTICLE FROM A DATABASE OR THE WEB
1. Author(s)	1. Author(s)
2. "Article Title"	2. "Article Title"
3. *Periodical Title*	3. *Periodical Title*
4. Volume and issue	4. Volume and issue
5. Date published	5. Date published
6. Page numbers	6. Page numbers, if any (usually present in versions also in print)
	7. *Website, Database*, or Sponsor
	8. URL or DOI
	9. Date of access (only if there is no clear publication date)
SAMPLE CITATION: PRINT ARTICLE	**SAMPLE CITATION: DATABASE ARTICLE**
Newcomb, Matthew. "Sustainability as a Design Principle for Composition." *College Composition and Communication,* vol. 63, no. 4, June 2012, pp. 593-614.	Newcomb, Matthew. "Sustainability as a Design Principle for Composition." *College Composition and Communication*, vol. 63, no. 4, June 2012, pp. 593-614. *JSTOR,* www.jstor.org/stable/23264230.

Format. Citations for magazines, journals, newspapers, and the like aren't much different from citations for books.

Author's Name. List the author(s) as you would for a book citation.

Article Title. Unlike book titles, article titles are usually enclosed in quotation marks.

Periodical Title. Italicize periodical titles, and include introductory articles (*The Aegis*, not *Aegis*). If you're citing a newspaper your readers may not be familiar with, include with the title—enclosed in brackets but not italicized—the city in which it is published. For example:

Barber, Rocky. "DEQ Responds to Concerns About Weiser Feedlot." *Idaho Statesman*

[Boise], 23 Apr. 2014, p. B1.

Volume and Issue Numbers. Most scholarly journals have both. Include the volume number preceded by *vol.* and the issue number preceded by *no.* in your citation. Popular periodicals frequently don't have issue numbers, and you're not required to use them.

Date. When citing popular periodicals, include the day, month, and year of the issue you're citing—in that order—following the periodical name. For academic journal articles, include the month or season, if available, and the year of publication. (See the example in the "A Journal Article" subsection). Use abbreviations for all months except May, June, and July.

Page Numbers. List the pages of the entire article, and use the abbreviations *p.* or *pp.* It's common for articles in newspapers and popular magazines *not* to run on consecutive pages. In that case, indicate the page on which the article begins, followed by a "+" (*p. 12+*).

Newspaper pagination can be peculiar. Some papers wed the section (usually a letter) with the page number (*p. A4*); other papers simply begin numbering anew in each section. (See the "A Newspaper Article" subsection.)

Online sources, which often have no pagination at all, present special problems. For guidance on how to handle them, see the "Citing Online and Other Sources" subsection.

Name of Website, Database, or Sponsor. If the name of the site is different from the title of the piece you're citing, include that name in italics. In addition, if the website's name is different from the name of the organization that hosts it, include the sponsor's name as well. The name of the site's sponsor isn't always obvious. Try looking at the bottom of the page or click on the "About Us" link if there is one. If you cannot locate the name of a publisher or sponsor, omit that element from your citation. Finally, if you found your source in a library database, identify the database (e.g., *ProQuest, JSTOR, Google Scholar*, etc.).

URL or DOI. For online periodicals, include a URL or DOI in your citation. Scholarly journal articles sometimes have a Digital Object Identifier (DOI) which functions as a permanent link to the work. If an article has a DOI, use the DOI in your citation (instead of a URL). Do not include *http://* or *https://* as part of any URLs in your citations.

Date of Access. If an online periodical does not have a publication date, include the date that you accessed the source at the end of your citation.

Sample Periodical Citations

A MAGAZINE ARTICLE

Elliott, Carl. "The New Drug Pushers." *The Atlantic,* Apr. 2006, pp. 82-93.

In-Text Citation: (Elliott 92)

Williams, Patricia J. "Unimagined Communities." *The Nation,* 3 May 2004, p. 14.

In-Text Citation: (Williams 14)

Citations for magazines that you find online should include the online publication date and the URL for the article. For example,

Zeldovich, Lina. "Robot Birds Haven't Taken Over Our Society...Yet." *Audubon,*

Summer 2016, www.audubon.org/magazine/summer-2016/robot-birds-

havent-taken-over-our-societyyet.

In-Text Citation: (Zeldovich)

Notice that both the website's name and its publisher are included in the online article below.

Schoen, John W. "How Hungry Is China for the World's Food?" *Nightly Business Report ,*

CNBC, 22 Oct. 2015, nbr.com/2015/10/22/how-hungry-is-china-for-the-

worlds-food/.

In-Text Citation: (Schoen)

A JOURNAL ARTICLE

There's a good chance that you found a journal article using your library's online database. If so, include the database name, italicized, in your citation. Remember to also include the volume and issue number whenever you cite a journal.

Here's an article from a library database with a DOI:

Allen, Rebecca E., and J. M. Oliver. "The Effects of Child Maltreatment on Language

Development." *Child Abuse and Neglect,* vol. 6, no. 3, 1982, pp. 299-305.

PsycNET, doi:10.1016/0145-2134(82)90033-3.

In-Text Citation: (Allen and Oliver 299-300)

If you need to cite the print version of this article, then follow the example above, but leave off the database information (*PsycNET,* doi:10.1016/0145-2134(82)90033-3).

A NEWSPAPER ARTICLE

Some newspapers have several editions (late edition, national edition), and each may feature different articles. If an edition is listed on the masthead, include it in the citation.

Mendels, Pamela. "Internet Access Spreads to More Classrooms." *The New York Times,*

morning ed., 1 Dec. 1999, pp. C1+.

In-Text Citation: (Mendels C1)

Some papers begin numbering pages anew in each section. In that case, include the section number if it's not part of pagination.

Brooks, James. "Lobsters on the Brink." *Portland Press,* 29 Nov. 2005, sec. 2: 4.

In-Text Citation: (Brooks 4)

For online newspaper articles, take careful note of the title and the publication date as they are listed online. Some publications, like *The New York Times*, offer permanent links for their articles; if your source has a permalink, use that in your citation.

Wald, Matthew. "Court Backs E.P.A. Over Emissions Limits Intended to Reduce Global Warming." *The New York Times,* 26 June 2012, nyti.ms/1F23s4w.

In-Text Citation: (Wald)

AN ARTICLE WITH NO AUTHOR

"The Understanding." *The New Yorker,* 2 Dec. 1991, pp. 34-35.

In-Text Citation: ("Understanding" 35)

AN EDITORIAL

"Downward Mobility." *The New York Times,* 27 Aug. 2006, p. 31. Editorial.

In-Text Citation: ("Downward" 31)

AN OPINION PIECE

Vanden Heuvel, Katrina. "Women Who Don't Have Anything Close to 'It All.'" *The Washington Post,* 26 June 2012, www.washingtonpost.com/opinions/katrina-vanden-heuvel-women-who-dont-have-anything-close-to-it-all/2012/06/26/gJQAMyAC4V_story.html?hpid=z7&utm_term=.133f4f4505a6.

In-Text Citation: (Vanden Heuvel)

A LETTER TO THE EDITOR

A published, untitled letter to the editor would be cited like this:

Boulay, Harvey. Letter to the editor. *The Boston Globe,* 30 Aug. 2006, p. 14.

In-Text Citation: (Boulay 14)

For a published letter to the editor with a title, use that title in your citation. Including a *Letter to the editor* description at the end of your citation is optional.

Jones, Maurice. "Ways to Help the Poor." *The New York Times,* 23 Sept. 2016, nyti.ms/2cuLkYP. Letter to the editor.

In-Text Citation: (Jones)

A REVIEW

Page, Barbara. "Theory and Historicity in Film Studies." Review of *Allegories of Cinema: American Film in the Sixties*, by David E. James. *College English,* vol. 54, no. 8, Dec. 1992, pp. 945-54.

In-Text Citation: (Page 945-46)

AN ABSTRACT

Edwards, Rob. "Air-Raid Warning." *New Scientist*, 14 Aug. 1999, pp. 48-49. Abstract.

    General OneFile, go.galegroup.com/ps/i.do?p=GPS&sw=w&u=nysl_me_wls&v=2

    .1&id=GALE%7CA55785479&it=r&asid=b4d33bce7d80a62332fc7b9a733ccf94.

In-Text Citation: (Edwards)

The following citation is from another useful source of abstracts, the *Dissertation Abstracts International*. In this case, the citation is from the print version of the index.

McDonald, James C. *Imitation of Models in the History of Rhetoric: Classical,*

    Belletristic, and Current-Traditional. 1988. U of Texas, Austin, PhD dissertation

    abstract. *Dissertation Abstracts International,* vol. 48, 1988, p. 2613A.

In-Text Citation: (McDonald 2613A)

Citing Online and Other Sources

AN INTERVIEW

If you conducted the interview yourself, list your subject's name first, indicate what kind of interview it was (telephone, e-mail, or personal interview), and provide the date.

Kelley, Karen. Personal interview. 1 Sept. 2015.

In-Text Citation: (Kelley)

If you're citing a published interview done by someone else (perhaps in a book or article), begin the citation with the subject's name, and then include the name of the person conducting the interview after the title of the book or periodical.

Pollan, Michael. "Michael Pollan on the Future of Food and Wood-Pulp Parmesan."

    Grub Street, interviewed by Chris Cowley, New York Media, 7 Mar. 2016, www

      .grubstreet.com/2016/03/michael-pollan-cooked-interview.html.

In-Text Citation: (Pollan)

As radio and TV interview programs are increasingly archived on the web, and more interviews are available as podcasts online, these can be great resources for a research essay. The following example shows an interview with a title that was found on *Fresh Air*'s website. Because this interview was used in its transcript form (vs. as an audio podcast), the description Transcript is added to the end of the citation.

Bakke, Gretchen. "Aging And Unstable, The Nation's Electrical Grid Is

    'The Weakest Link.'" *Fresh Air,* interviewed by Dave Davies, National

    Public Radio, 22 Aug. 2016, www.npr.org/2016/08/22/490932307/aging-

    and-unstable-the-nations-electrical-grid-is-the-weakest-link. Transcript.

In-Text Citation: (Bakke)

SURVEYS, QUESTIONNAIRES, AND CASE STUDIES

If you conducted the survey or case study, list it under your name and give it an appropriate title.

Ball, Helen. "Internet Survey." Boise State U, 2012.

In-Text Citation: (Ball)

RECORDINGS

Generally, cite a recording using the name of the artist, the name of the song in quotation marks, and the name of the album. Include the recording company and the year of the recording. If the recording you are citing is a re-release, include the date of the original release after the album title.

The Beatles. "Here Comes the Sun." *Abbey Road*. 1969. Capitol Records, 1990.

In-Text Citation: (Beatles)

TELEVISION EPISODES AND SHOWS

Include the title of the episode (if appropriate) and the title of the program (italicized). If your research essay focuses on the work of particular people associated with the episode or show, then include their names and roles. Then, depending on your rhetorical emphasis, list either the company that produced the show and the year it was produced (as in the first example below), or the distribution company and the date the show was broadcast (as in the second example below).

"Walking Big and Tall." *The Simpsons,* season 26, episode 13, Gracie

Films, 2015.

"Walking Big and Tall." *The Simpsons,* performance by Dan Castellaneta, season 26,

episode 13, Fox Network, 8 Feb. 2015.

In-Text Citation: ("Walking")

ONLINE VIDEO

National Aeronautics and Space Administration. "ScienceCasts: Electric Blue Sun-

sets." *YouTube*, 16 Aug. 2016, youtu.be/EAVJrLRBRPY.

In-Text Citation: (National Aeronautics and Space Administration)

ONLINE IMAGES

Forns, Alfred. "Atlantic Puffin." *Audubon,* www.audubon.org/content/2012-photo-

awards-top-100-0#92. Accessed 5 Oct. 2016.

In-Text Citation: (Forns)

ONLINE AUDIO OR PODCAST

> "What Are Gender Barriers Made Of?" *Freakonomics Radio,* narrated by Stephen
>
> J. Dubner, WNYC Studios / Dubner Productions, 20 July 2016, freakonomics
>
> .com/podcast/gender-barriers/.
>
> *In-Text Citation:* ("What Are Gender Barriers")

WIKI

Include the date that the wiki page was most recently updated, and because wikis do change frequently, include the date you accessed the page. For Wikipedia, use the permanent link provided for each page instead of copying the URL from your browser.

> "Emily Dickinson." *Wikipedia, The Free Encyclopedia,* 22 Sept. 2016, en.wikipedia
>
> .org/w/index.php?title=Emily_Dickinson&oldid=740594151. Accessed 23 Sept.
>
> 2016.
>
> *In-Text Citation:* ("Emily Dickinson")

FILMS

Begin with the title (italicized), the name of the company that distributed the film, and the year the film was released. If your research essay discusses the contributions of specific people associated with the film, then include their names and roles in the citation as well.

> *Saving Private Ryan.* Directed by Steven Spielberg, performance by Tom Hanks,
>
> Paramount, 1998.
>
> *In-Text Citation:* (*Saving*)

If you accessed the film online, include the name of the website and the URL for the film in your citation.

> *Saving Private Ryan.* Paramount, 1998. *Amazon Video,* www.amazon.com/dp/
>
> B00DQJPI00.

ARTWORK

List each work by artist. Then cite the title of the work (italicized) and where it's located (institution and city). If you've reproduced the work from a published source, include that information as well.

Homer, Winslow. *Breezing Up (A Fair Wind)*. 1873-86. National Gallery of Art,

Washington, D.C.

In-Text Citation: (Homer)

LECTURES AND SPEECHES

List by the name of the speaker, followed by the title of the address (if any) in quotation marks, the name of the sponsoring organization, the date, and the location. Be sure to indicate what kind of address it was (Lecture, Speech, etc.).

Naynaha, Siskanna. "Emily Dickinson's Last Poems." English 106: Introduction to

Poetry, 15 Nov. 2014, Lane Community College, Eugene. Lecture.

Avoid the need for parenthetical citation by mentioning the speaker's name in your text.

PAMPHLETS

Cite a pamphlet as you would a book.

New Challenges for Wilderness Conservationists. Wilderness Society, 2006.

In-Text Citation: (New Challenges)

A Sample Paper in MLA Style.

Burns 1

Laura Burns
Professor Ballenger
English 101
15 January 2015

The "Unreal Dream":
True Crime in the Justice System

1   I love true crime shows. The formula for these shows is simple: learn about the crime itself, investigate a few leads, find a suspect, prove the suspect is guilty, and go home, congratulating ourselves on a job well-done. Not only are these stories entertaining and chock-full of good guys, bad guys, cliff hangers, red herrings, and constant danger, but we are also granted the release of knowing that we are safe and snuggled into the couch, with the bad guys in jail and the good guys always on the right side. But the neat, pat conclusions of most of these cases masks a frightening reality. According to a recent study from the National Academy

of Sciences, 4.1% of all those who are sentenced to death in the United States are innocent (Gross et. al. 7230). In 1923, Judge Learned Hand said, "Our [justice system] has always been haunted by the ghost of the innocent man convicted. It is an unreal dream" (7230). However, Hand's "unreal dream" is a reality for many. How does wrongful conviction occur, and why does it occur so frequently? And even more importantly, how can we prevent it?

First, we need to examine what "wrongful conviction" really means. According to legal scholar Michael Risinger, there are three categories. The first is "Conviction Despite Serious Legal Error." In this case, a conviction is wrongful because a legal error was made (for example, the suspect's home was [searched] without a warrant). The second category is "Conviction Despite Lack of Legal Culpability." According to this definition, a conviction is wrongful because the convicted party was not legally culpable (for example, a crime was committed by someone with severe mental illness). The third definition is the most problematic: "Conviction Despite Factual Innocence." In these cases, one of two things occurs: either no crime was committed, so there is no offender, or, more commonly, a crime was committed, but not by the convicted party (Risinger 762).

How can this happen? Although there are countless ways an investigation and trial can veer off course, most wrongful convictions occur for one or more of the following reasons: eyewitness misidentification, false confessions, jailhouse snitches, poor forensic science, government and prosecutorial misconduct, and ineffective counsel. If I've learned anything from TV crime shows, it's that DNA is a powerful tool for convicting the guilty and exonerating the innocent. However, according to the National Registry of Exonerations, only 18 of the 91 exonerations in 2013 occurred due to DNA evidence, and the number of DNA exonerations decline annually ("Exonerations by Year"). So, although DNA evidence is an excellent tool for uncovering and proving wrongful convictions, its most effective use is uncovering the underlying causes of those wrongful convictions. It['s] only through understanding the issues and mending the fissures in the criminal justice system that allow for them, that we can slow the rate of wrongful convictions in the United States.

The most common cause of wrongful conviction is mistaken eyewitness identification. Nearly three-quarters of wrongful convictions overturned through DNA testing were caused in part by incorrect eyewitness testimony ("Innocence Project"). In order to truly understand why this is the case, we need to look at how memory works. There are two kinds of human memory: short-term and long-term. Long-term memory involves the storage of memory which can later be retrieved (Green). This is the type of memory most often accessed in eyewitness identifications, and also the type that is most easily distorted.

Take the case of Ronald Cotton. In July 1984, a young woman named Jennifer Thompson was attacked and raped in her home. Thompson made a point to try and get a good look at her rapist. She turned on lights, making sure to see his face, and immediately reported the crime to the police. Thompson was shown a photo array and informed that her assailant "may" be in the array. She identified Ronald Cotton, and the officer with her responded, "We thought this might be the one["] ("Innocence Project"). Thompson was then shown a live lineup of seven men, including Cotton. Thompson struggled with the selection, but eventually picked out Cotton— the only man who appeared in both the photo array and live lineup. The police informed

Thompson that she'd selected the same person as she had in the photo array. Based on these identifications and other circumstantial evidence, Cotton was convicted and sentenced to life in prison. Ten years later, in 1994, DNA evidence from the case exonerated Cotton. Now, Thompson and Cotton travel the country to speak about eyewitness misidentification (Cotton et. al.).

6   So, what happened here? Jennifer Thompson did everything in her power to be an excellent eyewitness, and she still misidentified Cotton. Eyewitness identification occurs because of two variables: *system* variables, which involve the criminal justice system, and *estimator* variables, which affect eyewitness accuracy but are not under the purview of the criminal justice system (Wells et. al.). Both variables were at play in the Ronald Cotton case. Some systemic factors included:

1. The second lineup. Ronald Cotton was the only person in both the photo array and the live lineup, which encouraged Thompson to identify him twice.

2. The officer's feedback. According to Thompson herself, her confidence in her identification grew after the officers provided positive feedback.

Some of the estimator factors included:

1. Weapon presence. Because her assailant had a weapon, Thompson was more inclined to focus on the weapon than on the assailant himself.

2. Own-race bias. Thompson is white, and her assailant was black (as is Ronald Cotton). Eyewitnesses are less accurate in their identifications when the person they are identifying is a race other than their own.

3. Passage of time. Memories decline in accuracy very quickly at first, then slower over time (Green).

7   Although many estimator variables cannot be controlled, system variables can be, and one of the most important systemic shifts to prevent misidentification is to ensure that the person who administers the lineup or photo array does not know the identity of the suspect. Frequently, body language cues or even (in the case of Thompson and Cotton) verbal clues from the administrator can influence a witness to identify the suspect.

8   Systemic issues in the criminal justice system cause wrongful convictions in other ways, too. While the vast majority of wrongful convictions occur due to honest mistakes or errors in judgment, there are also cases of police misconduct and government negligence. One of the most notorious of these took place in Chicago between the 1970s and 1990s under the supervision of Police Commander Jon Burge. In 1973, Anthony Holmes was arrested by Burge and brought to a police station. There, Holmes was tortured: beaten, verbally brutalized, suffocated with a bag, and subjected to a contraption of electro-shock torture, which Burge called the "nigger box" (Taylor). Eventually, under extreme duress, Holmes confessed to murder. Later, Holmes's interrogation was cited by the police department in one of Burge's commendations as demonstrating "skillful questioning" (Conroy). Journalist James Conroy wrote a series of exposes on these offenses in the *Chicago Reader* beginning in 1990, detailing the horrifying torture and the victims' failed attempts to seek justice. Burge was later fired in 1993 and

retired with pension to his boat in Florida. In 2003, Governor George Ryan commuted the sentences of all 167 men on death row in Illinois, out of concern that some of their confessions were coerced through torture. Burge was not arrested until 2008, when he was charged not for the torture, but for his involvement in covering it up (Shelton). Although the Burge case is an extreme example of government and police misconduct, it is a clear example of the importance of the public holding officers and government accountable for their actions.

Prosecutors, who represent the government in court, also occasionally exhibit misconduct. This can range from the malicious (such as the destruction of evidence) to the subtle (such as overstating the value of evidence). The most common form of prosecutorial misconduct is a Brady violation, which is defined as: "Suppression by the prosecution of evidence favorable to an accused who has requested it violates due process where the evidence is material either to guilt or to punishment, irrespective of the good faith or bad faith of the prosecution" ("Brady vs. Maryland"). Consider the case of Dewey Bozella, who was convicted of murder in 1983. In 2009, Bozella's lawyers conducted an independent investigation in which they uncovered testimony from multiple witnesses that would exonerate Bozella—all of which was withheld by the prosecution. The case was overturned (Denzel). Ineffective counsel can also be a cause of wrongful conviction. For example, an ineffective defense lawyer may fail to call witnesses who might support the defense, fail to obtain and submit DNA evidence for testing, fail to conduct independent investigations on behalf of their client, and more ("Ineffective Assistance").

While these examples demonstrate willful negligence, other causes of wrongful conviction are perfectly legal. Eighteen percent of wrongful convictions involve the testimony of a jailhouse snitch: a prisoner who allegedly learns information from another prisoner about an event that occurred outside the institution (Canada, Public Prosecution Service of Canada, Federal/Provincial/Territorial Heads of Prosecutions Committee). So, why snitch? The main reason is that snitching is incentivized. According to *USA Today*, 48,895 federal convicts received reduced sentences for their testimony against other convicts between 2006 and 2011; that is one in every eight convicts (Heath). You could argue that jailhouse snitches should not be permitted to testify at all, but occasionally, they do help expose a wrongful conviction, such as Ronald Cotton's. While incarcerated for another crime, the actual perpetrator of the crimes Cotton was convicted of bragged about his activities to other inmates. A snitch told a prosecutor what he heard, and Cotton was granted a new trial—the one that exonerated him ("Innocence Project").

The final element in many wrongful convictions (around 30% of DNA exonerations) is also the most misunderstood: false confessions ("Innocence Project"). How could someone confess to a crime they didn't commit, and why would they? First, we should understand the three different errors that can lead to false confessions:

1. <u>Misclassification error</u>: This occurs when investigators wrongly decide a suspect is guilty, and the interrogation turns into an effort not to determine a suspect's guilt, but to convince the suspect to confess.

2. <u>Coercion error</u>: This occurs when the interrogator uses coercive techniques (isolation, deception, sleep deprivation, etc.) to elicit a confession.

3. <u>Contamination error</u>: This is the error that most often leads to false confessions. In a contamination error, the interrogator influences the suspect's narrative by filling in certain details that an innocent person would not know (Leo and Drizen 13-20).

12   Of course, while not all interrogations end in false confessions, there are a number of indicators for interrogations that may lead to them. For example, the length of interrogations can affect the rate of false confessions. Though typical interrogations last around two hours, 84% of interrogations leading to false confessions lasted over six hours (and averaged around 16 hours) (Drizen and Leo 946). Additionally, all suspects are read their Miranda rights prior to interrogation, which is familiar to any of us who love "Law & Order": "You have the right to remain silent. Anything you say can and will be used against you in a court of law. You have the right to an attorney. If you cannot afford an attorney, one will be provided for you. Do you understand these rights?" The delivery and exact content of this statement varies from state to state, with some states making a point to emphasize a benefit to waiving one's rights or make the statement sound like an afterthought. Also, due to the impression many people have that "the truth will set me free," innocent people are significantly more likely to waive their rights and speak to police (Kassin 253).

13   Certain populations are more vulnerable to making false confessions. Juveniles are considered the most vulnerable: 42% of juvenile exonerees confessed to crimes they did not commit (Kassin 252). Minors tend to have more difficulty understanding legal wording (such as in the Miranda warning), are more susceptible to suggestion from interrogators, and have a less clear understanding of the consequences of their actions. Similarly, those with intellectual difficulties and mental illness are more vulnerable to false confessions. The case of Eddie Joe Lloyd is a clear example of this. While Lloyd was hospitalized for a mental illness, he wrote a series of letters to police, trying to help them solve local crimes. Officers selected one of Lloyd's letters and told him that if he confessed to that crime, it would help them find the real perpetrator. He did so, and was convicted and sent to prison for 17 years before his exoneration ("Innocence Project"). At least 22% of the false confessions currently known were made by those with a mental illness or intellectual disability (Drizen and Leo 918).

14   As I explored the many reasons why wrongful convictions occur, I began to wonder about the influence of the true crime shows I, and so many others, love so much. We love the drama and the human interest, but we also love seeing justice done. Does our obsession with these stories and our easy comfort with the way they end somehow add to the problem of wrongful convictions? My investigation into this issue led me to what is known in legal circles as the "CSI Effect," named for the famous TV crime show. According to the 2006 Nielsen ratings, five of the top ten television shows that year were related to forensics and criminal investigations. That's about 100 million viewers (Shelton). The "CSI effect" generally holds that due to these forensic science-focused shows, juries have excessively high expectations of the accuracy, quality, and utility of scientific evidence in the courtroom. They also tend to expect more certainty from scientific evidence, despite the fact that in most cases, there is no such thing as 100% forensic certainty. Despite how alarmist all of this sounds, no scientists can seem to agree on the extent

Burns 6

of this effect, and many even argue that shows like this may help improve juries' understanding of the justice system.

15 There's no easy solution to stymying wrongful convictions. Stopping them entirely would require a complete overhaul in our criminal justice system, down to the very words officers use in their day-to-day interactions. I concede that it is probably impossible to accomplish a goal of that magnitude, but there are small changes we can make that might help. One change that was recently implemented in some states is the requirement that all interrogations be videotaped. According to Illinois Public Act 97-1150, a confession resulting from interrogation will be allowed *only* if: "(1) an electronic recording is made of the custodial interrogation; and (2) the recording is substantially accurate and not intentionally altered" (Illinois State, General Assembly, House). Remember that Illinois is the state where Jon Burge committed so many atrocities in interrogation rooms. This requirement makes torture on that scale very close to impossible.

16 Finally, considering the "CSI effect" and juries' lack of understanding about the inner workings of the justice system, an improved set of jury instructions would be useful. Juries with a clearer understanding of eyewitness misidentification, incentivized snitching, and false confessions may help them make a more informed ruling. In other words, *more information*. That is the only overarching conclusion I can make: more information not only for juries, but for law enforcement officers, for lawyers, for government officials, and for the public. Navigating the process of the justice system requires far more than just to "learn about the crime itself, investigate a few leads, find a suspect, prove the suspect is guilty, and go home." We must navigate numerous uncertainties, take time to verify everything we learn, and most of all, understand the grey areas in a system that prefers the black and white, the right and wrong, the guilty and not guilty. Only once we understand why wrongful convictions occur can we begin to work on how to stop them.

Burns 7

Works Cited

"Brady v. Maryland." *Justia*, vol. 373, 1963, supreme.justia.com/cases/federal/us/373/83/case.html. 373 U.S. 83, U.S. Supreme Court.

Canada, Public Prosecution Service of Canada, Federal/Provincial/Territorial Heads of Prosecutions Committee. *The Path to Justice: Preventing Wrongful Convictions*. 2011, www.ppsc-sppc.gc.ca/eng/pub/ptj-spj/ptj-spj-eng.pdf.

Conroy, John. "House of Screams." *ChicagoReader*, 25 Jan. 1990, www.chicagoreader.com/chicago/house-of-screams/Content?oid=875107.

Denzel, Stephanie. "Dewey Bozella." *The National Registry of Exonerations*, UCI Newkirk Center for Science & Society / U of Michigan Law School / Michigan State U College of Law, 16 Nov. 2014, www.law.umich.edu/special/exoneration/Pages/casedetail.aspx?caseid=3038. Accessed 17 Jan. 2015.

Drizin, Steven A. and Richard A. Leo. "The Problem of False Confessions in the Post-DNA World." *North Carolina Law Review*, vol. 82, Mar. 2004, pp. 891-1004.

"Exonerations by Year: DNA and Non-DNA." *The National Registry of Exonerations*, UCI Newkirk Center for Science & Society / U of Michigan Law School / Michigan State U College of Law, www.law.umich.edu/special/exoneration/Pages/Exoneration-by-Year.aspx. Accessed 17 Jan. 2015.

Green, Marc. "Eyewitness Memory Is Unreliable." *Visual Expert*, 2013, www.visualexpert.com/Resources/eyewitnessmemory.html.

Gross, Samuel R., et al. "Rate of False Conviction of Criminal Defendants Who Are Sentenced to Death." *PNAS*, vol. 111, no. 20, May 2014, pp. 7230-35.

Heath, Brad. "Federal Prisoners Use Snitching for Personal Gain." *USAToday*, 14 Dec. 2012, www.usatoday.com/story/news/nation/2012/12/14/jailhouse-informants-for-sale/1762013/.

Illinois State, General Assembly, House. Public Act 097-1150. Sec. 103-2.1, 1 Jan. 2013, ww.ilga.gov/legislation/publicacts/97/097-1150.htm.

"Ineffective Assistance of Counsel." *California Innocence Project*, California Western School of Law, 2015, californiainnocenceproject.org/issues-we-face/ineffective-assistance-of-counsel/.

"The Innocence Project." *Benjamin N. Cardozo School of Law*, Yeshiva U, 2015, www.cardozo.yu.edu/innocenceproject.

Kassin, Saul M. "False Confessions: Causes, Consequences, and Implications for Reform." *Current Directions in Psychological Science*, vol. 17, no. 4, Aug. 2008, pp. 249-53.

Leo, Richard A., and Steven A. Drizin. "The Three Errors: Pathways to False Confession and Wrongful Conviction." *Police Interrogations and False Confessions: Current Research, Practice, and Policy Recommendations*, edited by G. Daniel Lassiter and Christian A. Meissner, American Psychological Association, 2010, pp. 9-30.

Risinger, D. Michael. "Innocents Convicted: An Empirically Justified Factual Wrongful Conviction Rate." *Journal of Criminal Law and Criminology*, vol. 97, no. 3, Spring 2007, pp. 761-806.

Shelton, Donald E. "The 'CSI Effect': Does It Really Exist?" *National Institute of Justice Journal*, no. 259, Mar. 2008, www.nij.gov/journals/259/pages/csi-effect.aspx.

MLA VERSUS APA: SOME BASIC DIFFERENCES

MLA Approach	APA Approach
(Author page #)—Example:	**(Author, year)—Example:**
According to Ackerman, there is an infatuation chemical (164).	According to Ackerman (1994), there is an infatuation chemical.
Usually no title page.	Usually title page and abstract. An abstract is a short summary of the paper's content, always less than 250 words in APA style.

MLA Approach	APA Approach
Pagination uses writer's last name and page number. For example:	Pagination uses running head and page number. The "running head" includes the paper's abbreviated title. For example:
Smith 5	EXPORTING JOBS 5
Figures and tables included within the paper.	Figures and tables included in section at the end of the paper.
Bibliography called Works Cited page.	Bibliography called References page.

APA Documentation Guidelines

The American Psychological Association's (APA) citation conventions are the other dominant approach to acknowledging sources. If you're headed for courses in the social sciences, then this is the system you'll use. It's no harder than the MLA system; in fact, the two systems are quite similar. Both use parenthetical citations. Their bibliography (or References page) formats are organized in very similar ways. But there are a few significant differences, some of which are summarized in the table. Detailed descriptions of the APA system are in the following sections.

How the Essay Should Look

Page Format. Papers should be double-spaced, with at least one-inch margins on all sides. Number all pages consecutively, beginning with the title page; put the page number in the upper right corner. Place an abbreviated title of the paper (fifty characters or less, including spaces), flush left and in all capital letters, on every page. As a rule, the first line of all paragraphs of text should be indented five to seven spaces.

Title Page. Unlike a paper in MLA style, an APA-style paper has a separate title page, containing the following information: the title of the paper, the author, and the author's affiliation (e.g., what university she is from). Each line of information should be centered and double-spaced. (See Figure 9.4.) At the top of the title page, flush left and in uppercase letters, you should include the *running head*, or the abbreviation of the title. (Note that "Running head:" should precede the paper's running head only on the title page.) The page number should appear in the upper right corner.

Abstract. Although it's not always required, many APA-style papers include an abstract (no longer than 250 words) following the title page. (See Figure 9.5.) An abstract is essentially a short summary of the paper's contents.

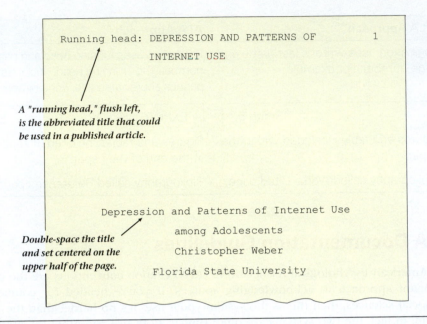

Figure 9.4   Title page in APA style

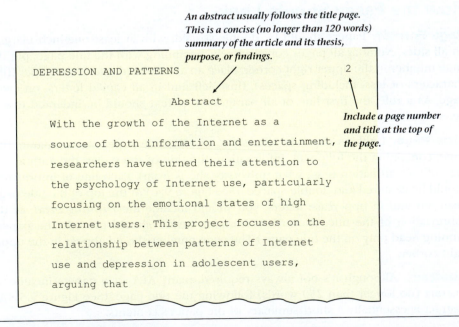

Figure 9.5   The abstract page

This is a key feature, because it's usually the first thing a reader encounters. The abstract should include statements about what problem or question the paper examines and what approach it follows; the abstract should also cite the thesis and significant findings. Type *Abstract* at the top of the page, and type the abstract's text in a single block, without indenting the first line.

Body of the Paper. The body of the paper begins with the centered title, followed by a double space and then the text. The running head should appear flush left, and the page number ("3" if the paper has a title page and an abstract) should appear in the upper right corner. (See Figure 9.6.)

You may want to use headings within your paper. If your paper is fairly formal, some headings might be prescribed, such as *Introduction, Method, Results,* and *Discussion.* Or create your own heads to clarify the organization of your paper.

If you use headings, the APA recommends the following hierarchy:

Centered, Boldfaced, Uppercase and Lowercase Letters

Flush Left, Boldfaced, Uppercase and Lowercase Letters

    Indented, boldfaced, lowercase except first letter of first word, end in period.

    Indented, boldfaced, italicized, lowercase except first letter of first word, end in period.

    Indented, italicized, lowercase except first letter of first word, end in period.

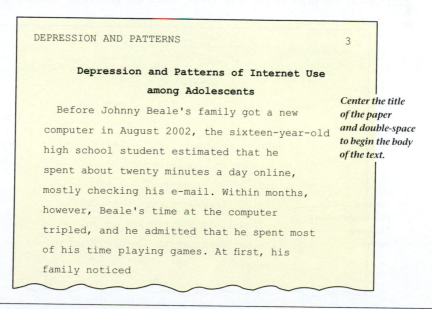

DEPRESSION AND PATTERNS   3

Depression and Patterns of Internet Use among Adolescents

Before Johnny Beale's family got a new computer in August 2002, the sixteen-year-old high school student estimated that he spent about twenty minutes a day online, mostly checking his e-mail. Within months, however, Beale's time at the computer tripled, and he admitted that he spent most of his time playing games. At first, his family noticed

Center the title of the paper and double-space to begin the body of the text.

Figure 9.6 The body of the paper in APA style

Papers rarely use all five levels of headings; two or three is probably most common, particularly in student papers. When you use multiple levels, always use them consecutively. In other words, a level 1 heading would always be followed by a level 2 heading (if there is one).

For example,

The Intelligence of Crows

Current Understandings of Crow Intelligence

References Page. All sources cited in the body of the paper are listed alphabetically by author (or by title, if there is no author) on a page titled *References*. See Figure 9.7. This list should begin a new page. Each entry is double-spaced; begin each entry flush left, and indent subsequent lines five to seven spaces. Explanations of how to cite various sources in the References are in the "Preparing the References List" section.

Appendix. This is a seldom-used feature of an APA-style paper, although you might find it helpful if you want to include detailed material or material that isn't central to the discussion in the body of your paper, such as a detailed description of a device mentioned in the paper, a copy of a survey, or the like. Each appendix should begin on a separate page and be labeled *Appendix*, followed by *A*, *B*, and so on, consecutively, if there is more than one appendix.

Notes. Several kinds of notes might be included in an APA-style paper. The most common is *content notes*, or brief commentaries by the writer keyed to superscript numbers in the body of the text. These notes are useful for discussing key points

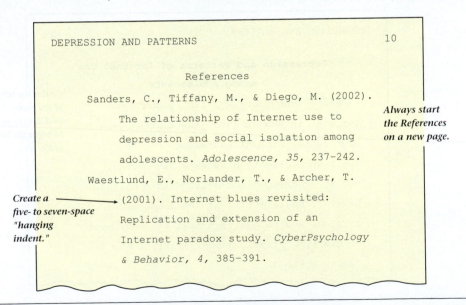

DEPRESSION AND PATTERNS   10

References

Sanders, C., Tiffany, M., & Diego, M. (2002).
The relationship of Internet use to
depression and social isolation among
adolescents. *Adolescence, 35,* 237-242.

Waestlund, E., Norlander, T., & Archer, T.
(2001). Internet blues revisited:
Replication and extension of an
Internet paradox study. *CyberPsychology
& Behavior, 4,* 385-391.

Always start the References on a new page.

Create a five- to seven-space "hanging indent."

Figure 9.7   The References page

that are relevant but might be distracting if explored in the text of your paper. Present all notes, numbered consecutively, on a page titled *Footnotes*. Each note should be double-spaced. Begin each note with the appropriate superscript number. Indent each first line five to seven spaces; consecutive lines run the full page measure.

Tables and Figures.   The final section of an APA-style paper includes the tables and figures that were mentioned in the text. All table text should be double-spaced. Type the table number at the top of the page, flush left. Number tables Table 1, Table 2, and so on, corresponding to the order in which they are mentioned in the text. A table may also include a title. Each table should begin on a separate page.

Figures (illustrations, graphs, charts, photographs, and drawings) are handled similarly to tables. Each should be titled *Figure* and numbered consecutively. Captions may be included, and should appear below each figure.

Language and Style.   The APA is comfortable with the italicizing and boldfacing functions of word processors, and underlining is a thing of the past. The guidelines for *italicizing* call for its use when writing the following:

- The titles of books, periodicals, and publications that appear on microfilm.

- When using new or specialized terms, but only the first time you use them (e.g., "the authors' *paradox study* of Internet users...").

- When citing a phrase, letter, or word as an example (e.g., "the second *a* in *separate* can be remembered by noticing the word *rat*").

The APA calls for quotation marks around the title of an article or book chapter when mentioned in your essay.

Been nagged all your life by the question of whether to spell out numbers or use numerals in APA style? Here, finally, is the answer: Numbers less than 10 that aren't precise measurements should be spelled out, and numbers 10 or more should be digits.

Citing Sources in Your Essay

When the Author Is Mentioned in the Text.   The author/date system is pretty uncomplicated. If you mention the name of the author in text, simply place the year his work was published in parentheses immediately after his name. For example:

Herrick (1999) argued that college testing was biased against minorities.

When the Author Isn't Mentioned in the Text. If you don't mention the author's name in the text, then include the name parenthetically. For example:

A New Hampshire political scientist (Sundberg, 2012) recently studied the state's

presidential primary.

Note that the author's name and the year of her work are separated by a comma.

When to Cite Page Numbers. If the information you're citing came from specific pages, chapters, or sections of a source, those specific elements may also be included in the parenthetical citation. Including page numbers is essential when quoting a source. For example:

The first stage of language acquisition is called "caretaker speech" (Moskowitz,

1985, pp. 50–51), in which children model their parents' language.

The same passage might also be cited this way if the author's name is mentioned in the text:

Moskowitz (1985) observed that the first stage of language acquisition is called

"caretaker speech" (pp. 50–51), in which children model their parents' language.

A Single Work by Two or More Authors. When a work has two authors, always mention them both whenever you cite their work in your paper. For example:

Allen and Oliver (1998) observed many cases of child abuse and concluded that

maltreatment inhibited language development.

If a source has more than two authors but fewer than six, mention them all the first time you refer to their work. However, any subsequent in-text references should include the surname of the first author followed by the abbreviation *et al*. When citing works with six or more authors, *always* use the first author's surname and *et al*.

A Work with No Author. When a work has no author, cite an abbreviated title and the year. Place article or chapter titles in quotation marks, and *italicize* book titles. For example:

The editorial ("Sinking," 2012) concluded that the EPA was mired in bureaucratic

muck.

Two or More Works by the Same Author. Works by the same author are usually distinguished by the date; one author's works are rarely published the same year. But if they are, distinguish among such works by adding an *a* or *b* immediately following the year in the parenthetical citation. The References list entries will also have these suffixes. For example:

> Douglas's studies (1986a) on the mating habits of lobsters revealed that the
>
> females are dominant. He also found that the female lobsters have the uncanny
>
> ability to smell a loser (1986b).

This citation alerts readers that the information came from two different studies by Douglas, both published in 1986.

An Institutional Author. When citing a corporation or agency as a source, simply list the year of the study in parentheses if you mention the institution in the text:

> The Environmental Protection Agency (2012) issued an alarming report on ozone
>
> pollution.

If you don't mention the institutional source in the text, spell it out in its entirety, along with the year. In subsequent parenthetical citations, you can abbreviate the name as long as the abbreviation will be understandable. For example:

> A study (Environmental Protection Agency [EPA], 2012) predicted dire consequenc-
>
> es from continued ozone depletion.

And later in the text:

> Continued ozone depletion may result in widespread skin cancers (EPA, 2012).

Multiple Works in the Same Parentheses. Occasionally, you'll want to cite several works at once that speak to a topic you're writing about in your essay. Probably the most common instance is when you refer to the findings of several relevant studies, something that is a good idea as you establish a context for what has already been said about your research topic. For example,

> A number of researchers have explored the connection between Internet use and
>
> depression (Sanders, Field, & Diego, 2000; Waestlund, Norlander, & Archer, 2001).

When listing multiple authors within the same parentheses, order them as they appear in the References. Semicolons separate each entry.

Interviews, E-Mail, and Letters. Interviews and other personal communications are not listed in the References at the back of the paper because they are not *recoverable data*, but they should be parenthetically cited in the text. Provide the initials and surname of the subject (if not mentioned in the text), the nature of the communication, and the complete date, if possible.

Nancy Diamonti (personal communication, November 12, 2012) disagrees with the critics of *Sesame Street*.

In a recent e-mail, Michelle Payne (personal communication, January 4, 2012) complained that....

New Editions of Old Works. For reprints of older works, include both the year of the original publication and that of the reprint edition (or the translation).

Pragmatism as a philosophy sought connection between scientific study and real

people's lives (James, 1906/1978).

A Website. When referring to an *entire* website (see the following example), cite the address parenthetically in your essay. As for e-mail, it isn't necessary to include a citation for an entire website in your References list. However, you should cite online documents that contribute information to your paper (see the "Sample References: Other" subsection).

One of the best sites for searching the so-called Invisible Web is the Librarians

Index to the Internet (http://www.lii.org).

Preparing the References List

All parenthetical citations in the body of the paper correspond to a complete listing of sources on the References page. The format for this section was described earlier (see the "References Page" subsection).

Order of Sources. List the References entries alphabetically by author or by the first key word of the title if there is no author. The only complication is when you have several articles or books by the same author. If the sources weren't published in the same year, list them in chronological order, the earliest first. If the sources *were* published in the same year, include a lowercase letter to distinguish them. For example:

Lane, B. (1991a). Verbal medicine...

Lane, B. (1991b). Writing...

While the alphabetical principle—listing authors according to the alphabetical placement of their last names—works in most cases, there are a few variations you should be aware of.

- If you have several entries by the same author, list them by year of publication, beginning with the earliest.

- Because scholars and writers often collaborate, you may have several citations in which an author is listed with several *different* collaborators. List these entries alphabetically according to the second author's last name. For example,

Brown, M., & Nelson, A. (2002)

Brown, M., & Payne, M. (1999)

Order of Information. A citation of a periodical in APA style includes this information, in this order: author, year of publication, article title, periodical title, volume and section numbers, and page numbers. A citation of a book in APA style includes the following information, in this order: author, year of publication, book title, and publication information.

Citations of electronic sources include some additional information. If you're harvesting your books and articles online or from a library database, you need to cite in a way that makes it clear how readers can find the book or document. That seems simple, right? It isn't always. Typically, you include the URL for an online document in your citation, even if it's long and ugly. But URLs can change, and they are vulnerable to transcription mistakes. To solve this problem, the APA uses something called the Digital Object Identifier (see the description in the paragraph headed "DOI or URL"). This is a number that is a permanent link to the document. But not all documents have them, and if they don't, cite their URLs.

One other bit of information you usually include in a citation for an electronic document is the retrieval date, or exactly when you accessed the work online. This can be omitted, however, when the document you're citing is "archival." An archival copy is a final version, and it's usually the version that appeared in print.

Author. List up to seven authors using last name, comma, and then initials. Invert all authors' names. Use commas to separate authors' names and add an ampersand (&) before the last author's name. When citing eight or more authors, list the first six, and then add ellipses ("…") and the name of the last author. When citing an edited book, list the editor(s) in place of the author(s), and add the abbreviation Ed. or Eds. in parentheses following the initials. End the list of names with a period.

Date. List the year the work was published along with the date, if it's a magazine or newspaper article (see the "Sample References: Articles" subsection), in parentheses, immediately after the last author's name. Add a period after the closing parenthesis.

Article or Book Title. APA style departs from MLA here. In APA style, only the first word of the article title is capitalized, and the title appears without italics or quotation marks. Book titles are italicized, with only the first word of the title and the first word of any subtitle capitalized. End all titles with periods.

Periodical Title and Publication Information. Italicize the complete periodical title, and use both uppercase and lowercase letters. Add the volume number (if any), also italicized. Separate the title and volume number with a comma (e.g., *Journal of Mass Communication, 10*, 138–150). If each issue of the periodical starts with page 1, then also include, in roman type, the issue number in parentheses immediately after the volume number (see examples following). End the entry with the page numbers of the article. Use the abbreviation *p.* or *pp.* if you are citing a newspaper. Other APA-style abbreviations include the following:

chap.	p. (pp.)
Ed./Eds. (Editor/Editors), ed. (edition)	Vol.
Rev. ed.	No.
2nd ed.	Pt.
Trans.	Suppl.

For books, list the city and state or country of publication (use postal abbreviations) and the name of the publisher; separate the city and publisher with a colon. End the citation with a period.

Remember that the first line of each citation should begin flush left, and all subsequent lines should be indented five to seven spaces. Double-space all entries.

Retrieval Date. If you're citing an electronic document, you often indicate when you accessed the book or article. This is important because online documents can change, and the retrieval date gives readers a "snapshot" of what version you were looking at when you did your research. When a citation includes a Digital Object Identifier (DOI), no other retrieval information is needed. In the absence of a DOI, and when a URL is included, don't include retrieval dates unless it's likely that the source material will change in the future (e.g., Wikis).

DOI or URL. These are more ingredients for your alphabet soup. So that readers can locate the electronic documents you're citing, you need to tell them where you found them. You frequently do this by including the URL. But more and more documents in the social sciences include a Digital Object Identifier (DOI), a permanent link to the work. The DOI is often listed on the article's first page. It may also be hidden under the "Article" button that appears with the work on certain library databases.

Here's a summary of the similarities and differences involved in citing print and electronic journals and magazines in APA style:

Print Periodical	Electronic Periodical
• Author(s)	• Author(s)
• (Date)	• (Date)
• Article title	• Article title
• Periodical title	• Periodical title
• Issue and volume number	• Issue and volume number
• Page numbers	• Page numbers
	• Retrieval date (unless archival)
	• DOI (if available) or URL (if DOI unavailable)

Sample References: Articles
A JOURNAL ARTICLE

When citing an online article, include information about how readers can find it. Use the DOI, if available. For example,

> Mori, K., Ujiie, T., Smith, A., & Howlin, P. (2009). Parental stress associated with caring for children with Asperger's syndrome. *Pediatrics International, 51*(3), 364–370. doi:10.1111/j.1442-200X-2008.0278.x

In-Text Citation: (Mori, Ujiie, Smith, & Howlin, 2009); (Mori et al., 2009) in subsequent citations. If authors are quoted, include page numbers.

If there is no DOI, include the document's URL.

> Wing, L. (1981). Asperger's syndrome: A clinical account. *Psychological Medicine, 11*(1), 115–129. Retrieved from http://search.ebscohost.com/login.aspx?direct=true&db=psyh&AN=1981-30537-001&site=ehost-live

In-Text Citation: (Wing, 1981)

Cite a print journal article like this:

> Blager, F. B. (1979). The effect of intervention on the speech and language of children. *Child Abuse and Neglect, 5*, 91–96.

In-Text Citation: (Blager, 1979)

If the author is mentioned in the text, just parenthetically cite the year:

Blager (1979) stated that. . . .

If the author is quoted, include the page number(s):

(Blager, 1979, p. 92)

A MAGAZINE ARTICLE

> Maya, P. (1981, December). The civilizing of Genie. *Psychology Today,* 28–34.

In-Text Citation: (Maya, 1981)

Maya (1981) observed that. . . .

When citing a magazine article from a database, include the URL. Many databases include a "permanent link" to the article on the citation page. Use that if available. Notice also that the database name is not included.

Horowitz, A. (July, 2008). My dog is smarter than your dog. *Discover Magazine,*

219(9), 71. Retrieved from http://search.ebscohost.com.libproxy.boisestate.

edu/login.aspx?direct=true&db=aph&an=32580478&site=ehost-live

In-Text Citation: (Horowitz, 2008)

If quoting, include page numbers:

(Horowitz, 2008, p. 71)

AN ARTICLE ON A WEBSITE
This article has no author, so the citation begins with the title.

Enhancing male body image. (2006). *Nationaleatingdisorders.org.* Retrieved July 9,

2009, from http://www.nationaleatingdisorders.org/

In-Text Citation: ("Enhancing," 2006)

If quoting, include the page number(s): ("Enhancing," 2006, p. 28)

A NEWSPAPER ARTICLE

Honan, W. (2004, January 24). The war affects Broadway. *The New York Times,* pp. C15–C16.

In-Text Citation: (Honan, 2004)

Honan (2004) argued that. . . .

Honan (2004) said that "Broadway is a battleground" (p. C15).

If there is no author, a common situation with newspaper articles, alphabetize the entry using the first "significant word" in the article title. The parenthetical citation will use an abbreviation of the title in quotation marks, then the year.

There's a good chance that you'll find newspaper articles online. Here's how you cite them:

Jennings, D. (2009, July 7). With cancer, you can't hurry recovery. *The New York*

Times. Retrieved from http://www.nytimes.com

In-Text Citation: (Jennings, 2009)

Sample References: Books
A BOOK

Lukas, A. J. (1986). *Common ground: A turbulent decade in the lives of three*

American families. New York, NY: Random House.

In-Text Citation: (Lukas, 1986)

According to Lukas (1986), . . .

If quoting, include the page number(s).

AN ONLINE BOOK

If you're citing an entire book you found online, include the URL. For example,

Suzuki, D. T. (1914). *A brief history of early Chinese philosophy*. Retrieved from

    http://www.archive.org/details/briefhistoryofea00suzuuoft

In-Text Citation: (Suzuki, 1914)

When citing a chapter from an online book, include a bit more information, including the name of the database (if any) from which you retrieved it.

Hollin, C. R. (2002). Criminal psychology. In C. R. Hollin (Ed.), *Oxford handbook of*

    criminology (pp. 144–174). Retrieved from Academic Research Premier database.

In-Text Citation: (Hollin, 2002)

A SOURCE MENTIONED BY ANOTHER SOURCE

Frequently you'll read an article that mentions another article you haven't read. Whenever possible, track down that original article and read it in its entirety. But when that's not possible, you need to make it clear that you know of the article and its findings or arguments indirectly. The APA convention for this is to use the expression *as cited in* parenthetically, followed by the author and date of the indirect source. For example, suppose you want to use some information from Eric Weiser's piece that you read about in Charlotte Jones's book. In your essay, you would write something like:

Weiser argues (as cited in Jones, 2002) that. . . .

A BOOK OR ARTICLE WITH MORE THAN ONE AUTHOR

Rosenbaum, A., & O'Leary, D. (1978). Children: The unintended victims of marital

    violence. *American Journal of Orthopsychiatry, 4,* 692–699.

In-Text Citation: (Rosenbaum & O'Leary, 1978)

Rosenbaum and O'Leary (1978) believed that. . . .

If quoting, include the page number(s).

A BOOK OR ARTICLE WITH AN UNKNOWN AUTHOR

The politics of war. (2004, June 1). *The New York Times*, p. 36.

In-Text Citation: ("Politics," 2004)

Or mention the source in the text:

In "The Politics of War" (2004), an editorialist compared Iraq to....

If quoting, provide page number(s) as well.

The Chicago manual of style (14th ed.). (1993). Chicago, IL: University of Chicago Press.

In-Text Citation: (*Chicago Manual of Style,* 1993)

According to the *Chicago Manual of Style* (1993),...

If quoting, include the page number(s).

A BOOK WITH AN INSTITUTIONAL AUTHOR

American Red Cross. (1999). *Advanced first aid and emergency care.* New York, NY: Doubleday.

In-Text Citation: (American Red Cross, 1999)

The book *Advanced First Aid and Emergency Care* (American Red Cross, 1999) stated that....

If quoting, include the page number(s).

A BOOK WITH AN EDITOR

Crane, R. S. (Ed.). (1952). *Critics and criticism.* Chicago, IL: University of Chicago Press.

In-Text Citation: (Crane, 1952)

In his preface, Crane (1952) observed that....

If quoting, include the page number(s).

A SELECTION IN A BOOK WITH AN EDITOR

McKeon, R. (1952). Rhetoric in the Middle Ages. In R. S. Crane (Ed.), *Critics and criticism* (pp. 260–289). Chicago, IL: University of Chicago Press.

In-Text Citation: (McKeon, 1952)

McKeon (1952) argued that....

If quoting, include the page number(s).

A REPUBLISHED WORK

James, W. (1978). *Pragmatism.* Cambridge, MA: Harvard University Press (Original work published 1907).

In-Text Citation: (James, 1907/1978)

According to William James (1907/1978), . . .

If quoting, include the page number(s).

AN ABSTRACT

The growth of online databases for articles has increased the availability of full-text versions and abstracts of articles. Although the full article is almost always best, sometimes an abstract alone contains some useful information. If the abstract was retrieved from a database or some other secondary source, include information about it. Aside from the name of the source, this information might involve the date, if different from the year of publication of the original article; an abstract number; or a page number. In the following example, the abstract was retrieved from an online database, Biological Abstracts.

Garcia, R. G. (2002). Evolutionary speed of species invasions. *Evolution, 56,* 661–668. Abstract retrieved from Biological Abstracts database.

In-Text Citation: (Garcia, 2002), or Garcia (2002) argues that. . . .

A BOOK REVIEW

Dentan, R. K. (1989). A new look at the brain [Review of the book *The dreaming brain*]. *Psychiatric Journal, 13,* 51.

In-Text Citation: (Dentan, 1989)

Dentan (1989) argues that. . . .

If quoting, include the page number(s).

An online book review would include the same information but with the phrase "Retrieved from" and the review's URL.

ONLINE ENCYCLOPEDIA

Turner, B. S. (2007). Body and society. In G. Ritzer (Ed.), *Blackwell encyclopedia of sociology.* Retrieved July 7, 2009, from http://blackwellreference.com

In-Text Citation: (Turner, 2007)

Because they are collaboratively written, Wikipedia articles have no single author. Usually, therefore, the citation should begin with the article title. For example,

Ticks. (n.d.). In *Wikipedia.* Retrieved July 9, 2009, from http://en.wikipedia.org<200b>/wiki/ticks

In-Text Citation: ("Ticks," n.d.)

Sample References: Other

A GOVERNMENT DOCUMENT

U.S. Bureau of the Census. (2004). *Statistical abstract of the United States* (126th ed.). Washington, DC: U.S. Government Printing Office.

In-Text Citation: (U.S. Bureau of the Census, 2004)

According to the U.S. Census Bureau (2004), . . .

If quoting, include the page number(s).

A LETTER TO THE EDITOR

Hill, A. C. (2006, February 19). A flawed history of blacks in Boston [Letter to the editor]. *The Boston Globe*, p. 22.

In-Text Citation: (Hill, 2006)

Hill (2006) complained that. . . .

If quoting, include page number(s).

A PUBLISHED INTERVIEW

Personal interviews are not cited in the References section of an APA-style paper, unlike published interviews. Here is a citation for a published interview:

Cotton, P. (2004, April). [Interview with Jake Tule, psychic]. *Chronicles Magazine*, 24–28.

In-Text Citation: (Cotton, 2004)

Cotton (2004) noted that. . . .

If quoting, include the page number(s).

A FILM OR VIDEOTAPE

Hitchcock, A. (Producer & Director). (1954). *Rear window* [Motion picture]. Los Angeles, CA: MGM.

In-Text Citation: (Hitchcock, 1954)

In *Rear Window*, Hitchcock (1954). . . .

PODCAST, VIDEO, AND AUDIO

Shier, J. (Producer & Director). (2005). Saving the grizzly: One hair at a time.

Terra: The nature of our world [Podcast]. Retrieved from http://www<200b>.

lifeonterra.com/episode.php?id=1

In-Text Citation: (Shier, 2005)

Uhry, A. (2009, July 6). Private education in America. *The Economist* [Podcast].

Retrieved from http://podcast.com/episode/40782102/5356/

In-Text Citation: (Uhry, 2009)

A TELEVISION PROGRAM

Burns, K. (Executive producer). (1996). *The west* [Television broadcast]. New York,

NY, and Washington, DC: Public Broadcasting Service.

In-Text Citation: (Burns, 1996)

In Ken Burns's (1996) film, . . .

For an episode of a television series, use the scriptwriter as the author, and provide the director's name after the scriptwriter. List the producer's name after the episode.

Hopley, J. (Writer/Director), & Shannon, J. (Writer/Director). (2006). Buffalo

burrito/Parkerina [Television series episode]. In J. Lenz (Producer), *Mr. Meaty*.

New York, NY: Nickelodeon.

In-Text Citation: (Hopley & Shannon, 2006)

Fans were appalled by the second episode, when Hopley and Shannon (2006). . . .

A MUSICAL RECORDING

Wolf, K. (1986). Muddy roads [Recorded by E. Clapton]. *On Gold in California* [CD].

Santa Monica, CA: Rhino Records. (1990).

In-Text Citation: (Wolf, 1986, track 5)

In Wolf's (1986) song, . . .

A COMPUTER PROGRAM

OmniPage Pro 14 (Version 14) [Computer software]. (2003). Peabody, MA: Scansoft.

In-Text Citation: (OmniPage Pro, Version 14, 2003)

Scansoft's new software, OmniPage Pro (2003), is reputed. . . .

DISCUSSION LISTS

Discussion lists abound on the Internet. They range from groups of flirtatious teenagers to those with a serious academic purpose. Although virtually all of these discussion lists are based on e-mail, they do vary a bit. The most useful lists for academic research tend to be e-mail discussion lists. Newsgroups, or Usenet groups, are extremely popular among more-general Internet users. Various search engines can help you find discussion groups appropriate for your topic. You can join or monitor the current discussion or, in some cases, search the archives for contributions that interest you. Google is a great search tool for newsgroups and includes an archive for many of them. *If there are no archives, don't include the citation in your References list, because the information isn't recoverable.* However, you may still cite these discussion groups in your essay as personal communications.

The method of citation varies slightly if it's a newsgroup, an online forum, or an electronic mailing list. For example, a newsgroup posting would be cited like this:

Hord, J. (2002, July 11). Re: Why do pigeons lift one wing up in the air?

[Online forum comment]. Message archived at rec.pets.birds.pigeons

In-Text Citation: (Hord, 2002), or Hord asks (2002). . . .

Note that the citation includes the subject line of the message as the title and the message number of the "thread" (the particular discussion topic). The prefix for this newsgroup is *rec*, which indicates the list is hobby oriented.

Electronic mailing lists would be cited this way:

Cook, D. (2002, July 19). Grammar and the teaching of writing [Electronic mailing

list message]. Retrieved from http://listserv.comptalk<200b>.boisestate.edu

In-Text Citation: (Cook, 2002), or According to Cook (2002). . . .

E-MAIL

E-mail is not cited in the list of references. But you should cite e-mail in the text of your essay. It should look like this:

In-Text Citation: M. Payne (personal communication, January 4, 2012) argued that

responding to personal writing. . . .

BLOG

Notice in this example that the blogger uses a screen name.

Rizaro. (2009, July 7). Anxiety and suicide [Web log post]. Retrieved from

HelptoHealth.co.cc

A Sample Paper in APA Style.

Kersti Harter

Beyond "Gaydar": How Gay Males Identify Other Gay Males

A Study with Four Boise, Idaho, Men

Introduction

While people who do not fit into the codified norms of behavior in contemporary urban life are often marginalized by the mainstream, this very fact often serves to empower and reinforce the behavior of its members in marginalized groups. This is the case within gay male culture in United States urban society. Because gay males remain heavily stigmatized, they have formed a large "outside" group with subtle yet unmistakably designated patterns and categories of behavior, action, clothing, and taste. These patterns and behaviors may not be identifiable to the larger society, but they are well-known among gay men. One of these social rituals is the patterns through which gay men attempt to identify other gay males. I had very little prior knowledge that this pattern existed, but through interviews and observations of several gay men in Boise, Idaho, aged 18–25, I discovered how some gay males identify others who are gay.

I was able to model this pattern and the categories of behavior that exist within it.

Background

Several studies suggest that so-called "gaydar," the use of intuition to determine the sexual orientation of someone without asking the person outright whether he or she is gay, might have a basis in fact. A recent study (Lawson, 2005) demonstrated that when provided with "neck-up" photographs of strangers who weren't wearing jewelry or makeup, homosexuals were better than heterosexuals in making the correct identification of the stranger's sexual orientation, making

1

2

BEYOND GAYDAR   2

this judgment in 2 seconds or less (p. 30). Martins et al. (2005) also reported that "gay men were found to be particularly good at detecting the scent of other gay men" (p. 694). In addition, another study argued that "eye gaze," with distinct variations, is "crucial to forces that either trigger or reinforce one gay's perception of another gay's identity during social encounters" (Nicholas, 2004).

Identifying Other Gay Males: Place

3   There are, however, other methods of gay identification used by male homosexuals that don't rely on "gaydar" or intuition. One such method, depicted in Figure 1, relies on contextual cues or markers. The number one identifier among the four contextual cues is place: if he's in the gay bar, he's likely gay. But

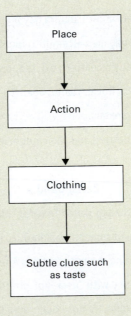

Figure 1. The sequence of judgments used by gay men to identify other gay men

BEYOND GAYDAR   3

this does not mean for sure that any man in a gay club is gay. Julian recounted a
story in which he accidentally "hit on" a straight male who was in a gay club:

> It was at a gay club, so I'm not entirely at fault. This guy was just sitting there,
> kind of like, I don't know, just sitting there at the bar, looking kind of, well,
> sitting there sulking I guess. And I thought he was pretty good looking, so
> I thought I'd go talk to him, I wasn't going to pick him up or anything. And
> so I went up and was talking to him, and he would answer me in one-syllable
> replies. And I just walked off and I found out that he was actually the bouncer
> that worked there and he had the night off.

Julian's story suggests that "gaydar" isn't always reliable. Sexual orientation   4
signaling is based on more than intuition. It also means that place is not the only
identifier of gay males, although it is often accurate. So what happens when the
identifier of place fails to confirm sexual orientation?

Action

Then we must move onto appearance. I use "appearance" here because my   5
participants claimed that movement as well as personal style played into identifying whether a man is gay. I have subdivided appearance into action, or movements
and other behaviors, and clothing, which I discuss below. During my group interview, both Aaron and Steven claimed that movement is the more important part of
appearance in determining a man's orientation:

> Me: Does clothing or movement clue you in more to whether or not a person
> is gay? Aaron: Movement . . . You can tell by the way a person gesticulates,
> by how they walk. I can tell how I walk . . . I'm like God, everyone knows I'm a
> homo [laughs]! Like I like it, but yeah, it's definitely how they move.

It seems that certain movements are ingrained qualities that help gay males   6
identify other gay males. So, in Figure 1, I've identified the next step my subjects

might use to identify another gay male as "Action." Some of these movements are evident even to straight observers, and occasionally the actions have to do with associations with other gay men. For example, another participant, Jeff, pointed out, "Well, if they are with a guy, then yeah, they're gay."

7   If action is not enough to identify the man's orientation, an observer might move on to more subtle parts of clothing style or even personal tastes. But this would probably not happen in such a situation, and actions are likely telling enough.

Clothing and Personal Style

8   There are times, however, when gay men are in places less exclusively gay, or in places not defined as gay at all. Then one must skip to the latter steps, identifying the less obvious markers of sexual orientation such as personal style.

9   When I began my research, I sat with my friend Steven in a popular downtown Boise coffee shop, The Flying M. While being widely known as the "gay" coffee shop, it is not exclusively so. Wednesday, according to Steven, has become known to some in the gay community as "Gay Night." This Wednesday was the first time that I met his friend Aaron, who later helped me in the group interview. I would ask Steven, "Is that guy over there gay?" and so on, and he would answer yes, because the man was simply at this coffee shop on Gay Night, or because he acted a certain way, or dressed a certain way.

10   When he would identify them as gay because of the way they looked, David would often cite things like button-down Abercrombie and Fitch shirts or spiky hair. There was a definite gay look that he was able to identify. Steven was able to identify gay males, even though we were in a setting that was not necessarily exclusively gay. Clothing, though it is used less than place and action, still can provide clues

BEYOND GAYDAR   5

about sexual orientation. There are also categories of gay male dress style that the men that I interviewed identified.

Stylistic Stereotypes Among Gay Males

To outsiders, clothing and personal style would be one of the easiest identi-   11
fiers of gay males. But it is actually, according to my subjects, a less obvious marker than place or action. Personal style also comes in many shapes and forms in the gay community. It's as if there is a set of emic values (distinctions that members of a group recognize that may not be apparent to outsiders) that are stereotypical of the gay male. This is an instance where the pattern of behavior in the group is broken down into diverse categories.

For example, Green and Ashmore, in "Taking and Developing Pictures in the   12
Head: Assessing the Physical Stereotypes of Eight Gender Types" (1998), asked college students to picture various stereotypes in their heads and describe what they saw. They asked them to picture both "nerd" and "homosexual," and they found that:

> Perceivers have similar pictures of the homosexual and the nerd in their
> heads. Both were frequently described as being slender and of average height,
> wearing glasses, and wearing the "uniform" of the male college student
> (e.g., button-down shirt, pants or jeans, sneakers or casual shoes). (p. 1627)

Though these college students pictured "the nerd" and "the homosexual"   13
together, the men I talked with identified a picture of the homosexual that was quite different from the one these college students identified. The men also emphasized that there were many different types of gay male style, not just one. They all identified several emic stereotypes, and disagreed with the "nerd" and "homosexual" being lumped together in similar stylistic categories.

BEYOND GAYDAR   6

14   When I mentioned this article to Julian, he explained to me why people might lump the "nerd" with the "homosexual":

> In Europe they used to associate Jews and homosexuals, they were kind of lumped together. And so maybe whoever's on the outside is kind of labeled together...I don't think that's a look that gay guys go for as far as trying to look like that...there's sort of that geek chic that a lot of people do, pretty much if you see that you know they're straight.

15   According to Julian, though the outside sees homosexuals and nerds having similar styles because of their roles as the "outsiders," homosexuals have a different view of their styles, one that is much more rich and varied.

16   In the essay "Gay Masculinity in the Gay Disco," Cheseboro and Klenk (1981) identify several categories of symbol-using in the gay disco. Though written more than twenty-five years ago, it gives insight into some incipient analyses of stylistic categories that gay men employ. Cheseboro and Klenk describe "The Virility Component":

> One concept asserted in the gay disco is an exaggerated, if not flagrant, form of masculinity in appearance...an extreme case of this composite image includes an explicitly displayed, muscularly developed body, a flannel shirt, a leather vest, denim or leather pants, construction or cowboy boots. (p. 95)

17   Though perhaps less in vogue now, the hyper-masculine male look is still a symbolic type that some gay males employ. At first, I described these men as "bears," a more masculine type of gay male, but Julian corrected me and said that perhaps I was referring to something more like a butch. Julian thought that perhaps butch gay males care about their appearance and attempt to look masculine while bears don't really care about their appearance at all, and are more like the general straight male.

BEYOND GAYDAR   7

Julian's uncertainty about what exactly the hyper-masculine gay man would be called perhaps reflects current fashion. With the rise of more males in high fashion, the advent of television programs such as *Queer Eye for the Straight Guy*, and the heterosexual adaptation of the homosexual stereotype, or the "metrosexual," it seems that the bear style has fallen out of favor. It seems that now, instead of taking its fashion cues from the heterosexual world, homosexuals are creating styles that are being used by the world of high fashion and by straight people, who dress more in the mainstream. Julian expressed this concern:

> Me and some of my friends were talking and we were mad because we feel that straight people are stealing our stuff, like have you noticed the guys wear-ing pink shirts? Yeah, I just don't think they have a right to do that. Like my friends and I were joking that we might go up to one of these guys and be like, "You better have put that in the laundry with something red," you know like it was white before.

There is a feeling of resentment within the gay community that symbols are being appropriated by the larger population. In *Gays, Lesbians, and Consumer Behavior* (1996), Wardlow explains the cause of this resentment:

> When the symbolism of the community becomes framed as the basis for a target market from an "outside" perspective, the styles become divorced of the meanings they once held . . . and the style takes on new or more vague meanings. Based on the perspectives expressed in our interviews, the issue is not so much that meaning has become diluted or that a symbol has been stolen, as it is that manufacturers are selling the product as "cool" or "hip" without reference to its meaning. (pp. 99–100)

18

19

20   The manufacturing world is taking symbols highly popularized in the gay community and making them available for the mainstream, for example, the pink shirts that Julian cited which are becoming increasingly popular with heterosexual males.

21   Appealing to both a homosexual and a heterosexual (or perhaps metrosexual) audience is a good strategy for a clothing manufacturer; it can target two highly valuable markets at once. Based on my research, it's obvious that no other company does this better than Abercrombie and Fitch, as every interviewee cited the popular clothing company and its ubiquity among gay males. This leads me to the associated stereotypes of "flamer" and "Abercrombie bitch." Both of these types would wear Abercrombie and Fitch clothing, but the flamer would not wear it exclusively. These two types would perhaps, if we could put all the different gay styles on a spectrum, fall closer to femininity than butch or bear would.

22   What happens when place, action, and personal style all fail to disclose a man's sexual orientation, or when one of these categories is missing or fragmentary? Then clues can be found in personal taste, or habitus.

Subtle Clues in Personal Taste

23   Among the gay men I interviewed, I found that there is a distinct musical taste that gay males recognize is characteristically gay. I focused on musical taste because my interviewees discussed it the most when I brought up gay preferences in things other than clothing. During the group interview, I asked them to comment on gay musical taste. Jeff mentioned that "they all listened to techno" and expressed his exasperation over it. They cited Barbara Streisand as gay music. Steven stressed that, "You can't be gay and not have Cher."

24   So how could musical taste signal sexual orientation? It's difficult to imagine such a situation when place, action, and personal style would fail to show sexual

BEYOND GAYDAR   9

orientation. Personal taste might be a more cultivated part of the gay habitus, one which would be formed later after the other qualifications were met, and therefore would not be present without the other gay qualities. In other words, musical taste cannot be seen as only a signal to other gay men of a man's orientation. For example, a man who contradicted the other gay qualities regarding place, action, and personal style would probably not be viewed by the others as gay, if he simply expressed an affection for alternative music.

Conclusions

In interviewing four gay males in Boise, Idaho, over a period of a month, I saw   25
some general patterns emerge. I discovered that the most importance in discovering sexual orientation was placed on the actual location where a man was seen. Behaviors and movements were also highly important, though being in a gay location might outweigh any straight symbolism that a certain man would possess, e.g., Julian's experience of assuming a man in a gay bar was gay, when in reality he was straight. Clothing can also be a signal to other males of sexual orientation, but it is not as telling as place and action. Personal tastes in things like music are less of a signal of sexual orientation and more of a cultivated gay taste.

In concluding my research, I also should point out that these things   26
I have observed have merely scratched the surface of gay male identification. I do not even attempt to explain verbal behavior and its relation to nonverbal clues. I did not consider hearsay among the gay community or when gay males have simply identified themselves verbally. I do not assume that these are the only ways that gay males identify each other or that they are the most commonly used. I also do not want to trivialize intuition or conclude that there is absolutely nothing to "gaydar."

BEYOND GAYDAR   10

References

Cheseboro, J. W., & Klenk, K. L. (1981). Gay masculinity and the gay disco.
    In J. W. Cheseboro (Ed.), *Gayspeak: Gay male and lesbian communication*
    (pp. 87–103). New York: Pilgrim Press.

Green, R. J., & Ashmore, R. D. (1998). Taking and developing pictures in the
    head: Assessing the physical stereotypes of eight gender types. *Journal of
    Applied Social Psychology, 28*(17), 1609–1636.

Lawson, W. (November–December 2005). Gay men really do find it easier to spot
    other gays. *Psychology Today,* 30.

Martins, Y., Crabtree, C. R., Runyan, T., Vainius, A. A., & Wysocki, C. J. (2005).
    Preference for human body odors is influenced by gender and sexual
    orientation. *Psychological Science, 16*, 694–701.

Nicholas, C. L. (2004). Gaydar: Eye-gaze as identity recognition among gay men
    and lesbians. *Sexuality and Culture, 8* (Winter), 60–86.

Wardlow, D. L. (1996). *Gays, lesbians, and consumer behavior: Theory, practice, and
    research issues in marketing.* New York: Harrington Park Press.

(All references to "Julian," Steven, Jeff, or Aaron come from either participant observation
or interviews collected between November 3, 2004, and November 29, 2004.)

Using What You Have Learned

1. **Use sources effectively and control sources so they don't control you.** In college you'll be writing about subjects you know little about. You need to understand what you read, evaluate its relevance, assess its credibility, and then deploy it in your own work. That's a lot. But now you have some tools to avoid doing this, and one of the most important is writing *while* you collect and read information.

2. **Practice summarizing, paraphrasing, and quoting and apply these to your own work.** A study by the Citation Project found that students almost never summarize their sources. Instead, they do something called "patchwriting"—they essentially reproduce what they read, changing some words and maybe some grammatical structures. Patchwriting doesn't involve much critical understanding of the source. Of the three strategies discussed in this chapter—summary, paraphrasing, and quoting—summary may be the most academically useful because it requires you to understand and think about a source.

3. **Understand and identify plagiarism to avoid it in your own work.** It's no secret that plagiarism is a huge problem on college campuses—but the vast majority of it is *unintentional*. If you ever have any questions about what constitutes plagiarism, return to this chapter and reread the definition on page 281 in the "Avoiding Plagiarism" section, or ask your instructor.

4. **Cite sources using MLA and APA documentation styles.** Citation can be mind-numbing. But remember that it's not just about following rules; it's about telling a story. When you cite an author, you are identifying the source of the ideas that changed the way you think.

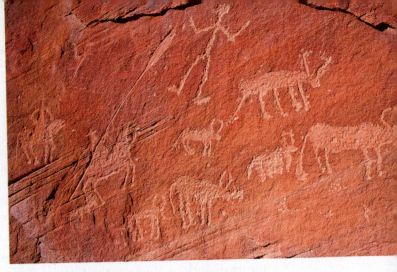

10

Re-Genre: Repurposing Your Writing for Multimedia Genres

Learning Objectives

In this chapter, you'll learn to

10.1 Analyze the rhetorical implications of repurposing a writing assignment into a different genre.

10.2 Develop rhetorical goals for a revision of an essay and use them to choose an appropriate multimodal genre.

10.3 Understand and apply the conventions of a multimodal genre.

An old professor of mine is retiring, and I was invited to write a short tribute. I did what I usually do: I sat down in front of my notebook and did some fastwriting to figure out what I might say, and then I started to craft a brief testimonial. "The best of my teachers I absorb into my own thinking in much the same way a successful transplant patient adapts to another's heart," I wrote. "They become a part of the way I think, and I find myself wondering from time to time whose idea was whose." This went on for a few paragraphs, and I was more or less pleased with it, when I received an e-mail. "We're going to do video tributes to Dr. Newkirk and show it at the conference," Barry wrote. "So send me a 30-second clip. I'll edit it as necessary." Certainly the easiest thing I could do, I initially thought, was to read my tribute in front of the camera. But this seemed off. Somehow the idea of reading my testimonial like a news anchor—a talking head—seemed inappropriate for the occasion and wouldn't adequately reflect how I feel about the man.

I don't know much about video. But I do know that it isn't a formal medium, and at the very least it demands that there is something to *see,* and watching me read a testimonial wouldn't be much to look at.

The problem I faced after Barry sent me his e-mail is exactly the challenge you'll explore in this chapter: How do you take something you've written and *re-purpose* it into another genre for a different audience and occasion? Actually, this is something we do all the time. Imagine, for example, that you wrote a narrative essay in English that you're really proud of, and at dinner that night you want to tell your partner the story. Without the text, you have to somehow capture in speech what you wrote. Since we're all practiced talkers, you intuitively know that you will tell this story not just with words but also with gestures. You might move in a little closer to emphasize a particularly poignant moment in your story, and change the register of your voice. What you're attempting to do is go from one mode of communication—a written text—to another—speech—and in the process you make adjustments in both the content of the message and its delivery. You are *repurpos-ing* your narrative essay in a different mode for a different rhetorical occasion: an informal conversation over the dinner table with someone you like and trust.

While this move might be a fairly common occurrence in our everyday lives, we rarely think much about what it demands, and this is especially true when we take something we've written and try to adapt it to other rhetorical situations. For example,

- When you shift from a written text to one that uses other modes—video, graphics, sound, and so on—how does that change the writing?
- What seems fundamentally different about writing in multimedia genres?
- If the choice of medium is yours, how do you choose the *right* form into which to repurpose your writing? What rhetorical considerations—purpose, audience, and message—might help in making that choice?

Then there's the question you might be asking yourself at this moment: Why would I want to experiment with repurposing a writing assignment in the first place?

10.1

Analyze the rhetorical implications of repurposing a writing assignment into a different genre.

What Writers Can Learn from Re-Genre: Knowledge Transfer

Practicing re-genre as a deep revision strategy in this class is useful to you as a writer. First, it builds your rhetorical muscle. Whenever you shift from one rhetorical situation to another, you have to reconsider all the elements that will make your message effective: What is my purpose in this situation, who is my audience, what do they know and what do they need to know about my topic, what do I want them to do? The rhetorical implications of this shift in situation become even more dramatic when you're remaking the *same material* for a different audience. In this case, though, you're not only shifting audiences, you're shifting genres. What does this mean?

The word "form" is often used interchangeably with "genre." That's okay, except that it implies that genre is merely a container into which your pour content, and like plaster in a mold, that content takes the shape of the form it's in. But genre isn't simply a container. It actively interacts with the content, changing the material it holds, and in turn being changed by the material. More important, though, is that the metaphor of form implies that genre is not only inert but opaque—and who can see through a plaster mold? The real power of genre is that it is something *through which we see* the things that interest us. It mediates our relationship to those things, changing what we notice. So when you're repurposing, say, a written proposal (Chapter 5) on campus sustainability to turn it into a video public service announcement, you'll return to the topic with new eyes. Suddenly, you'll see the visual possibilities of a chart in your written proposal that illustrates food waste at the campus cafeteria. Might the waste be dramatized by filming people throwing food into garbage bins, and editing the video so that this action is quickly replayed over and over again in a ten-second clip?

Rather than just talk about this shifting in the abstract, I'll tell you a re-genre story about one of my students.

Transfer from Blog Essay to Podcast: A Case Study

Andrea is a blogger, something that she describes as a form of "essaying" (see Chapter 3) that helps her to figure out what she thinks and feels, although sometimes, she says, "I don't hit the mark." In the midst of a breakup with her boyfriend, Andrea stumbled onto a box of old photographs in her garage, including some pictures of Jon, an old high school flame. This coincidental convergence of events—the abrupt end of a current relationship and the nostalgic recollection of an old one—naturally inspired a blog post that explored a familiar story: "the love that got away." But it had a contemporary twist. Andrea did what many of us do these days when we think of an old friend or lover: She looked on Facebook to see where Jon is and what he is doing now. The writing became not just a meditation on "the love that got away" theme but on how social media have turned this searching into a peculiar nostalgic exercise, one that involves sending out the hounds to pick up the scent of old lovers on Facebook. Andrea wrote the essay and posted the blog.

That might have been the end of it, but then Andrea thought that the essay might lend itself nicely to a podcast (or radio essay), a form that she had experimented with in several of my classes. In some ways, it was a logical rhetorical move. The blog, like the personal essay, establishes a relatively intimate relationship with its audience. The radio essay is intimate, too. The narrator's voice enters listeners' private worlds, much like a good friend does. But Andrea knew enough about this re-genre to know that it would change the original, written text in some basic ways. First, imagine the dramatic change in the rhetorical situation between a text that will be read and one that will only be heard once. With a written text, we can re-read, circling back to make sure that we understand. In an audio essay, we can't and this challenges the writer of an audio essay to use language that is engaging, clear, and memorable. There are also implications for the structure of the work. Information has to be arranged so it is easy to follow. In addition, this is a genre that exploits sound in ways that written texts can't—along with the spoken voice, with all of its emotional range and nuance, audio essays can include music tracks, ambient sound, and even interview clips.

Keeping all of this in mind, Andrea wrote a new version of her blog as a radio essay script, and when I asked her how this repurposing changed things, she told me about how the new genre changed the *structure* of her blog:

- She revised the beginning. In the original blog essay, the opening line was "My name is Andrea, and I suffer from nostalgia." She realized that this lacked tension and interest, things that are essential to catch a listener's ear, so she rewrote the opening to begin with this sentence: "Jon Berger will never be my husband."

- Andrea also realized that the structure of the original essay, which relied largely on exposition, simply wouldn't work well in an audio essay. Exposition isn't easy for listeners to retain, and it slows things down. The obvious solution, she thought, was to rewrite the original to emphasize the story, exploiting anecdotes rather than a lot of explanation.

Andrea also told me that the re-genre forced her to reconsider the *language and syntax* of the original blogged essay. Two things became obvious to her immediately: The language should be relatively simple and exclude words that we tend not to use in speech, and it must also be "punchy." "In writing, it's easy to add a long string of introductory clauses," Andrea said. "But in a radio essay you need an actor and an action, actor/action/actor/action." She offered this example:

Original essay: "I don't know what it feels like for most scorned lovers when they find their boyfriends-of-the-past hiding in a box in their garage, but for me, it was fun and sad and unnerving and uncomfortable." While there is a subject in the beginning, we don't get to the meat of the sentence until "but for me, it was fun and sad and...."

Radio essay: "When I think of Jon now, I get a lump in my throat."

All writing has qualities of speech, something that at times we describe as "voice," but it's also true that writing is *not* speech. An audio essay, however, encourages writers to move more towards the qualities of speech in their prose (simplicity and punchiness), *and* to exploit the sound of their voices for rhetorical effect. Here's what Andrea said about this: "I think the coolest aspect of the audio essay is the listener can hear emotion in your voice. They can hear exactly how your voice wavers and they can hear the rawness that doesn't necessarily come across in writing. They can hear the inflection and tone and pauses: that's one of the best parts. In this piece, I think you'd hear a bit of heartbreak come through, but also a good sense of embarrassment at the realization that I was stalking someone on Facebook because it was like this nostalgia infection I had contracted."

"Re-genre" is an act of imagination. But it is also a calculated move that requires an analysis of the genre's conventions, and the rhetorical implications of the shift in purpose and audience. In the sections that follow, I'll walk you through some of these calculations, beginning with a consideration of the "modes" of expression beyond written words that open new avenues for communication.

Beyond Words: Communicating in Other Modes

It's easy to forget, especially in the text-centric world of writing papers in college, that all writing is "multimodal"; we not only compose words but we design, often by habit, how they will look on the page. But even this is merely scratching the surface. The digital spaces in which we write these days make it possible to combine words with animated graphics, pictures, sound, and video. We can design brochures, posters, slide shows, and video trailers—genres that range from relatively static (little movement) to dynamic, all using a single device we can carry anywhere. The result, of course, is that there's a proliferation of multimedia everywhere we look, except perhaps in the one place we might most expect innovation: the college classroom. But that's changing. Not only are professors incorporating technology like video into classroom instruction, they're asking students to create multimedia projects as well. Writing may always be central to college assignments, but it is increasingly combined with other modes of expression.

What are these modes? In 1996, a group of international theorists convened in New London, Connecticut, to come up with language to describe the multiple literacies that students might need to develop for the twenty-first century. They came up with five basic modes in which we might communicate:

- Linguistic (i.e., writing)
- Visual (images but also things like graphic design and layout)
- Audio
- Spatial (physical spaces)
- Gestural (body language)

Most important of all, they concluded, is "multimodal" expression, or forms that combine more than one of these types of expression. It's not hard to see that human communication has always been a multimodal affair. What *is* different, however, is the range and accessibility of forms through which we can now communicate with one another; you'll experiment with these multimodal genres in this chapter.

The Problem of Definition

In the last few paragraphs, you encountered a scattering of terms—*form, genre, mode, multimodal, multimedia*—and before we go much further, let's tentatively agree on some definitions. But first, a basic problem: Some of these are contested concepts (none more than *genre*), and so whatever definitions we come up with will be necessarily inexact. I hope you'll revisit these definitions, particularly in the reflective writing you do in the course of this assignment, to explore how workable they are for you.

- **Form.** Often used interchangeably with *genre* (see the discussion of problems with that usage on page 348), form can also describe the structure of a composition.

- **Genre.** A loose category or classification of compositions that have "family resemblances"—similar aims, audiences, conventions, structures, and so on. For our purposes, however, a more rhetorical definition of genre seems best, one that is useful not just for describing the characteristics of a genre but also for describing what the genre can *do*. Theorist Carolyn Miller argues that genre is a rhetorical response to "recurrent situations." If the situation keeps coming up—say, the need to communicate using a limited number of characters about fast-breaking events to large numbers of people—then the response may become a genre, in this case a tweet. We learn to recognize both the recurring situations and the genre they demand. Keep in mind, though, that genres aren't necessarily stable; they change all the time.

- **Mode.** A particular way of communicating what we want to say. Modes include using writing, images, audio, and so on (see page 347).

- **Multimodal.** Using more than one mode to communicate meaning. This can be quite simple—combining written text with pictures—or quite complicated—a film that combines a written script, audio and visual elements, and gestures.

- **Multimedia.** This term is often used interchangeably with *multimodal*, and is more common outside of academia. The difference between multimedia and multimodal is subtle but significant.[1] When we talk about designing multimedia, we typically focus on the technical skills involved in production. The term implies a product focus. In contrast, multimodal is typically used to describe the *process* of designing a communication. Though we're all about examining the process of composing in *The Curious Writer,* I've decided to rely on the more familiar term "multimedia" rather than "multimodal" in this chapter.

---

[1] Lauer, Claire. "Contending with Terms: 'Multimodal' and 'Multimedia' in the Academic and Public Spheres." *Computers & Composition*, vol. 26, no. 4, Dec. 2009, pp. 225-39.

Re-Genre Is Deep Revision

This is a book about genres. For weeks now, you've drafted essays on some of the more common genres of writing inside school and out—personal essays, proposals, arguments, ethnographies, and so on. This is a chapter about genres, too, but this time you'll be *switching* genres as a revision strategy, one that in some ways radically shifts the way you see your topic, what you say about it, and also *how* you say it. In making this shift, there's an opportunity to learn a lot about two important things:

- **Rhetorical strategies for addressing big changes in purpose and audience.** These strategies include how to choose an appropriate genre and what that choice might mean about how you change the approach you took in the original writing assignment.

- **How genres differ.** Why does knowing that matter? Because we are all genre travelers. We do it every day, moving from e-mail to text message, from analytical essay in English to biology lab report, and from memorandum to PowerPoint presentation at work. Research on how we transfer knowledge from writing situation to writing situation suggests that genre knowledge is a particularly powerful vehicle for adapting to new types of writing and applying what we've already learned.

Genre as a Way of Knowing and Seeing

Taylor is interested in sports medicine, and last semester she wrote a research essay on the growing problem of concussions in team sports, especially their impact on women. She decided to re-genre her paper into an infographic, thinking that was the best way to tell the story of what happens to a young woman's brain when she's hit repeatedly in the head by a soccer ball. Since an infographic is a genre that combines text and image, Taylor had to reimagine a ten-page research paper as a visual story. In other words, she had to turn 2,000 words into a series of graphics with only 250 words. What did she see? A brain, of course, and a ball, and the story of what a brain looks like when it violently collides with a ball. In a way, this is the drama that was at the heart of those ten pages, but with all those words it wasn't easy to see. Taylor's switch to an infographic shifted her gaze and helped her to see the topic freshly.

Switching genres is a form of *reseeing*. Each genre provides us with a particular orientation towards the world, which is a powerful thing. For example, imagine that in an English class you are asked to write a paper that analyzes a short story. You wrote a lot of these kinds of papers in high school, and the genre that you might have used was the deductive, thesis-proof paper: thesis in the introduction, then a series of paragraphs that follow, each sporting a topic sentence that supports the thesis, and finally ending with a restatement of the thesis. The thesis-proof essay orients you and your reader towards the literary in a very particular way. Using this genre, as the theorist Keith Fort wrote, literature becomes, first and foremost, a "source of theses," a site to mine for main points. Imagine, as an alternative, writing about a literary text using a genre like the exploratory essay (see Chapter 3). Instead of beginning with the hunt for a point to prove, the essay genre urges the writer to begin with questions, to seek out what is complicated in the short story, and to use writing to sort out that complication. One genre prompts a writer to see a short story as a mine and the other to see it as a maze.

The implications of this shift in genres is even more profound when you're not going from one form of writing to another but from a form of writing that relies mostly on writing to a form of writing that uses multimedia. This is what Andrea learned when repurposing her blog as an audio essay and what Taylor learned when her research paper became an infographic.

Genre and Its Conventions

The optics of a magnifying glass and of a pair of binoculars limit their effectiveness to certain—and quite different—situations. One is for close work and the other for seeing from a distance. Similarly, genres are constructed to work best in certain situations and for particular purposes. One of the most useful kinds of genre knowledge is an awareness of these different conventions, and that awareness is something you've been practicing since the beginning of *The Curious Writer*. Your particular purpose in writing about a topic points the way to an appropriate form for exploring it and sharing your conclusions with others. The genre you choose, in turn, influences both how you see your topic and what approach you take to writing about it, from what kinds of evidence you use to how (and often where) you state your conclusions. The "Features of the Form" box in each assignment chapter helped you become aware of different genres' conventions. Many of these conventions arise from what an audience *expects* of a particular genre, including how it should be read and what its method of inquiry is.

For example, a podcast may begin as an essay that was intended to be read. But because a podcast is an audio genre meant to be *listened to* only once (and

Inquiring into the Details

Re-Genre and Re-Flect

Thinking about your thinking while doing this project will both maximize your learning and help you to transfer what you learn to other situations. Here are some things to think and write about:

1. *Your experience.* Tell the story of what you understood when you began the project and what you're starting to understand now. Update this narrative regularly.
2. *Rhetoric.* How does the shift in purpose and audience change things (e.g., language, treatment of topic, ethos/pathos/logos, approach to persuasion)?
3. *Genre.* What do you notice about how the genre shift influences how and what you see? Can you identify how "conventions" (e.g., rules of evidence, types of questions asked, voice, structure, roles of writer/designer and audience) change?

Write regularly about these (and other) questions.

never read), there are conventions to consider, things like repeating key lines and ideas for clarity, and using anecdotes to break up stretches of exposition so listeners stay tuned in. The speaking voice also plays a key role in this genre. While you may read a script, an authoritative monotone will not do; listeners expect some of the same things they experience in conversation—a sense of intimacy with the speaker, and evidence of feeling in the spoken words. These are all design considerations you'll consider for the genre you choose, but they grow from conventions that arise, in part, from what audiences *expect* from their prior experiences with that form. Once you choose a multimedia genre for this project, you'll do some quick research on the design conventions for the genre (see Exercise 10.2).

Re-Genre: The Assignment

You've considered a case study in re-genre, the modes of communication beyond writing, and some basic concepts about how genres work. But what exactly is your assignment in this chapter? (Your instructor may have other guidelines as well.)

1. You will choose a written assignment you completed earlier in the semester and revise it into a genre that uses *at least* one other mode of communication in addition to writing (audio, visual, spatial, gesture).

2. The choice of the new genre will be based on a rhetorical decision. You will define the purpose of the re-genre, and from this definition you will identify appropriate audiences for whom you can fulfill that purpose. This will in turn lead to the choice of the multimodal genre that is best for the project. In the "Planning the Re-Genre" section, we'll look more closely at how to do this rhetorical analysis, but for now, think of it this way: *What do I want a particular audience to think or do with respect to my topic? What form is best suited for accomplishing that goal?*

3. As part of the assignment, you will write about your experience with this kind of revision. (See "Inquiring into the Details: Re-Genre and Re-Flect" for questions to explore.)

Now for a reality check: There is too little time in a course like this to become an expert on any multimedia genre. (It's hard enough to develop expertise in writing in a single course, even though writing is something we've all done much of our lives.) But this assignment is a great learning opportunity—you'll develop new perspectives on revision, genre, and rhetoric—and in the process be introduced to some powerful new ways to communicate. That's why the writing you do about working on this project is as important as the multimedia project you design.

10.2
Develop rhetorical goals for a revision of an essay and use them to choose an appropriate multimedia genre.

Planning the Re-Genre

This assignment begins with a plan that is built around a clear goal. In general, what do you want your re-genre *to do*? More specifically, which of the following rhetorical goals might the re-genre help you accomplish?

1. To dramatize a problem or idea for certain audiences. To encourage certain audiences *to feel* something.

2. To change behavior. To persuade certain audiences *to do* something.

3. To inform a particular audience about an aspect of a topic *in a timely way.* When and where might the information be most persuasive or most relevant?

If you're thinking about a re-genre of earlier writing assignments that are more or less argumentative—review, proposal, argument, research essay, analysis, ethnography—it's likely that you won't have much trouble applying any of these goals. But what about the less explicitly argumentative forms like the profile and the personal essay? These writing assignments often lend themselves to dramatizing an idea or problem (goal #1) by using story to move an audience emotionally.

Tying goals to particular audiences will give any re-genre more rhetorical power. Use Table 10.1 as a way to start thinking about this.

Applying Rhetorical Goals

This semester, Rebecca wrote a research essay on the relationship between the emotional toll on nurses working in labor and delivery and professional burnout. Her essay celebrated the role of compassion and courage in good nursing practice but also identified some of the emotional costs to the practitioner. It's easy to imagine several purposes of a re-genre that involves both timely information and behavior change. Would it be helpful to design a communication to nurses that helps them to identify the causes of burnout and how to avoid them? Alternatively, should patients be better informed about the roles that nurses play in the birthing experience, and is there a time when and place where this information might be most persuasive (birthing classes)? In another of my classes, Emery wrote a personal essay that begins, "I hate weddings." The piece goes on to explore her experiences and observations at a recent wedding in which she noted the many "contradictions" that the ritual entails. How might she re-genre this essay? I'm not sure that she would want to persuade people not to attend weddings—good luck with that—but might she use other modes to *dramatize* the idea that weddings are rich in contradictions?

Table 10.1

Goal	What?	Who?
Dramatize	What dilemma, idea, problem?	Audiences who might be most receptive to the story?
Persuade	To do what? What action or behavior?	Audiences whose action on the problem is needed?
Inform	About what? What information will be most relevant and useful?	Audiences who can *use* the information?

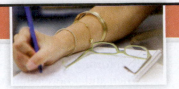

Inquiring into the Details

Levels of Content

Graphic designer Bill Shander argues that an essential part of design is thinking about how much information you'll include, and this depends on the main purpose of your communication. He believes there are essentially "four levels of content," and these levels should prove useful when thinking about your re-genre:

1. *Level One:* This level uses the least amount of information because it's an "attention grabber" meant to dramatize a topic (rhetorical goal #1) and help it to find an audience. A short video or photo essay might be a great genre for level one information.
2. *Level Two:* Once you've got the attention of an audience, some of them will be more interested in your topic, though not yet particularly invested in learning a lot more. They'd be game for a brief conversation, the kind that you facilitate with a blog or an infographic, something with a little more information.
3. *Level Three:* Audiences that are engaged with a topic will be actively information-seeking. You can provide information with multimedia genres like brochures or slide presentations.
4. *Level Four:* There are people who are passionate information-seekers on a topic. They're convinced it's important and relevant and would gladly dig into a web page with multiple links and documents.

A nearly irresistible temptation is to think about the appeal of doing one multimedia genre or another ("I want to do a podcast!") before defining your purpose. But this would be a mistake. Your choice of multimedia genre should be driven by your rhetorical goals. Keeping these goals in mind, make a preliminary pitch (written or verbal) about the writing assignment you'd like to re-genre and why.

Exercise 10.1

Re-Genre Pitch

If you want to sell a film idea, you make a pitch. Do the same for the choice of genre you made to repurpose your writing assignment. Here are the key parts your re-genre pitch should address:

10.3

Understand and apply the conventions of a multimodal genre.

1. What earlier writing assignment would you like to re-genre? Why? What is it about this topic that lends itself to a multimodal approach?
2. Which of the three rhetorical goals seems most relevant? Develop brief answers to the questions for each relevant goal (see Table 10.1 on page 355).
3. Make a case for your choice of a multimodal genre that will best meet these goals. In your pitch, explain how the genre is rhetorically appropriate for

your topic, your aims, and your potential audiences. What genres should you consider? Table 10.2 summarizes some of the multimedia genres my students have used and some rhetorical characteristics of each genre.

Table 10.2

Multimedia Genre	Typical Content Level (see p. 356)	Typical Rhetorical Goals (see Table 10.1)
Slide presentation (PowerPoint, etc.)	Level three	Persuade and inform
Infographic	Level one or two	Dramatize and persuade
Brochure	Level three	Persuade and inform
Conference Poster	Level three and four	Persuade and inform
Photographic Essay	Level one	Dramatize
Radio essay or podcast	Level two	Dramatize and persuade
Web page	Level three or four	Persuade and inform
Video Public Service Announcement	Level one or two	Dramatize

Exercise 10.2

Genre Analysis: Conventions and Best Practices

In a relatively short time, you will need to acquire enough knowledge about your chosen genre to plan, design, and produce it. This exercise should help. Unless your instructor tells you otherwise, this is a class presentation. Begin by searching online (or elsewhere) to find at least **three** examples of the genre you've chosen for this project. Try to find extremes—for example, a bad slide presentation and a really good one—because the comparison can be instructive. (For some of the genres, these aren't hard to find. Just search for "best" and "worst" or "reviews of.")

STEP ONE: Draw comparisons.

1. **Purpose and audience.** Do the purposes and audiences of each example differ? What are the implications of those differences in terms of design?

2. **Conventions.** Ignoring the differences between the examples for a moment, what features do they seem to have *in common*? Be specific.

3. **Rhetorical effectiveness.** Keeping audience and purpose in mind, which of the examples do you think is most rhetorically effective and why?

STEP TWO: Which example seems best? Make the case in a class presentation using the examples you chose.

Analyzing Your Examples

- **Movement.** How is the example designed to guide the audience through the material?
- **Modes.** What is the balance between different modes of communication? Which does the example seem to emphasize?
- **Ethos, pathos, logos.** Which does the example emphasize?
- **Content.** What level of content (1–4) does the example emphasize?
- **Usability.** How well does the example encourage users to interact with the content?
- **Best practices.** Based on what you've learned about the genre, how well does the example reflect the techniques considered by experts to be the prevailing "standard"?

Reflecting on Re-Genre

One of the reasons you're taking this course is that it will help you to use what you've learned in other writing situations, and you're likely to have plenty of those both in college and after. You've done a lot of reflective writing in *The Curious Writer*, and one reason is this: There's growing research that suggests that we *transfer* knowledge from one situation to another, related situation if we pause to consider what we're learning and how we're learning it. As I noted in the beginning of the chapter, we're all genre travelers, so what you learn by repurposing an earlier writing assignment should prove helpful if you take the time to reflect on the experience. End your experiment in re-genre by writing about how your thinking has changed, what you've learned, and how you might apply that learning in the future. Return to "Inquiring into the Details: Re-Genre and Re-Flect" on page 353 for some ideas about how to do this metacognitive work.

You can reflect on what you've done narratively—the story of your experience—but look for opportunities in telling your story to do what narrative essayists often do: Look back from time to time when remembering what happened to talk about what you know *now* that wasn't apparent to you *then*. You might also consider reflecting on what you've learned by returning to some key concepts we've touched on again and again, including genre, rhetoric, and revision. If the theories of transfer are true, then all of this thinking about your thinking in this assignment—and all the others in this book—will make you not only a curious writer, but a flexible and imaginative one, too.

Using What You Have Learned

1. **Analyze the rhetorical implications of repurposing a writing assignment into a different genre.** We are all genre travelers, often communicating the same information in different ways to different audiences. In this chapter, you were encouraged to do this consciously, with an awareness of how a shift like this changes the message, the messenger, and the messenger's purpose. This is knowledge that you can apply often. For instance, in other classes you might be asked to develop an oral presentation for a written assignment; at work you might be asked to take an annual report and rewrite it as web content; and in life, you might turn a late-night conversation into a podcast.

2. **Develop rhetorical goals for a revision of an essay and use them to choose an appropriate multimodal genre.** Throughout *The Curious Writer* I've challenged you to build a writing assignment around a specific purpose, one that in an inquiry-based project you often *discover as you write*. In this chapter, I asked you to do this up front—to define your rhetorical goals first and then to use them to make choices about what you will write and in what form. A lifetime of school writing that is less focused on discovery than on reporting what you already know has prepared you well for this. But I hope what you learned here is how powerful a change in rhetorical goals can be as "deep" revision, transforming your work and making it available to new audiences by exploiting new modes of communication and new genres.

3. **Understand and apply the conventions of a multimodal genre.** In a way, this chapter works from a crazy premise: In a few weeks' time, you will take something you've written and transform it into a multimedia genre with which you may have no experience. Not only do you have to try to revise your writing, you also have to engage in a crash course on design. While the result often isn't polished (how could it be?), what you learn in the process is powerful: new revision strategies and something about how genres work. But most important, you flex your rhetorical muscles, and these muscles will make you a better communicator, one who can slide from one rhetorical situation to the next appropriately and effectively.

11

Revision Strategies

Learning Objectives

In this chapter, you'll learn to

11.1 Understand the meaning—and value—of revision and apply it to your own work when appropriate.

11.2 Recognize five types of revision and apply the most relevant strategies to a particular draft.

Why Revise?

The motive for revision is like a photographer's inclination to take more than one shot—both writer and photographer know not to trust their first look at something.

One draft and done. That was Shauna's motto about revision, and when she said it nearly everyone in the class nodded. "I know I should revise but usually I write papers at the last minute, so I don't really have the time," she added.

Surprisingly, one of the least discussed topics in writing classes is *time*. Perhaps no other factor influences a writer's success more than having the time to do the work, and the academic culture doesn't provide a lot of time to write. You may have multiple writing assignments at the same time in different classes, with deadlines that may fall on the same day. Getting a single draft done by the due date, much less a revision, seems like a major accomplishment. And in some classes (though not this one), it isn't even clear that instructors expect students to revise their work before they hand it in. So why bother revising?

Before I make a pitch for revision, let's be clear on a few things. Revision isn't a virtue, nor is it always a necessary step in the writing

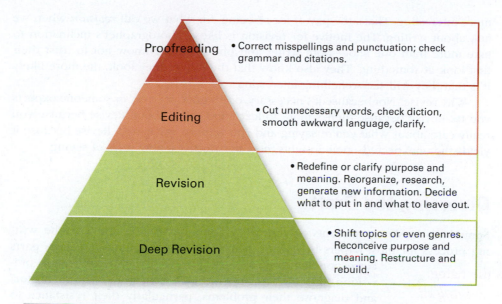

Figure 11.1   Four levels of rewriting

process; it also doesn't always occur at the end of the process. In addition, revision is more than "fixing" things. In Figure 11.1, you can see that "proofreading" and "editing," while very important parts of rewriting, may not involve revision. They are, instead, activities that help burnish the surface of prose and make it easier to see the subject underneath it.

Revision involves "reseeing." You started with a certain idea about what you were writing and now you realize, no, that's not it at all. Or perhaps when you began writing, you had one inquiry question, but the draft now tells you that another, better question is lurking there. "Deep revision" might lead you to start all over, or shift subjects entirely, or even switch genres. Sometimes revision helps you to resee not just the subject but the draft itself: It's apparent that the beginning is all wrong, or that essential information is missing, or that the strongest part of the paper is something you can build on in the next draft.

One of the most powerful analogies for revision comes from photography, a word from Greek that means "light writing." Typically, most of us take only one picture of a subject, even in the digital age, when it's cheap and easy to shoot multiple images. In other words: one draft and done. But what would happen if you took ten pictures of the same subject—say, an old wagon in a field—varying angle, distance, and time of day? Your first shot would likely be the most obvious image, the one everyone takes of the wagon. But by the fourth or fifth image, you have to strain a bit to find a fresh shot. Maybe you lie on the ground and shoot upwards, or you try a close-up of the wooden wheel in the evening when the light is thick. The more shots you take, the more likely it is that you start seeing your subject in a way that you hadn't initially seen it. The wagon becomes infinitely more interesting. That's the payoff for reseeing, for what we call *revision* when we talk about writing. The motive for revision is like a photographer's inclination to take more than one shot—both writer and photographer know not to trust their first look at something. They also know that the longer they look, the more likely it is that they will see something interesting.

Why revise? Not because it's necessary, or it's good for you, or someone expects you to. Revise because there's more to learn and think about. Revise because you really care about what you're saying and you want to say it well. Revise because it yields the unexpected—new insights, new perspectives, new ways of seeing.

Divorcing the Draft

Sometimes I ask my students to generalize about how they approach the writing process for most papers by having them divide a continuum into three parts

Revision, as the name implies, is a reseeing of the paper's topic and the writer's initial approach to it in the draft.

corresponding to how much time, roughly, they devote to prewriting, drafting, and rewriting. Then I play "writing doctor" and diagnose their problems, particularly their resistance to revision. Figure 11.2 depicts a typical example of the writing processes of most of my first-year students.

The writing process shown in Figure 11.2 obviously invests lots of time in the drafting stage and very little time in prewriting or rewriting. For most of my students, this means toiling over the first draft, starting and then starting over, carefully hammering every word into place. Strong resistance to revision is a typical symptom of students who use this process. It's easy to imagine why. If you invest all that time in the first draft, trying to make it as good as you can, you'll be too exhausted to consider a revision, delusional about the paper's quality, or, most likely, so invested in the draft's approach to the topic that revision seems impossible or a waste of time.

There also is another pattern among resistant revisers. Students who tend to spend a relatively long time on the prewriting stage also struggle with revision. My theory is that some of these writers resist revision as a final stage in the process

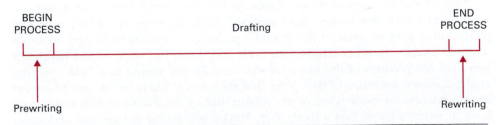

Figure 11.2   How some writers who resist revision typically divide their time among the three elements of the writing process: prewriting, drafting, and rewriting. The most time is devoted to writing the first draft, but not much time is given to prewriting or rewriting.

because *they already practiced some revision at the beginning of the process*. We often talk about revision as occurring only after you've written a draft, which of course is a quite sensible idea. But the process of revision is an effort to *resee* a subject, to circle it with questions, to view it from fresh angles; and many of the open-ended writing methods we've discussed in *The Curious Writer* certainly involve revision. Fastwriting, clustering, listing, and similar invention techniques all invite the writer to resee. Armed with these discoveries, some writers may be able to write fairly strong first drafts.

What is essential, however—whether you revise at the beginning of the writing process or, as most writers do, after you craft the draft—is achieving some separation from what you initially thought, what you initially said, and how you said it. To revise well, writers must divorce the draft.

Strategies for Divorcing the Draft

You can do some things to make separation from your work easier, and spending less time on the first draft and more time on the revision process is one of them. But aside from writing fast drafts, what are other strategies for reseeing a draft that already has a hold on you?

11.1
Understand the meaning—and value—of revision and apply it to your own work when appropriate.

1. **Take some time.** Absolutely the best remedy for overcoming revision resistance is setting the draft aside for a week or more. Professional writers, in fact, may set a piece aside for several years and then return to it with a fresh, more critical perspective. Students simply don't have that luxury. But if you can take a week or a month—or even a day—the break from looking at the work is almost always worth it.

2. **Attack the draft physically.** A cut-and-paste revision that reduces a draft to pieces is often enormously helpful, because you're no longer confronted with the familiar full draft, a version that may have cast a spell on you. By dismembering the draft, you can examine the smaller fragments more critically. How does each piece relate to the whole? Might there be alternative structures? What about gaps in information? (See Revision Strategy 11.18 later in this chapter for a useful cut-and-paste exercise.)

3. **Put it away.** Years ago I wrote a magazine article about alcoholism. It was about twenty-five pages long and it wasn't very good. I read and reread that draft, completely puzzled about how to rewrite it. One morning, I woke up and vowed I would read the draft just once more, then put it away in a drawer and start all over again, trusting that I would remember what was important. The result was much shorter and much better. In fact, I think it's the best essay I've ever written. Getting a troublesome draft out of sight—literally—may be the best way to find new ways to see it.

4. **Ask readers to respond.** Bringing other people's eyes and minds to your work allows you to see your drafts through perspectives other than your own. Other people have a completely different relationship with your writing

than you do. They will see what you don't. They easily achieve the critical distance that you are trying to cultivate when you revise.

5. **Write different leads.** The nonfiction writer John McPhee once talked about beginnings as the hardest thing to write. He described a lead as a "flashlight that shines down into the story," illuminating where the draft is headed. Imagine, then, the value of writing a new beginning, or even several new beginnings; each may point the next draft in a slightly different direction, perhaps one that you hadn't considered in your first draft.

6. **Conduct research.** One of the central themes of *The Curious Writer* is that research isn't a separate activity, but rather a source of information that can enrich almost any kind of writing. Particularly in genres such as the personal essay, in which the writer's voice, perspective, and experience dominate the draft, listening to the voices and knowledge of others can deepen and shift the writer's thinking and perspectives.

7. **Read aloud.** I always ask students in workshop groups to read their drafts aloud to each other. I do this for several reasons, but the most important is the effect that *hearing* a draft has on the writer's relationship to it. In a sense, we often hear a draft in our heads as we compose it or reread it, but when we read the words aloud, the draft comes alive as something separate from the writer. As the writer listens to herself—or listens to someone else read her prose—she may cringe at an awkward sentence, suddenly notice a leap in logic, or recognize the need for an example. Try reading your draft aloud to yourself, and the same thing may happen.

8. **Write in your journal.** One of the strategies you can use to divorce the draft is to return to your notebook and fastwrite about what you might do to improve the piece. You can do this by asking yourself questions about the draft and then—through fastwriting—attempt to answer them. The method can help you see a new idea, which may become key to the structure of your next draft. Too often we see the journal exclusively as a prewriting tool, but it can be useful throughout the writing process, particularly when you need to think about ways to solve a problem as you revise.

Later in this chapter, we'll build on some of these basic strategies by using specific revision methods that may work with particular kinds of writing and with drafts that have particular problems. All of these methods encourage a separation between the writer and his or her draft and rely on that critical distance to be effective.

11.2

Recognize five types of revision and apply the most relevant strategies to a particular draft.

Five Categories of Revision

The following kinds of writers are typically the ones who most need to revise:

1. Writers of fast drafts
2. Writers who compose short drafts
3. Writers who indulge in creative, but not critical, thinking

4. Writers who rarely go past their initial way of seeing things

5. Writers who have a hard time imagining a reader other than themselves

6. Writers who rely on limited sources of information

7. Writers who still aren't sure what they're trying to say

8. Writers who haven't found their own way of saying what they want to say

9. Writers who haven't delivered on their promises

10. Writers who think their draft is already "perfect"

These are the usual suspects whose drafts need revision, but there are many others. In general, if you think there's more to think about, more to learn, more to say, and better ways to say it, then revision is your route to surprise and discovery. Most writers agree that rewriting is a good idea but don't know where to start.

Problems in drafts vary enormously but tend to involve concerns in five general areas: purpose, meaning, information, structure, and clarity and style. Here are some typical reader responses to drafts with each kind of problem:

1. **Problems with Purpose**

   - "I don't know why the writer is writing this paper."
   - "The beginning of the essay seems to be about one thing, and the rest of it is about several others."
   - "I think there are about three different topics in the draft. Which one do you want to write about?"
   - "So what?"

2. **Problems with Meaning**

   - "I can't tell what the writer is trying to say in the draft."
   - "There doesn't seem to be a point behind all of this."
   - "I think there's a main idea, but there isn't much information on it."
   - "I thought the thesis was saying something that's already pretty obvious."

3. **Problems with Information**

   - "Parts of the draft seemed pretty vague or general."
   - "I couldn't really *see* what you were talking about."
   - "That could use more explanation."
   - "It seemed like you needed some more facts to back up your point."
   - "It needs more detail."

4. **Problems with Structure**

   - "I couldn't quite follow your thinking in the last few pages."
   - "I was confused about when this happened."
   - "I understood your point, but I couldn't figure out what this part had to do with it."
   - "The draft doesn't really flow very well."

5. **Problems with Clarity and Style**

   - "This seems a little choppy."

- "You need to explain this better. I couldn't quite follow what you were saying in this paragraph."
- "This sentence seems really awkward to me."
- "This doesn't have a strong voice."

Problems with Purpose

A draft that answers the *So what?* question is a draft with a purpose. Often enough, however, writers' intentions aren't all that clear to readers, who then don't have a strong incentive to keep reading.

It's a little like riding a tandem bike. The writer sits up front and steers while the reader occupies the seat behind, obligated to pedal but with no control over where the bike goes. As soon as the reader senses that the writer isn't steering anywhere in particular, the reader will get off the bike; why do all that work if the bike seems to be going nowhere?

Frequently when you begin writing about something, you don't have any idea where you're headed; that's exactly *why* you're writing about the subject in the first place. When you write such discovery drafts, revision often begins by looking for clues about your purpose. What you learn then becomes a key organizing principle for the next draft and for trying to clarify this purpose for your readers. The first question, therefore, is one writers must answer for themselves: "Why am I writing this?" Of course, if it's an assignment, it may be hard to get past the easy answer—"Because I have to"—but if the work is going to be any good, there must be a better answer than that. Whether your topic is your choice or your instructor's, you have to find your own reason to write about it, and what you discover will become an answer to your bike partner's nagging question, yelled into the wind from the seat behind you: "If I'm going to pedal this hard, you'd better let me know where we're going."

When we write, we may begin with wide-ranging motives: to explore, to argue, to analyze, to explain, or to reflect. Each of these motives is often associated with a particular genre. But in each draft, no matter what the genre, we also have narrower purposes. For example, you might want to explore the idea of gender roles in video gaming, or make a claim about the reasons behind climate change denial. In your first draft, you might be able to identify your wide-ranging motive behind writing, but you need to make your narrower purposes clear when you revise your draft.

Revision Strategy 11.1: Dialogue with Dave

Dave is a good sort. He's curious about the world and a pretty good listener. But his patience isn't endless. Imagine that you're in a conversation with Dave about the topic of your essay. Naturally, one of the first things he wants know is why you're writing about this topic in the first place. Write your half of the following dialogue in a Word document or in your notebook:

Dave	You
Alrighty then, what exactly is this draft on? What were you writing about?	
Hmmm…. That's interesting. What surprised you most when you wrote about that topic?	
Okay. Cool. But what I really want to know is why I should care about this as much as you do. Why is it important? Why does it matter? What does it have to do with someone like me?	

This exercise has helped you to think through your answer to that vital question that all writing must answer: So what? Examine your answers to Dave's questions, particularly the questions in the third box. Somewhere in your answers, do you see a clear statement of your purpose? Can you include that purpose somewhere near the beginning of your draft so that readers like Dave know where you're headed and why?

Revision Strategy 11.2: What Do You Want to Know About What You've Learned?

Because inquiry-based writing is usually driven by questions rather than answers, one way to discover your purpose in a sketch or draft is to generate a list of questions your topic raises for you. Of course, you hope that one of those questions might lead to your purpose in the next draft. Try the following steps with a draft that needs a stronger sense of purpose.

1. Choose a draft or sketch you'd like to revise, and reread it.
2. On the back of the manuscript, craft an answer to the following question: *What do I understand about this topic now that I didn't understand before I started writing about it?*
3. Next, if you can, build a list of questions—perhaps new ones—that this topic raises for you. Make this list as long as you can, and don't censor yourself (see "One Student's Response").
4. Use one or more of the questions as a prompt for a fastwrite. Follow your writing to see where it leads and what it might suggest about new directions for the revision.

One Student's Response

Julia's Draft

What do I understand about this topic now that I didn't understand before I started writing about it?

After writing this essay, I understand more clearly that there's a relationship between a girl's eating disorders and how her father treated her as a child.

LIST OF QUESTIONS

- Why the father and not the mother?

- What is it about father/daughter relationships that makes daughters so vulnerable to believing in so-called "ideal" feminine body types?

- Is a father's influence on a girl's body image greater at certain ages or stages in her life?

- How can a father be more informed about his impact on his daughter's body image?

5. If you can't think of any questions, or find that you didn't learn much from writing about the topic (step 2), you still have several options. One is to abandon the draft altogether. Is it possible that this topic simply doesn't interest you anymore? If abandoning the draft isn't possible, then you need to find a new angle from which to write about it. Try Revision Strategy 11.3.

Revision Strategy 11.3: Finding the Focusing Question

The best topics, and the most difficult to write about, are those that raise questions for you. In a sketch or first draft, you may not know what those questions are. But if your subsequent drafts are going to be purposeful and focused, then discovering the main question behind your essay is essential. This discovery is particularly important in essays that are research based, because the drafts are longer and you're often trying to manage a lot of information. This revision strategy works best when it's a class activity.

1. Begin by putting your essay topic at the top of a large piece of paper such as newsprint or butcher paper. If yours is a research topic—say, Alzheimer's disease—jot that down. Post your paper on the classroom wall.

2. Spend a few minutes writing a few sentences explaining why you originally chose to write about this topic.

3. Make a quick list of everything you *already know* (if anything) about your topic—for instance, facts or statistics, the extent of the problem, important people or institutions involved, key schools of thought, common misconceptions, familiar clichés that apply to the topic, observations you've made, important trends, and typical perspectives. Spend about five minutes on this.

4. Now spend fifteen to twenty minutes brainstorming a list of questions about your topic that you'd love to learn the answers to. Make this list as long as possible.

5. As you look around the room, you'll see a gallery of topics and questions on the walls. You can help your fellow students. Circulate around the room and do two things: Add a question that you're interested in about a particular topic, and put a checkmark next to the question (yours or someone else's) that seems most interesting.

When you return to your own newsprint or butcher paper, it should be covered with questions. How will you decide which of them might provide the best focus for the next draft? Generally, there are two kinds of questions: factual questions and questions that attempt to *do* something with information. What you're mostly going to see are factual questions. When we know little about a topic, it's natural to begin with fact or definition questions: What is known about this? What *is* it? Look at your piece of paper and identify which factual questions you might want to pursue. Ultimately, though, for a research essay you'll need to use what you're learning about your topic to frame a *doing* question, a question that will purposefully *use* the factual information you've gathered. These questions include the following:

- What should be done about this? (policy question)
- What is the value of this? (value question)
- What might this mean? (interpretation question)
- What is the relationship? (relationship question)
- Might this be true? (hypothesis question)

Try to draft a question about your topic that might fit into one of these doing question categories. Because relationship questions are particularly powerful guides to research, the next exercise looks more closely at how your topic might use cause and effect or comparison and contrast to analyze your topic.

Revision Strategy 11.4: What's the Relationship?

One of the more common purposes for all kinds of essays is to explore a relationship between two or more things. We see this purpose in research all the time: What's the relationship between AIDS and IV drug use in China? What's the relationship between gender and styles of collaboration in the workplace?

What's the social class relationship between Huck and Tom in *The Adventures of Huckleberry Finn*?

One way, then, to clarify your purpose in revision is to try to identify the relationship that may be at the heart of your inquiry. Relationships between things can be described in a couple different ways.

- **Cause and effect.** What is the relationship between my father's comments about my looks and my eating disorder when I was a teenager? What is the relationship between the second Iraqi war and destabilization in Saudi Arabia? What is the relationship between the decline of the Brazilian rain forest and the extinction of the native eagles? What is the relationship between my moving to Idaho and the failure of my relationship with Kevin?
- **Compare and contrast.** How is jealousy distinguished from envy? How might writing instruction in high school be distinguished from writing instruction in college? What are the differences and similarities between my experiences at the Rolling Stones concert last month and my experiences at the Stones concert fifteen years ago?

Review your sketch or draft to determine whether what you're really trying to write about is the relationship between two (or more) things. In your journal, try to state this relationship in sentences similar to those listed here. With this knowledge, return to the draft and revise from beginning to end with this purpose in mind. What do you need to add to the next draft to both clarify and develop the relationship you're focusing on? What should you cut that is irrelevant to that focus?

Problems with Meaning

Fundamentally, most of us write something in an attempt to say something to someone else. The note my wife, Karen, left for me yesterday said it in a sentence: "Bruce—could you pick up some virgin olive oil and a loaf of bread?" I had no trouble deciphering the meaning of this note. But it isn't always that easy. Certain poems, for example, may be incredibly ambiguous, and readers may puzzle over them for hours, coming up with a range of plausible interpretations of meaning. (See Figure 11.3.)

Where Does Meaning Come From?

Depending on the writing situation, you may know from the start what you want to say, or you may *discover* what you think as you write and research. Inquiry-based projects usually emphasize discovery, while more-conventional argument papers may rely on arriving at a thesis earlier in the process. It's something like the difference between sledding with a saucer or a flexible flyer. The saucer is

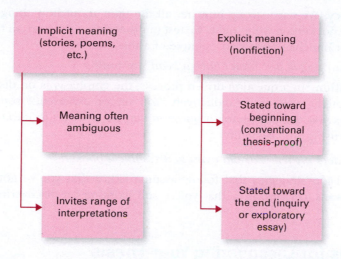

Figure 11.3 Depending on the genre, writers say it straight or tell it slant. In short stories, for example, the writers' ideas may be ambiguous, inviting interpretation. Nonfiction genres—the kind you will most often write in college and beyond—usually avoid ambiguity. Writers say what they mean as clearly and as persuasively as they can.

likely to veer off course, and you might find yourself somewhere unexpected, yet interesting.

Terms to Describe Dominant Meaning

- Thesis
- Main point
- Theme
- Controlling idea
- Central claim or assertion

No matter what you think about a topic when you start writing—even when you begin with a thesis to which you're committed—you can still change your mind. You *should* change your mind if the evidence you've gathered leads you away from your original idea. Unfortunately, writers of thesis-driven papers and other deductive forms are far more resistant than other writers to any change in their thinking. In some writing situations—say, essay exams—this isn't a problem. But it's often important in academic writing, including arguments, to continuously be open to new insight.

Ideas about what we want to say on a writing topic grow from the following:

1. **Thesis.** This is a term most of us know from high school writing, and it's most often associated with types of writing that work deductively from a main idea. Here's a sample thesis:

   The U.S. Securities and Exchange Commission is incapable of regulating an increasingly complex banking system.

2. **Theory.** We have strong hunches all the time about how things work, but we're not certain we're right. We test our theories and report on the accuracy of our hunches. Here's an example of a theory:

Certain people just "don't have a head" for math.

3. **Question.** In a question-driven process, the emphasis is on discovery, and you might work more inductively. You see or experience something that makes you wonder. Here's a question that led a writer to ideas about girls, advertising, and sexuality.

Why does my ten-year-old want to dress like a hooker?

The revision strategies that follow assume either that you've got a tentative thesis and want to refine it or that you're still working on discovering what you want to say.

Methods for Discovering Your Thesis

Use the following strategies if you're not quite sure whether you know what you're trying to say in a sketch or draft. How can you discover clues about your main point or meaning in what you've already written?

Revision Strategy 11.5: Harvest Meanings from the Draft

Sometimes when you're uncertain about what you're trying to say, the draft holds clues. But where do you look for them?

1. **Look in the end.** Discovery drafts—those you write to explore a topic—are end-weighted with meaning. It's in the final paragraphs, after you've worked your way through the material, that you often feel obligated to somehow reflect on what things might mean. Frequently there will be two or three ideas, all of which surface as you move to summarize. Choose the idea that is most important, and rebuild the revision *from the beginning* around that idea.

2. **Find the "instructive line."** Every draft is made up of many sentences. But which is *the most important sentence or passage?* Which line or passage points to an idea, theme, or feeling that seems to rise above much of the draft and illuminate the significance or relevance of everything else? Go through your draft and underline the one sentence or passage that you think is the most important in the entire piece. You must underline only one. In your journal, explain why you chose it, and answer this question: *In the end, what might this mean? What does it indicate about what I think is important to say?*

3. **Highlight the road signs.** In any draft there are two kinds of language: concrete, specific language and the language of abstraction. It is the language of abstraction—the words we use when we summarize, generalize, reflect, and comment—that holds the seeds of thought. On your computer,

highlight every passage in your draft that involves abstraction. Then cut and paste each passage into a new document. Examine the list of passages and move them around so that similar ideas are grouped together. What do you see? Which ideas seem most important? Which are secondary?

Revision Strategy 11.6: Looping Toward a Thesis

I've argued throughout *The Curious Writer* for a dialectical approach to writing: moving back and forth between creative and critical modes of thinking, between your observations of and your ideas about, between generating and judging, between specifics and generalities. This is how writers can make meaning. This approach can also be used as a revision strategy, in a technique called *loop writing*. When you loop write, you move back and forth dialectically between two modes of thought—opening things up and then trying to pin them down. I imagine that this way of thinking looks like an hourglass. (See Revision Strategy 11.7 for a variation on loop writing.)

1. **First steps.** Reread the draft quickly, and then turn it upside down on your desk. You won't look at it again but should trust that you'll remember what's important.

2. **Narrative of thought.** Begin a three-minute fastwrite on the draft in which you tell yourself the story of your thinking about the essay. When you first started writing it, what did you think you were writing about, and then what, and then…? Try to focus on your ideas about what you were trying to say and how those ideas evolved.

3. **Summary.** Sum up what you said in your fastwrite by answering the following question in a sentence: *What seems to be the most important thing I've finally come to understand about my topic?*

4. **Examples.** Begin another three-minute fastwrite. Focus on scenes, situations, case studies, moments, people, conversations, observations, and so on that stand out for you as you think about the draft. Think especially of the details that led to your understanding of the topic, which you stated in the preceding step. Some of these details may be in the draft, but some may *not* yet be in the draft.

5. **Summary.** Finish by restating the main point you want to make in the next draft. Begin the revision by thinking about a lead or introduction that dramatizes this point. Consider using an evocative scene, case study, finding, profile, description, comparison, anecdote, conversation, situation, or observation that points the essay toward your main idea. For example, if your point is that your university's program to help second-language learners is inadequate, you could begin the next draft by telling the story of Maria, an immigrant from Guatemala who was a victim of poor placement into a composition course that she was virtually guaranteed to fail. Follow this lead into the draft, always keeping your main point or thesis in mind.

Revision Strategy 11.7: Reclaiming Your Topic

When you do a lot of research on your topic, you may reach a point where you feel awash in information. It's easy at such moments to feel as if you're losing control of your topic—besieged by the voices of experts, a torrent of statistics and facts, and competing perspectives. Your success in writing the paper depends on your making it your own again, regaining control over the information for your own purposes, in the service of your own questions or arguments. This revision strategy, a variation of Revision Strategy 11.6, should help you regain control of the material you collected for a research-based inquiry project.

1. Spend ten to fifteen minutes reviewing all of the notes you've taken and skimming key articles or passages from books. Glance at your most important sources. If you have a rough draft, reread it. Let the information swim in your head.

2. Now clear your desk of everything but your journal. Remove all your notes and materials. If you have a rough draft, put it away.

3. Fastwrite about your topic for seven full minutes. Tell the story of how your thinking about the topic has evolved. When you began, what did you think? What were your initial assumptions or preconceptions? Then what happened, and what happened after that? Keep your pen moving.

4. Skip a few lines in your notebook, and write *Moments, Stories, People, and Scenes*. Now fastwrite for another seven minutes, this time focusing on specific case studies, situations, people, experiences, observations, facts, and so on that stand out in your mind from the research you've done so far, or perhaps from your own experience with the topic.

5. Skip a few more lines. For another seven minutes, write a dialogue between you and someone else about your topic. Choose someone who you think is typical of the audience you're writing for. (You might resurrect "Dave" from Revision Strategy 11.1.) Don't plan the dialogue. Just begin with the question most commonly asked about your topic, and take the conversation from there, writing both parts of the dialogue.

6. Finally, skip a few more lines and write this two-word question in your notebook: *So what?* Now spend a few minutes trying to summarize the most important thing you think your readers should understand about your topic, based on what you've learned so far. Distill this summary into a sentence or two.

As you work your way to the last step, you're reviewing what you've learned about your topic without being tyrannized by the many voices, perspectives, and facts in the research you've collected. The final step, step 6, leads you toward a thesis statement. In the revision, keep this statement in mind as you reopen your notes, reread your sources, and check on facts. Remember in the rewrite to put all of this information in the service of this main idea—as examples or illustrations, necessary background, evidence or support, counterexamples, and ways of qualifying or extending your main point.

Revision Strategy 11.8: The Believing Game

In school, we're often told that doubt is at the heart of critical thinking. But what this emphasis on doubting can lead to is the assumption that we have to pick sides, and that once we do, we have to suppress the impulse to consider any virtues in the ideas of those with whom we disagree. Compositionist Peter Elbow suggested that we can develop a richer understanding of a subject when we at least entertain other points of view. He called this "the believing game." *This exercise is particularly helpful when revising drafts that make an argument.*

Set aside seven minutes for an episode of fastwriting in your journal or on the computer. The "believing game" involves quieting your doubting mind to "try on" the ways of thinking of people with whom you might disagree.

- Quickly jot down some of the claims or ideas on your topic with which you disagree or have questions about.

- Begin your fastwrite by choosing one of these ideas and responding in writing to the following two questions:

  - Why might someone see things this way?

  - If I assume there might be some truth to this idea, how does that change the way I think about the topic?

Many things might emerge from this writing that will help you revise. Start with the following:

1. Take another look at your thesis. Should it be revised? Should you qualify your claim or idea to reflect a more nuanced understanding of the arguments on your topic?

2. Should you import some of this material into a section of the draft where you examine points of view you don't share, or that don't fit neatly in your argument?

Methods for Refining Your Thesis

You may emerge from writing a draft with a pretty clear sense of what you want to say in the next one. But does this idea seem a little obvious or perhaps too general? Does it fail to adequately express what you really feel and think? Use one or more of the following revision strategies to refine a thesis, theme, or controlling idea.

Revision Strategy 11.9: Questions as Knives

Imagine that your initial feeling, thesis, or main point is like an onion. Ideas, like onions, have layers, and to get closer to their hearts you need to cut through the most obvious outer layers to reveal what is less obvious, probably more specific, and almost certainly more interesting. Questions are to ideas as knives are to onions: They help you slice past your initial impressions. The most important question—the sharpest knife in the drawer—is simply *Why? Why* was the Orwell essay interesting? *Why* do you hate foreign films? *Why* should the university do more for second-language speakers? *Why* did you feel a sense of loss when the old cornfield was paved over for the mall?

Why may be the sharpest knife in the drawer, but there are other W questions with keen blades, too, including *What?, Where?, When?,* and *Who?* These questions can cut a broad thesis down to size. The result is a much more specific, more interesting controlling idea for the next draft.

1. Subject your tentative thesis to the same kind of narrowing. Write your theme, thesis, or main point as a single sentence in your notebook.

2. Slice it with questions and restate it each time.

3. Continue this process until your point is appropriately sliced—that is, when you feel that you've gone beyond the obvious and stated what you think or feel in a more specific and interesting way.

As before, rewrite the next draft with this new thesis in mind, reorganizing the essay around it from beginning to end. Add new information that supports the thesis, provides the necessary background, offers opposing views, or extends it. Cut information that isn't relevant to the new thesis.

Revision Strategy 11.10: Qualifying Your Claim

In your research you discovered that, while 90 percent of Americans think that their fellow citizens are too "fat," only 39 percent would describe themselves that way. This evidence leads you to make the following claim: *Although Americans agree that obesity is a national problem, their response is typical: It's somebody else's problem—an attitude that will cripple efforts to promote healthier lifestyles.* This seems like a logical assertion to make, if the evidence is reliable. But if you're going to try to build an argument around that assertion, it should be rigorously examined. Toulmin's approach to analyzing arguments provides a method for doing this rigorous examination.

1. Toulmin observes that sometimes a claim should be *qualified* so that it is more accurate and persuasive. The initial question is simple: *Is what you're asserting always or universally true?* Essentially, you're being challenged to examine your certainty about what you're saying. This might lead you to add "hedging" words or phrases that acknowledge your degree of certainty: *sometimes, always, mostly, in this case, based on available evidence,* and so on. In this example, the claim is already qualified because of its specification that it is limited to Americans, but the claim is also based on evidence from a single source. The claim, therefore, might be further qualified by saying this: *One survey suggests that although Americans agree that obesity is a national problem, their response is typical: It's somebody else's problem—an attitude that will cripple efforts to promote healthier lifestyles.*

2. Imagining how your claim might be rebutted is another way to strengthen it. (Revision Strategy 11.8, "The Believing Game," can help you with this.) How might someone take issue with your thesis? What might be the exceptions to what you're saying is true? For example, might someone object to the assertion that Americans "typically" respond by putting their heads in the sand when personally confronted with problems? You must decide, then, whether this clever aside in your claim is something you're prepared to support. If you're not, cut it.

Problems with Information

Writers who've spent a lot of time generating or collecting information about their topics can work from abundance rather than scarcity. This is an enormous advantage, because the ability to throw stuff away means you can be selective about what you use, and the result will be a more focused draft. But as you revise, your purpose and assertion might shift, and you may find yourself in the unhappy position of working from scarcity again. Most of your research, observation, or fastwriting was relevant to the triggering subject in your initial sketch or draft, not to the generated subject you decide is the better direction for the next draft. In some cases, you may need to research the new topic or return to the generating activities of listing, fastwriting, clustering, and so on that will help provide information for the next draft.

More often, however, writers don't have to begin from scratch in revision. Frequently, shifting the focus of or refining the thesis in the first draft just means emphasizing different information or perhaps filling in gaps in later drafts. The strategies that follow will help you solve this problem.

Revision Strategy 11.11: Explode a Moment

The success of essays that rely on stories, observations, or case studies frequently depends on how well the writer renders an important scene, situation, moment, or description. In an ethnography on women in rodeo, for example, "deep" descriptions of these women interacting with men in the arena might help illuminate gender differences. This takes efficient observation (and note-taking) skills but also requires the appropriate treatment: building a scene with concrete details. To create such a scene, you need to "explode the moment."

1. Choose a draft that relies on description, scene, or stories.

2. Make a list in your journal of the moments (for example, scenes, situations, and turning points) that stand out in the draft.

3. Circle one moment that you think is the most important to your purpose in the essay. It could be the situation that is most telling, a dramatic turning point, the moment of a key discovery that is central to what you're trying to say, or a scene that illustrates the dilemma or raises the question you're exploring in the draft.

4. Write that moment at the top of a blank journal page (for example, *the rodeo riders prepare*).

5. Now put yourself back into that moment and fastwrite about it for seven full minutes. Make sure that you use as much detail as possible, *drawing on all your senses*. Write in the present tense if it helps.

6. Use this same method with other moments in the draft that might deserve more emphasis in the next draft. Remember that real time means little in writing. An experience that lasted seven seconds can easily take up three pages of writing if it's described in enough detail. Rewrite and incorporate the best of the new information in the next draft.

Revision Strategy 11.12: Beyond Examples

When we decide to add information to a draft, we normally think of adding examples. If you're writing a research essay on living with a sibling who suffers from Down syndrome, you might mention that your brother typically tries to avoid certain cognitive challenges. Members of your workshop group wonder, "Well, what kind of cognitive challenges?" In revision, you add an example or two from your own experience to clarify what you mean. This is, of course, a helpful strategy; examples of what you mean by your assertion are a kind of evidence that helps readers more fully understand your work. But also consider adding other types of information to the next draft. Some of the following additions present opportunities for new research.

- **Presenting counterarguments.** Typically, persuasive essays include information that represents an opposing view. (See Revision Strategy 11.8, "The Believing Game," for help in generating material on other points of view.) Say you're arguing that except for "avoidance" behaviors, there really aren't personality traits that can be attributed to most people with Down syndrome. You include a summary of a study that says otherwise. Why? Because it provides readers with a better understanding of the debate, and enhances your ethos because you appear fair.

- **Providing background.** When you drop in on a conversation between two of your friends, you initially may be clueless about the subject. Naturally, you ask questions: "Who are you guys talking about? When did this happen? What did she say?" Answers to these questions provide a context that allows you to understand what your friends are saying and to participate in their conversation. Such background information is often essential in written communication, too. In a personal essay, readers may want to know when and where the event occurred or the relationship between the narrator and a character. In an analytical essay, it might be necessary to provide background information on the short story because readers may not have read it. In a research essay, it's often useful to provide background information about what has already been said on the topic and the research question.

■ **Establishing significance.** Let's say you're writing about the problem of obesity in America, something that most of us are generally aware of these days. But the significance of the problem really strikes home when you add information from research suggesting that 30 percent of American adults are overweight, up from 23 percent just six years ago. It is even more important to establish the significance of a problem about which there is little awareness or consensus. For example, most people don't know that America's national park system is crumbling and in disrepair. Your essay needs to provide readers with information that establishes the significance of the problem. In a profile, readers need to have a reason to be interested in the profile subject—perhaps he or she represents a particular group of people of interest or concern.

■ **Giving it a face.** One of the best ways to make an otherwise abstract issue or problem come to life is to show how it affects someone. We can't fully appreciate the social impact of deforestation in Brazil unless we are introduced to someone such as Chico Mendes, a forest defender who was murdered for his activism. Obesity might be an abstract problem until we meet Carl, a 500-pound 22-year-old who is "suffocating in his own fat." To make your essay more interesting and persuasive, add case studies, anecdotes, profiles, and descriptions that put people on the page.

■ **Defining it.** If your essay is on a subject your readers know little about, you'll likely use concepts or terms that readers will need you to define. What exactly do you mean, for example, when you say that the Internet is vulnerable to cyberterror? What exactly is cyberterror anyway? In your personal essay on your troubled relationship with your mother, what do you mean when you call her a narcissist? Frequently, your workshop group will alert you to terms and concepts in the draft that need defining, but also go through your draft and ask yourself, *Will my readers know what I mean?*

Revision Strategy 11.13: Research the Conversation

Your draft opens a door to a room in which there is an "unending conversation" about your topic, one that you've just dropped into. This is Kenneth Burke's "parlor metaphor" for how knowledge about the world is made: Imagine that all the people who share an interest in your question are in one room and are engaged in a lively debate and dialogue that has been going on for a long time. Drafts help us to figure out what parlor we've stumbled into, and when we know this, we also know what conversations to listen in on.

An example: You're writing about the campus's sustainability projects. This is a door into a conversation where a range of people are talking: college administrators who have implemented recycling programs, scholars who have researched ways of calculating carbon footprints, editorialists who opine about why it's a good idea—or not—to invest student funds in such projects. You may have already found some of this in your research, but there are always more voices to hear. In fact, this is the research that will have the biggest impact in strengthening your draft.

Research the conversation about your topic in the following ways:

1. **Mine bibliographies.** Often there is a scholarly article or book that is spot on and speaks directly to your research question. Look at its bibliography and scan the titles. Search for relevant articles or books among those that your favorite source cited. Pursue the promising titles. Can you use any of this new information somewhere in your draft?

2. **Gather names.** Who has said the most on your topic? Whose work is most influential? Collect these names, and using your library's database or Google Scholar, find the original works by these experts that caused the stir. Skim the articles and books that get cited most by others.

3. **Drill down from Wikipedia.** Wikipedia has its faults, but it's also a portal to relevant articles, websites, and organizations. Search for your topic on Wikipedia, hunting for relevant links in the text and bibliography. Use thelinks to find other voices who have shaped the conversation on your topic.

Revision Strategy 11.14: Backing Up Your Assumptions

Targeted research is particularly important when you're making an argument. In addition to providing evidence that is relevant to your thesis, an argument frequently is based on the assumptions behind that thesis. Stephen Toulmin calls these assumptions *warrants*. A warrant bridges the evidence with a related claim that reveals the assumptions on which the argument rests. A warrant essentially answers this question: What do you have to believe is true to believe a claim? For example, suppose your claim is the following: *Reading a lot makes people better writers.* And here's the evidence supporting the claim: *English majors read a lot and they are also strong writers.* What do you need to assume is true to believe this assertion? Lots. One particularly key warrant is that what's true of English majors is true of all "people." Warrants are often implicit, so it can be really helpful to bring them out into the open and see if they're sound.

1. Write your claim at the top of a journal page, and then list the assumptions or warrants on which it seems to rest. For example, consider this claim: *Teacher salary increases should be tied to student performances on tests.*

2. Now list the warrants behind your claim. In other words, what does one have to believe is true to buy the argument? In our example about teacher salaries and test scores, one warrant would be that *the quality of teaching is reflected in how students perform on tests.* Is there backing for that assumption?

3. Review your list of warrants. Which of them are assumptions that need supporting evidence? Focus your research on finding that evidence.

Problems with Structure

When it's effective, the structure of a piece of writing is nearly invisible. Readers don't notice how the writer is guiding them from one piece of information to the next. When structure is a problem, though, the writer asks readers to walk out on a shaky bridge and trust that it will help them get to the other side—but the walkers can think of little else but the shakiness of the bridge. Some professional writers, such as John McPhee, obsess about structure, and for good reason; when you're working with a tremendous amount of information, as McPhee often does in his research-based essays, it's important to have a clear idea about how you'll use that information.

It's helpful to distinguish between two basic structures for writing. One typically organizes the information of our experiences, and the other organizes our thinking so that it's clear and convincing. Typically, we use narrative, and especially chronology, to organize our experiences, though how we handle time can vary considerably. Writing that presents information based on the writer's reasoning—perhaps making an argument or reporting on an experiment—is logically structured. The most common example is the thesis-example or the thesis-proof paper. Much formal academic writing relies on logical structures that use deduction or induction.

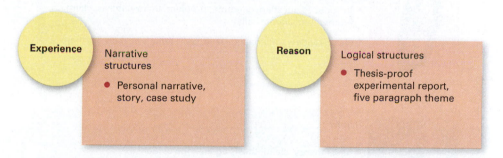

And yet some kinds of writing, such as the researched essay or ethnography, may *combine* both patterns, showing how the writer reasoned through to the meaning of an experience, observation, reading, and so on. These essays tell a "narrative of thought."

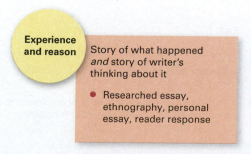

Formal Academic Structures

In some academic writing, the structure is prescribed. Scientific papers often have particular sections—Introduction, Methodology, Results, Discussion—but within those sections, writers must organize their material. Certain writing assignments may also require you to organize your information in a certain way. The most common of these arrangements is the thesis/support structure. In such essays, you typically establish your thesis in the first paragraph, spend the body of the paper presenting evidence that supports the thesis, and conclude the essay with a summary that restates the thesis in light of what you've presented.

Thesis/support is a persuasive form, so it lends itself to arguments, analytical essays, reviews, proposals, and similar pieces. In fact, you may have already structured your draft using this approach. If so, the following revision strategy may help you tighten and clarify the draft.

Beginning

- Establishes purpose (answers So what? question)
- Introduces question, dilemma, problem, theory, thesis, claim (sometimes dramatically)
- Helps readers understand—and feel—what's at stake for them

Middle

- Tests theory, claim, thesis against the evidence
- Develops reasons, with evidence, for writer's thesis or claim
- Tells story of writer's inquiry into question, problem, or dilemma

End

- Proposes answer, even if tentative, for writer's key question
- Revisits thesis or claim, extending, qualifying, contradicting, or reconfirming initial idea
- Raises new questions, poses new problems, or offers new understanding of what is at stake for readers

Revision Strategy 11.15: Beginnings, Middles, Ends, and the Work They Do

Stories, we are often told, are structured in three acts: They always have a beginning, middle, and end. This may be the most fundamental structure of all, and it doesn't just apply to narratives. The illustration with the butterfly explains what a beginning, middle, and end might contribute to making nearly any piece of writing coherent and convincing. Apply some of these ideas to your draft.

1. Draw a line in the draft where you think Act 1 ends and another line where you think Act 2 ends. Where you decide to divide the draft is entirely up to you; there's no formula to this. But you may change your mind as you go along.

2. Now use the illustration with the butterfly to analyze your beginning, middle, and end. Does each section do at least *one* of the listed tasks? If not, revise the section so that it does. This may involve adding a sentence or two—or possibly a couple paragraphs—of new information, perhaps moving some from elsewhere in the draft.

3. Generally speaking, Act 2 does the most work, and so proportionally it should have the most information.

If you find, for example, that your beginning takes three pages of a five-page essay, then you might want to remove material from the first few pages and concentrate on developing the body of your essay.

Revision Strategy 11.16: Reorganizing Around Thesis and Support

Because the thesis/support structure is fairly common, it's useful to master. Most drafts, even if they weren't initially organized in that form, can be revised into a thesis/support essay (personal essays would be an exception). The order of information in such an essay generally follows this design:

- **Lead paragraph:** This paragraph introduces the topic and explicitly states the thesis, usually as the last sentence in the paragraph. For example, a thesis/support paper on the deterioration of America's national parks system might begin this way:

  Yellowstone National Park, which shares territory with Idaho, Montana, and Wyoming, is the nation's oldest park and, to some, its most revered. Established on March 1, 1872, the park features the Old Faithful geyser, which spouts reliably every 76 minutes on average. What isn't nearly as reliable these days is whether school groups will get to see it. Last year 60% of them were turned away because the park simply didn't have the staff. <u>This essay will argue that poor funding of our national park system is a disgrace that threatens to undermine the Park Service's mission to preserve the areas "as cumulative expressions of a single national heritage"</u> ("Famous Quotes").

The thesis (underlined) is the final sentence in the paragraph, for emphasis.

- **Body:** Each succeeding paragraph until the final one attempts to prove or develop the thesis. Often, each paragraph is devoted to a single *reason* why the thesis is true, frequently stated as the topic sentence of the paragraph. Specific information then explains, clarifies, and supports the reason. For example, here's a typical paragraph from the body of the national parks essay:

    <u>One aspect of the important national heritage at risk because of poor funding for national parks is the pride many Americans feel about these national treasures.</u> *Newsweek* writer Arthur Frommer says the national park system is among the "crowning glories of our democracy." He adds, "Not to have seen them is to have missed something unique and precious in American life" (12). To see the crumbling roads in Glacier National Park, or the incursion of development in Great Smoky Mountains National Park, or the slow strangulation of the Everglades is not just an ecological issue; it's a sorry statement about a democratic nation's commitment to some of the places that define its identity.

    The underlined sentence is the topic sentence of the paragraph and is an assertion that supports and develops the thesis in the lead paragraph of the essay. The rest of the paragraph offers supporting evidence of the assertion, in this case a quotation from a *Newsweek* writer who recently visited several parks.

- **Concluding paragraph:** This paragraph reminds the reader of the central argument, not simply by restating the original thesis from the first paragraph, but also by reemphasizing some of the most important points. This reemphasis may lead to an elaboration or restatement of the thesis. One common technique is to find a way at the end of the essay to return to the beginning. Here's the concluding paragraph of the essay on national park funding:

    We would never risk our national heritage by allowing the White House to deteriorate or the Liberty Bell to rust away. <u>As the National Park Service's own mission states, the parks are also "expressions" of our "single national heritage," one this</u>

<u>paper contends is about preserving not only trees, animals, and habitats, but also our national identity.</u> The Old Faithful geyser reminds Americans of their constancy and their enduring spirit. What will it say about us if vandals finally end the regular eruptions of the geyser because Americans didn't support a park ranger to guard it? What will we call Old Faithful then? Old Faithless?

Note that the underlined sentence returns to the original thesis but doesn't simply repeat it word for word. Instead, it amplifies the original thesis, adding a definition of "national heritage" that includes national identity. It returns to the opening paragraph by finding a new way to discuss Old Faithful. Revise your draft to conform to this structure, beginning with a strong opening paragraph that explicitly states your thesis and concluding with an ending that somehow returns to the beginning without simply repeating what you've already said.

Revision Strategy 11.17: Multiple Leads

The element that may affect a draft more than any other is the beginning. There are many ways into the material, and of course you want to choose a beginning, or lead, that a reader would find interesting. You also want to choose a beginning that makes some kind of promise and provides readers with a sense of where you intend to take them. But a lead also has a less-obvious influence on both readers and writers. How you begin often establishes the voice of the essay; signals the writer's emotional relationship to the material (the writer's ethos); and might suggest the form the essay will take.

This is, of course, why beginnings are so hard to write. But the critical importance of where and how to begin suggests that examining alternative leads can give writers more choices and more control over their essays. To borrow John McPhee's metaphor, if a lead is a "flashlight that shines down into the story," then pointing that flashlight in four different directions might reveal four different ways to write about the same subject. This can be a powerful revision strategy.

1. Choose a draft that has a weak opening, doesn't have a strong sense of purpose, or needs to be reorganized.

2. Compose four *different* openings to the *same* draft. One way to generate ideas for this is to cluster your topic and write leads from four different branches. Also consider varying the type of lead you write.

3. Bring a typed copy of these four leads (or five, if you want to include the original lead from the first draft) to class and share them with a small group. First, simply ask your classmates to choose the lead they like best.

4. Choose the lead *you* prefer. It may or may not be the one your classmates chose. Find a partner who was not in your small group and ask him or her the following questions after sharing the lead you chose:

   - Based on this lead, what do you predict that this paper is about?
   - Can you guess the question, problem, or idea I'm writing about in the rest of the essay?
   - Do you have a sense of what my thesis is?
   - What is the ethos of this beginning? In other words, how do I come across as the narrator or author of the essay?

If the reader's predictions, using the lead you preferred, were fairly accurate, this lead might be a good opening of the next draft. Follow it in a fastwrite in your notebook to see where it leads you. Go ahead and use the other leads elsewhere in the revision, if you like.

If your reader's predictions were off, the lead may not be the best choice for the revision. However, should you consider this new direction an appealing alternative for the next draft? Or should you choose another lead that better reflects your current intentions rather than strike off in new directions? Either way, follow a new lead to see where it goes.

Revision Strategy 11.18: The Frankenstein Draft

One way to divorce a draft that has you in its clutches is to dismember it; that is, cut it into pieces and play with the parts, looking for new arrangements of information or new gaps to fill. Writing teacher Peter Elbow's cut-and-paste revision strategy can be a useful method, particularly for drafts that don't rely on narrative structures (although sometimes playing with alternatives, particularly if the draft is strictly chronological, can be helpful). Research essays and other pieces that attempt to corral lots of information seem to benefit the most from this strategy.

1. Choose a draft that needs help with organization. Make a one-sided copy.

2. Cut apart the copy, paragraph by paragraph. (You may cut it into smaller pieces later.) Once you have completely disassembled the draft, shuffle the paragraphs to get them wildly out of order so the original draft is just a memory.

3. Now go through the shuffled stack and find the *core paragraph*. This is the paragraph the essay really couldn't do without because it helps answer the *So what?* question. It might be the paragraph that contains your thesis or establishes your focusing question. It should be the paragraph that explains, implicitly or explicitly, what you're trying to say in the draft. Set this paragraph aside.

4. With the core paragraph directly in front of you, work your way through the remaining stack of paragraphs and make two new stacks: one of

paragraphs that don't seem relevant to the core paragraph (such as unnecessary digressions or information) and those that do (they support the main idea, explain or define a key concept, illustrate or exemplify something important, or provide necessary background).

5. Put your reject pile aside for the moment. You may later decide to salvage some of those paragraphs. But for now, focus on your relevant pile, including the core paragraph. Now play with order. Try new leads, ends, and middles. Consider trying some new methods of development as a way to organize your next draft (see the "Methods of Development" box). As you spread the paragraphs out before you and consider new arrangements, don't worry about the lack of transitions; you can add those later. Also look for gaps, places where more information might be needed. Consider some of the information in the reject pile as well. Should you splice in *parts* of paragraphs that you initially discarded?

6. As a structure begins to emerge, tape together the fragments of paper. Also splice in scraps in appropriate places and jot down what you might add in the next draft that is currently missing.

Methods of Development

- Narrative
- Problem to solution
- Cause to effect, or effect to cause
- Question to answer
- Known to unknown, or unknown to known
- Simple to complex
- General to specific, or specific to general
- Comparison and contrast
- Combinations of any of these

Now you've created a Frankenstein draft. But hopefully this ugly mess of paper and tape and scribbled notes holds much more promise than the monster did. On the other hand, if you end up with basically the original organization, perhaps your first approach wasn't so bad after all. In that case, maybe you at least found places where more information is needed.

Revision Strategy 11.19: Reverse Outline

While outlines can be a useful tool for planning a formal essay, they can also help writers revise a draft. The "reverse outline" is one method for doing this.

1. Number every paragraph in the draft.

2. Put your inquiry question or thesis at the top of a separate piece of paper, and then write a one- or two-sentence summary of each paragraph's

purpose. For an argumentative piece, the purpose will likely be the central point of the paragraph. For other essays, the summary might identify the category of information the paragraph represents and what work the paragraph is intended to do, such as "present definition of autism to provide background information" or "present case study of autistic child to dramatize the problem," etc.

3. Analyze the list of your summaries.

    - **Is the order of information logical?** Does it move effectively from claims to reasons to evidence? Does it have three acts (see Revision Strategy 11.15)?
    - **Are some paragraphs about more than one thing?** Should they be two paragraphs instead?
    - **Is every paragraph *relevant* to the research question or thesis?** If a paragraph digresses, is it a useful digression?
    - **Is the emphasis off?** Do you provide too much information on a minor purpose or idea and not enough on more central purposes or ideas?

Problems with Clarity and Style

One thing should be made clear immediately: Problems with clarity and style need not have anything to do with grammatical correctness. You can have a sentence that follows all the rules and still lumbers, sputters, and dies like a Volkswagen bug towing a heavy trailer up a steep hill. Take this sentence, for instance:

> Once upon a point in time, a small person named Little Red Riding Hood initiated plans for the preparation, delivery, and transportation of foodstuffs to her grandmother, a senior citizen residing at a place of residence in a wooded area of indeterminate dimension.

Strong writing at the sentence and paragraph levels always begins with clarity.

This beastly sentence opens Russell Baker's essay "Little Red Riding Hood Revisited," a satire about the gassiness of contemporary writing. It's grammatically correct, of course, but it's also pretentious and unnecessarily wordy, and would be annoying to read if it wasn't pretty amusing. This section of the chapter focuses on revision strategies that will improve the clarity of your writing and help you consider the effects you want to create through word choice and arrangement.

Because we often think that revision work with paragraphs, sentences, and words always involves problems of correctness, it may be hard to believe at first that writers can actually manage readers' responses and feelings by using different words or by rearranging the parts of a sentence or paragraph. Once you begin to play around with style, however, you will realize that style is much more than cosmetic. In fact, style in writing is a lot like music in movies. Chris Douridas, a Hollywood music supervisor who picked music for *Shrek* and *American Beauty*, said recently that he sees "music as an integral ingredient to the pie. I see it as helping to flavor the pie and not as whipped cream on top." Certainly, people don't decide to see a movie because of its music, but we know that music is central to our experience of a film. Similarly, *how* you say things in a piece of writing powerfully shapes the reader's experience of *what* you say.

But style is a secondary concern. Strong writing at the sentence and paragraph levels always begins with clarity. Do you say what you mean as directly and economically as you can? This can be a real problem, particularly with academic writing, in which it's easy to get the impression that a long word is always better than a short word and that the absence of anything interesting to say can be remedied by sounding smart. Nothing could be further from the truth.

Solving Problems of Clarity

Begin revising your draft for clarity by using one or more of the following revision strategies, any of which will make your writing more direct and clear.

Revision Strategy 11.20: The Three Most Important Sentences

Writers, like car dealers, organize their lots to take advantage of where customers are most likely to look and what they're most likely to remember. In many essays and papers, there are three places to park important information and to craft your very best sentences. These are:

- the very first sentence
- the last line of the first paragraph
- the very last line of the essay

The Very First Sentence. Obviously, there are many important places in a piece of writing—and longer essays, especially, have more and different locations—for your strongest sentences. But in an informal piece of modest length, the first sentence not only should engage the reader, it should, through strong language and voice, introduce the writer as well. For example, here's the first line of Richard Conniff's researched essay "Why Did God Make Flies?": "Though I've been killing them for years now, I have never tested the folklore that, with a little cream and sugar, flies taste very much like black raspberries." In more formal writing, the first line is less about introducing the writer's persona than about introducing the subject. Here's the first line of an academic piece I'm reading at the moment: "Much of the international debate about the relationship between research and teaching is characterized by difference." This raises an obvious question—"What is this difference?"—which is exactly what the author proposes to explore.

The Last Line of the First Paragraph. The so-called "lead" (or "lede" in journalism speak) of an essay or article does three things: It establishes the purpose of the work, raises interesting questions, and creates a register or tone. A lead paragraph in a shorter essay is just that—the first paragraph—while a lead in a longer work may run for paragraphs, even pages. Whatever the length, the last sentence of the lead launches the work and gets it going in a particular direction. In conventional, thesis-proof essays, then, this sentence might be where you state your main claim. In inquiry-based forms such as the essay, this sentence might be where you post the key question you're exploring or illuminate the aspect of the problem you're looking at.

The Very Last Line of the Essay. If it's good, this is the sentence readers are most likely to remember.

Try this revision strategy:

1. Highlight or underline each of the three key sentences in your draft.

2. Ask yourself these questions about the first line and, depending on your answers, revise the sentence:

   ■ Is the language lively?

   ■ Does it immediately raise questions the reader might want to learn the answers to?

   ■ Will readers want to read the second sentence, and why?

3. Analyze the last sentence of your "lead" paragraph for ideas about revision. Ask yourself this:

   ■ Is the sentence well crafted?

   ■ Does it hint at or explicitly state your motive for asking readers to follow along with you in the paragraphs and pages that follow?

4. Finally, scrutinize your last sentence:

   ■ Is it one of the best-written sentences in the piece?

   ■ Does it add something to the piece?

Revision Strategy 11.21: Untangling Paragraphs

One of the things I admire most in my friends David and Margaret is that they both have individual integrity—a deep understanding of who they are and who they want to be—and yet they remain just as profoundly connected to the people close to them. They manage to exude both individuality and connection. I hope my friends will forgive the comparison, but good paragraphs have the same qualities: Alone, they have their own identities, yet they are also strongly hitched to the paragraphs that precede and that follow them. This connection happens quite naturally when you're telling a story, but in expository writing the relationship between paragraphs is related more to content than to time.

The following passage is the first three paragraphs of Paul de Palma's essay on computers, with the clever title "http://www.when_is_enough_enough?.com."

In the misty past, before Bill Gates joined the company of the world's richest men, before the mass-marketed personal computer, before the metaphor of an information superhighway had been worn down to a cliché, I heard Roger Schank interviewed on National Public Radio. Then a computer science professor at Yale, Schank was already well known in artificial intelligence circles. Because those circles did not include me, a new programmer at Sperry Univac, I hadn't heard of him. Though I've forgotten details of the conversation, I have never forgotten Schank's insistence that most people do not need to own computers.

That view, of course, has not prevailed. Either we own a personal computer and fret about upgrades, or we are scheming to own one and fret about the technical marvel yet to come that will render our purchase obsolete. Well, there are worse ways to spend money, I suppose. For all I know, even Schank owns a personal computer. They're fiendishly clever machines, after all, and they've helped keep the wolf from my door for a long time.

It is not the personal computer itself that I object to. What reasonable person would voluntarily go back to a typewriter? The mischief is not in the computer itself, but in the ideology that surrounds it. If we hope to employ computers for tasks more interesting than word processing, we must devote some attention to how they are actually being used, and beyond that, to the remarkable grip that the idol of computing continues to exert.

A paragraph should be unified, focusing on a single topic, idea, or thing. It's like a mini-essay in that sense.

Note how the first sentence in the new paragraph links with the last sentence in the preceding paragraph.

As before, the first sentence links with the last sentence in the previous paragraph.

The final sentence is the most important one in a paragraph. Craft it carefully.

Notice the integrity of each paragraph—each is a kind of mini-essay—as well as the way each one is linked to the paragraph that precedes it.

Well-crafted paragraphs such as these create a fluent progression, all linked together like train cars; they make readers feel confident that this train is going somewhere. Paragraphs might do this by including information that clarifies, extends, proves, explains, or even contradicts. Do the paragraphs in your draft work well on their own *and* together?

1. Check the length of every paragraph in your draft. Are any too long, going on and on for a full page or more? Can you create smaller paragraphs by breaking out separate ideas, topics, discussions, or claims?

2. Now examine each paragraph in your draft for integrity. Is it relatively focused and unified? Should it be broken down into two or more paragraphs because it covers too much territory?

3. Often the first sentence is the second most important sentence in a paragraph. The third most important sentence follows immediately thereafter. The most important sentence usually comes at the end of the paragraph. Is each of your paragraphs arranged with that order in mind? In particular, how strong is the final sentence in each paragraph? Does it prepare readers to move into the next paragraph? In general, each paragraph should add some kind of new information to the old information in the paragraphs preceding it. This new information may clarify, explain, prove, elaborate on,

contrast, summarize, contradict, or alter time. Sometimes you should signal the nature of this addition using transition words and phrases (see the "Inquiring into the Details: Transition Flags" box). Are there any awkward transitions? Should you smooth them using transition flags?

Revision Strategy 11.22: Cutting Clutter

Russell Baker's overinflated version of "Little Red Riding Hood," which we looked at earlier, suffers from what writer and professor William Zinsser called "clutter." This disease afflicts much writing, particularly in academic settings. Clutter, simply put, is saying in three or four words what you might say in two, or choosing a long word when a short one will do just as well. It grows from the assumption that simplicity means simplemindedness. This assumption is misguided. Simplicity is a great virtue in writing. It's respectful of the readers, for one thing, who are mostly interested in understanding what you mean without having to deal with unnecessary detours or obstacles.

In case Russell Baker's tongue-and-cheek example of cluttered writing isn't convincing because it's an invention, here's a brief passage from a memo I received from a fellow faculty member some years ago. I won't make you endure more than a sentence of it.

> While those of us in the administration are supporting general excellence and consideration of the long-range future of the University, and while the Faculty Senate and Caucus are dealing with more immediate problems, the Executive Committee feels that an ongoing dialogue concerning the particular concerns of faculty is needed to maintain the quality of personal and educational life necessary for continued educational improvement.

That's a sixty-three-word sentence, and while there is nothing inherently wrong with long sentences, I'm pretty sure that at least half of the words are

---

Inquiring into the Details

Transition Flags

One way to connect paragraphs is to use words that signal to a reader what the relationship is between them.

- **Clarifying:** *for example, furthermore, specifically, also, to illustrate, similarly*
- **Proving:** *in fact, for example, indeed*
- **Time:** *first…second…finally, subsequently, following, now, recently*
- **Cause or effect:** *therefore, consequently, so, accordingly*
- **Contrast or contradiction:** *on the other hand, in contrast, however, on the contrary, despite, in comparison*
- **Summarizing:** *finally, in the end, in conclusion, summing up, to conclude*

unnecessary. For the fun of it, see if you can cut at least thirty words from the sentence without compromising the writer's intent. Look for ways to say the same things in fewer words, and look for short words that might replace long ones. What kinds of choices did you make to improve the clarity of the sentence?

Now shift your attention to one of your own drafts and see if you can be as ruthless with your own clutter as you were with the memo writer's:

1. One of the most common kinds of clutter is stock phrases, things we mindlessly say because we've simply gotten in the habit of saying them.

Stock Phrase	Simpler Version
Due to the fact that…	Because
At the present time…	Now
Until such time as…	Until
I am of the opinion that…	I think
In the event of…	When *or* If
Referred to as…	Called
Totally lacked the ability to…	Couldn't
A number of…	Many
There is a need for…	We must

2. Try choosing a shorter, simpler word rather than a long, complicated word. For example, why not say *many* rather than *numerous*, or *ease* rather than *facilitate*, or *do* rather than *implement*, or *found* rather than *identified*? Go through your draft and look for opportunities such as these to use simpler, more direct words.

3. In his book *Style: Ten Lessons in Clarity and Grace*, Joseph Williams cleverly calls the habit of using meaningless words "verbal tics." My favorite verbal tic is the phrase *in fact*, which I park at the front of a sentence when I feel I'm about to clarify something. Williams mentions a few other common ones, including *kind of, actually, basically, generally, given, various,* and *certain*. Go through your draft and search for words and phrases that you use out of habit, and cut them if they don't add meaning.

Revision Strategy 11.23: The Actor and the Action Next Door

I live in a relatively urban neighborhood, and so I can hear Kate play her music across the street and Gray powering up his chainsaw to cut wooden pallets next door. I have mixed feelings about this. Kate and I have different tastes in music, and Gray runs the chainsaw at dusk. But I am never confused about who is doing what. That's less obvious in the following passage:

> A conflict that was greeted at first with much ambivalence by the American public, <u>the war in Iraq</u>, which caused a tentativeness that some experts call the "Vietnam syndrome," <u>sparked protests</u> among Vietnam veterans.

The subject, or actor, of the sentence (*the war in Iraq*) and the action (*sparked protests*) are separated by a few city blocks. In addition, the subject is buried behind a long introductory clause. As a result, it's a bit hard to remember who is doing what. Putting actor and action next door to each other makes writing livelier, and bringing the subject up front helps clarify who is doing what.

> <u>The</u> war in Iraq sparked <u>protests</u> among Vietnam veterans even though the conflict was initially greeted with public ambivalence. Some experts call this tentativeness the "Vietnam syndrome."

Review your draft to determine whether the subjects in your sentences are buried or are in the same neighborhood as the verbs that modify them. If they're too far away from each other, rewrite to bring the actors up front in your sentences and to close the distance between actors and actions.

Improving Style

The revision strategies in this section will improve the style of your writing. Writers adopt a style because it serves a purpose, perhaps encouraging a certain feeling that makes a story more powerful; enhancing the writer's ethos and making an essay more convincing; or simply giving certain information particular emphasis. For example, here's the beginning of an article about Douglas Berry, a Marine drill sergeant.

> He is seething, he is rabid, he is wound up tight as a golf ball, with more adrenalin surging through his hypothalamus than a cornered slum rat, he is everything these Marine recruits with their heads shaved to dirty nubs have ever feared or ever hoped a drill sergeant might be.

The style of this opening is calculated to have an obvious effect—the reader is pelted with words, one after another, in a breathless sentence that almost simulates the experience of having Sgt. Douglas Berry in your face. There's no magic to this. It is all about using words that evoke action and feeling, usually verbs or words based on or derived from verbs.

Revision Strategy 11.24: Actors and Actions

Academic writing sometimes lacks strong verbs and relies instead on old, passive standbys such as *it was concluded by the study* or *it is believed*. Not only are the verbs weak, but the actors—the people or things engaged in the action—are often missing completely from the sentences. *Who* or *what* did the study? *Who* believes?

This is called *passive voice*, and while it's not grammatically incorrect, it can suck the air out of a room. One of the easiest ways to locate passive voice in your drafts is to conduct a *to be* search. Most forms of the verb *to be* signal passive voice.

1. Conduct a *to be* search of your own draft. Whenever you find passive construction, try to put the actor into the sentence.

2. Try to use lively verbs as well. Can you replace weak verbs with stronger ones? How about *discovered* instead of *found*, or *seized* instead of *took*, *shattered* instead of *broke*? Review every sentence in your draft and, when appropriate, revise with a stronger verb.

Revision Strategy 11.25: Smoothing the Choppiness

Consider the following sentences, each labeled with the number of syllables it contains:

> When the sun finally rose the next day I felt young again.(15) It was a strange feeling because I wasn't young anymore.(15) I was fifty years old and felt like it.(10) It was the smell of the lake at dawn that thrust me back into adolescence.(19) I remembered the hiss of the waves.(9) They erased my footprints in the sand.(9)

The cause of the plodding rhythm is the unvarying length of the pauses. The last two sentences in the passage each have nine syllables, and the first two sentences are nearly identical in length as well (fifteen syllables each).

Now notice how this choppiness disappears by varying the lengths of the pauses through combining sentences, inserting other punctuation, and dropping a few unnecessary words.

> When the sun finally rose the next day I felt young again,(15) and it was a strange feeling because I wasn't young.(13) I was fifty years old.(6) It was the smell of the lake at dawn that thrust me back into adolescence and remembering the hiss of the waves as they erased my footprints in the sand.(39)

The revision is much more fluent, and the reason is simple: The writer varies the pauses and the number of syllables within each sentence—15, 13, 6, 39.

1. Choose a draft of your own that doesn't seem to flow or seems choppy in places.

2. Mark the pauses in the problem areas. Put slash marks next to periods, commas, semicolons, dashes, and so on—any punctuation that prompts a reader to pause briefly.

3. If the intervals between the pauses seem similar in length, revise to vary them, combining sentences, adding punctuation, dropping unnecessary words, or varying long and short words.

Revision Strategy 11.26: Fresh Ways to Say Things

It goes without saying that a tried-and-true method of getting to the heart of revision problems is to just do or die. Do you know what I mean? Of course you don't, because the opening sentence is laden with clichés and figures of speech that obscure meaning.

Removing clichés and shopworn expressions from your writing will make it sound as if you are writing with your own voice rather than someone else's.

1. Reread your draft and circle clichés and hand-me-down expressions. If you're not sure whether a phrase qualifies for either category, share your circled items with a partner and ask: Have you heard these things before?

2. Cut the clichés and overused expressions and rewrite your sentences by finding your own way to say things. In your own words, what do you really mean by "do or die" or "striking while the iron is hot" or becoming a "true believer"?

Using What You Have Learned

Take a few moments to reflect on what you have learned in this chapter and how you can apply it to your writing.

1. **Understand the meaning—and value—of revision and apply it to your own work when appropriate.** Even if an instructor doesn't explicitly require a revision for a writing assignment, you now have experience with what a difference revision can make in the quality of your work.

2. **Recognize five types of revision and apply the most relevant strategies to a particular draft.** As you continue to develop as a writer, you'll become a more critical reader of your own work, and assessing the quality of your writing will get easier. Learn to recognize your weaknesses—maybe you're not great at organizing drafts or you're wordy—and find strategies that help you address those problems.

Credits

Text

Chapter 1
Olivas, Bernice, "Bernice's Journal." Reprinted by permission of the author.

Chapter 2
Ballenger, Bruce, The Curious Writer, 5th Ed., Pearson Education, Inc., 2016.

Chapter 3
Zazulak, Laura, "Every Morning for Five Years." Reprinted by permission of the author.

Blanford, Virginia, "My Turn: The Dog That Made Us a Family," Newsweek, March 16 © 2009 IBT Media. All rights reserved. Used by permission and protected by the Copyright Laws of the United States. The printing, copying, redistribution, or retransmission of this Content without express written permission is prohibited.

Stewart, Amanda, "Learning a Sense of Place." Reprinted by permission of the author.

Marlin, Seth, "Smoke of Empire." Reprinted by permission of the author.

Chapter 4
Ebert, Roger, "A Christmas Story." © 2000 The Ebert Company. Dist. By UNIVERSAL UCLICK. Reprinted with permission. All rights reserved.

Schiesel, Seth: "Grand Theft Auto Takes on New York," The New York Times, April 28 © 2008 The New York Times. All rights reserved. Used by permission and protected by the Copyright Laws of the United States. The printing, copying, redistribution, or retransmission of this Content without express written permission is prohibited.

Burns, Laura, "Recipe for a Great Film: Unlikeable People, Poor Choices, and Little Redemption." Reprinted by permission of Becca Ballenger.

Burns, Laura, "How to Not Feel Good and Feel Good About It: A Review of Young Adult." Reprinted by permission of Becca Ballenger.

Chapter 5
Bissinger, Buzz, "Why College Football Should Be Banned," The Wall Street Journal, May 8, 2012. Reprinted with permission of the author.

Saltz, Robert F., "Preventing Alcohol-Related Problems on College Campuses—Summary of the Final Report of the NIAAA Task Force on College Drinking," National Institute on Alcohol Abuse and Alcoholism.

Appleman, Jenna, "Loving and Hating Reality TV." Reprinted by permission of Becca Ballenger.

Appleman, Jenna, "Avoidable Accidents: How to Make Reality TV Safer." Reprinted with permission of Becca Ballenger.

Chapter 6
"Is College Worth It? Clearly, New Data Say" from The New York Times, May 27 © 2014 The New York Times. All rights reserved. Used by permission and protected by the Copyright Laws of the United States. The printing, copying, redistribution, or retransmission of this Content without express written permission is prohibited.

Mohammed, Khalid Sheikh, "The Language of War is Killing," Department of Defense.

Sabat, Kevin, "Colorado Will Show Why Legalizing Marijuana Is a Mistake," The Washington Times, Jan 17, 2014. Reprinted with permission. Copyright © 2015 The Washington Times LLC. This reprint does not constitute or imply any endorsement or sponsorship of any product, service, company or organization. License # 48577

Thompson, Rebecca, "Twitter a Profound Thought?" Reprinted by permission of Becca Ballenger.

Thompson, Rebecca, "Social Networking Social Good?" Reprinted by permission of Becca Ballenger.

Chapter 7
Momaday, N. Scott, "The Shield that Came Back." From "In the Presence of the Sun" by N. Scott Momaday. Copyright © 2009 University of New Mexico Press, 2009

Brinkman, Bartholomew, "On 'The Shield That Came Back'", © 2004, in Modern American Poetry Site http://www.english.illinois.edu/maps/poets/m_r/momaday/shield-came-back.htm

Pang, Alex Soojung-Kim: "What Does Apple's 'Misunderstood' Advertisement Mean?" Huffington Post. Reprinted with permission of the author.

Bishop, Bryan: "'Why won't you die?!' The art of the jump scare" published on The Verge website on October 31, 2012 (http://www.theverge.com/2012/10/31/3574592/art-of-the-jump-scare-horror-movies). Copyright © 2012. Used by permission of Vox Media, Inc.

Johnson-Waskow, Hallie, "All About That Hate."

Chapter 11
de Palma, Paul, "http://www.when_is_enough_enough?.com," The American Scholar, Winter 1992, pp. 61-72.

Photo

Chapter 1
Zurijeta/Shutterstock

Richard Sharrocks/Alamy

Chapter 2
Balazs Kovacs Images/Shutterstock

Chapter 3
Elzbieta Sekowska/Shutterstock

Neufeld, Josh, "A Matter of Perspective," Unexpected World of Nature #3 (Thirteen/WNET, 2008). Copyright © 2008 Josh Neufeld

Lupien, Craig, Doll "Mable". Reprinted with permission.

Chapter 4
Christian Bertrand/Shutterstock

Dorthea Lange/Library of Congress (5 images)

Tatsuya Ishida, "One Shade of Grey: A Feminist Fantasy." Reprinted by permission of Tatsuya Ishida.

Everett Collection

Everett Collection

Stephen Trupp/Starmaxinc.com/AP Images

Chapter 5
Atm2003/Shutterstock

Used with the permission of the San Francisco Bicycle Coalition: sfbike.org (6 images)

Chapter 6
Rena Schild/Shutterstock

Joe Heller/PoliticalCartoons.com

Photo B.D.V./Corbis

Chapter 7
Rob Hyrons/Fotolia

James Steidl/Fotolia

Gift of Walter and Naomi Rosenblum/Brooklyn Museum

Chapter 8
WDG Photo/Shutterstock

Brian Jackson/Fotolia

Tim/Fotolia

Xuejun li/Fotolia

Chapter 9
Veronika Mannova/Shutterstock

Chapter 10
Nicholas Pitt/Getty Images

Chapter 11
Peter Souza/White House Photo Office

Steven Russell Smith Photos/Shutterstock

DelMonaco/Shutterstock

Rafael Ben-Ari/Fotolia

Inquiring into the Details icon. Frederick Bass/Getty Images

One Student's Response icon. Purestock/Getty Images

Writing Beyond the Classroom icon. Fuse/Getty Images

Index